# Financial Analysis

## A User Approach

GARY GIROUX
*Texas A&M University*

www.wiley.com/college/giroux

Acquisitions Editor *Jay O'Callaghan*
Marketing Manager *Keari Bedford*
Production Manager *Lari Bishop*
Designer *Shoshanna Turek*
Illustration Editor *Michele Chancellor*
Copy Editor *Leon Unruh*
Indexer *Sandy Schroeder*
Cover Design *Benjamin Reece*
Cover Images Milan main gallery: Copyright ©Corbis,
All others: Copyright ©PhotoDisc

This book was set in Minion and printed and bound by Malloy, Inc.. The cover was printed by Phoenix Color Corp.

This book is printed on acid free paper.∞



This textbook was published by John Wiley & Sons, Inc. under exclusive license from Leyh Publishing, LLC.



ISBN 0-471-22990-3

*This book is dedicated to the memory of Michael, Sunny, and Louis Giroux.*

# Contents

# Preface

Why study financial analysis? Technology has made financial information plentiful and cheap to collect, but skilled analysis of this information is just as valuable and critical as ever. The purpose of using financial and other information is to make informed financial decisions and recommendations, based on professional financial analysis.

This book is geared toward the user of financial information, as opposed to the preparer. Within the user approach, the concentration can be on financial analysis that is internal or external to the company. The internal focus is usually associated with financial and managerial accounting and typically deals with the preparation of original financial data. The focus of this book is external, concerning analysis performed on financial data by parties outside the company.

The purpose of this book is to develop a framework for the comprehensive analysis of financial, equity market, and subjective measures of corporations to make specific financial recommendations and decisions. The most common types of decisions are credit and investment decisions, and these will be the primary focus of analysis. The emphasis is on processes and on the data needed to make professional decisions.

This book is written for finance and accounting undergraduate students in a financial analysis course or in other courses that emphasize a professional perspective on financial analysis processes. The book can also be used as part of graduate courses to stress professional emphasis, or by other readers who want this perspective. The reader is assumed to have a reasonable understanding of basic accounting and finance principles. The book is short enough to be used as a supplement in a variety of contexts, but is fairly comprehensive and coverage will be detailed enough to assist in informed analysis and decision-making.

## Organization and Coverage

The structure of the book follows a formal six-step process for financial analysis. This process is introduced in Chapter 1. In order to employ the six-step process, the user must be comfortable with the basic events and data of accounting and finance. This reasoning forms the basis of the topical organization of the first part of this book, and is well illustrated by the "value chain" of information, as identified by Robert Elliot, partner at KPMG.

| Business Event | Data | Information | Knowledge | Decisions |
|---|---|---|---|---|
| Stage 1<br>$10 | Stage 2<br>$30 | Stage 3<br>$100 | Stage 4<br>$300 | Stage 5<br>$1,000 |

Source: Robert Elliot, KPMG

In the "value chain" of information, one can see that the "Decision" stage is considered the most valuable. From the collecting of information through decision-making, all of Elliot's 5 stages are important, but the real value is found in the analysis at the end, which is based on knowledge gained from previous stages.

Hence, the rationale for the book's organization: just as in this value chain, we move from fundamental to the most significant, so we will build quickly in this book from the student's fundamental knowledge of basic accounting and finance, to the critical thinking and analysis used in knowledge and decision-making. Although the strategy is to move as quickly as possible to these higher stages, there is no substitute for the fundamental information.

Therefore, after Chapters 1 and 2 provide an introduction and describe the environment, Chapters 3 through 6 present basic financial statements and financial analysis tools and techniques. The background of the reader should determine how much time is spent on the problems in these chapters.

From this foundation, the book builds to present the student with financial and accounting analysis techniques from a variety of perspectives. A limited amount of financial and economic theory is described, where it helps explain incentives of corporate managers and how economic markets work. For example, the efficient markets hypothesis is an important perspective to understand market response to new information. To some extent, finance and economic tools have been adopted by finance professionals, and these tools should be understood. Managers have incentives for earnings management. Understanding these incentives is useful to evaluate the adequacy of financial reporting. Most ratios and models assume that the raw data is completely accurate, but this is not necessarily the case. Analysts should be aware of incentives to manipulate financial data and how to analyze companies when data is suspect. A number of potential earnings management examples are presented throughout the book.

Discussion of financial accounting and reporting standards will be included, but only where their understanding is necessary to interpret relevant information for decision-making. For example, analysts must know how to read pension footnotes. For most decisions, however, it is not necessary to be an expert in pension accounting. The perspective and markets of most large corporations are global and complex. This global perspective will be treated seriously, but not in detail.

## Textbook Features

Every chapter begins by stating learning objectives and then providing an introduction to the topics that follow. At the end of the book, a glossary of key terms is provided.

## CURRENT FINANCIAL INFORMATION

The reader can expect to find that most of the discussion and the problems in the book involve very recent financial data, usually fiscal year 2001, first quarter 2002, and May 1, 2002 stock prices.

The book emphasizes taking full advantage of the valuable information and tools currently available on the Internet. As information on the Internet is always changing, we have taken pains to see that the analysis in the book is as up to date as possible.

## EXAMPLES

Chapter discussions typically illustrate points using the same three computer companies (Dell, Apple, and Gateway), for consistency.

## PROBLEMS

Closely paralleling chapter content, problems are set in the manufacturing and service industries. For consistency, they focus on a few industries and major companies within them:

- Manufacturing problems use chemical companies (DuPont, Dow, and PPG)
- Service industry problems use the hotel and resort industry (Hilton, Marriott, and Mandalay)
- Some additional problems use the automotive industry

## END OF CHAPTER MATERIAL

End of chapter material includes financial ratio summaries and discussion questions.

## CASES

The cases are designed to challenge the student, and present what are often more difficult financial and accounting issues to which no obvious solution exists. Enron, GE, and Amazon.com appear in the cases.

## ETHICAL CONSIDERATIONS

When covering an area in which ethical issues may have a significant impact on financial analysis, we have included an ethical considerations feature.

## INTERNET PROJECTS AND EXPLORATION

Because of the importance of finance-related Web sites, many Internet projects are included throughout the text. Also, references to Web sites for additional reading or research are listed in the course of discussion. These are then summarized at the end of the book for easy access.

# WEB SITE

You can find a complete support Web site at http://www.wiley.com/college/giroux. One of the advantages of the Web page is to keep up to date with the changing environment and events as they occur. As I'm writing this, the stock price of TXU (formerly Texas Utilities) has dropped 30 percent in a matter of hours. Bad news was reported, but 30 percent? Is this a great buying opportunity, or do the sellers know something the rest of us don't? Enron was another Texas-based energy company, whose dramatic stock price drop in 2001 preceded bankruptcy and one of the biggest financial scandals ever. A TXU case can be expected on the Web site in the near future. This is an on-going process. Standards change. New regulations are passed. Company and market news have an impact on stock prices.

In my financial analysis course, an equity financial analysis is used as a major project. The PC companies are presented as an example. The classes are divided into groups of four or five and each group selects an industry based on the Fortune 500 industry list. Each individual selects a company from the group's industry for analysis. The format for this analysis is the same as the PC example, which is updated each semester and available on the Web site. The best of the student projects also will be presented on the Web site.

## WEB SITE MATERIALS FOR THE INSTRUCTOR

### Instructor's Solutions Manual

The solutions manual will provide instructors with answers to the conceptual questions and the problems at the end of each chapter. In addition, instructors will find suggested answers to the cases for each chapter. This manual is available for download from an instructor's area of the Web site.

### Test Bank

Over two hundred multiple choice questions are presented, chapter by chapter. Suggested answers are available.

### PowerPoint Slides

Over 140 PowerPoint slides are available to aid instructors in their lectures.

## WEB SITE MATERIALS FOR STUDENTS

### Well-Developed Group Projects

In the three group projects, each group is instructed to choose an industry. Each student in the group chooses a specific company within the industry, and students are asked to write executive summaries, evaluate financial data, and provide complete industry analysis. The final projects challenge students to use all the tools and techniques learned. Sample completed projects are provided as guidance to students.

### Excel Problem

A comprehensive case problem is provided to demonstrate the use of Microsoft Excel® in the financial analysis process. The student will prepare a series of twenty financial ratios, like return on assets, market to book, EPS, and fixed asset turnover, for the thirty companies that make up the Dow Jones Industrial Average.

### Self-quiz Questions

A generous number of additional multiple-choice questions offer students the opportunity to test their understanding of the material and study for exams. Suggested answers are available.

### Directory of Online Resources

This extensive directory includes: Web sites providing stock information and financial services; information on derivatives; mutual funds and economics; industry and banking links; analysis sites; licensing information; libraries; and government sites.

### Hyperlinks

All sites discussed in the textbook are hyperlinked on the Web site for convenient access.

### Relevant Articles

Current articles keep students informed about topics like industry outlooks, mutual funds, and cash flow statements.

### Reference Material

The financial statements of Dell Computer Corporation are used as examples extensively throughout the text. Therefore, the Web site provides the complete Dell 2002 SEC annual report (10-K) for students to access for further reference.

### Accounting History Enrichment

Accounting is a vibrant, current field, at the center of current news stories week after week. But many do not know about accounting's fascinating history! Accounting is as old as civilization. I write about accounting history as well, and have provided articles, links, and historical timelines. Pieces like "The Big Five—Where Were They Then?" will deepen students' understanding of and interest in the field.

## ACKNOWLEDGMENTS

I would like to acknowledge the support of a number of people in the creation of this textbook.

I must thank Jim Byrne for his help in compiling the solutions manual. At Leyh Publishing, my thanks go to Rick Leyh for his encouragement to publish a user-friendly book with Web support. I would like to recognize the hard work of the Leyh editorial team: Lari Bishop, Michele Chancellor, Shoshanna Turek, and Camille McMorrow. In addition, I would like to thank Susan Elbe, Jay O'Callaghan, Keari Bedford, and the other talented people at John Wiley & Sons Publishers.

The development of *Financial Analysis: A User Approach* has benefited greatly from the comments and evaluations of colleagues throughout the country. I would like to thank the following people who provided their time and energy in reviewing the book:

M.J. Abdolmohammadi, Bentley College
Murad Antia, University of South Florida
Leroy W. Ashorn, Sam Houston State University
Florence Atiase, University of Texas at Austin
Michael Dalbor, University of Nevada–Las Vegas
Frank Flanegin, Robert Morris University
Steve Grossman, Texas A&M University
G.P. Hruby, University of Akron
Mallory McWilliams, San Jose State University
Lawrence Metzger, Loyola University
Elisa Moncarz, Florida International University
Dennis Profitt, Grand Canyon University
Kevin Prykull, Duquesne University
Terry Shevlin, University of Washington
Uma Velury, University of Delaware

# About the Author

Gary Giroux is Shelton Professor of Accounting at Texas A&M University. He received his Ph.D. from Texas Tech University and has been at Texas A&M for about twenty-five years. He teaches financial analysis and other financial and governmental courses in the undergraduate program. He also teaches research methods in the Ph.D. program.

Dr. Giroux has published over fifty articles, including publications in *Accounting Review, Journal of Accounting Research, Accounting, Organizations and Society, Journal of Accounting and Public Policy,* and numerous other journals. He is the author of three earlier books, including *Dollars & Scholars, Scribes & Bribes: The Story of Accounting.* His primary research areas are governmental and financial accounting. He also is interested in accounting and business history.

He has a number of outside interests, including collecting revenue documents and stamps, reading, golf, and scuba diving. He and his wife Naomi travel regularly, in part based on international research projects and presentations.

# CHAPTER 1

# What Is Financial Analysis?

**Objectives**

- Identify and define financial analysis.
- Distinguish between internal and external financial analysis perspectives.
- Understand the comprehensive six-step financial analysis process for decision-making.
- Evaluate the focus on a specific purpose for a financial analysis. Consider lending and equity investing as potential contexts for decision-making.
- Analyze the corporate overview process and distinguish between industry analysis and business strategy.
- Evaluate the use of quantitative financial analysis techniques: how are they used and why they can be effective.
- Evaluate the detailed accounting analysis process and identify the importance of detecting existing earnings management techniques.
- Understand the importance of comprehensive analysis to summarize key financial analysis findings.

## INTRODUCTION

Financial analysts use financial and other information to make recommendations and decisions. The process can be used for equity investments, credit decisions, company acquisition decisions, and so on. Analysis is a fundamental part of business decision-making. Analysts use financial statements, detailed accounting information, stock market information, economic and industry information, and other sources.

Basic tools are used to standardize financial information. These include common-size analysis, financial ratios, financial models, forecasts of operations and valuation techniques. Analysts typically are skeptical of raw financial information and use methods to reevaluate or reestimate existing financial information when necessary. These tools and methods are needed to make sound decisions.

The purpose of this book is to present a comprehensive approach to financial analysis with the intent of providing systematic procedures for making reasonable decisions. Most techniques are fundamental to financial analysis decisions, with modifications and additional analysis for each decision type.

A six-step approach is suggested for a systematic financial analysis process:

1. Purpose. Identify the purpose of the specific financial analysis decision.
2. Corporate overview. Develop an overview of the company to be analyzed in the context of the industry and specific purpose of the analysis.
3. Quantitative financial analysis techniques. Calculate common-size statements, financial ratios, financial models, and forecasts using the financial statements as the raw materials for analysis. Include appropriate multiperiod, industry, and market comparisons.
4. Detailed accounting analysis. Consider the relative confidence that should be given to financial statements, given earnings management incentives. Specific accounting topics are reviewed for key issues to evaluate.
5. Comprehensive analysis. Summarize all analytical components, perhaps as an executive summary. Emphasize key decision points, including red flags—major concerns from earlier steps.
6. Financial analysis decision. The recommendation or decision is based on the key factors discovered from the analysis above. A written analysis should support the specific decision made.

All six steps will be described in detail throughout the book, beginning with a brief description in this chapter. The most common purposes of financial analysis are presented in Chapters 12 (Credit Analysis) and 13 (Equity Investment Analysis). Quite a bit of time is spent in Chapter 1 on the corporate overview, with specific examples in Chapters 12 and 13. Quantitative financial analysis techniques (financial ratios, common-size analysis, trends, market analysis, and so on) are described in detail in Chapters 4–6.

Step 4, the **detailed accounting analysis,** primarily studies the complexity of the corporate operations and financial position and determines the relative accuracy and reliability of the financial information. Four chapters, 7 through 10, consider a variety of accounting issues. Chapter 11 considers credit risk. The comprehensive analysis is a summary of the first four steps, emphasizing what's particularly important. This is dealt with in greater detail in Chapters 12 and 13. Finally, the financial decision—the $1,000-an-hour step! Again, this is in Chapters 12 and 13.

In summary, the fundamentals of financial analysis are described in reasonable detail in Chapter 2–11, leading to the knowledge-based analysis and decision-making of Chapters 12 and 13. A reasonable strategy is to get to these final two chapters as soon as possible. However, they become meaningful only with a thorough understanding of the first eleven chapters.

## PURPOSE

Financial analysis requires a context: stock investment, a credit decision, a government giving economic incentives to a corporation, considering the job opportunities of a company, a corporate merger decision, and so on. The detailed components of the analysis depend on the unique objectives required (e.g., a commercial loan for a specific amount of money for some purpose, or a possible investment decision specifically for a 30-year-old woman's aggressive portfolio). Once the purpose is identified, the financial analysis components for the company can be specified.

Consider a lending example. A midsize regional bank (total assets of $250 million) with a specialty in commercial lending to retailers within the state has a request for a 90-day, $100,000 working capital loan from Piles of Tiles. A thorough analysis can be structured to determine whether the line of credit should be granted, what the interest rate should be, and what other terms (such as collateral and debt covenants) are required.

Linda, a thirty-year-old computer analyst at a high technology company, has stock options valued at over $1 million. She wants to convert 25 percent of her vested options into an equity growth portfolio of large companies to diversify her long-term investment holdings. Linda is looking at *Fortune* 500 companies for investment opportunities. She can screen these companies based on specific criteria, such as earnings growth rates, and then conduct a thorough financial analysis of the companies found most promising from her initial search.

These are two of an unlimited number of scenarios. The key point is that the decision-making criteria differ for each. The general focus of analysis will be the same, based on the six-step approach identified above, but the specifics will be unique for each analysis.

## CORPORATE OVERVIEW

The **corporate overview** can be divided into two major sections—industry and business strategy. The purpose is to identify the competing industry and its primary characteristics and to analyze how the company attempts to compete, given the industry characteristics. Financial analysis needs a qualitative perspective of the company analyzed. What industry does the company operate in? What are the unique economic and financial conditions of the company and industry? How does the company compete in this industry? How is the company positioned for the future?

### INDUSTRY ANALYSIS

The relevant industry sometimes can be easy to identify: airlines, banks, chemicals, or food. However, large corporations can have diverse operations, making them more difficult to classify. The *Fortune* 500 companies (www.fortune.com) are broken into sixty-two industries, a useful starting point for **industry analysis** of the largest U.S. corporations. Dell Computer is categorized in the Computers–Office Equipment industry, along with IBM, Hewlett-Packard, Xerox, Sun Microsystems, Gateway, NCR, Apple Computer, and Pitney Bowes. All of these companies manufacture high technology equipment, mainly computer related. Gateway is a direct competitor of Dell, with emphasis on manufacturing personal computers (PCs) using the "wintel" standard. Apple is a direct competitor, except it uses its proprietary software. However, International Business Machines (IBM) and Hewlett-Packard are in the same basic industry. It should be noted that large companies could have many segments across several industry categories. Coca-Cola and Pepsi are not direct competitors in many of their market segments. General Electric essentially is a conglomerate, operating in many diverse fields. USX (formerly United States Steel) acquired Marathon Oil and was classified as a petroleum company in the *Fortune* 500. (U.S. Steel and Marathon now trade separately).

There are no universal standards to define industry. The most comprehensive is the use of **standard industrial classification (SIC) codes,** available through the Department of Labor (www.osha.gov). This method is much more detailed than the *Fortune* 500 list and more comprehensive. The list can be broken into one-, two-, three-, and four-digit codes. The one-digit codes are:

0. Agriculture, forestry, and fishing
1. Mining and construction
2. Manufacturing
3. Manufacturing
4. Transportation, communications, electronic, gas and sanitary services
5. Wholesale and retail trade
6. Finance, insurance and real estate
7. Services
8. Services
9. Public administration

The PC companies are categorized under 3571, using the four-digit code, electronic computers:

3—Manufacturing

35—Industrial machinery and equipment

357—Computers and office equipment

3571—Electronic computers

The complete list of SIC codes is available at asbdc.ualr.edu/sic.

It should be noted that the SIC codes are being replaced by the North American Industry Classification System (NAICS, www.naics.com). These codes first went into effect in 1997 and were revised in 2002. The NAICS codes use a six-digit code. The first two digits identify a major economic sector, the third a subsector, the fourth an industry group, the fifth the NAICS industry, and the sixth, when used, a subdivision of an industry. The NAICS code for the PC companies is 334111, electronic computers manufacturing.

What are the key characteristics of a specific industry? Several questions are obvious. What is the specific industry? What do companies in this industry do? How concentrated is this industry, and how competitive are the companies? Are there obvious economies of scale (that is, do increased production levels reduce unit costs)? What factors are unique to a given industry? Are there unique customer or supplier characteristics? How do U.S. and global economic conditions affect this industry? For example, durable goods manufacturers are directly affected by the business cycle—when economic conditions decline, sales drop precipitously.

Determining key industry characteristics can be difficult, but a number of Web sites can be a good starting point. The *Fortune* 500 list tabulates basic financial data for the firms in each industry. Hoovers (www.hoovers.com) describes each company and has limited industry information. Quicken (www.quicken.com) has company profiles and lists comparison companies. Yahoo (quote.yahoo.com) provides similar information in a somewhat different format. Sector Updates (www.sectorupdates.com) has substantial information for some industries under "Sector News."

Manufacturing industries differ from service industries. Economies of scale are more likely in manufacturing rather than service industries. Concentration ratios can be significant. Some industries deal directly with the public (retail) and others don't (wholesalers). Some industries are inherently regional or national (utilities); others are global (automotive manufacturers) and perhaps have most of their success outside the United States. How many direct competitors exist?

There can be any number of unique conditions associated with an industry. Are there legal barriers such as patent or copyright protections, or do specific industry regulations exist? Pharmaceutical companies depend on patent protection for their new drugs. Utilities are highly regulated (as natural monopolies). Environmental regulations and potential lawsuits are especially significant for chemical companies.

The personal computer industry was quite successful in the 1990s, but it has hit hard times since. The PC is a durable good (as a major acquisition, the decision to buy a computer can be put off when economic conditions are bad or uncertain). The PC also is basically a commodity; most buyers can easily replace one brand name with another. A limited number of large firms are primarily PC manufacturers, including the three analyzed in this book—Dell, Gateway, and Apple. There also are several large computer companies, such as IBM, where PC manufacturing represents only a small business segment. And there are perhaps hundreds of very small computer manufacturers. Consequently, it is an unusual but highly competitive industry.

Dell, Apple, and Gateway are direct competitors, competing against large companies that produce PCs as a business segment and small companies that produce rival products. Most of their effort (Apple is the exception) is production of IBM-compatible PCs based on "wintel" components (a Microsoft Windows operating system and Intel chips). These companies compete fiercely at producing a narrow range of virtually identical (homogeneous) computer products. None of the companies has a dominant market share (Dell is the market leader, with a market share over 10 percent), but most experienced dramatic sales growth in the 1990s as PC demand exploded. Major factors were falling prices and increasing performance of PCs. Demand slowed early this century, and there has been something of a price war started by Dell. This is a dynamic industry where success results in expanding earnings and stock prices and failure can mean being bought out at a bargain price or Chapter 11 bankruptcy.

In this new century, competition may be stronger in this industry. Consumers expect higher performance and lower prices, but both seem to be harder to find. Supplies of key components can be problematic. Growth rates for PCs can be expected to decline at some point and, eventually, the market for PCs should be relatively saturated.

## BUSINESS STRATEGY

Three factors are particularly important to **business strategy:** (1) cost leadership, (2) product differentiation, and (3) core competencies. Lower production costs may be the result of efficient production methods, low input prices, or economies of scale. The low-cost producer has considerable advantages, since this company has the most flexibility in determining selling price. A higher price means higher markups, which should result in greater net income for the price leader and all competitors. A lower price can mean increasing sales at the expense of competitors, which should result in a greater market share. If economies of scale exist, higher sales should be associated with lower unit cost.

If the product is a commodity, such as oil, agricultural products or electricity, there is little or no product differentiation. Presumably, a Jaguar is different from a Ford (although Jaguar is owned by Ford), but is that true for an Olds Intrigue compared to a Toyota Camry? Pharmaceutical companies develop specific drugs that are patent protected, an example of high product differentiation.

Core competencies are what the companies do well. Usually, these are industry specific. Dell should be successful by building a high-quality PC at a low price combined with an effective delivery system. In the case of Dell, the direct model is used—Dell sells directly to end users rather than to distributors. Companies need to identify what their business is and what they do well. Amazon.com decided it was an Internet distribution company rather than a bookstore and expanded rapidly into many other products.

## DELL'S BUSINESS STRATEGY

What is Dell's competitive strategy in the difficult PC industry, and where can information be found to analyze the effectiveness of its business strategy? Analysts use multiple sources, including company information, the business press, and other analysts. They also talk directly to company executives. Dell's Web page (www.dell.com) emphasizes an e-commerce strategy. Dell sells computers directly to individuals and businesses, with a growing share purchased on-line. In the Dell Vision section of the site is a discussion of "The Dell Direct Model," emphasizing price, customization, and service and support. In addition to PCs, Dell is a major provider of servers and enterprise computer products. The company's annual report (10-K for fiscal year 2001) focuses on current operations. Management discussion and analysis (MD&A), an important feature in the annual reports, describes operations from the company's perspective. Dell emphasizes growth and expanding e-commerce with both customers and suppliers:

> The Company's business strategy is based on its direct business model. The Company's business model seeks to deliver a superior customer experience through direct, comprehensive customer relations, cooperative research and development with technology partners, computer systems custom-built to customer specifications and service and support programs tailored to customer needs.
>
> The direct model eliminates the need to support an extensive network of wholesale and retail dealers, thereby avoiding dealer mark-ups; avoid the higher inventory costs associated with the wholesale/retail channel and the competition for retail shelf space. …
>
> The Company is committed to refining and extending the advantages of its direct model approach by moving even greater volumes of product sales, service and support to the Internet. …
>
> The Company's primary product offerings include enterprise systems, notebook computers and desktop computer systems. Enterprise systems include

> PowerEdge servers; PowerApp server appliances; PowerVault storage products; PowerConnect network switchers; and Dell Precision desktop and mobile workstations. The company also markets and sells Dell/EMC storage products under a long-term strategic relationship with EMC Corporation. The Company offers Latitude and Inspiron notebook computers and Dimension, OptiPlex and SmartStep desktop computer systems.
>
> The Company enhances its product offerings with a number of specialized services, including professional consulting services, custom hardware and software integration, leasing and asset management, network installation and support and onsite service. ... The Company offers warranty and technical support for all of its products.
>
> The Company offers specialized custom factory integration services designed to address specific hardware and software integration requirements of customers. These services allow the Company to satisfy a customer's particular integration requirements.
>
> The Company has established a broad range of customers based on continuing relationships with large corporations, government, healthcare and educational institutions and small-to-medium businesses. The Company maintains a field sales force throughout the world to call on business and institutional customers.
>
> The Company's manufacturing process requires a high volume of quality components that are produced from third party suppliers. ... The Company has several single-sourced supplier relationships, either because alternative sources are not available or the relationship is advantageous due to performance, quality, support, delivery, capacity or price considerations (Dell's 2002 10-K, pp. 2–10).

The company's analysis is hardly unbiased. Generally, MD&A and other sources are not critical of the company's business strategy. The financial press is expected to take a more balanced look at Dell's current performance and future. Articles on Dell and its competitors can be found in *Fortune, Business Week, The Wall Street Journal,* and other publications. Additional information is found on the Web sites of these and other financial organizations. The financial press has generally been favorable to Dell, but concerns have been expressed about the company's ability to meet future expectations of sales and income growth and Dell's ability to penetrate business markets dominated by other companies.

An article in *The Wall Street Journal* stated:

> Dell's strategy is collapsing profit margins throughout the PC market, a dire development for rivals who can't keep up. Dell is pricing its machines not much like lucrative high-tech products, but more like airline tickets and other low-margin commodities. That puts pressure on Dell to push up sales volume to compensate for the thinner margins.
>
> For Dell, the strategy is paying off. In the first quarter of 2001, shipments of personal computers worldwide grew by 852,000 units, to 31.6 million, while Dell's unit sales alone grew by 957,000 units (June 8, 2001, p. A1).

Dell's performance dropped since this was written. The 2002 results are lower than in previous years, but still in the black on slightly declining sales.

Dell's corporate overview can be summarized this way for industry and business strategy:

| Industry Issue | Discussion |
|---|---|
| 1. What is the industry? | Personal computer industry, specializing in PCs and related computer hardware and technical support |
| 2. What is the relative size and significance, based on *Fortune* 1000 list? | This is a relatively small industry. It is a part of the Computers, Office Equipment industry in the *Fortune* 1000 list. Most of these firms are broad-based manufacturers, providing software and technical support for a large range of products. |
| 3. What are the largest companies in the industry? | Dell is the largest PC company, but only third largest under Computers, Office Equipment, following IBM and Hewlett-Packard. Gateway and Apple are somewhat smaller. |
| 4. What is the geographic presence in this industry (local, U.S. only, multinational or global)? | The PC firms are multinational, with primary focus on the U.S. market. The larger computer companies, such as IBM, are global. |
| 5. How does the business cycle affect this industry? Future potential? | These are durable goods, and production follows the business cycle closely. Consequently, all have been hurt by the recent recession. |

| Business Strategy Issues | Discussion |
|---|---|
| 1. Brief historical perspective on this company. | Michael Dell started assembling PCs in his dorm room at the University of Texas in the 1980s. The company has continued to grow by stressing efficiency, speed, and direct selling |
| 2. What is the primary focus of operations? | Dell stresses efficient production and quick delivery at low prices using the "wintel" formula for computers. |
| 3. What is the most important strategy used by this company (e.g., low-cost producer, product differentiation, quality, or service)? | Dell is the low-cost producer and continues to lower prices to increase market share. Dell has remained profitable and substantially increased market share, while all competitors are struggling. |
| 4. What are the major operating segments? | Dell's operations are split between consumers and businesses. Dell has expanded production into servers and other products for business. |
| 5. What is the ou ecast) for this company over one to five years? | Excellent. The low cost, direct sell strategy is working; margins and net income are off a bit, but market share has substantially increased. During a period of economic recovery, Dell should substantially increase profitability. |

## Quantitative Financial Analysis

The primary source of financial analysis data is the financial statements of the company. **Quantitative financial analysis** techniques, which are a host of ratios, models, time series, and forecasts to identify key financial characteristics that can be compared to competitors or other standards, serve three basic functions. First, financial information is standardized. Common-size analysis and financial ratios convert raw numbers into percentages. Cash can be stated as a percent of current liabilities. The relationship of debt to equity can be analyzed as leverage percentages. Net income as a percent of sales is one of many profitability measures. Second, financial trends can be analyzed over time. Has return on sales gone up over the last five years? Are liquidity ratios higher this year relative to last year? Third, ratios and other measures can be compared with direct competitors, industry averages, or marketwide averages.

This information is historical. That is, it is based on financial events that have already occurred. Ironically, this is the primary source of analysis to determine how the company will perform in the future. Virtually all financial analysis decisions are based on expectations and forecasts of future performance, using historical data.

Dell's income statement for the fiscal year ended February 1, 2002, shows a net income of $1.25 billion on sales of $31.1 billion. Thus, return on sales (net income/sales or $1.25/$31.1) is 4.0 percent. Is this good? In the previous year, Dell has a return on sales of 6.8 percent, based on sales of $31.9 billion (sales essentially flat, down $800 million or 2.5 percent for the year). For a comparable period (year ended December 31, 2001), Gateway lost $1.0 billion on sales of $6.1 billion. Thus, Dell avoided the performance disaster of its closest competitors, but it had a lower return rate than the previous year. This provides useful information on Dell's performance, but a complete financial analysis is needed before meaningful investment decisions can be attempted.

## Detailed Accounting Analysis

Detailed accounting analysis is the analysis of financial statements and other sources of information to further evaluate how corporations compete in complex environments. The financial statements provide the basic data for the preceding financial analysis. The income statement and balance sheet numbers are based on a complex set of accounting standards called generally accepted accounting principles (GAAP). GAAP allows alternative procedures, such as inventory methods and depreciation, and gives considerable leeway to management on how to report the financial data. Thus, differences can arise because the companies do not use the same procedures.

Large corporations operate in complex environments. Financial statements condense and simplify financial position and results from operations. Additional accounting and financial details are available in the footnotes. Management discussion and analysis (MD&A) and the president's letter should be reviewed for the company's perspective on operating performance and business strategy.

Another problem is the potential for **earnings management.** Managers have incentives to show good earnings (to improve bonuses and boost stock prices that make stock options more attractive, for example). This can be achieved through successful business strategies and improved operating efficiencies. Alternatively, improved earnings numbers can be reported by manipulating the accounting numbers: more aggressive revenue recognition, using methods to reduce current period expenses, recording one-time gains as operating revenue, or recording losses as nonrecurring items. The disclosure of bad news may be avoided or discounted, thus understating financial risks, such as potential losses from lawsuits and other contingencies. Liabilities may be understated by using off-balance-sheet financing, such as operating leases.

Analysts must understand accounting differences across firms, potential financial risks, and the likelihood for earnings management. Effectively, this means that each financial statement item and all footnotes must be analyzed for potential problems. Does Dell use accounting policies similar to the industry? Does Dell management have incentives that suggest potential earnings management? Does Dell have potential contingencies that increase financial risk? Are there uncertainties concerning Dell's foreign operations? Are there other areas of concern?

Answers to these questions may be found in the notes in the latest annual report. Notes present detailed financial data not obvious from the financial statements. The first note summaries Dell's accounting procedures, which can be compared with industry competitors for similarities and differences. Specific accounting issues can be learned through a detailed analysis of the relevant notes. Special charges from workforce reduction are described in Note 2. Dell's stock options, described in Note 6, are a potential concern.

Analysts should remain skeptical of financial information presented and should base their judgments on the detailed information available. Under some circumstances, ratios can be adjusted or new ratios calculated to provide more useful comparisons.

## Comprehensive Analysis

The findings from the steps above are summarized in the comprehensive analysis, stressing the most relevant information for determining whether or not to invest in Dell. In other words, what's really important? It is recommended that this be a formal process with a brief analytical write-up of all components. Emphasis is on the key points, both good and bad. Particularly important is the discussion of any red flags that were recognized. These are the areas of particular concern, where the company underperforms based on trend or industry comparisons or other factors that suggest increased financial risk. Green flags for really good news also can be used. In a written report, it is useful to start with an executive summary, followed by detailed analysis of each component. It can be useful to rate all categories of the financial analysis section. If a 1–10 scale is used with 10 representing excellence, it might be expected that ratings of 8 and above be achieved on most important categories.

## Financial Analysis Decision

The decision is based on the initial purpose of the analysis. A commercial loan for a specific purpose is approved or denied by a commercial bank. If approved, the loan terms must be specified based on the relative credit risk of the borrower and possibly other factors such as the long-term relationship with this customer. The analysis is based on the probability that the loan principal and interest will be paid when due. A stock for an investment portfolio is recommended to be acquired (or held or sold) based on the investor's criteria. The most relevant criterion, in most cases, is the ability of the company to generate earnings growth.

All decisions are based on a thorough **financial analysis.** The company's future is predicted largely on what has happened in the past and how the company has positioned itself for future competition and business opportunities. The analyst needs to combine all the information effectively. Generally, information from the various sources corroborates the relative financial health of the firm. Successful companies are expected to excel in all dimensions. Poor performers should have multiple problem areas identified and several red flags.

Of course, positive recommendations may be made for poor performers and vice versa. A bank loan may be extended to a poorly performing company if the probability of default is low and the company provides adequate collateral. An investor may decline to invest in a successful company if the price earnings ratio is too high or the company does not meet the investment goals of the portfolio. A poor performer can be a buy if reorganization is expected to be successful and the current stock price is low relative to future earnings expectations.

## SUMMARY

This chapter describes the importance of financial analysis as a systematic procedure to arrive at specific recommendations and decisions based on qualitative and quantitative techniques. Although the specific tools used will vary by purpose, the same basic process is suggested for each financial analysis decision. The focus is on two important categories of financial analysis: credit and investment decisions.

A six-step process is used as a systematic procedure for all financial analysis decision:

1. Purpose of financial analysis
2. Overview of company analyzed
3. Quantitative Financial analysis techniques used for analysis
4. Detailed accounting analysis on specific issues, potential earnings management and relative confidence in the financial numbers
5. Comprehensive analysis, usually including an executive summary
6. Financial analysis decision

Each step is summarized to identify why it's important and how it fits into the overall analysis. A consistent approach for all financial decisions is suggested, modified for the specific analysis at hand.

## KEY TERMS

business strategy
corporate overview
detailed accounting analysis
earnings management
external financial analysis
financial analysis
industry analysis
internal financial analysis
quantitative financial analysis
Standardized Industry Classification (SIC) codes

## QUESTIONS

1. What is financial analysis and how can it be used to make a recommendation about a company asking for a loan? For an equity investment decision?
2. Give an example of an internal financial analysis decision. An external decision.
3. Assume you are asked to develop a financial analysis strategy for a forty-year-old manager who is restructuring her 401K retirement portfolio. Identify the purpose of the analysis and the key points needed.

4. You are asked to evaluate the chemical industry as part of a corporate overview of Dow Chemical. How would you go about this analysis?
5. Why are quantitative financial analysis techniques important for both internal and external financial analysis projects?
6. Why is specific accounting knowledge important for external financial analysis?
7. What is comprehensive analysis and why is it a necessary step in the financial analysis process?

## PROBLEMS

Throughout the book most problems will focus on (1) the chemical industry using Du Pont, Dow, and PPG, (2) the Hotel and Resort Industry using Hilton, Marriott and Mandalay Resorts, and (3) the automotive industry using Ford and General Motors.

### Problem 1.1 Du Pont's Corporate Overview and Business Strategy

The following are excerpts from various sources.

**Industry:** The chemical industry is global, with corporations producing both commodities and specialty products. A vast number of products are produced, with companies specializing in everything from bulk products with low margins to high-margin specialty products resulting from research and development. In the *Fortune* 1000, thirty-four chemical companies are listed (thirteen in the *Fortune* 500), with combined sales of $154 billion. Du Pont is the largest with revenues of $29 billion. Economic conditions have a moderate effect on this industry, but they have a differential impact on companies' specific products. Environmental regulations and other legal concerns have a major impact on this industry, again with differential effects by company.

From Hoover's Company Capsule (www.hoovers.com)

> E. I. du Pont de Nemours is the largest chemical company in the U.S. Developer of Lycra, Dacron, and Teflon, Du Pont has operations in about 65 countries. Its eight business units make products including coatings, nylon, specialty polymers, and pigments and chemicals.

History: From Hoover's Handbook (1993, p. 249):

> E. I. Du Pont fled the French Revolution . . . [and] founded E. I. Du Pont de Nemours [1802] and set up a gunpowder plant [in Delaware]. Within a decade the plant grew to be the largest of its kind in the U.S. . . . In 1902 Du Pont cousins Pierre, Alfred, and Coleman bought Du Pont and in 1903 instituted a centralized structure with functionally organized departments, an innovation that big business widely adopted. . . . In the 1920s Du Pont bought and improved French cellophane technology and began production of rayon. Du Pont's inventions include neoprene synthetic rubber (1931), Orlon, Dacron, and many others.

DuPont's Web page:

> DuPont is a science company, delivering science-based solutions in markets such as food and nutrition, health care, apparel, home and construction, electronics and transportation.
>
> Two hundred years ago, DuPont was primarily an explosives company. One hundred years ago, our focus turned to global chemicals, materials and energy. Today,

entering our third century, we deliver science-based solutions that make real differences in real lives. Look closely at the things around your home and, chances are, you'll find a DuPont imprint.

Our ability to adapt to change and our foundation of unending scientific inquiry enabled this two-century journey to becoming one of the world's most innovative companies. But, in the face of constant change, innovation and discovery, our core values have remained constant: commitment to safety, health and the environment; integrity and high ethical standards; and treating people with fairness and respect.

From DuPont's 2001 10-K:

DuPont was founded in 1802 and was incorporated in Delaware in 1915. DuPont is a world leader in science and technology in a range of disciplines including high-performance materials, synthetic fibers, electronics, specialty chemicals, agriculture and biotechnology. The company operates globally through some 22 strategic business units. Within the strategic business units, a wide range of products are manufactured for distribution and sale to many different markets, including the transportation, textile, construction, motor vehicle, agricultural, home furnishings, medical, packaging, electronics and the nutrition and health markets.

The company and its subsidiaries have operations in about 75 countries worldwide and, as a result, about 50 percent of consolidated sales are made to customers outside the United States. Subsidiaries and affiliates of DuPont conduct manufacturing, seed production, or selling activities, and some are distributors of products manufactured by the company.

In February 2002, the company announced the realignment of its businesses into five market- and technology-focused growth platforms and its plans for the creation of a Textiles and Interiors subsidiary. The growth platforms are: DuPont Electronic & Communication Technologies; DuPont Performance Materials; DuPont Coatings & Color Technologies; DuPont Safety & Protection; and DuPont Agriculture & Nutrition. Du Pont will consider a full range of options to separate Du Pont Textiles & Interiors from the company by year-end 2003, market conditions permitting.

Sales in 2001 were $24,726, down from $28,268 in 2000. Net income in 2001 was $4,339 million, up from $2,314; however, $3,866 million was a gain on the sale of DuPont Pharmaceutials.

We faced the worst economic environment in two decades, unusually high energy prices and unfavorable currency exchange rates. . . . Overall mission is substantial growth—creating value for our shareholders.

From DuPont's MD&A (2000 Annual Report)

Consolidated sales in 2000 were a record $28.3 billion, $1.4 billion or 5 percent above 1999. Specialty Fibers, Specialty Polymers and Pigments & Chemicals segments had the most positive impact on volume.

Net income for the year 2000 was $2,314 million compared with $7,690 million in 1999. The decrease in net income principally reflects the absence of a $7,471 million after-tax gain recorded in 1999 of discontinued business . . .

> Income from continuing operations was $2,314 million or $2.19 per share in 2000, compared to $219 million of $.19 per share in 1999.

Use this information (plus other Internet searches) to write a one-page Corporate Overview for Du Pont (one paragraph on industry and one paragraph on business strategy). Be sure to answer the following questions.

**Industry**

1. What is the industry?
2. What is the relative size and significance, based on the *Fortune* 1000 list?
3. What are the largest companies in the industry?
4. What is the geographic presence in this industry (local, U.S. only, multinational, or global)?
5. What is the impact of the business cycle on this industry? Future potential?

**Business Strategy**

1. Give a brief historical perspective on this company.
2. What is the primary focus of operations of this company?
3. What is the most important strategy used by this company (e.g., low-cost producer, product differentiation, quality, or service)?
4. What are the major operating segments?
5. What is the outlook (operating forecast) for this company (1–5 years)?

## Problem 1.2 Hilton's Corporate Overview and Business Strategy

The following are excerpts from various sources.

**Industry:** The hotel, casino, and resort industry includes nine companies on *Fortune's* 1000 list, with Hilton at No. 499 based on revenue. Total revenues for the group were $35 billion in 2001, with income down substantially to $791 million. Marriott is the largest of the group, at No. 189. These companies have global operations, although their primary focus usually is in the United States. The corporations operate in somewhat different sectors, although all have major hotel operations. This is a capital-intensive industry and depends on tourism for most of its revenue and growth. They were hit hard by the recession of 2001 and the September 11 attacks. From Hoover's Company Capsule (www.hoovers.com):

> The company's lodging empire includes some 2,000 hotels (about 80% are franchised), mostly located in the U.S. Hilton operates 21 vacation resorts [but] has completely cashed out of the gaming industry.

History: From Hoover's Handbook (1993, p. 326)

> Conrad Hilton got his start in hotel management by renting rooms in his family's New Mexico home. [He bought] his first hotel in Cisco, Texas. He survived the Great Depression. He began buying hotels again. He founded Hilton International to manage his foreign business (1948) and realized his ambition to run New York's Waldorf-Astoria (1949). The company began to franchise in 1965. Conrad's son Baron became president in 1966.

From Hilton's MD&A, 2001 10-K

> We are primarily engaged in the ownership, management and development of hotels, resorts and timeshare properties and the franchising of lodging properties. Our brands include Hilton, Hilton Garden Inn, Doubletree, Embassy Suites,

Hampton, Homewood Suites by Hilton. In addition, we develop and operate timeshare resorts through Hilton Grand Vacations Company.

Our operations consist of three reportable segments, which are based on similar products or services: Hotel Ownership, Managing and Franchising, and Timeshare. The Hotel Ownership segment derives revenue primarily from the rental of rooms as well as food and beverage operations at our owned, majority owned and leased hotel properties and equity earnings from unconsolidated affiliates. The Management and Franchising segment provides services including hotel management and licensing of the Hilton family of brands. This segment generates its revenue from management and franchise fees charged to hotel owners. The Timeshare segment consists of multi-unit timeshare resorts.

Development: We intend to grow our hotel brands primarily through franchising and the addition of management contracts, which require little or no capital investment. In addition, we will continue to invest in normal capital replacement and select major renovation projects at our owned hotels, and we may seek to acquire hotel properties on a strategic and selective basis.

Fiscal 2001 compared with fiscal 2000 (in millions):

| | **2000** | **2001** | **% Change** |
|---|---|---|---|
| Revenue | $3,451 | $3,050 | **—12%** |
| Operating Income | 830 | 632 | **—24** |
| Net Income | 272 | 166 | **—39** |
| EPS, Basic | 0.73 | 0.45 | **—39** |

Note: particularly important numbers are in bold. Usually these suggest "bad news."

All operating numbers are down, due to a combination of the recession and September 11 attacks.

From Hilton's Web page (www.hilton.com):

Conrad Hilton purchased his first hotel in Cisco, Texas back in 1919. The first hotel to carry the Hilton name was built in Dallas in 1925. In 1943, Hilton became the first "coast-to-coast" hotel chain in the United States; and in 1949, open its first hotel outside the U.S. in San Juan, Puerto Rico. Hilton went on the New York Stock Exchange in 1946, and Conrad Hilton purchased the Waldorf Astoria in 1949. Hilton has several world-renowned, marquee properties; some of which are: Beverly Hilton, Cavalieri Hilton in Rome, Hilton Athens, Hilton San Francisco, Hilton New York, Hilton Hawaiian Village, Hilton Waikoloa Village, Paris Hilton, and others.

Hilton Hotels Corporation is recognized around the world as a preeminent lodging hospitality company, offering guests and customers the finest accommodations, services, amenities and value for business or leisure. While the Hilton brand has, for more than 80 years, been synonymous with excellence in the hospitality industry, our acquisition in 1999 of Promus Hotel Corporation expanded our family of brands to include such well-known and highly respected brand names as Hampton Inn®, Doubletree®, Embassy Suites Hotels®, and Homewood Suites® by Hilton. Through ownership of some of the most recognized hotels in the world and our newly enhanced brand portfolio, Hilton is now able to offer guests the widest possible variety of hotel experiences, including four-star city center hotels, convention properties, all-suite hotels, extended stay, mid-priced focused service, destination resorts, vacation ownership, airport hotels and conference centers.

Today's Hilton can be viewed as a major industry competitor in a number of areas:

- Owning hotels. Hilton owns such unique, irreplaceable hotel assets as New York's Waldorf-Astoria, The Hilton Hawaiian Village® on Waikiki Beach, Chicago's Palmer House Hilton and the Hilton San Francisco on Union Square. These large-scale properties occupy the best locations in the nation's best markets.
- Managing/franchising hotels. The company is a prominent franchisor of hotels across its entire brand family, with income from management or franchise fees accounting for some 30 percent of Hilton's total cash flow. The company will open, through its franchisees, approximately 430 hotels and sixty-three thousand rooms in 2000–01, consisting primarily of Hampton Inn, Homewood Suites by Hilton and Hilton Garden Inn hotels.
- Vacation ownership. Hilton Grand Vacations Club, the company's vacation ownership business, operates properties across the country including such desirable locales as Las Vegas, Orlando, Miami and (in 2001) Honolulu.
- International. A global strategic alliance with Hilton International, the London-based company that owns the rights to the Hilton brand outside of the U.S., brings to customers a single, seamless Hilton system of two thousand hotels in more than fifty countries throughout the world. Additionally, Conrad International offers five-star luxury hotels in England, Ireland, Belgium, Hong Kong, Singapore, Turkey and Egypt.

Use this information (plus other Internet searches) to write a one-page Corporate Overview for Hilton (one paragraph on industry and one paragraph on business strategy). Be sure to answer the following questions.

### Industry

1. What is the industry?
2. What is the relative size and significance, based on *Fortune* 1000 list?
3. What are the largest companies in the industry?
4. What is the geographic presence in this industry (local, U.S. only, multinational, or global)?
5. What is the impact of the business cycle on this industry? Future potential?

### Business Strategy

1. Give a brief historical perspective on this company.
2. What is the primary focus of operations of this company?
3. What is the most important strategy used by this company (e.g., low-cost producer, product differentiation, quality, or service)?
4. What are the major operating segments?
5. What is the outlook (operating forecast) for this company (1–5 years)?

## Problem 1.3 Ford's Corporate Overview and Business Strategy

The following are excerpts from various sources.

> **Industry:** The 100-year-old motor vehicle industry is global, with major North American, European, and Asian markets. Auto manufacturing is among the largest and most complex of the heavy industrials in the world and companies complete is auto, truck, SUV, and other markets. Competition is fierce with all companies attempting to gain market share in the major markets. These are durable goods, subject to business cycle conditions. When economic conditions are robust, these companies tend to be immensely profitable. But during recession, massive losses are the rule. Only Ford and General Motors are listed on the *Fortune* 1000 list. However, the *Fortune* Global 500 has sixteen listed manufacturers, including DaimlerChrysler, Toyota, Volkswagen, Honda, and Nissan. Globally, this is a trillion-dollar industry (in sales). Individual companies have their own strengths and weakness by geographic area and product. The industry is subject to safety, fuel economy, and environmental regulations. Lawsuits also are common.

From Hoover's Company Capsule (www.hoovers.com)

> Ford Motor started a manufacturing revolution with its mass production assembly lines in the early 1900s. Now Ford is firmly entrenched in the status quo as the world's largest truck maker and the #2 maker of cars and trucks, behind General Motors. It makes vehicles under the Aston Martin, Ford, Jaguar, Lincoln, Mercury, and Volvo brands. Two of its biggest successes are the Ford Taurus and the F-Series pickup. Ford also owns a controlling (33 percent) stake in Mazda and has purchased BMW's Land Rover SUV operations. Ford's finance subsidiary, Ford Motor Credit, is the U.S.'s #1 auto finance company. Ford also owns 81 percent of Hertz, the #1 car rental firm in the world. The Ford family owns about 34 percent of the firm's voting stock.

History: From *Hoover's Handbook* (1993, p. 280)

> Henry Ford began the Ford Motor Company in 1903 in Dearborn, Michigan, hoping to design a car he could mass-produce. In 1908 he introduced the Model T. ... Ford perfected the moving assembly line. ... By 1916 the cars cost $360; by 1920—60 percent of all vehicles were Fords. ... It was 1956 before the Ford allowed outside ownership. [During the Depression] market share slipped behind GM and Chrysler. ... In 1950 Ford recaptured 2nd place from Chrysler.

From Ford's Management Discussion and Analysis (2001 Annual Report)

> Our worldwide sales and revenues were $162.4 billion in 2001, down $7.7 billion from 2000, reflecting primarily lower vehicle sales in North America, offset partially by higher vehicle sales in Europe. We sold 6,991,000 cars and trucks in 2001, down 433,000 units. ... The Company lost $5,453 million in 2001 after a net income of $3,467 in 2000.

Results summary: Automotive

- North America, return on sales of –2.3 percent
- Europe, return on sales of 0.8 percent
- Rest of world, earned $156 million
- Financial services: earnings declined 22 percent

Stockholders' equity was $7.8 billion 12/31/01, down $10.8 billion due to net losses, dividend payments, foreign currency translation, etc.

Bond ratings were lowered by Moody's in 2002 (from A3 to Baa1 on long-term debt), S&P (from A– to BBB) and Fitch (from A+ to A–).

From Ford's Review of Major Operations (2000 Annual Report)

**2000 Operating Highlights**

- Improved worldwide automotive sales of $170.1 billion in 2000, up $9.4 billion from 1999
- Record 7.4 million vehicles sold worldwide
- Income from operations for automotive $3.6 billion and $5,410 billion overall

**Competitive Strengths**

- Worldwide truck leadership
- Total cost management
- Global product development capability and distribution network
- Global platforms/great brands
- Strong union relations
- Strong balance sheet
- Highest U.S. customer loyalty

**Breakthrough Priorities**

- E-business
- Customer Satisfaction

From the Ford CEO's Letter (2000 Annual Report)

At the start of last year we reconfirmed our commitment to being the leading consumer company for automotive products and services. This makes customers the foundation of everything we do and superior shareholder returns the ultimate measure of our success.

Our two breakthrough strategic priorities—customer satisfaction and e-business—are aligned with the customer-driven vision. We made tremendous progress on both initiatives in 2000.

Use this and other Internet sources to write a one-page Corporate Overview for Ford (one paragraph on industry and one paragraph on business strategy). Be sure to answer the following questions.

### Industry

1. What is the industry?
2. What is the relative size and significance, based on the *Fortune* 1000 list?
3. What are the largest companies in the industry?
4. What is the geographic presence in this industry (local, U.S. only, multinational, or global)?
5. What is the impact of the business cycle on this industry? Future potential?

### Business Strategy

1. Give a brief historical perspective on this company.
2. What is the primary focus of operations of this company?
3. What is the most important strategy used by this company (e.g., low-cost producer, product differentiation, quality, or service)?
4. What are the major operating segments?
5. What is the outlook (operating forecast) for this company (1–5 years)?

## CASES

### Case 1.1 Is IBM a Direct Competitor of Dell's?

IBM is the world's largest provider of computer hardware, everything from notebooks to mainframes and network servers. It's number two to Microsoft in software and also a major player in peripherals and computer services. About 60 percent of IBM's sales are outside the United States. IBM PC sales (part of IBM's personal systems division) represent a 4 percent market share, up 1.1 percent from 1999. IBM is shifting to Internet sales. An operating summary from IBM's 2000 segment reporting note (in millions) is:

| | Personal Systems Segment | Total Segments |
|---|---|---|
| Revenue | $16,250 | $96,370 |
| Pre-tax income | –148 | 10,891 |
| Total assets | 2,442 | 69,263 |

Is IBM a direct competitor of Dell's? Answer yes or no and explain. For more information see www.ibm.com and www.dell.com.

## ETHICS CONSIDERATIONS

Many industries are associated with specific public policy issues. Tobacco companies produce products that cause health problems and governments and individuals have sued the companies for billions. Chemical companies produce some dangerous chemicals, some that cause environmental damage. Perhaps the most significant problem is chemical dumping in water and land sites. Environmental Protection Agency damage assessments, lawsuits, and regulatory fines have cost the chemical industry hundreds of millions of dollars. Other industries have various public policy problems. Autos cause pollution and are subject to fuel mileage and safety issue, utilities are air polluters, pharmaceutical companies produce drugs with unexpected side effects.

a. These are industry problems important to analysts. What should be the major focus? The specific public policy issues involved? Or should the focus be exclusively on the potential for damages that reduce earnings?
b. Take the position of a specific user, either potential creditor or equity investor. Does this perspective change your answer from (a) above?

## INTERNET PROJECTS

### Project 1.1

Pick a company for a Corporate Overview and Business Strategy. Use the company's annual report, Hoover's Company Capsule (www.hoovers.com), *Fortune's Fortune* 500 industry (www.fortune.com) and other sources to write a one-page Corporate Overview for this company (one paragraph on the industry and one paragraph on the business strategy).

CHAPTER

# 2 The Financial Environment

### Objectives

- Describe capital markets and distinguish between the equity and debt markets and between the primary and secondary markets. Understand the key decisions involved in credit and equity markets.
- Understand the mission of the Securities and Exchange Commission in regulating securities markets and the role of the Financial Accounting Standards Board and other regulatory bodies in establishing generally accepted accounting principles.
- Interpret management incentives for disclosure; specifically, know why managers may not be willing to provide complete and accurate financial information.
- Evaluate the role of finance theory in determining expected financial behavior, including efficient markets, random walk, portfolio theory, and beta (ß) analysis.
- Interpret why efficient contracting is important for corporations and understand the relationship of efficient contracting to transaction cost. Understand the relationship between economic behavior and opportunism.
- Describe agency theory and evaluate the importance of agency costs.
- Evaluate the relationship between economic consequences and accounting choice, including the standard-setting process.

## INTRODUCTION

The financial environment is complex, but it must be understood by the analyst. The capital markets are central to this environment, the source of long- and short-term financing for companies, governments, and individuals. The capital markets include commercial and investment banks, stock and bond markets, and other financial institutions. The Securities and Exchange Commission (SEC), Federal Reserve, and other national and state organizations regulate capital markets.

The SEC and Financial Accounting Standards Board (FASB) regulate financial accounting. The codification of standards issued by the FASB is one definition of **generally accepted accounting principles** (GAAP). Analysts need a general familiarity with GAAP and knowledge of how to research complex accounting issues.

Equity and other capital markets have characteristics that should be known by analysts. Financial economists who viewed the market (at least the one for the largest corporations) as efficient developed investment "portfolio" theories to maximize the rate of return for different risk levels. Considerable controversy exists on this academic perspective, but it offers useful insight to potential market behavior.

Managers have incentives to behave in their own best interests, which may or may not benefit investors and other users of financial statements. This has been demonstrated by recent financial scandals involving large corporations, including WorldCom, Enron, Xerox, Tyco, and Merrill Lynch, to name a few. Analysts need a conceptual and practical knowledge of anticipated behavior based on incentives if they are to predict the type of earnings management techniques expected and how that may influence financial analysis conclusions.

## Capital Markets

Capital markets can be divided into equity and debt markets and **primary** and **secondary markets.** Companies first issue stock in the primary equity market as initial public offerings (IPOs). Shares of stock of large public corporations are bought and sold on the secondary equity markets that include the three major exchanges: New York Stock Exchange (NYSE), National Association of Securities Dealers Automated Quotations system (NASDAQ), and the American Stock Exchange (Amex). A bank loan or the initial issue of bonds part of the primary debt market, while the buying and selling of existing debt securities is done on the secondary debt market. This can be summarized as follows in Exhibit 2.1.

This book focuses on two capital market areas: (1) bank loans and (2) buying and selling stock on the secondary equity market. The Federal Reserve, Federal Deposit Insurance Corporation (FDIC), and other federal and state regulators regulate banks. The **Securities and Exchange Commission** regulates the securities markets. Regulation adds confidence for individuals making decisions in these markets. Many types of transactions are regulated, limiting transaction flexibility and how they are reported. Thus, business acquisitions must be reported using the purchase method. Regulations disallow certain types of decisions and behavior, such as insider trading. In extreme cases, violators can be prosecuted as criminals.

**EXHIBIT 2.1 THE CAPITAL MARKETS**

| | Equity | Debt |
|---|---|---|
| **Primary** | Initial public offerings | Bank loan, initial debt securities offering |
| **Secondary** | Buying and selling of stocks on securities markets | Secondary debt market |

## Credit Decisions

Commercial banks are a major provider of short-term commercial loans. Banks take in deposits and invest this money in commercial and consumer loans and other allowed investments such as Treasury and municipal securities. Commercial loans typically make up a large percentage of a bank's investment portfolio, since they are profitable when credit risks are limited.

A small but growing business may ask for a revolving loan to borrow up to some maximum amount to fund inventory or other current operations. The bank's credit department would complete a financial analysis of the firm to determine creditworthiness and potential credit risk. The major concern is the ability of the company to pay back interest and principal when due. If the company is considered worthy of a loan, an interest rate is determined along with necessary collateral and debt covenants, which are contractual terms to protect the bank from potential default. Interest rates often are based on the prime rate, the interest rate granted to the bank's premier customers. Interest rates could be 1 percent to 3 percent over prime, with the 3 percent increase assigned to riskier companies. Company assets, such as accounts receivable, inventory, or fixed assets, could be required for collateral. The debt covenant could require minimum levels of liquidity or maximum leverage ratios.

U.S. commercial banks at the beginning of 2000 had $1,012.5 billion in commercial loans outstanding and $3,520.3 billion in total loans. Total assets of commercial banks were $5,644.2 billion. There were about 3,400 banks with assets over $100 million.

## Equity Investment Decisions

Buy, sell, and hold decisions for common stock (and related securities) are based on prices determined in the secondary equity markets. Public securities trade on formal market exchanges. Most large companies trade on the New York Stock Exchange (NYSE), while high technology companies often trade on NASDAQ.

Investors can use investment brokers for transactions involving individual securities. Historically, buy and sell transactions were relatively expensive. Now investors can use the Internet to find discount brokers who may charge $10 or less per transaction. A useful alternative is mutual funds, portfolios of securities managed by investment professionals.

At the turn of the century (2000), NASDAQ listed 4,829 companies, with a total market capitalization (market cap) over $5 trillion. The dollar volume of NASDAQ was $10.8 trillion in 1999 (51 percent of the volume for the three major exchanges) on 270 billion shares. NYSE listed 3,025 companies, with a market cap of $16 trillion, while Amex listed 769 companies.

Stock investing has high short-term risks, since individual stocks (or the entire market) can drop substantially in a single day. On October 19, 1987, the Dow Jones Industrial Average (DJIA) dropped 508 points and, in a matter of days, the market lost about a quarter of its value. However, professionals claim that the best long-term investment returns come from a diversified stock portfolio. The Standard & Poor's 500 companies represent one definition of the market—and an investor can buy an S&P 500 index fund. S&P companies have a long-term annual return (dividends plus market appreciation) of about 12 percent.

# SEC Regulation

As stated by the SEC on its Web page (www.sec.gov): "The primary mission ... is to protect investors and maintain the integrity of the securities markets." When the stock market crashed in October 1929 and the Great Depression followed, people lost faith in both the stock market and the banking system. Franklin Roosevelt won the presidential election of 1932 by promising a New Deal to end the depression and restore confidence in basic capitalistic institutions. Along with bank reform, the SEC was established in 1934 to enforce the new securities laws. The major legislation included the Securities Act of 1933, the Securities and Exchange Act of 1934, and the Investment Company Act of 1940.

The SEC has five commissioners, each appointed to five-year terms. Joseph P. Kennedy (father of John F. Kennedy) was the first chairman of the SEC. Arthur Levitt was the chairman until the election of George W. Bush as president. Levitt was an activist, and views are mixed about his tenure, depending on whether SEC activism was appreciated. Generally, financial analysts favor an active SEC, the result of which is additional corporate disclosure. President Bush appointed Harvey Pitt, a securities lawyer, as chairman.

Public corporations must register with the SEC's Division of Corporation Finance. Newly offered securities require a registration statement. Annual and quarterly filings (**Forms 10-K** and **10-Q** for companies with over $10 million in assets and securities held by more than five hundred owners), as well as proxy statements, merger and acquisition filings, and other documents are required from all public companies. Registration statements and other information are available to the public shortly after filing on the EDGAR database (www.sec.gov). Several Internet sources can be used to access 10-Ks and other EDGAR filings.

The Division of Enforcement investigates potential violations of securities laws. Common violations include insider trading, misrepresenting or omitting important securities information, manipulating the stock price, and sales of securities without SEC registration. After the Enron debacle, the SEC increased its enforcement effort. Enron's problems became public in 2001. Enron restated 2000 and 2001 earnings in its third quarter 2001 10-Q and declared bankruptcy on December 2, 2001. The SEC proposed new disclosure rules, which were adopted in the Sarbanes-Oxley Act of 2002. The SEC required CEO and CFO certification of SEC filings by August 2002. Other actions are summarized on the SEC's press release Web page (www.sec.gov/news/press.shtml).

# Financial Reporting

Full financial disclosure is central to the mission of the SEC. Corporations must issue annual and quarterly reports to the public and to the SEC. Annual and quarterly reports are issued based on GAAP as currently established by the FASB, while the SEC annual (10-K) and quarterly (10-Q) reports are based on additional SEC requirements beyond GAAP. Earnings announcements generally are issued shortly after the end of the accounting period, while reports tend to become available about three months after the end of the period. Thus, this represents historical data available after a lag. Dell's 2002 10-K is presented on the support Web site for this text, at www.wiley.com/college/giroux.

## THE FASB

In 1973 the **Financial Accounting Standards Board** (FASB) was created to promulgate accounting standards, in place of the Accounting Principles Board (APB). The FASB's predecessor bodies, the Committee on Accounting Procedure (1938–59) and APB (1959–73) had weaknesses. To correct these perceived weaknesses the relatively complex FASB has a full-time board, a research staff, and due process with public input. The Financial Accounting Foundation (FAF) was established to appoint the members of the FASB and provide financial support. Funding comes from corporations and various accounting and industry organizations. The FASB and its structure have a number of critics, and vocal complaints increased since the Enron bankruptcy.

The seven members of the board are appointed by the FAF to five-year terms, and members can be reappointed for an additional term. The Board has a director of research and a staff of about forty professionals. The mission of the FASB is "to establish and improve standards of financial accounting and reporting for the guidance and education of the public, including issuers, auditors, and users of financial information" ("Facts about FASB," p. 1).

The FASB's rules of procedure require extensive **due process.** When the board agrees to add a topic to its agenda, an advisory task force is appointed under a project manager. An appointed staff usually prepares a discussion memorandum (DM), which defines the problem, the scope of the project, issues involved, a research analysis, and alternative solutions. The DM is distributed and public hearings are held. The board reaches a tentative conclusion and the staff prepares an exposure draft (ED), which is the proposed solution. The ED includes a discussion of the problem, a proposed solution and effective date, and the rationale for the decision. As with the DM, it is publicly exposed. If controversy is avoided, a final statement is prepared, usually with modification to the ED. A "super majority" of five members is required for approval. The pronouncement becomes GAAP as a statement of financial accounting standards (SFAS).

The FASB Web site (www.fasb.org) includes its procedures and current issues. It is an important starting point for recent pronouncements and current issues that may change GAAP in the near future. Also available are summaries of all FASB statements issued, 146 by the end of July 2002.

## FINANCIAL STATEMENTS

Analysts focus most attention on the financial statements. The income statement represents current period performance (compared to prior years), with particular emphasis on the bottom line usually measured as net income. Revenue levels, revenue growth and the relationship of the various categories of expenses explain the level of earnings and the potential for future earnings. Since income statement numbers rely on estimates, various arbitrary allocations, and management "judgment," the overall accuracy of this "performance summary" can be called into question. The balance sheet describes the firm's assets, obligations, and net book value, all based on GAAP. Limitations of balance sheet information are numerous, including assets not measured at current values and both assets and obligations not reported at all. Cash flow information available from the Statement of Cash Flows can be useful to "see through" accounting accruals.

The financial statements are central to Dell's 2002 10-K (fiscal year ended February 1, 2002). The income statement includes three years of comparative data in a simplified format. Only a dozen or so categories exist between net revenues and net income. This is partially based on relatively simple operations. The balance sheet is almost equally short, with only 10 asset line items balanced against six liability and six equity lines. Dell's statements of cash flows and stockholders' equity are more complex and contain specialized information.

Detailed accounting information is available in the footnotes. The first note, a little over three pages for Dell, describes the accounting policy, which helps the analyst compare the company to competitors and others. The remaining notes describe specific issues such as marketable securities, pension, and contingencies. Notes, which can be quite extensive, provide necessary information on specific financial and accounting issues. The usefulness of notes tends to be company-specific, providing key information for some companies and not as much for others. Dell's notes will be examined in Chapters 7–10.

Management discussion and analysis (MD&A) is the company's discussion of current operations and future strategies. This can be a comprehensive analysis of operations, business and geographic segments, and future plans and expectations. A company's MD&A is not unbiased, but it is an essential source for determining managers' expectations. MD&A is a primary source for understanding a corporation's industry and business strategy. Dell's MD&A was reviewed in Chapter 1.

The financial statement results are based on GAAP, and analysts need a good understanding of the recording and reporting requirements. Important issues vary by firm and industry. Automobile companies have large pension obligations and diverse business and geographic segments. They also provide auto loans, and their lending operations represent major components of their balance sheets. Analysis of contingencies is significant to tobacco, chemical, and other companies, which are subject to a multitude of lawsuits and government regulations. Airlines and retail chains often use operating leases, which may distort the analysis of actual liabilities.

Financial statement information is reviewed in detail in Chapters 7–10 with a major focus on Dell. For a given company certain specific issues will be crucial, while others are minor. Stock options are important to Dell's analysis. Since Dell does not have a defined benefit pension plan, the issue of future pension obligations is irrelevant.

## Management Incentives for Disclosure

Managers are expected to run corporations in the best interests of the shareholders. Presumably, the firm should maximize long-term economic earnings. More immediate goals include a pragmatic business strategy; successful long-term relationships with suppliers; a focus on employee competence, welfare, training and career opportunities; innovative customer products and service; and planning for the use of the Internet and other high tech business objectives.

It is assumed that managers behave in their own best (perceived) interests. This should be identical to the long-term interests of shareholders, but that sometimes is not the case. Managers may focus on short-term incentives, rather than long-term economic success. Managers can attempt to maximize salary, bonuses, and other short-term compensation. This can be accomplished through improved business strategy and successful operations.

It can also be accomplished, at least in the short-term, through **earnings management**—modifying earnings and other accounting numbers to change the operating perspectives concerning the firm. **Earnings manipulation** (essentially extreme earnings management) is almost always considered detrimental by financial analysts.

Most earnings management techniques represent timing differences. Revenues and expenses can be increased or decreased in the current period rather than in future periods. Revenues can be increased through aggressive revenue recognition, and expenses can be avoided temporarily by capitalizing certain costs or by not recording losses in the current period. Troubled companies likely manipulate earnings to indicate they are still solvent. However, even successful companies are tempted to manipulate operating numbers when quarterly earnings are not up to analysts' forecasts.

Recent examples of earnings manipulation have lead to considerable distrust of corporate financial information. World Com announced that it had capitalized $3.85 billion in operating expenses and then declared bankruptcy in July 2002. Enron hid a multitude its operating problems by using special-purpose entities to keep the bad news off the balance sheet. Global Crossing sold fiber cable capacity using long-term contracts to other telecommunications companies and booked the proceeds immediately as operating revenues. Dynergy was subject to a federal probe based on sham trades, again to boost revenues.

## Theoretical Perspectives from Financial Theory

Financial and economic theories and empirical testing provide assumptions and evidence for important perspectives on financial behavior. Equity capital markets are assumed to be efficient, which means that information is impounded in share price quickly and in an unbiased fashion. Not everyone believes in efficient markets, but it explains behavior in many cases such as market response to earnings announcements by major corporations. Agency theory and transactions cost economics indicate the importance of contracts in business environments and the evaluation of costs associated with these contracts. The incentives of the key actors involved in contracts are key elements in these theoretical perspectives. Earnings management is a related perspective of particular importance to financial analysts, since analysts rely on reported financial information. Finally, new regulations have economic consequences. In many cases these are unintended.

### EFFICIENT MARKETS

Markets are efficient if information is impounded immediately in capital prices in an unbiased fashion. Most important to financial disclosure is the semistrong form of **efficient markets,** which is based on publicly available information. Thus, stock prices are assumed to "fully reflect" publicly available information almost immediately.

Finance and accounting research generally supports the efficient market hypothesis. Considerable testing has been conducted on earnings announcements. Before actual earnings are announced, analysts have expectations or forecasts. The difference between analysts' expectations (or other earnings forecasts) and actual earnings is the **"earnings**

**surprise.**" If the surprise is "good news" (actual earnings are greater than expected), the stock price should go up—and down for "bad news." These results are found with reasonable consistency, supporting efficient markets in the semistrong form (Watts and Zimmerman, 1986).

On June 26, 2000, the television company CNNFN reported: "Building materials company Owens Corning Monday warned that sales and operating income for the second quarter will be below Wall Street forecasts and year-earlier levels, blaming the soft housing market and rising raw material costs" (www.cnnfn.com). Owens Corning (www.owenscorning.com) said fully diluted earnings per share (EPS), before a charge-off of $700 million to $1 billion for asbestos-related liabilities, would be $1. Actual EPS for the same quarter the previous year was $0.77, and consensus analysts' estimates for the June 2000 quarter were $1.24 (the estimate had been falling for the previous ninety days). Thus, this bad news should result in a substantial stock price decline. Exhibit 2.2 shows the stock chart for Owens Corning (OWC) for the five-day period ending June 27.

As expected, the stock price of Owen Corning stumbled badly on June 26, dropping from below $15 to below $11, then rising to $12 at the close.

Why are efficient markets expected? For the largest companies, dozens of analysts follow the operations and reporting of the firm and present earnings forecasts. Public information is incorporated in their expectations and, therefore, this should be impounded in stock price. By this logic, the impounding of information in stock prices should be less efficient in smaller companies followed by few if any analysts.

A key question: if markets are efficient, how can investors earn an "abnormal return" (that is, greater than market averages)? This has sparked controversy. Opponents of market efficiency often claim the concept is nonsense, while some proponents claim that investors should essentially buy portfolios equivalent to stock indexes and hold these for the long term. For example, Motley Fool (www.fool.com), an analysis company popular on the Internet, is a proponent of stock indexes.

**EXHIBIT 2.2 OWENS CORNING STOCK CHART**

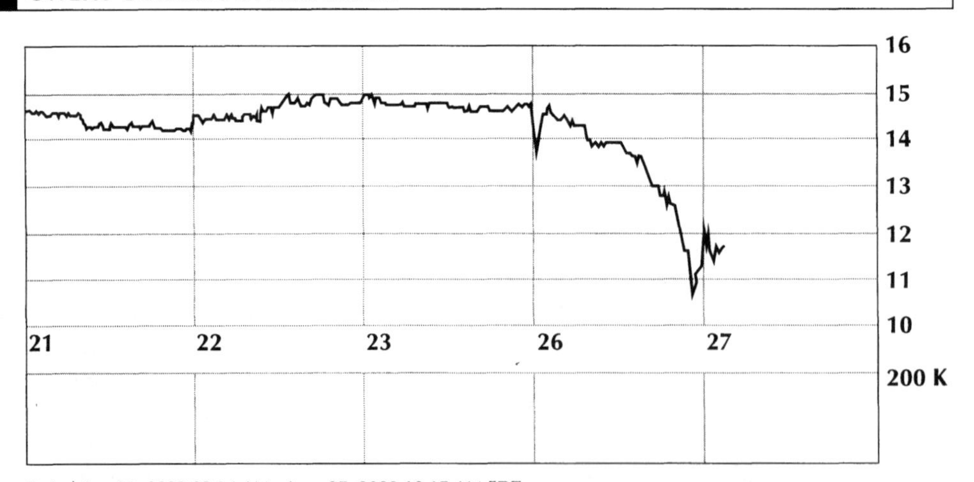


Period. Jun 21, 2000 09:34 AM – June 27, 2000 10:17 AM EDT

Source: www.quicken.com

## RANDOM WALK THEORY

The efficient markets hypothesis is consistent with **random walk,** the concept that a professional analysts and portfolio managers cannot outperform a randomly selected stock portfolio. As stated by Malkiel (1975, p. 171):

> Fundamental analysis of publicly available information cannot produce investment recommendations that will enable an investor consistently to outperform a buy-and-hold strategy in managing a portfolio.

This takes on various forms, such as throwing darts at the *Wall Street Journal;* better yet if a chimpanzee throws the darts. That portfolio should work as well as a professional's fund. Various simulation and other academic studies have generally confirmed this result. The fit of random walk to efficient markets is that all information is quickly impounded in stock price, making it difficult to realize excess profit from fundamental analysis.

## PORTFOLIO THEORY AND THE CAPITAL ASSET PRICING MODEL

Harry Markowitz introduced the concept of portfolio diversification with his 1952 dissertation, *Portfolio Selection.* **Portfolio theory** insists that investment portfolios should be diversified. Markowitz discovered that the variance of return (a standard measure of risk) for a portfolio is less than the variance of individual stocks. The concept is to maximize return for some level of risk. A simple model incorporating this concept is the **capital asset pricing model** (CAPM), an equation of risk and return:

$$E(R_i) = R_f + ß[E(R_m) - R_f]$$

where

$R_i$ = rate of return on stock $i$
$R_f$ = risk-free rate of return
$R_m$ = rate of return on the market
ß = "beta," the coefficient of the relationship of the company's return with that of the market
E = expected value or forecast

Thus the expected rate of return for a given stock is associated with a risk-free rate (which might be approximated by the interest rate on a short-term Treasury bill) and its relationship with the stock market as a whole.

The **market model** gives the realized stock return as:

$$R_{it} = \alpha_i + \alpha_i R_{mt} + e_{it}$$

where

$R_i$ = rate of return on stock $i$
$R_m$ = rate of return on the market
$e$ = unexpected or abnormal return (unsystematic risk)
ß = the relationship between individual stock and market return (systematic risk)
$\alpha$ = intercept
$t$ = time period

For a portfolio of securities, return = $\Sigma R_{it}$ and risk is a combination of systematic risk (ß) and unsystematic or abnormal risk ($e$). Unsystematic risk is associated with characteristics of the specific company. The concept is to match ß with the investor's level of preferred risk, where ß = 1 should match the market as a whole and ß > 1 should result in a greater return in both directions, higher than the market when stock prices rise while declining faster when prices fall. Unexpected returns (those associated with unsystematic risk; that is, related to specific companies) can be diversified away in a well-selected portfolio.

## BETA (ß) ANALYSIS

This ß comes directly from the coefficient (slope) of the market model above. (This is based on regression analysis, a statistical technique.) **Beta analysis** is a measure of the relationship of price movements of individual securities to market price movements. This is a measure of systematic risk. There is always risk with stock investments. Individual stocks and the market as a whole can drop in price, sometimes by considerable amounts. Using ß as a guide, an investor willing to assume the normal risks of the stock market wants a portfolio with an average ß = 1. An investor willing to take greater risks should construct a portfolio with a ß greater than one. An investor willing to take no risk can invest in a ninety-day Treasury bill, presumably with a ß = 0. According to some academic studies, the only way to beat the market consistently long-term is to invest in a diversified portfolio with a high ß.

Beta is calculated in long-term regression analysis. Several sources present ß for firms; for example, there is a sixty-month ß at Quicken's Fundamentals (www.quicken.com /investments/stats). The ß of several Dow Jones industrial companies from Quicken (as of May 2002) is shown in Exhibit 2.3.

Assuming that these ß calculations are correct, this is a start to pick portfolios by relative risk. It's debatable whether ß can be accurately measured for individual securities. That is, ß is based on the statistical relationship of the stock to the market for the last five years. It's not clear that this is a good predictor of future risk. Using ß analysis, risk-adverse investors presumably pick stocks such as Eastman Kodak or Procter & Gamble. High-risk investors would prefer Microsoft or Citigroup. An average-risk portfolio could include companies with ßs between 0.9 and 1.1. A high-risk portfolio would include stocks with ßs above 1.1; a low-risk portfolio, below 0.9. Alternatively, one could pick companies with diverse ßs, as long as the portfolio average results in the desired risk preference (with an average ß of about 1.0 for an average-risk portfolio).

Dell and its competitors are high tech personal computer companies that should be growth stocks and, therefore, have high ßs. Dell had a ß of 2.14 on Quicken (May 2002),

**EXHIBIT 2.3 THE BETAS OF SELECT COMPANIES**

| Lower Risk | | Market Average | | Higher Risk | |
|---|---|---|---|---|---|
| **Company** | **ß** | **Company** | **ß** | **Company** | **ß** |
| Eastman Kodak (EK) | .45 | General Motors (GM) | 1.08 | General Electric (GE) | 1.18 |
| Procter & Gamble (PG) | .22 | Ford (F) | 1.06 | Citigroup (C) | 1.42 |
| Merck (MRK) | .40 | International Paper (IP) | .98 | Microsoft (MSFT) | 1.74 |

and Gateway and Apple had ßs of 2.15 and 1.54, respectively. As expected, all are high-risk companies, according to ß analysis.

## EFFICIENT CONTRACTING AND AGENCY THEORY

**Transaction cost** economics focuses on the transaction—goods and services transferred across a technologically separate interface (Williamson, 1985)—as the basic unit of analysis. (). Transaction costs are contracting costs and transactions are optimized through **efficient contracting,** or writing contracts to accomplish something with minimum transaction and agency costs. Contracting costs include drafting, negotiating, safeguarding a contract, costs of governance structures, and agency costs.

Contracts have a principal and an agent. In a corporation, owners are principals and employees are agents. The principal attempts to maximize wealth and contracts to avoid conflicts. **Agency costs** include (1) information asymmetries (limited or misinformed information by one side—note the role of accounting to limit asymmetries), (2) adverse selection (such as the "market for lemons"), and (3) moral hazard (such as shirking or ethics violations). Agency costs can be reduced by (1) better acquisition decisions, (2) monitoring such as a financial audit, (3) aligning preferences of agents with principals (such as management compensation based on performance or employee stock ownership), and (4) control devices (such as budgets).

## ECONOMIC RATIONALITY AND BEHAVIOR

Standard economic theory suggests that individuals and organizations behave rationally. Older theories often assumed perfect knowledge and perfect decision making with no transaction or other extraneous costs. More recent finance models instead tend to assume **bounded rationality;** that is, people intend to be rational but are limited in their ability to make optimal choices. Decisions must be made, even when all relevant information is not available. Despite behavioral deficiencies and imperfect knowledge, individuals are still expected to make rational (but not necessarily optimal) decisions.

According to Williamson (1985) there are three levels of individual behavior: obedience, self-interest, and opportunism. Socialist economists assume that people will obey directives for the best interest of society. Capitalist economists assume people behave in their own self-interest. **Opportunism** is "self-interest with guile." In other words, people are willing to violate normal ethical boundaries for personal benefit. Analysts should be on the lookout for opportunistic behavior.

Agents are expected to act in their own self-interest; therefore, understanding agent incentives is important when writing contracts. The principal wants efficient contracts that limit transaction costs, including agency costs. From the perspective of principals, contracts should be written to (1) limit expected agency costs and (2) align agent interests with those of the principal. Employment contracts may have incentives for managers to enhance earnings performance such as bonus plans or stock options. Bonus plans pay cash bonuses for some achieved levels of performance, usually based on some definition of accounting income. Thus, bonus plans provide incentives for short-term profit (with limits at maximum bonuses and "big bath" potential when losses are generated). Stock options should align managers' interests with shareholders', a long-term focus. There is some debate on how effective these techniques are in aligning managers' interests to those of investors. Managers may focus on short-term performance rather than long-term earnings growth.

## EARNINGS MANAGEMENT AND ACCOUNTING CHOICE

Given management incentives for self-interest or opportunism, managers can manipulate accounting earnings to achieve their own best interests, such as bonuses. The basic incentive is to raise current bonuses by increasing accounting earnings. Aggressive revenue recognition (recognizing revenues early in the business cycle), capitalizing rather than expensing current costs, and allocating costs over longer periods (e.g., straight-line rather than accelerated depreciation) are common examples of potential earnings management techniques. A potential component of earnings management is income smoothing, attempting to generate consistent revenue and earnings growth rather than erratic changes. Capitalizing costs and allocating these costs over time using a straight-line method tends to smooth income.

It is expected that managers would behave in their own self-interest. Therefore, it would be expected that the concept of earnings management is normal. That is, managers are going to present the operating and financial conditions in the best possible light. If managers take this too far (in overly aggressive use of nonrecurring items or revenue and expense recognition), this opportunistic behavior can be considered earnings manipulation. Generally, when earnings manipulation is detected, the earnings quality of the firm is in question and analysts may have to reevaluate and restate financial information (a process called normalizing income).

Since many accounting techniques allow alternatives and professional judgment, **accounting choice** is an important component of earnings management. Inventory methods, depreciation, and accounting for marketable securities are examples of areas that allow accounting choice. It is expected that managers will use accounting choices to promote their own self- interest.

What are the incentives for earnings management? Manipulating current earnings might increase cash bonuses tied to income performance. Companies that don't quite meet quartering earnings expectations have incentives to tweak earnings to meet expectations. Companies that are close to violating debt covenants based on accounting numbers can manipulate earnings to avoid violations.

**Income smoothing** is an earnings management technique to maintain earnings at a specified level or to increase them at a steady pace. This gives the appearance of high earnings quality or earnings persistence, which indicate that core earnings are likely to continue. Managers can increase current income (borrowing future earnings) by techniques such as aggressive revenue recognition (e.g., recording revenues before they have been earned and extending credit to customers with poor credit risks) and by decreasing expenses (e.g., reducing bad debts, reducing or eliminating maintenance, and capitalizing rather than expensing).

Techniques to decrease current earnings also can be used. An extreme example is the "big bath" write-offs. Why would managers do this? When the corporation is losing money in the current period and no cash bonuses will be paid, it may be a good time to take a large write-off. This is especially effective when the company is in the process of reorganizing. Generally, these write-offs are nonrecurring items that are not considered part of continuing operations. Recording big losses from extraordinary items or discontinued operations when the company is losing money anyway is an example. These losses highlight the reorganization attempt and, since these losses are recorded in the current year, make it more likely that profitability will happen next year—allowing the managers to get larger future bonuses.

Potential areas of earnings management often are industry specific: the understatement of warranty liabilities for manufacturers; credit losses and loan loss provisions of banks; contingencies for tobacco litigation; technological change, which is especially important in high tech companies (e.g., potential for inventory losses); high receivables and bad debts in retailing; and product liability for chemical or drug companies.

## ECONOMIC CONSEQUENCES

New regulations have economic consequences. When a luxury tax was placed on large boats, new boat sales plummeted. Presumably, buyers could afford it but would not pay the tax, a situation that almost drove the boat building industry out of business (fortunately, the tax was repealed). Thus, we have the concept of unintended consequences. When new accounting standards are issued, **economic consequences** become apparent. When pension accounting became more stringent and federal requirements were imposed, many corporations abandoned their pension plans. When SFAS No. 2 required expensing all research and development (R&D), it was claimed that the level of R&D dropped (for earnings management reasons).

## SUMMARY

The financial environment is complex. Capital markets include both primary and secondary markets, with most investment decisions taking place in the major stock exchanges (secondary equity markets). Since the 1930s, the SEC has regulated capital markets. Accounting regulations (GAAP) have expanded over the past six decades. The FASB establishes GAAP, which benefit investors but make analysis more complex. A good understanding of GAAP and the standard-setting process is an important component of financial analysis.

Finance and accounting theory suggest the existence of efficient markets, which has implications on how markets behave. Agency theory suggests that market participants, including managers and stockholders, behave in their own best interests. Earnings management and other incentives by managers suggest certain behaviors that may not be in the best interest of stockholders. A basic understanding of these theories can improve financial insights and specific decisions.

## KEY TERMS

10-K
10-Q
accounting choice
agency costs
agency theory
beta analysis
bounded rationality
capital asset pricing model
due process
earnings management
earnings manipulation
earnings surprise
economic consequences
efficient contracting
efficient markets
Financial Accounting Standards Board
generally accepted accounting principles
income smoothing
market model
opportunism
portfolio theory
primary market
random walk
secondary market
Securities and Exchange Commission
transaction cost

## QUESTIONS

1. What is a capital market? What's the difference between a primary and secondary market?
2. What is the mission of the SEC? The FASB?
3. Why would managers have different financial disclosure objectives than stockholders?
4. Finance theory has been important in evaluating capital markets, especially related to stock prices and investment strategies? Why? Consider portfolio theory, efficient markets and ß analysis.
5. What is efficient contracting? What is its relationship to agency cost?

## PROBLEMS

### Problem 2.1 Capital Market Components

Where would the following information be found?

| | MD&A | Financial Statements | Notes | Market Analysis |
|---|---|---|---|---|
| Next Year's Expected Operating Performance | | | | |
| Business Strategy | | | | |
| Retained Earnings | | | | |
| Derivatives | | | | |
| Gross Profit | | | | |
| Projected Benefits Obligation | | | | |
| Operating Leases | | | | |
| Company's ß | | | | |
| Contingencies | | | | |
| Stock Price Trends, Last 12 Months | | | | |
| Other Comprehensive Income | | | | |
| Analysts' Forecasts | | | | |
| Number of Common Shares Outstanding | | | | |

### Problem 2.2 Earnings Expectations and Surprise (PC Companies)

The following table relates to quarterly earnings for three companies:

| | Quarterly Earnings, Last Period | Quarterly Earnings, Current Period (Analysts Forecasts) | Quarterly Earnings, Current Period (Actual) | Change in Actual Quarterly Earnings ($) | Earnings Surprise, in $ (Actual – Forecast) | % Earnings Surprise (Actual – Forecast) / Forecast |
|---|---|---|---|---|---|---|
| Dell | $0.16 | $0.17 | $0.17 | | | |
| Gateway | 0.02 | –0.19 | –0.20 | | | |
| Apple | 0.11 | 0.10 | 0.11 | | | |

Current quarter for Dell January 2002; March 2002 for all other companies

Complete this table. Are the stock prices likely to go up or down on the day of the earnings announcement? Explain.

### Problem 2.3 Earnings Expectations and Surprise (Chemical Companies)

The following table relates to quarterly earnings for three companies:

| | Quarterly Earnings, Last Period | Quarterly Earnings, Current Period (Analysts Forecasts) | Quarterly Earnings, Current Period (Actual) | Change in Actual Quarterly Earnings ($) | Earnings Surprise, in $ (Actual – Forecast) | % Earnings Surprise (Actual – Forecast) / Forecast |
|---|---|---|---|---|---|---|
| DuPont | $0.12 | $0.56 | $0.55 | | | |
| DOW | –0.01 | 0.07 | 0.07 | | | |
| PPG | 0.49 | 0.52 | 0.58 | | | |

Current quarter March 2002 for all companies

Complete this table. Are the stock prices likely to go up or down on the day of the earnings announcement? Explain.

### Problem 2.4 Earnings Expectations and Surprise (Hotel and Resort Companies)

The following table relates to quarterly earnings for three companies:

| | Quarterly Earnings, Last Period | Quarterly Earnings, Current Period (Analysts Forecasts) | Quarterly Earnings, Current Period (Actual) | Change in Actual Quarterly Earnings ($) | Earnings Surprise, in $ (Actual – Forecast) | % Earnings Surprise (Actual – Forecast) / Forecast |
|---|---|---|---|---|---|---|
| Hilton | $0.01 | $0.05 | $0.09 | | | |
| Marriot | 0.25 | 0.27 | 0.32 | | | |
| Mandalay | 0.10 | 0.68 | 0.71 | | | |

Current quarter March 2002 for Hilton and Marriott, April 2002 for Mandalay

Complete this table. Are the stock prices likely to go up or down on the day of the earnings announcement? Explain.

### Problem 2.5 Earnings Expectations and Surprise (Motor Vehicles Companies)

The following table relates to quarterly earnings for Ford and GM:

| | Quarterly Earnings, Last Period | Quarterly Earnings, Current Period (Analysts Forecasts) | Quarterly Earnings, Current Period (Actual) | Change in Actual Quarterly Earnings ($) | Earnings Surprise, in $ (Actual – Forecast) | % Earnings Surprise (Actual – Forecast) / Forecast |
|---|---|---|---|---|---|---|
| Ford | $–0.48 | $–0.14 | $–0.06 | | | |
| GM | 0.60 | 1.09 | 1.29 | | | |

Current quarter March 2002 for both companies.

Complete this table. Are the stock prices likely to go up or down on the day of the earnings announcement? Explain.

## Problem 2.6 Beta and Growth Analysis for the Chemical Industry

Given below are the ßs and five-year earnings growth forecasts:

| | ß | ß Portfolio (low, average, or high risk) | 5-Year Earnings Growth | 5-Year Growth Portfolio (low, average, or high risk) |
|---|---|---|---|---|
| DuPont | .73 | | 11.0% | |
| DOW | .76 | | 10.0 | |
| PPG | .83 | | 8.0 | |

Assume that the average-risk portfolio has ßs between .9 and 1.1 and earnings growth between 11% and 14%. Low-risk portfolios would be lower and high-risk higher. Classify the companies in the correct portfolio for each indicator. Do the two measurements indicate the same portfolio for each company or are the signals mixed? Explain.

## Problem 2.7 Beta and Growth Analysis for the Hotel and Resort Industry

Given below are the ßs and five-year earnings growth forecasts:

| | ß | ß Portfolio (low, average, or high risk) | 5-Year Earnings Growth | 5-Year Growth Portfolio (low, average, or high risk) |
|---|---|---|---|---|
| Hilton | .72 | | 13.9% | |
| Marriott | .93 | | 14.4 | |
| Mandalay | .92 | | 13.6 | |

Assume that the average risk portfolio has ßs between .9 and 1.1 and earnings growth between 11 percent and 14 percent. Low risk portfolios would be lower and high risk higher. Classify the companies in the correct portfolio for each indicator. Do the two measurements indicate the same portfolio for each company or are the signals mixed? Explain.

## Problem 2.8 Beta and Growth Analysis

Given below are several Dow Jones Industrial companies, with industries, ßs, and projected five-year earnings growth (www.quicken.com). Assume that an average risk portfolio has companies with ßs between 0.9 and 1.1.

| Company | Industry | ß | 5-Year Growth |
|---|---|---|---|
| 3M | Conglomerate | 59 | 11.1 |
| Johnson & Johnson | Pharmaceuticals | .80 | 13.0 |
| Boeing | Aerospace | .83 | 16.4 |
| Disney | Entertainment | .88 | 14.8 |
| McDonald's | Restaurant | .92 | 12.5 |
| Caterpillar | Machinery | .94 | 10.3 |
| AT&T | Long Distance | 1.09 | 12.8 |
| IBM | Computers | 1.10 | 13.4 |
| Wal-Mart | Discount | 1.18 | 14.4 |

Classify these companies into an investment portfolio based on ß: (1) low risk or low ß, (2) average (market) risk, and (3) high risk or high ß. Presumably risk levels should relate to industry and earnings growth rates. On average the S&P 500 companies are expected to grow 12.8 percent annually over the next five years (the "average" portfolio is expected to have securities with five-year average growth rates of 11 percent to 14 percent). Assuming this is true, which companies seem to be misclassified based on projected five-year earnings growth rates? (Note: neither ß nor projected earnings is necessarily very accurate.)

| Company | Which Portfolio (based on ß) | Misclassified (relative to 5-year growth rate)? | Explain |
|---|---|---|---|
| 3M | | | |
| Johnson & Johnson | | | |
| Boeing | | | |
| Disney | | | |
| McDonald's | | | |
| Caterpillar | | | |
| AT&T | | | |
| IBM | | | |
| Wal-Mart | | | |

## CASES

### Case 2.1 Where are financial statements found?

Dell's 10-K appears on the support Web site for this text at www.wiley.com/college/giroux. Where can financial statements for Dell's competitors, Gateway and Apple, be found? How can Dell's accounting policies be compared with other PC companies?

### Case 2.2 Financial theory concepts

Are financial economists nuts? Peter Lynch makes the following statement in *One Up on Wall Street* (1989): "I also found it difficult to integrate the efficient-market hypothesis (that everything in the stock market is 'known' and prices are always 'rational') with the random-walk hypothesis (that the ups and downs of the market are irrational and entirely unpredictable)." What's wrong with this statement?

### Case 2.3. Stock price response to earnings announcement

NCR reported quarterly earnings on July 25, 2002, of $0.34, up from $0.04 the previous quarter. Analysts expected $0.34 for the quarter. Is the "earnings surprise" good news or bad news? On July 26, NCR's stock price dropped $2.27 to $23.75. Was this expected? Why?

## ETHICS CONSIDERATIONS

### Earnings management and earnings manipulation

Corporations are expected to use earnings management to promote their self-interest. At some point, accounting and reporting adjustments severely misstate the financial position and performance of the firm. This is commonly called earnings manipulation. Can the distinction be made between earnings management and earnings manipulation in most cases? Explain.

## INTERNET PROJECTS

### Project 2.1

Go to Project Activities on the FASB Web site (www.fasb.org) and pick a project. Use the staff summary to analyze the project in one page or less. Use the following format:

- Background, purpose of project
- Project description
- Accounting scope (what the FASB intends to do)
- Time to complete, planning

CHAPTER

# 3 The Financial Statements

**Objectives**

- Identify and evaluate the required financial statements in an annual report.
- Understand the ten elements of financial statements as defined in SFAC No. 6.
- Understand the importance of the balance sheet.
- Evaluate assets, liabilities, and equity. Understand how they are recorded relative to the conceptual framework definitions.
- Evaluate the components of the income statement and the concept of earnings.
- Evaluate alternative concepts of the "bottom line."
- Describe the components of the statement of cash flows. Ascertain how this information relates to the balance sheet and income statement.
- Describe the composition of the statement of stockholders' equity.

## INTRODUCTION

Accounting has developed over several hundred years as a pragmatic approach to document the financial position and operations of business enterprises. As companies became more complex, accountants have struggled to maintain a reliable structure to portray economic reality. Accounting complexity expanded, compromises were made, and accounting and reporting systems today are respected as reasonable summary portrayals of corporate financial structure. As demonstrated in Chapter 4, the financial statements are the starting points for a thorough financial analysis.

Examining accounting details is an important financial analysis step for several reasons. Quantitative techniques assume that financial statement information is correct and a true picture of economic reality. Financial statements are supposed to be "transparent," but complexity is detailed in the footnotes. High earnings quality (an accurate measure of current operating activity) is subject to interpretation and requires analysis. The self-interest of managers suggests incentives for earnings management techniques that can inflate earnings and reduce earnings quality. Also, the business environment of large companies is complex, resulting in difficult accounting issues such as revenue recognition criteria, recording liabilities, and nonrecurring items.

The Financial Accounting Standards Board (FASB) promulgates generally accepted accounting principals (GAAP), primarily by issuing standards after a formal public review procedure. FASB also developed its **Conceptual Framework** by issuing Statements of Financial Accounting Concepts (SFACs), a useful starting point to financial accounting theory. Whether trained as accountants or not, financial analysts need: (1) a basic understanding of accounting fundamentals, (2) a general knowledge of specific accounting issues likely to affect analysis decisions, and (3) the knowledge of how to access detailed accounting information when necessary.

The financial statements include four required statements: balance sheet, income statement, statement of cash flows, and statement of stockholders' equity. These will be evaluated individually based on the 10 elements defined by the FASB. They are interrelated and a fundamental understanding of their significance is essential to financial analysis. The financial statements of Dell Computer for fiscal year 2002 are presented on pages 32–35 of its 10-K, which is provided on the support Web site for this text at www.wiley.com/college/giroux. The various components will be evaluated below.

The ten elements of financial statements are defined in SFAC No. 6 (para. 25–89) and summarized as:

- *Asset*—Probable future economic benefits obtained or controlled by a particular entity as a result of past transactions or events.
- *Liabilities*—Probable future sacrifices of economic benefits arising from present obligations of a particular entity to transfer assets or provide services to another entity in the future as a result of past transactions or events.
- *Equity (or net assets)*—Residual interest in the assets of an entity that remains after deducting its liabilities. In a business enterprise, the equity is the ownership interest.
- *Investments by owners*—Increases in equity ... resulting from transfers to it from other entities of something valuable to obtain or increase ownership interests (or equity) in it.
- *Distributions to owners*—Decrease in equity of a particular business enterprise resulting from transferring assets, rendering services, or incurring liabilities by the enterprise to owners.
- *Comprehensive income*—Change in equity of a business enterprise during a period from transactions and other events and circumstances from nonowner sources. It includes all changes in equity during a period except those resulting from investments by owners and distributions to owners.
- *Revenues*—Inflows or other enhancements of assets of an entity or settlement of its liabilities (or a combination of both) from delivering or producing goods, rendering services, or other activities that constitute the entity's ongoing major or central operations.
- *Expenses*—Outflows or other using up of assets or incurrence of liabilities (or a combination of both) from delivering or producing goods, rendering services,

or carrying out other activities that constitute the entity's ongoing major or central operations.

- *Gains*—Increases in equity (net assets) from peripheral or incidental transactions of an entity and from all other transactions and other events and circumstances affecting the entity except those that result from revenues or investments by owners.
- *Losses*—Decreases in equity (net assets) from peripheral or incidental transactions of an entity and from all other transactions and other events and circumstances affecting the entity except those that result from expenses or distributions to owners.

The first five terms relate to the balance sheet and the last five to the income statement. Comprehensive income "crosses over" to balance the two statements. **Comprehensive income** is the return on financial capital, which includes all changes in net assets not between the firm and its owners. In practice, comprehensive income is not the same as net income, and reconciling the two takes additional analysis.

The practice of regulating financial accounting through standard setting started after the formation of the Securities and Exchange Commission (SEC) in the mid-1930s. The primary focus became historical cost accounting, an approach well defended by Paton and Littleton (1940). Historical (acquisition) values are easily verified, tend to be conservative (e.g., book values are not raised to current values), and emphasize the income statement rather than the balance sheet. That is, emphasis is on revenue recognition, matching cost of goods sold and other expenses on a cost basis, and attempting to measure earnings as accurately as possible. Consequently, somewhat less emphasis is placed on the balance sheet. Fixed assets (property, plant, and equipment) are recorded net of accumulated depreciation, and no attempt is made to determine current value. The cost of using these assets is allocated as depreciation, an arbitrary but systematic procedure. Items such as deferred taxes are placed in the balance sheet to offset the tax expense in the income statement. Although the FASB requires more items stated at current value, the fundamental historical cost approach still dominates financial accounting.

# The Balance Sheet

The balance sheet shows the financial position of a company at a particular point in time. It is composed of assets, liabilities, and stockholders' equity. The assets are the resources of the firm. The liabilities and equity are the "sources" of assets, in other words, how they were financed by creditors or owners. This is demonstrated in the accounting equation: Assets = Liabilities + Stockholders' Equity.

## ASSETS

According to the FASB's Conceptual Framework, **assets** have probable future economic benefit. A basic problem is the poor match of this definition to how assets are recorded under GAAP. The definition suggests that some measure of current or market value should be used. A few assets are recorded at current values, such as marketable securities (if trading securities or available for sale), pension assets, and derivatives. Most items are capitalized (i.e., recorded as an asset) based on original cost, such as fixed assets and inventory. Several items that meet the FASB definition of assets are not recorded, such as patents and other research and development costs and human resources.

The present GAAP structure can be defended by arguing that GAAP provides a reasonable starting point for approximating economic reality. The historical cost process (including depreciation and other allocations) is conservative: the dollar amounts can be verified and defended as "real costs," while valuations based on current cost often cannot. Human capital is expensed, although companies spend considerable sums on employee training and development. Again, this is conservative. The costs are expensed as incurred, reducing current earnings. They are not capitalized, in part, because they are difficult to value and employees can leave the firm at any time. The value of human capital is important to the analyst, but it is not available from the balance sheet. Internal research and development (R&D) costs may be the most important spending categories by high tech companies and result in real economic assets (patents, new products, improved processes, and so on). These are almost always expensed, since it is difficult to measure specific benefits. The analyst must estimate the importance of R&D, partially available from a variety of sources. These include footnotes, management discussion and analysis, the president's letter, and media/analyst write-ups.

Several unusual asset items discussed in future chapters are difficult to analyze conceptually. Goodwill is recorded in a purchase acquisition of another firm as the difference between the actual purchase price and the fair value of restated net assets, making it a plug figure. Goodwill has no obvious meaning except to balance debits and credits. Deferred tax assets (and liabilities) represent the timing difference between income tax according to GAAP and the Internal Revenue Code. Deferred tax assets are taxes paid in advance relative to income statement figures, while deferred tax liabilities are not yet paid. The Internal Revenue Service doesn't want the money this year for these deferred tax liabilities, but recording them is a necessary part of GAAP.

Some assets are recorded at fair value. Inventory is recorded at the lower of cost or market value, a "one-direction current cost." Revaluing inventory to a lower market value is somewhat uncommon and a possible red flag. Marketable securities (if trading or available for sale) are recorded at fair value, since market values are easily determined and verifiable. These can be considered exceptions to historical cost. The result is, despite the Conceptual Framework, little consistent guidance from accounting theory to financial practice on valuing assets. Derivatives must be stated at fair value, a complex calculation based on economic models such as Black-Scholes—values that change continuously and can move swiftly.

In summary, from an economic value analysis (as probable future economic benefits), many assets are misstated or not recorded on the balance sheet. This creates problems for the analysts who need to value the economic resources of the firm. However, considerable information is available in other financial statements and footnotes for evaluation. There is some consistency in information being reported conservatively (usually expensed rather than capitalized) and verifiable. Therefore, assets recorded on the balance sheet are a reasonable starting point for economic valuation of the firm. Considerable amounts of relevant information have to be estimated, but various sources are available for this analysis.

**EXHIBIT 3.1 ASSETS OF DELL, FISCAL YEAR-END 2002**

| | February 1, 2002 | February 2, 2001 |
|---|---|---|
| **Assets** | | |
| Current assets: | | |
| Cash and cash equivalents | $ 3,641 | $ 4,910 |
| Short-term investments | 273 | 525 |
| Accounts receivable, net | 2,269 | 2,424 |
| Inventories | 278 | 400 |
| Other | 1,416 | 1,467 |
| Total current assets | 7,877 | 9,726 |
| Property, plant and equipment, net | 826 | 996 |
| Investments | 4,373 | 2,418 |
| Other non-current assets | 459 | 530 |
| Total assets | $13,535 | $13,670 |

Consider the asset position for Dell, based on the 2002 10-K in Exhibit 3.1. Comparative information is presented, for both the current and previous year. The assets are divided into two major categories, current and noncurrent. Current assets usually are defined as cash and items that will be converted to cash within one year. Items generally are listed by liquidity, the relative ability to be converted to cash. Dell has a large cash position and considerable current assets. Dell has a small inventory position (part of the company's business strategy) but fairly substantial accounts receivable. All current asset categories are lower than the previous year. The determination of whether these amounts are too much or too little is a significant part of financial analysis. Property, plant, and equipment (or fixed assets) are a relatively small part of noncurrent assets. This is unusual for a manufacturing company, but comparable to competitors. Investments represent the largest asset category, made of the noncurrent investments.

Assets can be categorized as physical, financial, or intangible. Physical assets include property, plant, and equipment and inventory. Financial assets include investments and accounts receivable. Intangible assets include goodwill, patents, and trademarks. Not listed as separate items for Dell, they are instead part of other noncurrent assets and are evaluated in the footnotes.

How useful are the asset values for Dell? Dell has assets of $13.5 billion (mainly current assets) and net assets (total stockholders' equity) of $4.7 billion. Dell has a market value of $68.9 billion, based on a May 1, 2002, stock price of $26.48 and 2,602 million shares outstanding, which is 12.8 times book value. The valuation can be explained by performance, but not by asset valuation. Apple Computer, on the other hand, had assets (fiscal year 2001) of $6.3 billion and net assets of $4.0 billion, compared to a market value of $8.4 billion. Apple's performance was less stellar than Dell's. Gateway, which lost $1.0 million in 2001, had total assets of $3.0 billion, net assets of $1.6 billion, and a market value of $1.7 million. A market-to-book ratio of 1.06× suggests that the asset values are particularly important when evaluating Gateway.

## LIABILITIES

**Liabilities** are defined by SFAC No. 6 as "probable future economic sacrifices". In most cases, these are payables with a due date and payable in dollars. For these items, the criteria for recording have been met: (1) an obligation has been incurred and (2) the amount and timing are measurable. Except for the time value of money, there are no conceptual problems between GAAP and the Conceptual Framework for these items.

Other categories of potential obligations exist that are problematic. A major category is contingencies, potential obligations recognized by rules established in Statement of Financial Accounting Standards (SFAS) No. 5. To record a liability, the loss must be probable and the amount reasonably estimated. Litigation is a primary example, since major corporations are subject to government regulations and lawsuits of various kinds. Another category is environmental hazards that are common to certain industries such as chemical and utilities. In most cases, companies claim that the SFAS No. 5 criteria are not met, so these go unrecorded but described in a contingency footnote.

Most companies describe contingencies in notes, usually explaining some details and denying allegations. Generally, contingencies are not recorded in the financial statements. Owens Corning, a building materials company, records liabilities related to personal injury suits from inhaling asbestos (Owens Corning stopped producing asbestos in 1972). The 1999 balance sheet showed a current liability of $900 million and long-term liabilities of $938 million for this contingency. Note 22 explained these contingencies in detail and states: "Owens Corning will continue to review the adequacy of its estimates of liability on a periodic basis and make such adjustments as may be appropriate" (p. 49). In June 2000, the company announced that it was increasing this reserve from $700 million to $1 billion for the second quarter. On October 5, 2000, the company filed for bankruptcy under Chapter 11.

Three chemical companies, DuPont, Dow, and PPG, have substantial contingencies associated with lawsuits, price fixing, environmental liabilities, and so forth. See Problem 5.4 to analyze footnote disclosure by these companies. A key question: is liability recognition adequate? As demonstrated by the chemical companies' notes, companies seem to understate potential legal obligations.

Some obligations are difficult to quantify. Product warranties are obligations, but specific timing and dollar amounts can be difficult to determine. Generally, companies use experience to determine probable costs. Insurance premiums prepay insurance coverage. The amount and timing of claims have to be estimated by insurance companies to record insurance reserves (a liability).

Dell's liabilities for 2002 and 2001 are shown in Exhibit 3.2. As with assets, liabilities are divided into current and noncurrent. Most of Dell's liabilities are current, primarily accounts payable. Current liabilities are expected to be paid using current assets (or by creating other current liabilities). Payables are short-term obligations based on acquisition of goods and services. Dell has some long-term debt and other noncurrent assets, but no commitments or contingencies are recognized. Most long-term liabilities are financing arrangements to acquire cash or other assets. These include notes and bonds payable. Operational obligations include warranties and deferred taxes.

**EXHIBIT 3.2** LIABILITIES OF DELL, FISCAL YEAR-END 2002

| | February 1, 2002 | February 2, 2001 |
|---|---|---|
| Current liabilities: | | |
| Accounts payable | $5,075 | $4,286 |
| Accrued and other | 2,444 | 2,492 |
| Total current liabilities | 7,519 | 6,778 |
| Long-term debt | 520 | 509 |
| Other | 802 | 761 |
| Commitments and contingent liabilities (Note 7) | — | — |
| Total liabilities | $8,841 | $8,048 |

## STOCKHOLDERS' EQUITY

Stockholders' **equity** represents ownership in a corporation. From the investors' perspective, this represents holding common (or preferred) shares. From the corporation's perspective, the accounting is more complicated. Dell's relatively simple equity position is shown in Exhibit 3.3.

Common stock and capital in excess are part of paid-in capital, the amount contributed by original investors, through public offerings and other sources. Thus, Dell has issued and outstanding 2,601 million shares with a total paid-in capital of $5.6 billion. Dell has a policy of buying back its own shares, which are recorded as treasury stock, a negative equity item totaling $2.2 billion. Therefore, Dell in 2002 had 2,602 million shares issued and outstanding (2,654 – 52). Retained earnings are accumulated earnings that are not distributed as dividends; Dell does not pay dividends. Other comprehensive income included foreign currency translation and marketable securities' gains and losses. **Comprehensive income** adjustments are called **"dirty surplus"** charges, since these are **gains** and **losses** recorded

**EXHIBIT 3.3** STOCKHOLDERS' EQUITY FOR DELL, FISCAL YEAR-END 2002

| | 2002 | 2001 |
|---|---|---|
| Common stock and capital in excess of $.01 par value; shares authorized: 7,000; shares issued: 2,654 and 2,601, respectively | $5,605 | $4,795 |
| Treasury stock, at cost; 52 shares and no shares, respectively | (2,249) | — |
| Retained earnings | 1,364 | 839 |
| Other comprehensive income | 38 | 62 |
| Other | (64) | (74) |
| Total stockholders' equity | $4,694 | $5,622 |

directly to equity rather than through the income statement. These are items that can vary substantially in amount from year to year, but they tend toward zero in the long run.

The detail associated with stockholders' equity can be found in the Consolidated Statement of Stockholders' Equity. The typical analyst perspective for equity is **net assets** as a residual amount equal to assets minus liabilities, a formula that provides what is often called book value of the firm.

Another problematic area is **hybrid securities,** which have characteristics of both debt and equity. Convertible bonds are the common example. These are bonds that pay interest and have a specific maturity date; however, they can be converted to (usually) common stock at some conversion rate. From the investors' perspective, interest is received in cash and they participate in the future performance of the company (that is, if the price of the stock rises high enough, the shares can convert to stock) with minimal risk (they don't convert if the stock price declines). From the corporation's viewpoint, lower interest payments are required and, if the company is successful, principal isn't repaid since the bonds will be converted to stock.

Should convertible bonds be classified as liabilities or equity? They have characteristics of both. The GAAP answer is simple: according to Accounting Principles Board (APB) Opinion 14, convertible bonds are liabilities and the equity provisions are ignored until the bonds are converted. Upon conversion, either book value or market value can be used for valuation of the new equity.

## INCOME STATEMENT

Equity financial analysts (primarily for buying and selling equity securities) will focus relatively more attention on the income statement as the key to evaluating operating performance and future earnings. Measures of the bottom line, including net income, earnings per share, or income from continuing operations, are crucial; however, all aspects of performance must be evaluated to arrive at the relative confidence to be placed in a single bottom-line number. This can be called earnings power.

An income statement summarizes the relative success of business performance for a specific period of time, usually annually and quarterly. The annual income statement is comparative, including the current and the two previous years. Basically, the form is sales and other revenue less all expenses (plus and minus gains and losses) to arrive at net income. Net income is then stated on a per share basis as earnings per share. The format is standardized based on GAAP to include several basic components.

Dell's 2002 income statement, shown in Exhibit 3.4, is fairly basic. Net **revenue** includes sales and other revenue items recognized during the fiscal year. Cost of revenue is deducted to arrive at gross margin (or gross profit). Cost of revenues for manufacturing sales is cost of goods sold. Associated with sale of services is cost of services. Gross margin is an important measure of operating performance, which will be compared over time and to other firms. Operating **expenses,** which include selling and administrative, research, and development costs, are then deducted to arrive at operating income. Investment and other income (loss) is added to arrive at income before income tax. The provision for income tax (income tax expenses) is deducted to arrive at **income from continuing operations,** called in this case income before cumulative effect of change in

**EXHIBIT 3.4 INCOME STATEMENT OF DELL, FISCAL YEAR 2002**

| | Fiscal Year Ended | | |
|---|---|---|---|
| | **February 1, 2002** | **February 2, 2001** | **January 28, 2000** |
| Net revenue | $31,168 | $31,888 | $25,265 |
| Cost of revenue | 25,661 | 25,445 | 20,047 |
| Gross margin | 5,507 | 6,443 | 5,218 |
| Operating expenses: | | | |
| Selling, general and administrative | 2,784 | 3,193 | 2,387 |
| Research, development and engineering | 452 | 482 | 374 |
| Special charges | 482 | 105 | 194 |
| Total operating expenses | 3,718 | 3,780 | 2,955 |
| Operating income | 1,789 | 2,663 | 2,263 |
| Investment and other income (loss), net | (58) | 531 | 188 |
| Income before income taxes and cumulative effect of change in accounting principle | 1,731 | 3,194 | 2,451 |
| Provision for income taxes | 485 | 958 | 785 |
| Income before cumulative effect of change in accounting principle | 1,246 | 2,236 | 1,666 |
| Cumulative effect of change in accounting principle, net | — | 59 | — |
| Net income | $ 1,246 | $ 2,177 | $ 1,666 |

accounting principal. The cumulative effect of change in accounting principle is a **nonrecurring item** (essentially not part of continuing operations), which is deducted to arrive at net income, the "bottom line." Note that 2002 net income is well below 2001 net income, which will be subject to considerable analysis in Chapter 4.

The net income is converted to a per share basis, as shown in Exhibit 3.5. Earnings per share (EPS) were calculated both on a basic (net income ÷ shares outstanding) and diluted (net income ÷ restated shares outstanding based on potential shares from stock options and other sources). EPS also were calculated before the accounting change, essentially on the basis of income from continuing operations.

## Statement of Cash Flows

The balance sheet and income statement depend on accrual accounting to measure of financial position and operating performance. Additional information can be evaluated based on cash flows, and SFAS No. 95 requires the statement of cash flows. The statement is comparative, the current year compared to the two previous years. Essentially this is restated information with a different perspective—cash. The statement provides additional

**EXHIBIT 3.5 EARNINGS PER SHARE FOR DELL, FISCAL YEAR 2002**

| Earnings per common share | | | |
|---|---|---|---|
| **Before cumulative effect of change in accounting principle:** | | | |
| Basic | $ 0.48 | $ 0.87 | $ 0.66 |
| Diluted | $ 0.46 | $ 0.81 | $ 0.61 |
| **After cumulative effect of change in accounting principle:** | | | |
| Basic | $ 0.48 | $ 0.84 | $ 0.66 |
| Diluted | $ 0.46 | $ 0.79 | $ 0.61 |
| **Weighted average shares outstanding:** | | | |
| Basic | 2,602 | 2,582 | 2,536 |
| Diluted | 2,726 | 2,746 | 2,728 |

information on the liquidity of the company and its ability to finance operations and growth from internal funds. It can highlight certain problems such as lagging cash collections or the relative need for operating capital.

The statement of cash flows evaluates cash receipts (inflows) and cash payments (outflows) into three categories: operations, investing, and financing activities. The focus of **cash flows from operations** (CFO) is cash effects of all transaction that involve net income. The indirect method starts with net income and then adds back nonitems such as depreciation and amortization as well as changes in noncash current items. Most often, CFO is positive because net income is normally positive and noncash expenses such as depreciation increase CFO. Cash flows from investing (CFI) include capital expenditures and investments. Generally, CFI is negative because investments are uses of cash. Cash flow from financing (CFF) includes the acquisition or disposal of equity or debt and the payment of dividends. Then cash is reconciled from the beginning balance to the ending balance.

Dell's cash flows from operating activities are presented in Exhibit 3.6. The income statement shows that 2002 net income was down from the previous year but still $1.2 billion. Most adjustments to add back noncash accrued items such as depreciation were positive, as expected. The changes to all current assets and liabilities were presented as a single line item called operating working capital. Consequently, CFO was positive all three years and substantially larger than net income. Thus, CFO was a major source of cash.

Cash from investing and financing for Dell is shown in Exhibit 3.7. Usually, capital expenditures was the largest item for cash from investing. For Dell it was only $303 million in 2002, since Dell had a small fixed asset base. Dell's investments include both debt and equity securities, and Dell was a net investor for all three years (that is, purchases were greater than maturities and sales). The primary use of cash from financing was Dell's repurchase of outstanding stock (**treasury stock**). In summary, both CFI and CFF were significant uses of cash.

Finally, Dell reconciled cash, as shown in Exhibit 3.8. After adjusting for exchange rate fluctuations, Dell had a net decrease in cash of $1.3 billion for 2002. The beginning cash balance was a large $4.9 billion, realizing an ending cash balance of $3.6 billion.

**EXHIBIT 3.6 CASH FLOWS FROM OPERATIONS FOR DELL, FISCAL YEAR 2002**

| | Fiscal Year Ended | | |
|---|---|---|---|
| | February 1, 2002 | February 2, 2001 | January 28, 2000 |
| Cash flows from operating activities: | | | |
| Net income | $1,246 | $2,177 | $1,666 |
| Adjustments to reconcile net income to net cash provided by operating activities: | | | |
| Depreciation and amortization | 239 | 240 | 156 |
| Tax benefits of employee stock plans | 487 | 929 | 1,040 |
| Special charges | 742 | 105 | 194 |
| (Gains)/losses on investments | 17 | (307) | (80) |
| Other | 178 | 135 | 56 |
| Changes in: | | | |
| Operating working capital | 826 | 642 | 812 |
| Non-current assets and liabilities | 62 | 274 | 82 |
| Net cash provided by operating activities: | $3,797 | $4,195 | $3,926 |

**EXHIBIT 3.7 CASH FLOWS FROM INVESTING AND FINANCING ACTIVITIES FOR DELL, FY 2002**

| | Fiscal Year Ended | | |
|---|---|---|---|
| | February 1, 2002 | February 2, 2001 | January 28, 2000 |
| Cash flows from investing activities: | | | |
| Investments: | | | |
| Purchases | $(5,382) | $(2,606) | $(3,101) |
| Maturities and sales | 3,425 | 2,331 | 2,319 |
| Capital expenditures | (303) | (482) | (401) |
| Net cash used in investing activities | (2,260) | (757) | (1,183) |
| Cash flows from financing activities: | | | |
| Purchase of common stock | (3,000) | (2,700) | (1,061) |
| Issuance of common stock under employee plans | 295 | 404 | 289 |
| Other | 3 | (9) | 77 |
| Net cash used in financing activities | $(2,702) | $(2,305) | $ (695) |

**EXHIBIT 3.8 CASH RECONCILIATION FOR DELL, FISCAL YEAR 2002**

| | | | |
|---|---|---|---|
| Effect of exchange rate changes on cash | (104) | (32) | 35 |
| Net (decrease) increase in cash | (1,269) | 1,101 | 2,083 |
| Cash and cash equivalents at beginning of period | 4,910 | 3,809 | 1,726 |
| Cash and cash equivalents at end of period | $3,641 | $4,910 | $3,809 |

# Statement of Stockholders' Equity

The final required statement is the statement of stockholders' equity, which reconciles the various component of equity for three years. The beginning balances for Dell's 2002 fiscal year start in the middle of the page (see page 35 of Dell's 10-K, provided at www.wiley.com /college/giroux). The first line is net income of $1,246 added to retained earnings. Then are the comprehensive income items, including losses on investments, foreign currency translation adjustments, and gain on derivative instruments (net $24 million loss). Total comprehensive income for the year was $1,222 million. Stock issuances and purchases reduced stockholders' equity by a net $2,147 million ($3 billion less $853 million). The result was that equity decreased from the start of the year at $5.6 billion to $4.7 billion at year-end.

## SUMMARY

This chapter reviewed the financial statement required under GAAP, including the balance sheet, income statement, cash flow statement, and statement of stockholders' equity. The balance sheet and income statement are the most significant and provide the most basic financial information. The cash flow statement and statement of stockholders' equity provide additional information useful to a thorough financial analysis of the firm. Dell's financial statements were reviewed in some detail to illustrate fundamental points of analysis.

## KEY TERMS

assets
cash flows from operations
comprehensive income
Conceptual Framework
dirty surplus
equity
expenses
gains
hybrid securities
income from continuing operations
liabilities
losses
net assets
nonrecurring items
revenues
treasury stock

## QUESTIONS

1. What are the 10 financial statement elements and why are they integral to accounting analysis?
2. The balance sheet also is called the statement of financial position. Why are both terms correct?
3. Does the definition of assets by SFAS No. 5 fit assets actually presented in the balance sheet? Explain.

4. What is the relationship between liabilities and equity?
5. What are the basic components of income? What is the bottom line?
6. How is the statement of cash flows useful for understanding both liquidity and performance?
7. How is comprehensive income presented on the financial statements?

## PROBLEMS

### Problem 3.1 Assets of DuPont

Below is the asset section of the balance sheet of DuPont for fiscal year 2001.

| | December 31 | |
|---|---|---|
| | 2001 | 2000 |
| ASSETS | | |
| CURRENT ASSETS | | |
| Cash and cash equivalents | $ 5,763 | $ 1,540 |
| Marketable debt securities | 85 | 77 |
| Accounts and notes receivable (Note 13) | 3,903 | 4,552 |
| Inventories (Note 14) | 4,215 | 4,658 |
| Prepaid expenses | 217 | 228 |
| Deferred income taxes (Note 9) | 618 | 601 |
| Total current assets | 14,801 | 11,656 |
| PROPERTY, PLANT AND EQUIPMENT (Note 15) | 33,778 | 34,650 |
| Less: Accumulated depreciation | 20,491 | 20,468 |
| Net property, plant and equipment | 13,287 | 14,182 |
| GOODWILL AND OTHER INTANGIBLE ASSETS (Note 16) | 6,897 | 8,365 |
| INVESTMENT IN AFFILIATES (Note 17) | 2,045 | 2,206 |
| OTHER ASSETS (Notes 9 and 18) | 3,289 | 3,017 |
| TOTAL | $40,319 | $39,426 |

This financial statement is much more complicated than Dell's. Why? What additional items are here, but not on the Dell balance sheet? Various items refer to specific notes. What does this mean, and why is it important? Is DuPont a bigger company than Dell, based on assets?

### Problem 3.2 Preferred Stock at DuPont

The balance sheet of DuPont includes the following:

| | | |
|---|---|---|
| STOCKHOLDERS' EQUITY | | |
| Preferred stock, without par value—cumulative; 23,000,000 shares authorized; issued at December 31: | | |
| $4.50 Series—1,672,594 shares (callable at $120) | $ 167 | $ 167 |
| $3.50 Series—700,000 shares (callable at $102) | 70 | 70 |
| Common stock, $.30 par value; 1,800,000,000 shares authorized; Issued at December 31, 2001— 1,088,994,789; 2000—1,129,973,354 | 327 | 339 |
| Additional paid-in capital | $7,371 | $7,659 |

DuPont has preferred stock. Is this different than common stock? Explain. Are the amounts of preferred stock material in terms of total paid-in capital? Explain.

## Problem 3.3 Revenue and Operating Expenses for Hilton Hotels

Below is abbreviated information from Hilton's income statement:

| | 2001 |
|---|---|
| Revenue | |
| Owned hotels | $1,813 |
| Leased hotels | 26 |
| Management and franchise fees | 120 |
| Other fees and income | 191 |
| | 2,150 |
| Expenses | |
| Owned hotels | 1,196 |
| Leased hotels | 26 |
| Depreciation and amortization | 187 |
| Other operating expenses | 173 |
| Corporate expenses, net | 73 |
| | 1,655 |
| Operating Income | $ 495 |

Hilton is a service company, not manufacturing. The format for revenue and operating expenses is much different than Dell. Why? What are the primary differences?

## Problem 3.4 Cash Flows from Operations for DuPont

CFO from operations for 2001 is presented below. Unlike at Dell, DuPont's CFO is considerably less than net income. Why?

| CASH PROVIDED BY CONTINUING OPERATIONS | |
|---|---|
| Net income | 4,339 |
| Adjustments to reconcile net income to cash provided by continuing operations: | |
| Cumulative effect of a change in accounting principle (Note 11) | (11) |
| Depreciation | 1,320 |
| Amortization of goodwill and other intangible assets | 434 |
| Gain on sale of DuPont Pharmaceuticals (Note 7) | (6,136) |
| Other noncash charges and credits – | |
| Accounts and notes receivable | 435 |
| Inventories and other operating assets | (362) |
| Increase (decrease) in operating liabilities: | |
| Accounts payable and other operating liabilities | (634) |
| Accrued interest and income taxes (Notes 4 and 9) | 2,069 |
| Cash provided by continuing operations | $ 2,419 |

## CASES

### Case 3.1 Income Statement Items for General Electric (GE)

GE is a conglomerate and on some dimensions the largest company in the United States. Below are 2001 income statement items (in millions):

| | |
|---|---|
| REVENUES | |
| Sales of goods | $ 52,677 |
| Sales of services | 18,722 |
| Other income (note 2) | 234 |
| GECS revenues from services (note 3) | 54,280 |
| Total revenues | 125,913 |
| COSTS AND EXPENSES (note 4) | |
| Cost of goods sold | 35,678 |
| Cost of services sold | 13,419 |
| Interest and other financial charges | 11,062 |
| Insurance losses and policyholder and annuity benefits | 15,062 |
| Provision for losses on financing receivables (note 13) | 2,481 |
| Other costs and expenses | 28,162 |
| Total costs and expenses | 106,212 |
| EARNINGS BEFORE INCOME TAXES AND ACCOUNTING CHANGES | $ 19,701 |

GE has both manufacturing and service subsidiaries. In addition, much of its operations involve the large financing operation, General Electric Capital Services (GECS). How it this reflected on the income statement? Compare GE to Dell.

## ETHICS CONSIDERATIONS

So what happened to corporate ethics? This was a question poised in a *Business Week* article (J. Byrne, "Restoring Trust in Corporate America," June 24, 2002). Byrne's analysis:

> The root of the deterioration dates back 20 years, to the start of an unprecedented era of prosperity that transformed CEOs into cult heroes. From a time when many feared the U.S. would be overwhelmed by a super-efficient Japan, America's business leaders helped to make the U.S. the world's most productive economy. A return to business basics, along with a flowering of innovation and entrepreneurship, led to a celebration of corporate chieftains. Capital freely flowed into a financial system based on trust, stability, transparency, and the assurance that checks and balances made the stock exchanges a marketplace for every player.
>
> Nobody got fatter during the boom than the newly invincible CEOs, who were increasingly compensated with massive stock-option grants. That meant their success—and take-home pay—became directly related to how high they could nudge their stock price. Indeed, the great paradox of the so-called "shareholder revolution" of the past two decades is that CEOs gained exponentially in power,

influence, and certainly pay. Pressures from institutional shareholders unwittingly led to massive transfers of wealth from investors to senior executives, all under the guise of lining up management's interests with those of shareholders.

a. Evaluate this perspective on corporate ethics.
b. If this perspective is correct, it suggests that traditional management incentives are a major component of the problem. Do you agree? If so, what can be done about it?

## INTERNET PROJECTS

### Internet Project 3.1

Annual reports can be found at the companies' Web sites, and their 10-Ks can be found at Lexis/Nexis (www.lexisnexis.com). Download the financial statements of one company and evaluate the financial statements. How does this company compare to Dell?

CHAPTER 4

# Quantitative Financial Analysis Using Financial Statement Information

**Objectives**

- Develop a systematic perspective for quantitative financial analysis for all key elements of analysis.
- Explain the rationale for standardization of financial information for comparative purposes.
- Identify basic comparative measures using benchmarks, trends, competitors, and industry and market averages.
- Evaluate the use of common-size analysis for a comprehensive overview of key balance sheet and income statement items.
- Calculate and identify the importance of ratios for comparative analysis and describe the major ratio categories, which are liquidity, activity, leverage (solvency), and performance.
- Describe the use and importance of the DuPont Model.
- Describe the limitations of ratio analysis and other techniques that standardize financial information.

## INTRODUCTION

When an analyst looks at a corporation, there is an immense amount of quantitative financial data available. Initially, the numbers have no particular significance. What does it mean if a company has earnings per share of $4, revenue of $9 billion, or accounts receivable of $3.5 billion? The strategy is to develop a structured approach that standardizes the relevant information for comparative purposes. Financial information is relevant when it is compared over time for the firm and then compared to the industry and economy-wide measures of performance and financial position. The approach used is the following:

- Common-size analysis
- Financial ratios

- DuPont model
- Growth analysis
- Quarterly analysis

It should be noted that balance sheet items are stated as levels at a specific point in time, while income statement items measure operating flows over the period analyzed. The cash flow statement also considers flows rather than levels.

What is a good ratio? Or a red flag? These can be difficult to know. However, there are several comparison measures that can be useful:

- **Benchmark**—These are "rules of thumb" that can be useful as a first pass, such as a current ratio of 2 being adequate. Industry and market averages also can be used as benchmarks. Dun & Bradstreet (www.dnb.com) publishes industry norms and key business ratios.
- Common sense—Some results are obvious. For example, red flags are usually associated with net losses, negative cash flows from operations, or negative working capital.
- Trend analysis—How does the current measure compare to previous years? In most cases, the measure should be similar. Growth rates are a measure of performance.
- Near competitors—It is expected that firms in the same industry should have similar measures. If not, problems or opportunities may be present.
- Industry averages—Instead of considering one or more direct competitors, the average for the industry can be calculated. This is a broader measure that may be more difficult to interpret because of differences across many companies.
- Market averages—This is the broadest measure of comparison and is useful to consider how close the firm is to an "average" company.

All of these measures can be useful, but have limitations. Therefore, the more comparisons made, the more "feel" the analyst should have for the comparisons.

The annual report (10-K) for Dell Corporation for the fiscal year ended February 1, 2002, is presented on the support Web site for this text, at www.wiley.com/college/giroux. Most calculations for this chapter will use this financial information, plus comparable information for close competitors Gateway and Apple, for calculations and interpretation.

Common-size, financial ratios, and models such as the DuPont Model convert financial information to percentages. Thus, relative size is ignored. As important as these techniques are, they are only part of the overall financial analysis. Size is important and included in the overall analysis.

## Common-size Analysis

The balance sheet and income statement, usually in a simplified format, can be presented in dollar amounts and then standardized as percentages. In **common-size analysis,** all balance sheet items are stated as a percentage of total assets and all income statement items as a percentage of sales or total revenues. Abbreviated financial statements for several years and across firms in the industry can provide a useful overview of the operating performance and financial health of the firm. Common-size analysis can be used as a useful starting point for a firm's operations and financial position.

Consider the abbreviated financial statement information (in millions) for Dell Computer and two competitors, Gateway and Apple, to be used in common-size analysis and financial ratios, in Exhibit 4.1.

The financial information is not complete, but it provides considerable information on Dell's current performance relative to the previous two fiscal years and Dell's two major competitors in personal computers and related hardware. In terms of performance, Dell has stable

**EXHIBIT 4.1 ABBREVIATED FINANCIAL STATEMENTS FOR THE PERSONAL COMPUTER COMPANIES**

**Income Statement**

| | Dell | Dell | Dell | Gateway | Apple |
|---|---|---|---|---|---|
| **Fiscal year ended** | 2/01/2002 | 2/02/2001 | 1/30/2000 | 12/31/2001 | 9/30/2001 |
| **Revenue** | $31,168 | $31,888 | $25,265 | $6,080 | $5,363 |
| **Cost of Goods Sold** | 35,661 | 25,445 | 20,047 | 5,041 | 4,026 |
| **Gross Profit** | 5,507 | 6,443 | 5,218 | 1,038 | 1,337 |
| **SG&A Expense** | 2,784 | 3,193 | 2,761 | 2,022 | 1,568 |
| **Interest Expense** | 29 | 47 | 34 | NA | 16 |
| **Tax Expense** | 485 | 958 | 785 | –276 | –15 |
| **Net Income** | 1,246 | 2,177 | 1,666 | **–1,034** | **–25** |

**Balance Sheet**

| | Dell | Dell | Dell | Gateway | Apple |
|---|---|---|---|---|---|
| **Fiscal year ended** | 2/01/2002 | 2/02/2001 | 1/30/2000 | 12/31/2001 | 9/30/2001 |
| **Cash and Marketable Securities** | $3,914 | $5,438 | $3,809 | $1,166 | $2,310 |
| **Receivables, net** | 2,636 | 2,895 | 2,608 | 220 | 466 |
| **Inventories** | 278 | 400 | 301 | 120 | 11 |
| **Total Current Assets** | 7,877 | 9,491 | 7,681 | 2,123 | 5,143 |
| **Fixed Assets, net** | 826 | 996 | 765 | 608 | 564 |
| **Total Assets** | 13,535 | 13,435 | 11,471 | 2,987 | 6,021 |
| **Total Current Liabilities** | 7,519 | 6,543 | 5,192 | 1,146 | 1,518 |
| **Total Liabilities** | 8,841 | 7,813 | 6,163 | 1,422 | 2,101 |
| **Total Equity** | 4,694 | 5,622 | 5,308 | 1,565 | 3,920 |

**Cash Flow Statement**

| | Dell | Dell | Dell | Gateway | Apple |
|---|---|---|---|---|---|
| **Fiscal year ended** | 2/01/2002 | 2/02/2001 | 1/30/2000 | 12/31/2000 | 9/30/2001 |
| **Cash Flows from Operations** | $3,797 | $4,195 | $3,926 | **$–270** | $185 |
| **Cash Flows from Investing** | –2,260 | –757 | –1,183 | 109 | 892 |
| **Cash Flows from Financing** | –2,702 | –2,305 | –695 | 405 | 42 |

revenues, but declining net income. However, both competitors had net losses for the current year, red flags (RF) (in bold in the tables). The cash flow statement shows that all companies had positive net increases in cash, although Gateway had negative cash from operations.

The analysis is limited when presented only in dollars. Standardizing the analysis into percentages provides additional information. Each income statement is standardized as a percentage of revenues (i.e., revenues = 100 percent) and balance sheet as a percentage of total assets (i.e., total assets = 100 percent). The restated, or common-size, financial statements are shown in Exhibit 4.2.

The standardized or common-size analysis provides considerable information and, with a little practice, can be interpreted quickly. Dell's profit margin declined to only 4.0 percent, down from 6.8 percent the previous year. Both of Dell's competitors have obvious operating problems, with net losses for the year. Dell's margin has been declining and is the same as Gateway at 17.7 percent. Apple is higher at 24.9 percent. Dell's selling, general, and administrative expenses (SG&A) are much lower than the competitors', associated with the company's direct selling and low-cost business strategy. A key question is: are the fiscal year 2001 (2002 for Dell) operations for this industry an anomaly or will this poor performance trend continue? The answer to this question may be the most important one to determine buy or sell equity decisions.

**EXHIBIT 4.2 COMMON-SIZE STATEMENTS FOR THE PC COMPANIES**

**Common-size Income Statement**

| | Dell | Dell | Dell | Dell | Gateway | Apple |
|---|---|---|---|---|---|---|
| **Fiscal year ended** | 2/01/2002 | 2/01/2002 | 2/02/2001 | 1/30/2000 | 12/31/2001 | 9/30/2001 |
| **Revenue** | $31,168 | 100% | 100% | 100% | 100% | 100% |
| **Cost of Goods Sold** | 25,661 | 82.3 | 79.8 | 79.3 | 82.9 | 75.1 |
| **Gross Profit** | 5,507 | 17.7 | 20.2 | 20.7 | 17.7 | 24.9 |
| **SG&A Expense** | 2,784 | 8.9 | 10.0 | 10.9 | 33.3 | 29.2 |
| **Net Income** | 1,246 | 4.0 | 6.8 | 6.6 | **–4.5 RF** | **–0.3 RF** |

**Common-size Balance Sheet**

| | Dell | Dell | Dell | Dell | Gateway | Apple |
|---|---|---|---|---|---|---|
| **Fiscal year ended** | 2/01/2002 | 2/01/2002 | 2/02/2001 | 1/30/2000 | 12/31/2001 | 9/30/2001 |
| **Cash and Marketable Securities** | $3,914 | 28.9% | 40.5% | 33.2% | 39.0% | 38.4% |
| **Receivables, net** | 2,636 | 19.5 | 21.5 | 22.7 | 7.4 | 7.7 |
| **Inventories** | 278 | 2.1 | 3.0 | 2.6 | 4.0 | 0.2 |
| **Total Current Assets** | 7,877 | 58.2 | 70.6 | 67.0 | 71.1 | 85.4 |
| **Fixed Assets, net** | 826 | 6.1 | 7.4 | 6.7 | 20.4 | 9.4 |
| **Total Assets** | 13,535 | 100 | 100 | 100 | 100 | 100 |
| **Total Current Liabilities** | 7,517 | 55.6 | 48.7 | 45.3 | 38.4 | 25.2 |
| **Total Liabilities** | 8,841 | 65.3 | 58.2 | 53.7 | 47.6 | 34.9 |
| **Total Equity** | 4,694 | 34.7 | 41.8 | 46.3 | 52.4 | 65.1 |

Dell's balance sheet is quite different from the standard manufacturing firm's. Current assets make up almost 60 percent of total assets for 2001, down from the previous year. Cash, including marketable securities, is down to 28.9 percent. Inventory is only 2.1 percent, down from 3.0 percent in 2001, and accounts receivable is 19.5 percent, down from 21.5 percent. Low inventory usually is a sign of good production control, low receivables a sign of good credit control. Dell's total current assets, at 58.2 percent, is the lowest of the group. Both Gateway and Apple have considerably more cash at 39.0 percent and 38.4 percent, respectively. Gateway and Apple have lower accounts receivable ratio at 7.4 percent and 7.7 percent. All three have very low inventory, 4.0 percent for Gateway and an incredible 0.2 percent for Apple. Apple seemingly has mastered the use of just-in-time inventory control.

Matching high current assets at Dell, current liabilities are 55.6 percent of total assets, up from 48.7 percent the previous year. Although there are few long-term liabilities, total liabilities are 65.3 percent of total assets. This means that equity is only 34.7 percent of assets, resulting in a high debt-to-equity position. This equity position is lower than the competitors'. Since most of the liabilities are current and there are plenty of current assets, especially cash, this may not be a problem. However, cash for the year is down and liabilities are up. Therefore, it is a concern and may require additional analysis. More will be learned from a thorough ratio analysis.

## Financial Ratios

Central to financial analysis is the calculation of financial ratios. A ratio has a numerator and a denominator, which converts the financial data to a percentage. This provides one approach to standardizing financial information for useful comparisons. The major ratio categories and the questions they attempt to answer are:

- *Liquidity*—Does the company have enough cash and current assets to pay obligations as they come due?
- *Activity*—How efficient are the operations of the company?
- *Leverage*—What is the mix of equity to debt?
- *Performance*—How profitable is the company?

Each ratio provides a somewhat different analysis. A company may have substantial current assets but little cash. A company with high leverage may or may not suggest a red flag. High leverage increases business and default risk, but it improves return on equity. High leverage could result from too many long-term bonds or high accounts payable. These would be interpreted differently.

Three significant points relate to ratio analysis: (1) the ratios overlap, so a red flag in one area will likely relate to red flags in other areas; (2) a thorough ratio analysis must be done, although most ratios end up in a normal range that needs little further analysis; and (3) the importance of specific ratios differs based on the objectives of the financial analysis (e.g., credit versus investment decision), industry involved (e.g., banks behave differently from high tech or automobile companies), and other factors (e.g., relative interest rates at the time of analysis).

Financial ratios for the most recent year (and most recent quarter when relevant) are the most important, since this represents the latest financial data available. As with other techniques, comparisons over time and with other companies and industries are useful, since ratios are evaluated in some context.

## LIQUIDITY

Does the company have the cash and other current assets to pay liabilities as they come due? Most current assets are converted to cash and most current liabilities are paid in cash when due. Current marketable securities generally are investments of excess cash into liquid debt securities to earn a return until the cash is needed for operations. Marketable securities are treated as cash (or near cash) for analysis. In most cases, relatively large cash balances are considered good news.

Accounts receivable are credit terms given to customers on sales. Some percentage of receivables will become delinquent and end up as bad debts. The credit terms that companies give is an important component related to revenue analysis. A company can increase sales by expanding credit sales to higher-risk customers. This will increase revenue in the short term, but receivables will increase and bad debts can be expected to rise in the near future.

Inventory represents goods available for sale, either purchased (merchandizing firms) or manufactured, plus raw materials and work in progress for manufacturing firms. There are different inventory accounting techniques (last-in first-out versus first-in first-out or average, perpetual, or periodic) plus all firms must use lower of cost or market. Large inventory may signal relatively inefficient operations. Also, excess inventory or rising inventory levels may be a red flag related to potentially obsolete inventory or operating problems.

Current liabilities are obligations to be paid or liquidated with current resources, usually within one year. The largest category usually is accounts payable, the amount owed to suppliers. Many companies have a policy to delay payment as long as possible to conserve cash.

**Working capital** is net current assets (total current assets – total current liabilities). This is one measure of liquidity. Since cash and other current assets are needed to pay current obligations, negative working capital is a potential red flag. Working capital and other measures of liquidity are particularly important when evaluating credit decisions. Common **liquidity ratios** are shown in Exhibit 4.3.

Liquidity ratios are calculated for Dell and competitors in Exhibit 4.4. Dell's ratios are adequate across the different calculations of liquidity and compare somewhat below Dell's previous year and competitors. Dell's current ratio for 2002 of 1.0 is down from the previous year and is the lowest in the industry. However, since over half of Dell's current assets are cash and

**EXHIBIT 4.3 LIQUIDITY RATIOS**

| Ratio | Calculation | Discussion |
|---|---|---|
| Current | Current Assets ÷ Current Liabilities | Standard ratio to evaluate working capital. |
| Quick (Acid Test) | (Cash + Marketable Securities + Net Receivables) ÷ Current Liabilities | This ratio eliminates inventory and other current assets from the denominator, focusing on "near cash" and receivables. |
| Cash | (Cash + Marketable Securities) ÷ Current Liabilities | Only cash and cash equivalents considered for payment of current liabilities. |
| Operating Cash Flow | Cash Flows from Operations ÷ Current Liabilities | Evaluates cash-related performance (as measured from the Statement of Cash Flows) relative to current liabilities. |

**EXHIBIT 4.4 LIQUIDITY RATIOS FOR THE PC COMPANIES**

| | Dell | Dell | Gateway | Apple |
|---|---|---|---|---|
| Year | 2002 | 2001 | 2001 | 2001 |
| Current | 7,877 ÷ 7,519 = 1.0 | 1.5 | 1.9 | 3.4 |
| Quick | (3,814 + 2,636) ÷ 7,519 = 81.7% | 1.3 | 83.0% | 1.8 |
| Cash | 3,914 ÷ 7,519 = 52.1% | 83.1% | 62.9% | 1.5 |
| Operating Cash Flow | 3,797 ÷ 7,519 = 50.5% | 64.1% | **–23.6% RF** | 12.2% |
| Rating (1–10) | 4 | 6 | 5 | 8 |

Notes: (1) All rounding to 0.1 or 0.1%; generally, ratios below 1.0 will be converted to percentages; (2) Dell's fiscal year-end for 2002 is 2/01/2002, so it is comparable to Gateway's 2001 fiscal year, which ends 12/31/2001, and Apple's, which ends 9/30/2001; ratings are from 1 for very poor to 10 for excellent, with the average between 4 and 6.

marketable securities, this does not seem to be a concern. The quick and cash ratios are good at 81.7 percent and 50.5 percent, respectively. Both are below the previous year and roughly comparable to Gateway's ratios but below Apple's. Operating cash flow ratio compares cash flows from operations to current liabilities, and Dell's is a healthy 50.5 percent but down from the previous year. Negative or low operating cash flow ratios (such as Gateway's–23.6 percent) suggest unusual accruals or other problems, often caused by earnings management techniques—a potential red flag. Gateway had a large net loss, which carried over to this ratio.

A rating scale is estimated by company for liquidity on a 1–10 scale. A 1 represents severe problems and 10 excellence. Ratings of 1–2 should be considered red flags, and ratings of 9–10 could be green flags. Apple's 8 is near excellence, showing very high liquidity. The others have average ratings. The use of ratings depends on judgment and can be based on a combination of rules of thumb (e.g., a current ratio below 1 can be considered "bad news"), industry comparisons, and market averages.

## ACTIVITY

Activity or turnover ratios are measures of efficiency and, generally, the higher the better. Typically, the numerator is an operating measure such as sales (revenues) or cost of goods sold and the denominator is a balance sheet measure such as inventory or receivables. Thus, operating flows are measured against asset and other levels. Time series trends and comparisons to other companies are useful to spot red flags or potential opportunities. Common **activity ratios** are shown in Exhibit 4.5.

The operating measures occur over the fiscal period. Therefore, the most appropriate comparison is the average balance sheet measure for the denominator. This is measured as ½ (beginning balance + ending balance), equivalent to half of this year's balance plus half of last year's balance. Note that inventory turnover uses cost of goods sold as the numerator; all other activity ratios use sales (or total revenue) as the numerator.

Activity ratios for Dell and competitors are shown in Exhibit 4.6. Dell's turnover ratios are extremely high on most measures, even when compared to Apple; Gateway is a bit less efficient. This is caused by a combination of good performance and growth and relatively low asset balances. Low inventory levels are part of Dell's operating strategy, resulting in a high inventory turnover. Note that Apple's inventory is even higher. Dell's receivables turnover and payables turnover are average to competitors', in both cases higher than Apple but below Gateway. Dell's working capital turnover is the highest of the group, resulting from Dell's low working capital for the current year. Fixed assets turnover is higher than competitors, since Dell has a low infrastructure strategy. Dell's total asset turnover is a bit above its competitors'. Future success for Dell will depend, in part, on maintaining high turnover ratios; that is, its low-cost business strategy.

Overall, Dell was given a rating of 9 for excellent efficiency, slightly above Apple's 8. Dell has consistently high turnover ratios, but Apple is relatively lower on some dimensions. Gateway has average efficiency.

**EXHIBIT 4.5 ACTIVITY RATIOS**

| Ratio | Calculation | Discussion |
|---|---|---|
| Inventory Turnover | COGS ÷ Average Inventory | Measures inventory management. Inventory should be turned over rapidly, rather than accumulating in warehouses. |
| Receivables Turnover | Sales ÷ Average Accounts Receivables | Measures the effectiveness of credit policies and needed level of receivables investment for sales. (Also called the collection period). |
| Payables Turnover | Sales ÷ Average Accounts Payables | Payables represent a financing source for operations. |
| Working Capital Turnover | Sales ÷ Average Working Capital | Measures how much working (operating) capital is needed for sales. |
| Fixed Asset Turnover | Sales ÷ Average Fixed Assets | Measures the efficiency of net fixed asset (property, plant, and equipment after accumulated depreciation) investments. |
| Total Asset Turnover | Sales ÷ Average Total Assets | Represents the overall (comprehensive) efficiency of assets to sales. |

**EXHIBIT 4.6 ACTIVITY RATIOS FOR THE PC COMPANIES**

| | Dell | Dell | Gateway* | Apple† |
|---|---|---|---|---|
| Year | 2002 | 2001 | 2001 | 2001 |
| Inventory Turnover | 25,661 ÷½(278 + 400) = 75.7 | 72.6 | 23.2 | 183.0 |
| Receivables Turnover | 31,168 ÷ ½(2,636 +2,895) = 11.3 | 11.6 | 15.9 | 7.6 |
| Payables Turnover‡ | 31,168 ÷ ½(5,075 +4,286) = 6.7 | 8.2 | 10.8 | 5.5 |
| Working Capital Turnover | 31,168 ÷ ½(358+ 2,948) = 18.9 | 11.7 | 7.7 | 1.5 |
| Fixed Asset Turnover | 31,168 ÷ ½(826+ 996) = 34.2 | 39.2 | 8.1 | 10.9 |
| Total Asset Turnover | 31,168 ÷ ½(13,535+ 13,435) = 2.3 | 2.6 | 1.7 | 83.6% |
| Rating | 9 | 9 | 6 | 8 |

*Gateway 2000 inventory = 315; receivables = 545; working capital = 608; fixed assets = 897; total assets = 4,181

†Apple 2000 inventory = 33; receivables = 953; working capital = 3,494; fixed assets = 419; total assets 6,803

‡Accounts payable for Dell are: fiscal year 2002 = 5,075; 2001 = 4,286; 2000 = 3,538; Gateway 2001 = 341; 2000 = 785; 2000 = 4,233; Apple 2001 = 801; 2000 = 1,157

Activity ratios can be converted to days "held," measures that are easily compared across firms, as shown in Exhibit 4.7.

Day's ratios for Dell and competitors are shown in Exhibit 4.8. Converting to days represents basically the same results, although it may be easier to evaluate based on number of days. Inventory stock for Dell is a low 4.8 days, lower than Gateway and Apple, but above the incredible two days of inventory at Apple. However, Dell's average days receivables is higher than Gateway's. Only Apple is higher. The length of the operating cycle may be a useful activity measure across firms. Both Dell and Gateway have extremely low operating cycles. Dell has a relatively long average days payable outstanding. The firm does not pay suppliers quickly, really a measure of policy rather than efficiency. Note that ratings are a bit different than the activity ratios. Dell is still a healthy 7, as is Gateway, while Apple is slightly lower at 6. Both Dell and Apple have relatively "average" operating cycles because of somewhat higher receivables turnovers.

## LEVERAGE/SOLVENCY

Leverage (also called solvency) considers the capital structure of the firm and the evaluation of the relative risk and return associated with liabilities (especially long-term debt) and equity (or ownership). Equity is associated with common stock, although preferred stock is part of the equity structure in some firms. Essentially, equity is a residual value, also called net assets (which are equal to total assets – total liabilities). Another way to consider

**EXHIBIT 4.7 ACTIVITY RATIOS IN DAYS**

| Ratio | Calculation |
|---|---|
| Average Days Inventory in Stock | 365 ÷ Inventory Turnover |
| Average Days Receivables Outstanding | 365 ÷ Receivables Turnover |
| Average Days Payable Outstanding | 365 ÷ Payables Turnover |
| Length of Operating Cycle | 365 [(1 ÷ Inventory Turnover) + (1 ÷ Receivables Turnover)]; equivalent to average days inventory + average days receivables outstanding |

**EXHIBIT 4.8 ACTIVITY RATIOS IN DAYS FOR THE PC COMPANIES**

| | Dell | Dell | Gateway | Apple |
|---|---|---|---|---|
| Year | 2002 | 2001 | 2001 | 2001 |
| Average Days Inventory in Stock | 365 ÷ 75.7 = 4.8 days | 5.0 days | 15.7 days | 2.0 days |
| Average Days Receivables Outstanding | 365 ÷ 11.3 = 32.3 days | 31.5 | 23.0 | 48.0 |
| Average Days Payable Outstanding | 365 ÷ 6.7 = 54.5 days | 44.5 | 33.8 | 66.4 |
| Length of Operating Cycle | 4.8 + 32.3 = 37.1 days | 36.5 | 38.7 | 50.0 |
| Rating | 7 | 7 | 7 | 6 |

the balance sheet is assets are on the left and the sources of the assets on the right. Both stockholders and creditors are stakeholders in the firm.

A number of technical accounting issues influence the evaluation of debt. However, it is worth noting that real and potential liabilities exist whether or not reported on the balance sheet. Contingencies, operating leases, defined benefit pension commitments, and other postemployment benefits are associated with liabilities that require additional analysis. These and other issues will be described in Chapters 5–7.

Common leverage ratios are shown in Exhibit 4.9. Debt is defined as total liabilities. This may be an oversimplification, but it is easy to determine and compare across firms. Other definitions of debt can be useful for additional analysis. Total equity at market value is defined as closing stock price at some specific date multiplied by the number of shares outstanding at the end of the fiscal period under study. It is further analyzed in Chapter 4.

Leverage ratios for Dell and competitors are shown in Exhibit 4.10. Dell's debt to equity ratio suggests that Dell has leverage problems with more debt than equity in 2002 and debt to equity higher than in 2001. The reason is the high level of current liabilities (offset by high levels of current assets), not long-term debt. Dell's 2002 leverage ratios were roughly similar to the competitors'. The interest coverage was extremely high, since Dell has relatively little long-term liability. Dell's long-term debt to equity was only 28.2 percent, but this was the highest of the three companies. When market equity is used rather than net assets, debt is 12.6% of market value. Overall, leverage is about average for Dell. Dell has relatively high leverage, but this is more a function of accounts payable rather than long-term debt. Overall, Gateway also had average leverage. Only Apple had low leverage levels, although the interest coverage ratio was not meaningful for the year.

Leverage ratios are relatively easy to interpret for credit decisions: the lower the better. As debt increases, the potential for credit default decreases. The interpretation for equity investment decisions is more difficult, since increasing debt would increase return on equity. From an equity perspective, the relative debt is evaluated. Too high increases credit risk, too low means reduced return on equity.

**EXHIBIT 4.9 LEVERAGE RATIOS**

| Ratio | Calculation | Discussion |
|---|---|---|
| Debt to Equity | Total Liabilities ÷ Total Stockholders' Equity | Direct comparison of debt to equity stakeholders and the most common measure of capital structure. |
| Debt Ratio | Total Liabilities ÷ Total Assets | A broader definition, stating debt as a percent of assets. |
| Interest Coverage (Times Interest Earned) | (Net Income + Interest Expense + Tax Expense) ÷ Interest Expense | This is a direct measure of the firm's ability to meet interest payments, indicating the protection provided from current operations. |
| Long-term Debt to Equity | Long-term Liabilities ÷ Total Stockholders' Equity | A long-term perspective of debt and equity positions of stakeholders. |
| Debt to Market Equity | Total Liabilities at Book Value ÷ Total Equity at Market Value | Market valuation may represent a better measure of equity than book value. Most firms have a market premium relative to book value. |

## PROFITABILITY

Profit is the most important criterion for evaluating commercial firms for investment decisions. The most significant predictor of firm market valuation is profitability and the likelihood of continuous profit growth. Thus, the future existence and success of corporations depends on this analysis. Consequently, there are several profitability ratios that consider different aspects of earnings performance. Common **profitability ratios** are shown in Exhibit 4.11.

Ratios for Dell and competitors are shown in Exhibit 4.12. Dell's 2002 profitability ratios were consistently lower than its 2001 results, a trend since 1999. This suggests that

**EXHIBIT 4.10 LEVERAGE RATIOS FOR THE PC COMPANIES**

| | Dell | Dell | Gateway | Apple |
|---|---|---|---|---|
| Year | 2002 | 2001 | 2001 | 2001 |
| Debt to Equity | 8,841 ÷ 4,694 = 1.9 | 1.4 | 90.9% | 53.6% |
| Debt Ratio | 8,841 ÷ 13,535 = 65.3% | 58.2% | 47.6% | 34.9% |
| Interest Coverage | (1,246 + 29 + 485) ÷ 29 = 60.7 | 67.7 | NM† | NM† |
| Long-term Debt to Equity | 1,322 ÷ 4,694 = 28.2% | 22.6% | 17.6% | 9.7% |
| Debt to Market Equity* | 8,841 ÷ 70,278 = 12.6% | 12.3% | 82.3% | 25.0% |
| Rating | 6 | 6 | 6 | 8 |

*Market equity for Dell is calculated as the current market price (in this case the May 1, 2002, closing price of $26.48) × number of shares outstanding: $26.48 × 2,654 million = $70,278 million. Market value for Gateway is $5.33 × 324 million = $1,727 million; and Apple is $23.98 × 351 = $8,417 million.

†NM = not meaningful; all have net losses and negative numerators. These ratios can be calculated (Apple's is (–25 + 16 - 15) ÷ 16 = –1.5×, but a negative interest coverage is NM.

**EXHIBIT 4.11 PROFITABILITY RATIOS**

| Ratio | Calculation | Discussion |
|---|---|---|
| Gross Margin | (Sales - COGS) ÷ Sales | This captures the relationship between sales and manufacturing (or merchandising) costs. Also called the gross profit margin. |
| Return on Sales | Net Income ÷ Sales | Measures the relationship of the bottom line to sales and thus captures sales to total costs of sales. Also called the net profit margin. |
| Return on Assets | Net Income ÷ Average Total Assets | Measures the firm's efficiency in using assets to generate earnings. Alternatively stated, it captures earnings to all providers of capital. |
| Pretax Return on Assets | Earnings before Interest and Taxes ÷ Average Total Assets | Measures earnings from operations on a pretax and pre-interest expense basis. |
| Return on Total Equity | Net Income ÷ Average Total Stockholders' Equity | Measures earnings to owners as measured by net assets. |
| Dividend Payout | Common Dividends ÷ Net Income | Measures the percent of earnings paid out to common stockholders. |

**EXHIBIT 4.12 PROFITABILITY RATIOS FOR THE PC COMPANIES**

| | Dell | Dell | Gateway | Apple |
|---|---|---|---|---|
| Year | 2002 | 2001 | 2001 | 2001 |
| Gross Margin | (31,168 – 25,661) ÷ 31,168 = 17.7% | 20.2% | 17.1% | 24.9% |
| Return on Sales | 1,246 ÷ 31,168 = 4.0% | 6.8 | **–17.0 RF** | **–0.5 RF** |
| Return on Assets* | 1,246 ÷ ½(13,535 + 13,435) = 9.2% | 17.5 | **–7.7 RF** | **–0.4 RF** |
| Pretax Return on Assets | (1,731 + 29) ÷ ½(13,535 + 13,435) = 13.1% | 25.6 | **–36.0 RF** | **–0.6 RF** |
| Return on Total Equity† | 1,246 ÷ ½(4,694 + 5,622) = 24.2% | 39.8 | **–14.0 RF** | **–0.6 RF** |
| Dividend Payout‡ | 0 | 0 | 0 | 0 |
| Rating | 6 | 8 | **1 RF** | **2 RF** |

*Gateway total assets for = 4,181; Apple = 6,803.
†2000 total equity for Gateway = 2,380; Apple = 4,107.
‡Dividends per share were 0 for all companies.

Dell's spectacular performance of the 1990s has leveled off to more normal levels. At some point this is a potential red flag, unusual because the numbers on almost any scale (except Dell's past performance) are excellent. On the other hand, competitors Gateway and Apple had net losses, obvious red flags.

Thus, Dell rates a 6 as an average performer for the year—down from an 8 for the previous year. Gateway's performance was a disaster, an obvious 1 rating. The key question is: will Gateway survive as an independent company? Apple had a slight net loss, a 2 rating but still a red flag. During the 1990s PC and other successful high tech companies had stellar profitability.

## DuPont Model

The **DuPont Model** was initially developed at DuPont and decomposes return on equity (ROE) by several ratios. Considered here is the three-component model (two-, four-, and five-component models can also be calculated). The purpose is to consider interrelated aspects of important financial ratios and how they overlap for analysis. The basic model is Profitability × Activity × Solvency = Return on Equity. Also, Profitability × Activity = Return on Assets. Note that ROE is really return on common equity in the DuPont Model, which is total stockholders' equity less preferred stock. The calculation for companies without preferred stock is based on total stockholders' equity. The specific ratios used are shown in Exhibit 4.13.

The DuPont Model calculations for Dell, Gateway, and Apple are shown in Exhibit 4.14. The DuPont Model considers several interrelated aspects of operating performance. Dell's 2002 return on sales is a respectable 4.0 percent, lower than the previous year. Gateway and Apple are both negative, which raises red flags. Asset turnover represents high efficiency for

**EXHIBIT 4.13 DUPONT MODEL**

| Ratio | Calculation |
|---|---|
| Profitability (Return on Sales) × | Net Income ÷ Sales |
| Activity (Asset Turnover) | Sales ÷ Average Total Assets |
| = Return on Assets | Net Income ÷ Average Total Assets |
| × Solvency (Common Equity Leverage) | Average Total Assets ÷ Average Common Equity |
| = Return on Equity | Net Income ÷ Average Common Equity |

**EXHIBIT 4.14 DUPONT MODEL FOR THE PC COMPANIES**

| | Dell | Dell | Gateway | Apple |
|---|---|---|---|---|
| Year | 2002 | 2001 | 2001 | 2001 |
| Profitability | 1,246 ÷ 31,168 = 4.0% | 6.8% | **–17.0% RF** | **–0.5% RF** |
| Activity | 31,168 ÷ ½(13,535 + 13,435) = 231.1 | 256.1 | 169.6 | 83.6 |
| Return on Assets | 1,246 ÷ 13,485 = 9.2 | 17.5 | **–7.7 RF** | **–0.4 RF** |
| Solvency | 13,485 ÷ ½(4,694 + 5,622 = 261.4 | 227.9 | 181.7 | 159.8 |
| Return on Equity* | 1,246 ÷ 5,158 = 24.2 | 39.8 | **–14.0 RF** | **–0.6 RF** |
| Rating | 6 | 8 | **1 RF** | **2 RF** |

*None of these companies has preferred stock; therefore, average total stockholders' equity is used.

Dell, the highest at 231.1 but lower than the previous year. Gateway is moderately efficient, but Apple has a ratio below 1. Combining these two ratios results in a return on assets of 9.2 percent, with the same relationships to competitors and the previous year. Solvency is relatively high for all three companies. The tradeoff is high leverage, increasing the credit risk, but also a higher ROE relative to return on assets (ROA). This results in a respectable return on equity ratios for Dell at 24.2 percent, but that is considerably lower than the previous year's 39.8 percent and also short of 2000's 43.7 percent. Both Gateway and Apple had losses, resulting in red flags. Note that none of these three companies had preferred stock.

## Limitations of Ratio Analysis

Ratio analysis and related techniques such as the DuPont Model and common-size analysis provide information on a percentage basis, useful for comparisons over time and across firms and industries. However, the limitations of ratio analysis also are important. Relative size is deemphasized. Being a large or small firm may be particularly important. The largest firm in a mature industry is less likely to achieve rapid growth, but it may continue to dominate an industry at adequate performance levels well into the future. A small firm is subject to both advantages and limitations. Growth would seem to be potentially unlimited. Consider the spectacular growth of Dell Computer over the last decade. On the other hand, market share may be hard to achieve when facing much larger competitors. Smaller firms typically have more trouble raising capital than larger, well-established firms and have a higher probability of bankruptcy.

A basic assumption of financial ratios and other financial analysis tools is that the numbers used are correct. Basic income statement and balance sheet numbers can be misstated or manipulated in a variety of ways. Managers have earnings management incentives, which suggests that basic financial statement numbers may be fallible. A primary purpose of the detailed accounting analysis is to determine to what degree the financial statement numbers can be relied upon. If not reliable, the ratio analysis is less useful for decision purposes.

## SUMMARY

An immense amount of quantitative financial data is readily available for firms on the major stock exchanges. A systematic analysis requires the use of standardizing techniques for comparative purposes, including common-size, financial ratios, and various financial models. A thorough financial analysis provides substantial information on performance and most aspects of financial position and growth. Common-size analysis converts financial statement line items to percentages for quick comparisons. Financial ratios are used for a more thorough analysis of key categories that include liquidity (available cash and other current items), leverage (relative debt), activity (operational efficiency), and performance (profitability). The DuPont Model is a formal decomposition of return on equity.

## KEY TERMS

activity ratio
benchmarks
common-size analysis
DuPont Model
leverage ratio
liquidity ratio
profitability ratio
working capital

## A SUMMARY OF FINANCIAL RATIOS

### Liquidity

Current: Current Assets ÷ Current Liabilities

Standard ratio to evaluate working capital.

Quick (Acid Test): (Cash + Marketable Securities + Net Receivables) ÷ Current Liabilities

This ratio eliminates inventory and other current assets from the denominator, focusing on "near cash" and receivables.

Cash: (Cash + Marketable Securities) ÷ Current Liabilities

Only cash and cash equivalents considered for payment of current liabilities.

Operating: Cash Flows from Operations ÷ Current Liabilities

Evaluates cash-related performance (as measured from the Statement of Cash Flows) relative to current liabilities.

### Activity

Inventory Turnover: COGS ÷ Average Inventory

Measures inventory management. Inventory should be turned over rapidly, rather than accumulating in warehouses.

Receivables Turnover: Sales ÷ Average Accounts Receivables

Measures the effectiveness of credit policies and needed level of receivables investment for sales.

Payables Turnover: Sales ÷ Average Accounts Payables
Payables represent a financing source for operations.

Working Capital Turnover: Sales ÷ Average Working Capital
Measures how much working (operating) capital is needed for sales.

Fixed Asset Turnover: Sales ÷ Average Fixed Assets
Measures the efficiency of net fixed asset (property, plant, and equipment after accumulated depreciation) investments.

Total Asset Turnover: Sales ÷ Average Total Assets
Represents the overall (comprehensive) activity measure of assets to sales.

**Leverage (Solvency)**

Debt to Equity: Total Liabilities ÷ Total Stockholders' Equity
Direct comparison of debt to equity stakeholders and the most common measure of capital structure.

Debt Ratio: Total Liabilities ÷ Total Assets
A broader definition, stating debt as a percent of assets.

Interest Coverage (Times Interest Earned):
(Net Income + Interest Expense+ Tax Expense) ÷ Interest Expense
This is a direct measure of the firm's ability to meet interest payments, indicating the protection provided from current operations.

Long-term Debt to Equity: Long-term Liabilities ÷ Total Stockholders' Equity
A long-term perspective of debt and equity positions of stakeholders

Debt to Market Equity: Total Liabilities at Book Value ÷ Total Equity at Market Value
Market valuation may represent a better measure of equity than book value. Most firms have a market premium relative to book value.

**Profitability (Performance)**

Gross Margin: (Sales – COGS) ÷ Sales
This captures the relationship between sales and manufacturing (or merchandising) costs.

Return on Sales: Net Income ÷ Sales
Measures the relationship of the bottom line to sales and thus captures sales to total costs of sales.

Return on Assets: Net Income ÷ Average Total Assets
Measures the firm's efficiency in using assets to generate earnings. Alternatively stated, it captures earnings to all providers of capital

Pretax Return on Assets: Earnings before Interest and Taxes ÷ Average Total Assets
Measures earnings from operations on a pretax and pre-interest expense basis.

Return on Total Equity: Net Income ÷ Average Total Stockholders' Equity
Measures earnings to owners as measured by net assets.

Dividend Payout: Common Dividends ÷ Net Income
Measures the percent of earnings paid out to common stockholders.

## QUESTIONS

1. Why is a systematic quantitative perspective important for financial analysis?
2. How is standardization achieved in the quantitative process? Why is this important?
3. After a set of ratios is calculated for a company, how can they be analyzed? When is a ratio "good" or "bad"?

4. For each of these financial ratio categories—liquidity, leverage, activity, and performance—describe the purpose of analysis and list at least three useful ratios.
5. What is the DuPont Model and why is it important?
6. Give examples of ratio analysis limitations.

## PROBLEMS

### Problem 4.1 Common-size Analysis

(Problems 4.1–6 relate to the chemical industry.)

Summary income statements and balance sheets are presented for the three largest companies in the chemical industry for fiscal year 2001 (in millions). For additional information, their Web sites (and ticker symbols) are www.dupont.com (DD), www.dow.com (DOW), and www.ppg.com (PPG).

**Income Statement**

| | DuPont | Dow | PPG |
|---|---|---|---|
| Revenues | $24,726 | $27,805 | $8,169 |
| COGS | 16,727 | 22,015 | 5,137 |
| Gross Profit | 7,999 | 5,790 | 3,032 |
| SG&A Expenses | 4,513 | 2,807 | 1,764 |
| Net Income | 4,339 | **–385** | 387 |

**Balance Sheet**

| | DuPont | Dow | PPG |
|---|---|---|---|
| Cash & Market Securities | $5,763 | $220 | $108 |
| Receivables, net | 3,903 | 5,098 | 1,416 |
| Inventories | 4,215 | 4,440 | 904 |
| Total Current Assets | 14,801 | 10,308 | 2,703 |
| Fixed Assets, net | 13,287 | 13,579 | 2,752 |
| Total Assets | 40,319 | 35,515 | 8,452 |
| Total Current Liabilities | 8,067 | 8,125 | 1,955 |
| Total Liabilities | 25,867 | 25,522 | 5,372 |
| Total Equity | 14,452 | 9,993 | 3,080 |

Complete the following tables using common-size analysis:

**Income Statement**

| | DuPont | Dow | PPG |
|---|---|---|---|
| Revenues | 100% | 100% | 100% |
| COGS | | | |
| Gross Profit | | | |
| SG&A Expenses | | | |
| Net Income | | | |

**Balance Sheet**

| | DuPont | Dow | PPG |
|---|---|---|---|
| Cash & Market Securities | | | |
| Receivables, net | | | |
| Inventories | | | |
| Total Current Assets | | | |
| Fixed Assets, net | | | |
| Total Assets | 100% | 100% | 100% |
| Total Current Liabilities | | | |
| Total Liabilities | | | |
| Total Equity | | | |

Summarize the highlights from common-size analysis for these companies and indicate possible red flags.

## Problem 4.2 Financial Ratios—Liquidity

Given the information from 3.1 above, calculate the liquidity ratios for the three chemical companies. Rate liquidity for each company from 1 (poor) to 10 (excellent).

| | DuPont | Dow | PPG |
|---|---|---|---|
| Current | | | |
| Quick | | | |
| Cash | | | |
| Operating Cash Flow* | | | |
| Ratings | | | |

*Operating cash flows (in millions) are: DuPont, $2,419; Dow, $1,789; PPG, $1,060.

## Problem 4.3 Financial Ratios—Activity

The following additional information is provided for fiscal year 2000:

| | DuPont | Dow | PPG |
|---|---|---|---|
| Inventory | $4,658 | $3,463 | $1,121 |
| Receivables, net | 4,552 | 5,385 | 1,563 |
| Working Capital | 2,401 | 1,387 | 550 |
| Fixed Assets, net | 13,287 | 13,579 | 2,752 |
| Total Assets | 39,426 | 27,645 | 9,125 |
| Total Equity | 13,299 | 9,686 | 3,097 |

Given the information above, calculate the activity ratios for the three chemical companies. Rate activity for these companies from 1 (poor) to 10 (excellent).

| | DuPont | Dow | PPG |
|---|---|---|---|
| Inventory Turnover | | | |
| Receivables Turnover | | | |
| Working Capital Turnover | | | |
| Fixed Asset Turnover | | | |
| Total Asset Turnover | | | |
| Ratings | | | |

| | DuPont | Dow | PPG |
|---|---|---|---|
| Average Days Inventory in Stock | | | |
| Average Days Receivables Outstanding | | | |
| Length of Operating Cycle | | | |
| Ratings | | | |

## Problem 4.4 Financial Ratios—Leverage

Here is information on stock price.

| | DuPont | Dow | PPG |
|---|---|---|---|
| Stock Price, 5/1/2002 | $44.63 | $31.49 | $52.22 |
| Shares Outstanding (millions) | 1,002 | 905 | 168 |

Given the information above, calculate the leverage ratios for the three chemical companies. Rate leverage for these companies from 1 to 10.

| | DuPont | Dow | PPG |
|---|---|---|---|
| Debt to Equity | | | |
| Debt Ratio | | | |
| Debt to Market Equity | | | |
| Ratings | | | |

## Problem 4.5 Financial Ratios—Profitability

Given the information above, calculate the profitability ratios for the three chemical companies. Rate profitability for these companies from 1 to 10.

| | DuPont | Dow | PPG |
|---|---|---|---|
| Gross Margin | | | |
| Return on Sales | | | |
| Return on Assets | | | |
| Return on Total Equity | | | |
| Dividend Payout* | | | |
| Ratings | | | |

*Dividends per share for 2001: DuPont, $1.40; Dow, $1.34; PPG, $1.68

## Problem 4.6 DuPont Model

Given the information above, calculate the DuPont Model for the three chemical companies. Rate DuPont performance for these companies from 1 to 10.

| | DuPont | Dow | PPG |
|---|---|---|---|
| Profitability | | | |
| Activity | | | |
| Return on Assets | | | |
| Solvency* | | | |
| Return on Equity* | | | |
| Ratings | | | |

*Only DuPont has preferred stock, of $237; deduct this amount from total stockholders' equity for total common equity; for other companies, common is the same as total.

## Problem 4.7 Common-size Analysis

Summary income statements and balance sheets are presented for three companies in the hotel and resort industry for fiscal year 2001 (in millions).

### Income Statement

| | Hilton | Marriott | Mandalay* |
|---|---|---|---|
| Revenues | $2,632 | $10,152 | $2,462 |
| COGS | 1,946 | 9,234 | 1,370 |
| Gross Profit | 686 | 918 | 1,092 |
| SG&A Expenses | 71 | 187 | 473 |
| Net Income | 166 | 236 | 53 |

*Fiscal year ends (FYE) January 2002.

### Balance Sheet

| | Hilton | Marriott | Mandalay |
|---|---|---|---|
| Cash & Market Securities | $35 | $817 | $106 |
| Receivables, net | 631 | 611 | 77 |
| Inventories | 148 | 96 | 31 |
| Total Current Assets | 996 | 2,130 | 267 |
| Fixed Assets, net | 3,986 | 2,930 | 3,050 |
| Total Assets | 8,785 | 9,107 | 4,037 |
| Total Current Liabilities | 902 | 1,802 | 309 |
| Total Liabilities | 7,002 | 5,629 | 3097 |
| Total Equity | 1,783 | 3,478 | 941 |

Complete these tables using common-size analysis:

**Income Statement**

| | Hilton | Marriott | Mandalay |
|---|---|---|---|
| Revenues | 100% | 100% | 100% |
| COGS | | | |
| Gross Profit | | | |
| SG&A Expenses | | | |
| Net Income | | | |

**Balance Sheet**

| | Hilton | Marriott | Mandalay |
|---|---|---|---|
| Cash & Market Securities | | | |
| Receivables, net | | | |
| Inventories | | | |
| Total Current Assets | | | |
| Fixed Assets, net | | | |
| Total Assets | 100% | 100% | 100% |
| Total Current Liabilities | | | |
| Total Liabilities | | | |
| Total Equity | | | |

Summarize the highlights from common-size analysis for these companies and indicate possible red flags.

## Problem 4.8 Financial Ratios—Liquidity

Given the information from 4.7 above, calculate the liquidity ratios for the three hotel and resort companies. Rate liquidity for each company from 1 (poor) to 10 (excellent).

| | Hilton | Marriott | Mandalay |
|---|---|---|---|
| Current | | | |
| Quick | | | |
| Cash | | | |
| Operating Cash Flow* | | | |
| Ratings | | | |

*Operating cash flows (in millions) are Hilton, $270; Marriott, $400; Mandalay, $351.

## Problem 4.9 Financial Ratios—Activity

The following additional information is provided for fiscal year 2000:

| | Hilton | Marriott | Mandalay* |
|---|---|---|---|
| Inventory | $137 | $97 | $31 |
| Receivables, net | 435 | 728 | 78 |
| Working Capital | 194 | **–502** | **–10** |
| Fixed Assets, net | 3,911 | 3,011 | 3,237 |
| Total Assets | 9,140 | 8,237 | 4,248 |
| Total Equity | 1,642 | 3,267 | 1,069 |

*FYE January 2002.

Given the information above, calculate the activity ratios for the three hotel and resort companies. Rate activity for these companies from 1 (poor) to 10 (excellent).

| | Hilton | Marriott | Mandalay |
|---|---|---|---|
| Inventory Turnover | | | |
| Receivables Turnover | | | |
| Working Capital Turnover | | | |
| Fixed Asset Turnover | | | |
| Total Asset Turnover | | | |
| Ratings | | | |

| | Hilton | Marriott | Mandalay |
|---|---|---|---|
| Average Days Inventory in Stock | | | |
| Average Days Receivables Outstanding | | | |
| Length of Operating Cycle | | | |
| Ratings | | | |

## Problem 4.10 Financial Ratios—Leverage

The following additional information is provided on stock price.

| | Hilton | Marriott | Mandalay |
|---|---|---|---|
| Stock Price, 5/1/2002 | 16.00 | 44.03 | 7.13 |
| Shares Outstanding (millions) | 369 | 245 | 68 |

Given the information above, calculate the leverage ratios for the three hotel and resort companies. Rate leverage for these companies from 1 to 10.

| | Hilton | Marriott | Mandalay |
|---|---|---|---|
| Debt to Equity | | | |
| Debt Ratio | | | |
| Debt to Market Equity | | | |
| Ratings | | | |

### Problem 4.11 Financial Ratios—Profitability

Given the information above, calculate the profitability ratios for the three hotel and resort companies. Rate profitability for these companies from 1 to 10.

| | Hilton | Marriott | Mandalay |
|---|---|---|---|
| Gross Margin | | | |
| Return on Sales | | | |
| Return on Assets | | | |
| Return on Total Equity | | | |
| Dividend Payout* | | | |
| Ratings | | | |

*Dividends per share for 2001: Hilton, $0.08; Marriott, $0.28; Mandalay, $0.

### Problem 4.12 DuPont Model

Given the information above, calculate the DuPont Model for the three hotel and resort companies. Rate DuPont performance for these companies from 1 to 10.

| | Hilton | Marriott | Mandalay |
|---|---|---|---|
| Profitability | | | |
| Activity | | | |
| Return on Assets | | | |
| Solvency* | | | |
| Return on Equity* | | | |
| Ratings | | | |

*None of the companies has preferred stock; common is the same as total.

### Problem 4.13 Common-size Analysis

(Problems 4.13 – 4.18 relate to the automotive industry.)

Summary income statements and balance sheets are presented for Ford and General Motors for fiscal year 2001 (in millions). For additional information, their Web sites (and ticker symbols) are www.ford.com (F) and www.gm.com (GM). Note that these numbers are for overall operations, not just automotive. For more analysis comparing automotive to financial services segments for Ford, see Case 4.4.

**Income Statement (in millions)**

| | Ford | Ford | GM | GM |
|---|---|---|---|---|
| Fiscal year | 12/31/2001 | 12/31/2000 | 12/31/2001 | 12/31/2000 |
| Revenue | $162,412 | $170,064 | $177,260 | $184,632 |
| COGS | 125,706 | 140,499 | 130,942 | 145,664 |
| Gross Profit | 36,706 | 29,565 | 46,318 | 38,968 |
| SG&A | 13,602 | 11,847 | 23,302 | 22,252 |
| Interest Expense | 10,848 | 10,902 | 8,590 | 9,552 |
| Tax Expense | –2,151 | 2,705 | 768 | 2,393 |
| Net Income | **–5,453 RF** | 3,467 | 601 | 4,452 |

**Balance Sheet (in millions)**

| | Ford | Ford | GM | GM |
|---|---|---|---|---|
| Fiscal year | 12/31/2001 | 12/31/2000 | 12/31/2001 | 12/31/2000 |
| Cash & Market Securities | $7,218 | $4,851 | $18,555 | $10,284 |
| Receivables, Trade (net) | 3,152 | 6,272 | 141,394 | 135,002 |
| Inventories | 6,191 | 7,514 | 10,034 | 10,945 |
| Total Current Assets | 36,260 | 39,310 | 193,843 | 208,920 |
| Total Fixed Assets | 33,121 | 37,508 | 34,908 | 33,977 |
| Total Assets | 276,543 | 284,421 | 323,969 | 303,100 |
| Total Current Liabilities | 44,546 | 43,327 | 64,246 | 63,156 |
| Total Liabilities | 268,757 | 265,811 | 304,262 | 272,925 |
| Total Equity | 7,786 | 18,610 | 19,707 | 30,175 |

**Cash Flow Statement (in millions)**

| | Ford | Ford | GM | GM |
|---|---|---|---|---|
| Fiscal year | 12/31/2001 | 12/31/2000 | 12/31/2001 | 12/31/2000 |
| Cash Flows from Operations | $22,764 | $33,764 | $9,166 | $10,871 |
| Cash Flows from Investing | –17,169 | –9,867 | –23,171 | –11,313 |
| Cash Flows from Financing | –2,976 | –8,521 | 22,372 | –890 |

Common-size analysis—complete the following tables:

**Income Statement—Common-size**

| | Ford | Ford | GM | GM |
|---|---|---|---|---|
| Fiscal year | 12/31/2001 | 12/31/2000 | 12/31/2001 | 12/31/2000 |
| Revenue | 100% | 100% | 100% | 100% |
| COGS | | | | |
| Gross Profit | | | | |
| SG&A | | | | |
| Net Income | | | | |

**Balance Sheet—Common-size**

| | Ford | Ford | GM | GM |
|---|---|---|---|---|
| Fiscal year | 12/31/2001 | 12/31/2000 | 12/31/2001 | 12/31/2000 |
| Cash & Market Securities | | | | |
| Receivables, net | | | | |
| Inventories | | | | |
| Total Current Assets | | | | |
| Fixed Assets, net | | | | |
| Total Assets | 100% | 100% | 100% | 100% |
| Total Current Liabilities | | | | |
| Total Liabilities | | | | |
| Total Equity | | | | |

## Problem 4.14 Financial Ratios—Liquidity

Given the information above, calculate the liquidity ratios for Ford and GM. Rate the liquidity from 1 to 10 for each company.

**Liquidity**

| | Ford | GM |
|---|---|---|
| Year | 2001 | 2001 |
| Current | | |
| Quick | | |
| Cash | | |
| Operating Cash Flow | | |
| Rating | | |

## Problem 4.15 Financial Ratios—Activity

Given the information above, calculate the activity ratios and rate the companies' efficiency from 1 to 10.

| | Ford | GM |
|---|---|---|
| Year | 2001 | 2001 |
| Inventory Turnover | | |
| Receivables Turnover | | |
| Working Capital Turnover | | |
| Fixed Asset Turnover | | |
| Total Asset Turnover | | |
| Average Days Inventory in Stock | | |
| Average Days Receivables Outstanding | | |
| Length of Operating Cycle | | |
| Ratings | | |

## Problem 4.16 Financial Ratios—Leverage

Given the information above, calculate the leverage ratios and rate the companies' solvency from 1 to 10.

| | Ford | GM |
|---|---|---|
| Year | 2001 | 2001 |
| Debt to Equity | | |
| Debt Ratio | | |
| Interest Coverage | | |
| Debt to Market Equity* | | |
| Ratings | | |

*Market price (5/1/02) for Ford, $16.34, and shares outstanding, 1,908 million; GM stock price, $65.51, and shares outstanding, 1,437.

### Problem 4.17 Financial Ratios—Profitability

Given the information above, calculate the profitability ratios and rate the companies' performance from 1 to 10.

| | Ford | GM |
|---|---|---|
| Year | 2001 | 2001 |
| Gross Margin | | |
| Return on Sales | | |
| Return on Assets | | |
| Return on Total Equity | | |
| Dividend Payout* | | |
| Ratings | | |

*Dividends for Ford, $0.40, and for GM, $2.00

### Problem 4.18 DuPont Model

Given the information above, calculate the DuPont Model and ratings.

**DuPont Model**

| | Ford | GM |
|---|---|---|
| Year | 2001 | 2001 |
| Profitability | | |
| Activity | | |
| Return on Assets | | |
| Solvency | | |
| Return on Equity | | |
| Ratings | | |

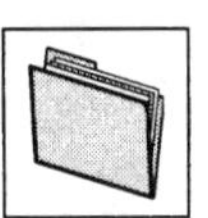

## CASES

### Case 4.1 Overview of Chemical Industry Quantitative Analysis

A complete quantitative financial analysis for the current year has been conducted for the chemical industry. Write a short overview for each company, including an overall rating from 1 to 10.

| | Rating | Summary |
|---|---|---|
| DuPont | | |
| Dow | | |
| PPG | | |

### Case 4.2 Overview of Hotel and Resort Industry Quantitative Analysis

A complete quantitative financial analysis for the current year has been conducted for the hotel and resort industry. Write a short overview for each company, including an overall rating from 1 to 10.

| | Rating | Summary |
|---|---|---|
| Hilton | | |
| Marriott | | |
| Mandalay | | |

## Case 4.3 Overview of Automotive Industry Quantitative Analysis

A complete quantitative financial analysis for the current year has been conducted for Ford and GM. Write a short overview for each company, including an overall rating from 1 to 10.

| | Rating | Summary |
|---|---|---|
| Ford | | |
| GM | | |

## Case 4.4 Ford's Industry Segments

Problems 4.13–18 included the total company. However, automotive and financial services are reported separately in their annual reports and have different characteristics. Consider the following abbreviated financial information for Ford for 2001.

| | Automotive | Financial Services | Companywide |
|---|---|---|---|
| Sales/Revenue | $131,528 | $30,884 | |
| Cost & Expenses | 139,096 | 29,432 | |
| Operating Income | **(7,568)** | 1,452 | |
| Net Income (Loss) | | | **$(5,453)** |
| Cash & Marketable Securities | 15,028 | 3,767 | |
| Total Current Assets | 33,121 | 64,917 | |
| Total Assets | 88,319 | 188,224 | |
| Total Current Liabilities | 44,546 | 3,397 | |
| Total Liabilities | 92,980 | 175,105 | |
| Stockholders' Equity | | | 7,786 |

Calculate common-size information for the segments:

| | Automotive | Financial Services |
|---|---|---|
| Sales/Revenue | 100% | 100% |
| Cost & Expenses | | |
| Operating Income | | |
| Net Income (Loss) | | |
| Total Current Assets | | |
| Total Assets | 100% | 100% |
| Total Current Liabilities | | |
| Total Liabilities | | |

a. Calculate the following ratios for the two segments:

| | Automotive | Financial Services |
|---|---|---|
| Operating Income to Sales | | |
| Operating Income to Total Assets | | |
| Current Ratio | | |
| Cash Ratio | | |
| Debt Ratio | | |

b. Evaluate the financial information for the two business segments. How are they different? What are the obvious red flags? Are they differences expected? Explain. How does this analysis change your perspective on Ford as a potential equity investment?

## INTERNET PROJECTS

### Project 4.1

Pick a company from the *Fortune* 500 list. Gather the financial information you need from the company's annual report and other sources. Do a complete financial analysis, using the same format as above.

**Suggestions:** Summary financial statements can be found at www.hoovers.com. Complete financial statements can usually be found on company Web sites and the SEC's EDGAR system, which is available from several sources. Considerable financial information can be found at financial Web sites, such as Quicken (www.quicken.com) and Yahoo Financial (quote.yahoo.com).

# Appendix: Other Financial Ratios and Considerations

This chapter lists most of the common ratios, although in some cases in a simplified form (e.g., debt is generally defined as total liabilities). There is no equivalent to GAAP for ratios, so different ratios and different definitions exist. Specific ratios and definitions are based on user needs and preferences of individuals and institutions.

For example, most of the leverage ratios in this book use total liabilities for debt. These are easy to calculate, and there is no misunderstanding about what to include or exclude. Alternatively, bonds outstanding or other definitions of long-term debt could be used. Bondholders (or all long-term creditors) can be considered stakeholders in the company, a somewhat different perspective from "all liabilities." However, it may be difficult to identify which liabilities are long-term and which calculate all bonded debt. These are valid leverage ratio substitutes, may represent preferred variables, and are commonly used by analysts. (See Cases 11.1 and 11.2 for a more detailed discussion on liabilities.)

Below are some alternative ratios:

**Liquidity**

Cash to Current Assets: (Cash + Marketable Securities) ÷ Current Assets

Cash Position: Cash ÷ Total Assets

Current Liability Position: Current Liabilities ÷ Total Assets

**Leverage**

Cash Turnover: Sales ÷ Average Cash (which usually inc-ludes marketable securities)

Payables Turnover: Sales ÷ Average Accounts Payable

**Activity**

Cash Turnover: Sales ÷ Average Cash (which usually includes marketable securities)

Payables Turnover: Sales ÷ Average Accounts Payable

**Profit**

Operating Profit Margin: Income from Continuing Operations (after tax) ÷ Sales

Pretax Profit Margin: Income before Tax ÷ Sales

Return on Common Equity: (Net Income – Preferred Dividends) ÷ Average Common Equity

Financial Leverage Index: Return on Equity ÷ Return on Assets

These are all valid ratios, although perhaps not as common as ratios described earlier. Even with these, this is hardly a complete list. Virtually any number (or set of related numbers) in the financial statements can be a numerator or denominator in a quantitative financial ratio.

CHAPTER 5

# Multiperiod Quantitative Financial Analysis

**Objectives**

- Evaluate the importance and use of multiple-period analysis.
- Calculate growth analysis for performance and explain how this enhances quantitative financial analysis.
- Calculate trend analysis for performance and explain how this enhances quantitative financial analysis.
- Distinguish between growth and trend analysis.
- Calculate quarterly analysis for the most recent periods and understand how this updates traditional annual financial quantitative analysis.
- Explain why quarterly analysis is particularly important and develop standard techniques for analyzing data on a quarterly basis.

## INTRODUCTION

Traditional quantitative financial analysis includes the most recent year or two, which are considered the most relevant. However, significant long-term trends may exist and be crucial to a complete financial analysis. Therefore, additional quantitative analysis is suggested for at least the previous five years. In addition, financial data are available on a quarterly basis, which becomes the most recent information available on performance and other aspects of financial conditions. Although these data are limited, a quarterly quantitative analysis is essential.

## GROWTH ANALYSIS

**Growth analysis** considers growth rates in dollars and growth rate percentages, especially for operations. Earnings and sales growth are particularly important for equity investment decisions. An understanding of the relationship of earnings to revenues and expenses is also important, because they are indicators of sustainability of earnings growth rates. Balance sheet changes and growth rates, which are important for credit decisions, provide information on sustainability of operating performance and indicators of future problems and risk. Accounts receivable growth may indicate the potential for aggressive revenue recognition. Increasing leverage suggests rising credit risk and potential problems if economic conditions worsen.

Several techniques can be used to analyze growth rates. First, as with the common-size analysis, the relevant numbers can be presented in a table. Alternatively, information can be presented as graphs or bar charts. This is largely a matter of taste. However, annual or quarterly data are relatively more useful in tabular form, while stock prices, which change daily, are usually presented in graph form. Growth rates can also be stated as annual (or total) changes for some period, such as five or ten years.

Consider income statement numbers for the last six years for the PC competitors, shown in Exhibit 5.1. It should be noted that these are the same fiscal years, except that Gateway's fiscal year ends December 31, 2001, Dell's February 1, 2002, and Apple's on September 31, 2001. All operating numbers are down in the current year for each company. Prior to 2002, Dell had an impressive record in sales growth and increases in gross profit and net income. This is the performance trend that analysts prefer to see. Both Gateway and Apple lost money in 2001, with somewhat erratic performance over the earlier years. Apple also lost money in both 1996 and 1997. Based only on limited multiyear performance numbers, Dell seems the most likely to recover quickly.

Can this information be presented in a more useful fashion? The annual growth percentages can be calculated, as shown in Exhibit 5.2. Thus, Dell's 1997–98 revenue growth rate was (12,327 – 7,759) ÷ 7,759 [(most recent – previous) ÷ previous]. All three companies showed

**EXHIBIT 5.1 ABBREVIATED INCOME STATEMENTS FOR THE PC COMPANIES, LAST SIX YEARS**

**Dell (in millions)**

| | 1997 | 1998 | 1999 | 2000 | 2001 | 2002 |
|---|---|---|---|---|---|---|
| Revenues | $7,759 | $12,327 | $18,243 | $25,265 | $31,888 | $31,168 |
| Gross Profit | 1,666 | 2,722 | 4,106 | 5,218 | 6,443 | 5,746 |
| Net Income | 518 | 944 | 1,460 | 1,666 | 2,177 | 1,246 |

**Gateway (in millions)**

| | 1996 | 1997 | 1998 | 1999 | 2000 | 2001 |
|---|---|---|---|---|---|---|
| Revenues | $5,035 | $6,294 | $7,468 | $8,646 | $9,601 | $6,079 |
| Gross Profit | 936 | 1,077 | 1,546 | 1,900 | 2,059 | 1,038 |
| Net Income | 251 | 110 | 346 | 428 | 241 | **–1,034 RF** |

**Apple (in millions)**

| | 1996 | 1997 | 1998 | 1999 | 2000 | 2001 |
|---|---|---|---|---|---|---|
| Revenues | $9,833 | $7,081 | $5,941 | $6,134 | $7,983 | $5,363 |
| Gross Profit | 968 | 1,368 | 1,479 | 1,781 | 2,250 | 1,337 |
| Net Income | **–816 RF** | **–1,045 RF** | 309 | 601 | 786 | **–25 RF** |

concerns over the last six years, particularly with poor performance in the most recent year relative to previous years.

The total 1997–2002 growth rate for Dell's net income was over 140 percent [(1,246 – 518) ÷ 518]. The percentage change can be interpreted more easily than dollar amounts. It should be noted that Dell's net income growth percentages were lower than either sales or gross profit growth, indicating that Dell's profitability rates were declining. Except for the most recent year, Dell had consistent performance improvements. Thus, the percentage changes for Dell were reasonably impressive, while both Gateway and Apple had significant performance problems. Gateway had severe problems in 2001 and more modest problems in earlier years. Apple's performance was erratic. Although Apple's 2001 net loss was relatively small compared to Gateway's, losses were recorded in three of the previous six years and sales declined in those same years.

It should be pointed out that acquisitions and divestitures influence trend analysis. For example, Dell acquired a number of relatively small high tech companies over the trend analysis period. Consequently, part of Dell's growth can be attributed to these acquisitions. On the other hand, in the chemical industry, DuPont divested two large holdings over the same time period, Conoco and DuPont Pharmaceutical. Consequently, DuPont appears to have declining performance.

In summary, the most recent year was a disaster for all of the PC companies, but Apple seemed to have recurring problems. Based solely on this limited analysis, Dell seems the most likely to recover quickly. Gateway's severe problems suggest the real possibility of failure. If Gateway can turn around quickly, the future should be promising. Apple's recurring performance problems indicate that other structural problems may be present. Thus,

**EXHIBIT 5.2 ANNUAL EARNINGS GROWTH RATES FOR THE PC COMPANIES**

**Dell Annual Growth Percentages**

| | 1997-1998 | 1998-1999 | 1999-2000 | 2000-2001 | 2001-2002 | Total 1997-2002 |
|---|---|---|---|---|---|---|
| Revenues | 58.9% | 48.0% | 38.5% | 26.2% | **–2.3%** | 301.7% |
| Gross Profit | 63.4 | 50.8 | 27.1 | 23.5 | **–10.8** | 244.9 |
| Net Income | 82.2 | 54.7 | 14.1 | 30.7 | **–42.8** | 140.5 |

**Gateway Annual Growth Percentages**

| | 1996-1997 | 1997-1998 | 1998-1999 | 1999-2000 | 2000-2001 | Total 1996-2001 |
|---|---|---|---|---|---|---|
| Revenues | 25.0% | 18.7% | 15.8% | 11.0% | **–36.7%** | 20.7% |
| Gross Profit | 15.1 | 43.5 | 22.9 | 8.4 | **–49.6** | 10.9 |
| Net Income | **–56.2** | 214.5 | 23.7 | **–43.7** | **–528.6 RF** | **-512.4 RF** |

**Apple Annual Growth Percentages**

| | 1996-1997 | 1997-1998 | 1998-1999 | 1999-2000 | 2000-2001 | Total 1996-2001 |
|---|---|---|---|---|---|---|
| Revenues | **–28.0%** | **–16.1%** | 3.2% | 30.1% | **–32.8%** | **–45.5%** |
| Gross Profit | 41.3 | 8.1 | 20.4 | 26.3 | **–40.6** | 38.1 |
| Net Income | NM | NM | 94.5 | 30.8 | **–103.2 RF** | NM |

Apple's long-term success would seem to depend more on restructuring and a changing business strategy.

## TREND ANALYSIS

A variation to the growth analysis is to use the earliest year as the base year. In **trend analysis,** the base year numbers are set equal to 100 and the remaining numbers are calculated relative to that base. Thus, Dell's 1997 revenues of $7,759 million are set equal to 100. The revenue index for 1998 is calculated as 12,327 ÷ 7,759 = 1.5887 (stated as 158.9). Dell's 2002 net income is 1,246 ÷ 518 = 2.4054 (240.5). A limitation is that the base year must be positive to be calculated meaningfully. (Note that if the base year number is abnormally large or small, the analysis is much less meaningful.) Because Apple had net losses in 1996 and 1997, 1998 is set as the based year for Apple's net income, as shown in Exhibit 5.3.

Although the same performance numbers are used, the trend analysis has a slightly different perspective than growth analysis and either or both can be evaluated. The tremendous operating growth of Dell is highlighted, with 2002 revenues four times 1997—a growth of 300 percent. Net income is more modest at 240.5. Note that the declines from 2001 to 2002 seem minor without minus signs.

The performance problems of both Gateway and Apple are also highlighted: Gateway was down in 2001, and the 2000 drop in net income is also obvious. Apple's revenues declined over the six years and never recovered to its 1996 level. Apple's bad performance in 2001 is emphasized. The long-term perspective of trend analysis is particularly useful in cyclical industries and companies with periodic problems. Compare the results for both

**EXHIBIT 5.3 TREND ANALYSIS FOR THE PC COMPANIES, LAST SIX YEARS**

| Dell | | | | | | |
|---|---|---|---|---|---|---|
| | **1997** | **1998** | **1999** | **2000** | **2001** | **2002** |
| Revenues | 100 | 158.9 | 235.1 | 325.6 | 411.0 | 401.7 |
| Gross Profit | 100 | 163.4 | 246.5 | 313.2 | 386.7 | 344.9 |
| Net Income | 100 | 182.2 | 281.9 | 321.6 | 420.3 | **240.5** |

| Gateway | | | | | | |
|---|---|---|---|---|---|---|
| | **1996** | **1997** | **1998** | **1999** | **2000** | **2001** |
| Revenues | 100 | 125.0 | 148.3 | 171.7 | 190.7 | **$120.7** |
| Gross Profit | 100 | 115.1 | 165.2 | 203.0 | 220.0 | **110.9** |
| Net Income | 100 | **43.8** | 137.8 | 170.5 | **96.0** | **–412.0 RF** |

| Apple | | | | | | |
|---|---|---|---|---|---|---|
| | **1996** | **1997** | **1998** | **1999** | **2000** | **2001** |
| Revenues | 100 | **72.0** | **60.4** | **62.4** | **81.2** | **54.5** |
| Gross Profit | 100 | 141.3 | 152.8 | 184.0 | 232.4 | **138.1** |
| Net Income | NM* | NM* | **100*** | **194.5** | **254.4** | **–8.1 RF** |

*Since Apple had net losses for both 1996 and 1997, 1998 is used as the base year for net income.

growth and trend analysis. They are based on the same numbers. Is the analysis the same? (See Question 3 at the end of the chapter.)

## QUARTERLY ANALYSIS

Financial statements are prepared quarterly. The information used in **quarterly analysis** is less complete than annual reports, and there are seasonality problem associated with quarterly information (e.g., a large percent of retail sales occur around Christmas). For most of the year, however, this is the most up-to-date information and a necessary part of financial analysis. Changes in performance trends and other important signals may be first discerned in the analysis of quarterly data. Particularly important are (1) the current quarter to the previous quarter and (2) the current quarter to the same quarter a year ago. Consider Dell's last five available quarters compared to its competitors', as shown in Exhibit 5.4.

Operating results for Dell were relatively consistent, except for the July 2001 quarter with its $100 million loss. Gateway showed major problems over the entire five quarters. Revenues and gross profit declined each quarter. Gateway had net losses in all but the December 2001 quarter, obvious red flags. Apple's performance was relatively consistent over the periods analyzed, with modest fluctuations in sales and net income. Dell's low-cost

**EXHIBIT 5.4 QUARTERLY ANALYSIS FOR THE PC COMPANIES**

**Dell Operations, Quarter Ended (in millions)**

| | February 2002 | October 2001 | July 2001 | May 2001 | January 2002 |
|---|---|---|---|---|---|
| Revenues | $8,061 | $7,468 | $7,611 | $8,028 | $8,674 |
| COGS | 6,591 | 6,095 | 6,221 | 6,515 | 7,047 |
| Gross Profit | 1,470 | 1,373 | 1,390 | 1,513 | 1,627 |
| SG&A | 822 | 769 | 785 | 860 | 970 |
| Net Income | 456 | 429 | **–101 RF** | 462 | 375 |

**Gateway Operations, Quarter Ended (in millions)**

| | March 2002 | December 2001 | September 2001 | June 2001 | March 2002 |
|---|---|---|---|---|---|
| Revenues | $992 | $1,135 | $1,410 | $1,501 | $2,034 |
| COGS | 829 | 853 | 1,245 | 1,166 | 1,836 |
| Gross Profit | 163 | 282 | 165 | 335 | 197 |
| SG&A | 338 | 240 | 675 | 334 | 773 |
| Net Income | **–123 RF** | 9 | **–520 RF** | **–21 RF** | **–503 RF** |

**Apple Operations, Quarter Ended (in millions)**

| | March 2002 | December 2001 | September 2001 | June 2001 | March 2002 |
|---|---|---|---|---|---|
| Revenues | $1,495 | $1,375 | $1,450 | $1,475 | $1,431 |
| COGS | 1,057 | 925 | 983 | 1,015 | 1,024 |
| Gross Profit | 438 | 450 | 467 | 460 | 407 |
| SG&A | 381 | 402 | 384 | 392 | 393 |
| Net Income | 40 | 38 | 66 | 61 | 43 |

business strategy and aggressive pricing has been successful, and Apple may be on the road to recovery. However, Gateway's performance continues to suffer.

A common-size and percentage change analysis, as shown in Exhibit 5.5, provides additional information. The focus is the current quarter relative to the previous quarter and the same quarter one year ago. This is essentially the "minimum" needed, and a more thorough analysis is encouraged.

The common-size and percentage change analysis reinforces the dollar amount and provides additional insight. Quarterly results were erratic for the industry. Dell's common-size percentages were roughly consistent, but percentage changes from the February 2001 quarter were down, –21.6 percent for net income. Gateway had negative percentage changes consistently from the previous quarter and the same quarter one year previous. The negative 1,500 percent net income from the previous quarter is striking, but it results from a negative current

**EXHIBIT 5.5 COMMON-SIZE ANALYSIS FOR THE PC COMPANIES, BASED ON QUARTERLY DATA**

**Dell Operations, Quarterly Analysis**

| | Common-size | Common-size | Common-size | % Δ from Previous Qtr | % Δ from Same Qtr, 1 Year Ago |
|---|---|---|---|---|---|
| **Period** | Feb. 2002 | Oct. 2001 | Feb. 2001 | Oct. 2001 | Feb. 2001 |
| **Revenues** | 100% | 100% | 100% | 7.9% | **–7.1%** |
| **COGS** | 81.8 | 81.6 | 82.0 | 8.1 | **–6.5** |
| **Gross Profit** | 18.2 | 18.4 | 18.0 | 7.1 | **–9.6** |
| **SG&A** | 10.2 | 10.3 | 11.2 | 6.9 | **–15.3** |
| **Net Income** | 5.7 | 5.7 | 4.3 | 6.3 | 21.6 |

**Gateway Operations, Quarterly Analysis**

| | Common-size | Common-size | Common-size | % Δ from Previous Qtr | % Δ from Same Qtr, 1 Year Ago |
|---|---|---|---|---|---|
| **Period** | March 2002 | Dec. 2001 | March 2001 | Dec. 2001 | March 2001 |
| **Revenues** | 100% | 100% | 100% | **–12.6** | **–51.2** |
| **COGS** | 83.8 | 75.2 | 79.3 | **–2.8** | **–54.8** |
| **Gross Profit** | 16.4 | 24.8 | 9.7 | **–42.2** | **–17.3** |
| **SG&A** | 34.1 | 21.1 | 38.0 | 40.8 | **–56.3** |
| **Net Income** | **–12.4 RF** | 0.8 | **–25.6 RF** | **–1,467.7 RF** | **NM** |

**Apple Operations, Quarterly Analysis**

| | Common-size | Common-size | Common-size | % Δ from Previous Qtr | % Δ from Same Qtr, 1 Year Ago |
|---|---|---|---|---|---|
| **Period** | March 2002 | Dec. 2001 | March 2001 | Dec. 2001 | March 2001 |
| **Revenues** | 100% | 100% | 100% | 8.7% | 4.5% |
| **COGS** | 70.7 | 67.3 | 71.6 | 14.3 | 3.2 |
| **Gross Profit** | 29.3 | 32.7 | 28.4 | **–2.7** | 7.6 |
| **SG&A** | 25.5 | 27.2 | 27.5 | **–5.2** | **–3.1** |
| **Net Income** | 2.7 | 2.8 | 3.0 | 5.3 | **–7.0** |

quarter and a small income the previous quarter. Apple's common-size performance was roughly comparable. Percentage change numbers for Apple was erratic. Sales were up from the previous quarter and one year ago, but gross margin was down from the previous quarter and net income was down from one year ago. In summary, poor operating results were a problem across the industry, although most severe for Gateway.

The above quarterly comparison is abbreviated. A thorough quarterly analysis could extend back two or three (or more) years to better understand the seasonal and cyclical relationships in operations and include more operating categories. Changing trends in operations need to be discovered as quickly as possible to make correct decisions. This is best done with quarterly analysis.

## SUMMARY

Comparisons over time and across firms place the analysis in some perspective. Long-term trends and changes in earlier trends can be analyzed only by using multiyear techniques. Growth analysis and trend analysis are common techniques. Generally, analysts prefer smooth performance trends upward and the indication that these will continue. Erratic performance or major downward trends are significant indicators and may represent red flags and the need for further analysis.

Most analysis is based on annual data, which can be updated using available quarterly financial statements. Although abbreviated, this is the most recent data available. Changing trends and other indicators of potential problems should first be spotted using quarterly analysis. Much of the quantitative analysis uses percentages, particularly useful for comparisons by time period. Although limitations exist, the quantitative perspective still represents the heart of the financial analysis process.

## KEY TERMS

growth analysis

quarterly analysis

trend analysis

## QUESTIONS

1. Why would a trend or growth analysis (both multiperiod) be useful?
2. Assume that basic performance data for the last six years is somewhat erratic. What does the analyst do then?
3. How much is enough? Is limited annual performance data for the last six years enough or should a thorough financial analysis be conducted for the last twenty years (or something else)? Explain.
4. Is quarterly analysis useful? Explain.
5. Compare the results for the PC companies for both growth and trend analysis. They are based on the same numbers. Is the analysis the same?

## PROBLEMS

### Problem 5.1 Growth Analysis

(Problems 5.1–3 focus on the chemical industry.)

Given are the three chemical companies' performance numbers for the last five years.

**DuPont**

| | 1997 | 1998 | 1999 | 2000 | 2001 |
|---|---|---|---|---|---|
| Revenue | $39,730 | $24,767 | $26,918 | $28,268 | $24,726 |
| Gross Profit | 10,511 | 7,651 | 8,237 | 8,201 | 7,999 |
| Net Income | 2,405 | 4,480 | 7,690 | 2,314 | 4,339 |

**Dow**

| | 1997 | 1998 | 1999 | 2000 | 2001 |
|---|---|---|---|---|---|
| Revenue | $20,018 | $18,441 | $18,929 | $23,008 | $27,805 |
| Gross Profit | 5,278 | 4,554 | 4,481 | 4,621 | 5,790 |
| Net Income | 1,808 | 1,310 | 1,331 | 1,513 | **–385 RF** |

**PPG**

| | 1997 | 1998 | 1999 | 2000 | 2001 |
|---|---|---|---|---|---|
| Revenue | $7,379 | $7,510 | $7,757 | $8,629 | $8,169 |
| Gross Profit | 2,634 | 2,680 | 2,623 | 2,848 | 3,032 |
| Net Income | 714 | 801 | 568 | 620 | 387 |

Calculate the annual growth percentages for these chemical companies and rate from 1 to 10.

**DuPont**

| | 1997–98 | 1998–99 | 1999–2000 | 2000–01 | Total 1997–2001 |
|---|---|---|---|---|---|
| Revenue | | | | | |
| Gross Profit | | | | | |
| Net Income | | | | | |

**Dow**

| | 1997–98 | 1998–99 | 1999–2000 | 2000–01 | Total 1997–2001 |
|---|---|---|---|---|---|
| Revenue | | | | | |
| Gross Profit | | | | | |
| Net Income | | | | | |

**PPG**

| | 1997–98 | 1998–99 | 1999–2000 | 2000–01 | Total 1997–2001 |
|---|---|---|---|---|---|
| Revenue | | | | | |
| Gross Profit | | | | | |
| Net Income | | | | | |

| Company | Rating |
|---|---|
| DuPont | |
| Dow | |

## Problem 5.2 Trend Analysis

An alternative to growth percentages is to set the earliest year as the base year = 100 and calculate the remaining years as percentage change. For DuPont, 1997 is set to 100. Revenues for 1998 are calculated as 24,767 ÷ 39,730 = .6234. 2001 revenues for Dow are 27,805 ÷ 20,018 = 1.3889.

**DuPont**

| | 1997 | 1998 | 1999 | 2000 | 2001 |
|---|---|---|---|---|---|
| Revenues | 100 | 62.3 | | | |
| Gross Profit | 100 | | | | |
| Net Income | 100 | | | | |

**Dow**

| | 1997 | 1998 | 1999 | 2000 | 2001 |
|---|---|---|---|---|---|
| Revenues | 100 | | | | 138.9 |
| Gross Profit | | | | | |
| Net Income | | | | | |

**PPG**

| | 1997 | 1998 | 1999 | 2000 | 2001 |
|---|---|---|---|---|---|
| Revenues | | | | | |
| Gross Profit | | | | | |
| Net Income | | | | | |

Analyze the trend data and compare it to the growth analysis from Problem 4.1.

## Problem 5.3 Quarterly Analysis

The following performance information is available for the last five quarters for the three chemical companies (in millions).

**DuPont**

| | March 2002 | Dec. 2001 | Sept. 2001 | June 2001 | March 2001 |
|---|---|---|---|---|---|
| Revenue | $6,142 | $5,229 | $5,641 | $6,997 | $6,859 |
| COGS | 3,984 | 3,668 | 3,958 | 4,428 | 4,486 |
| Gross Profit | 2,158 | 1,561 | 1,683 | 2,269 | 2,373 |
| SG&A | 932 | 956 | 1,128 | 1,262 | 1,167 |
| Net Income | 479 | 3,915 | 142 | **–213 RF** | 495 |

**Dow**

| | March 2002 | Dec. 2001 | Sept. 2001 | June 2001 | March 2001 |
|---|---|---|---|---|---|
| Revenue | $6,262 | $6,346 | $6,729 | $7,344 | $7,386 |
| COGS | 4,919 | 4,981 | 5,236 | 5,743 | 6,055 |
| Gross Profit | 1,343 | 1,365 | 1,493 | 1,601 | 1,331 |
| SG&A | 641 | 662 | 694 | 727 | 724 |
| Net Income | 105 | **–37 RF** | 57 | 280 | **–685 RF** |

**PPG**

| | March 2002 | Dec. 2001 | Sept. 2001 | June 2001 | March 2001 |
|---|---|---|---|---|---|
| Revenue | $1,875 | $1,907 | $1,999 | $2,164 | $2,099 |
| COGS | 1,288 | 875 | 1,372 | 1,454 | 1,436 |
| Gross Profit | 587 | 1,032 | 627 | 710 | 663 |
| SG&A | 408 | 420 | 414 | 409 | 418 |
| Net Income | 52 | 83 | 93 | 155 | 56 |

Complete the following common-size and percentage change table.

**DuPont**

| | Common-size | Common-size | Common-size | % Δ from Previous Qtr. | % Δ Same Qtr. 1 Year Ago |
|---|---|---|---|---|---|
| Period | March 2002 | Dec. 2001 | March 2001 | Dec. 2001 | March 2001 |
| Revenue | | | | | |
| COGS | | | | | |
| Gross Profit | | | | | |
| SG&A | | | | | |
| Net Income | | | | | |

| | | | | | |
|---|---|---|---|---|---|
| Revenue | | | | | |
| COGS | | | | | |
| Gross Profit | | | | | |
| SG&A | | | | | |
| Net Income | | | | | |

Does the quarterly analysis indicate any red flags? Explain.

## Problem 5.4 Growth Analysis

(Problems 5.4-5.6 focus on the Hotel and Resort Industry.)

Given are performance numbers for the last five years to the three chemical companies.

**Hilton**

| | 1997 | 1998 | 1999 | 2000 | 2001 |
|---|---|---|---|---|---|
| Revenues | $1,475 | $1,769 | $1,959 | $3,177 | $2,632 |
| Gross Profit | 395 | 464 | 567 | 1,008 | 686 |
| Net Income | 250 | 297 | 174 | 272 | 166 |

**Marriott**

| | 1997 | 1998 | 1999 | 2000 | 2001 |
|---|---|---|---|---|---|
| Revenues | $10,172 | $12,034 | $8,739 | $10,017 | $10,152 |
| Gross Profit | 452 | 569 | 992 | 1,117 | 918 |
| Net Income | 306 | 335 | 400 | 479 | **236** |

**Mandalay***

| | 1997 | 1998 | 1999 | 2000 | 2001 |
|---|---|---|---|---|---|
| Revenues | $1,355 | $1,480 | $2,051 | $2,524 | $2,462 |
| Gross Profit | 271 | 275 | 898 | 1,133 | 1,092 |
| Net Income | 90 | 85 | 42 | 120 | 53 |

*FYE Jan. 02.

Calculate the annual growth percentages for these chemical companies and rate from 1 to 10.

**Hilton**

| | 1997–98 | 1998–99 | 1999–2000 | 2000–01 | Total 1997–01 |
|---|---|---|---|---|---|
| Revenues | | | | | |
| Gross Profit | | | | | |
| Net Income | | | | | |

**Marriott**

| | 1997–98 | 1998–99 | 1999–2000 | 2000–01 | Total 1997–01 |
|---|---|---|---|---|---|
| Revenues | | | | | |
| Gross Profit | | | | | |
| Net Income | | | | | |

**Mandalay**

| | 1997–98 | 1998–99 | 1999–2000 | 2000–01 | Total 1997–01 |
|---|---|---|---|---|---|
| Revenues | | | | | |
| Gross Profit | | | | | |
| Net Income | | | | | |

| Company | Rating |
|---|---|
| Hilton | |
| Marriott | |
| Mandalay | |

## Problem 5.5. Trend Analysis

An alternative to growth percentages is to set the earliest year as the base year = 100 and calculate the remaining years as percentage change. For Hilton, 1997 is set to 100. Revenues for 1998 are calculated as 1,769 ÷ 1,475 = 1.1993. 2001 revenues for Marriott are 10,152 ÷ 10,172 = .9980.

**Hilton**

| | 1997 | 1998 | 1999 | 2000 | 2001 |
|---|---|---|---|---|---|
| Revenues | 100 | 119.9 | | | |
| Gross Profit | 100 | | | | |
| Net Income | 100 | | | | |

**Marriott**

| | 1997 | 1998 | 1999 | 2000 | 2001 |
|---|---|---|---|---|---|
| Revenues | 100 | | | | 99.8 |
| Gross Profit | | | | | |
| Net Income | | | | | |

**Mandalay**

| | 1997 | 1998 | 1999 | 2000 | 2001 |
|---|---|---|---|---|---|
| Revenues | | | | | |
| Gross Profit | | | | | |
| Net Income | | | | | |

Analyze the trend data and compare it to the growth analysis from 4.1.

## Problem 5.6. Quarterly Analysis

The following performance information is available for the last five quarters for the three chemical companies (in millions).

**Hilton**

| | March 2002 | Dec. 2001 | Sept. 2001 | June 2001 | March 2001 |
|---|---|---|---|---|---|
| Revenue | $822 | $579 | $610 | $744 | $699 |
| COGS | 680 | 460 | 466 | 489 | 531 |
| Gross Profit | 142 | 119 | 144 | 255 | 168 |
| SG&A | 17 | 23 | 16 | 16 | 16 |
| Net Income | 34 | 4 | 21 | 86 | 55 |

**Marriott**

| | March 2002 | Dec. 2001 | Sept. 2001 | June 2001 | March 2001 |
|---|---|---|---|---|---|
| Revenue | $2,364 | $2,868 | $2,373 | $2,450 | $2,461 |
| COGS | 2,178 | 2,740 | 2,144 | 2,161 | 2,189 |
| Gross Profit | 186 | 128 | 229 | 289 | 272 |
| SG&A | 29 | 115 | 13 | 29 | 30 |
| Net Income | 82 | **–116** | 101 | 130 | **121** |

**Mandalay**

| | April 2002 | Jan. 2002 | Oct. 2001 | July 2001 | April 2001 |
|---|---|---|---|---|---|
| Revenue | $638 | $629 | $581 | $644 | $669 |
| COGS | | 324 | 337 | 355 | 365 |
| Gross Profit | | 305 | 244 | 290 | 305 |
| SG&A | | 112 | 117 | 123 | 112 |
| Net Income | | 49 | **–48** | 23 | 47 |

Complete the following common-size and percentage change table.

**Hilton**

| | Common-size | Common-size | Common-size | % Δ from Previous Qtr. | % Δ Same Qtr., 1 Year Ago |
|---|---|---|---|---|---|
| Period | March 2002 | Dec. 2001 | March 2001 | Dec. 2001 | March 2001 |
| Revenue | | | | | |
| COGS | | | | | |
| Gross Profit | | | | | |
| SG&A | | | | | |
| Net Income | | | | | |

**Marriott**

| | Common-size | Common-size | Common-size | % Δ from Previous Qtr. | % Δ Same Qtr., 1 Year Ago |
|---|---|---|---|---|---|
| Period | March 2002 | Dec. 2001 | March 2001 | Dec. 2001 | March 2001 |
| Revenue | | | | | |
| COGS | | | | | |
| Gross Profit | | | | | |
| SG&A | | | | | |
| Net Income | | | | | |

**Mandalay**

| | Common-size | Common-size | Common-size | % Δ from Previous Qtr. | % Δ Same Qtr., 1 Year Ago |
|---|---|---|---|---|---|
| Period | April 2002 | Jan. 2002 | April 2001 | Jan. 2002 | April 2001 |
| Revenue | | | | | |
| COGS | | | | | |
| Gross Profit | | | | | |
| SG&A | | | | | |
| Net Income | | | | | |

Does the quarterly analysis indicate any red flags? Explain

## Problem 5.7 Growth Analysis

(Problems 5.7–5.9 focus on the auto industry.)

Given are performance numbers for the last five years for Ford and GM.

**Ford**

| | 1997 | 1998 | 1999 | 2000 | 2001 |
|---|---|---|---|---|---|
| Revenue | $145,348 | $142,666 | $162,558 | $170,064 | $162,412 |
| Gross Profit | 36,441 | 37,884 | 44,798 | 45,514 | 36,706 |
| Net Income | 6,088 | 5,939 | 7,237 | 3,467 | **–5,453 RF** |

**GM**

| | 1997 | 1998 | 1999 | 2000 | 2001 |
|---|---|---|---|---|---|
| Revenue | $172,580 | $155,445 | $167,369 | $184,632 | $177,260 |
| Gross Profit | 44,355 | 40,903 | 35,115 | 52,379 | 46,318 |
| Net Income | 6,698 | 2,956 | 6,002 | 4,452 | 601 |

Calculate the annual growth percentages for these companies and rate from 1 to 10.

**Ford**

| | 1997–98 | 1998–99 | 1999–2000 | 2000–01 | Total 1997–2001 |
|---|---|---|---|---|---|
| Revenue | | | | | |
| Gross Profit | | | | | |
| Net Income | | | | | |

**GM**

| | 1997–98 | 1998–99 | 1999–2000 | 2000–01 | Total 1997–2001 |
|---|---|---|---|---|---|
| Revenue | | | | | |
| Gross Profit | | | | | |
| Net Income | | | | | |

| Rating | Ford | | GM | |
|---|---|---|---|---|

### Problem 5.8 Trend Analysis

An alternative to growth percentages is to set the earliest year as the base year = 100 and calculate the remaining years as percentage change. For Ford, 1997 is set to 100. Revenues for 1998 are calculated as 142,666 ÷ 145,348 = .9815. 2001 revenues for GM are 177,260 ÷ 172,580 = 1.0271.

**Ford**

| | 1997 | 1998 | 1999 | 2000 | 2001 |
|---|---|---|---|---|---|
| Revenues | 100 | 98.2 | | | |
| Gross Profit | 100 | | | | |
| Net Income | 100 | | | | |

**GM**

| | 1997 | 1998 | 1999 | 2000 | 2001 |
|---|---|---|---|---|---|
| Revenues | 100 | | | | 102.7 |
| Gross Profit | | | | | |
| Net Income | | | | | |

Analyze the trend data and compare it to the growth analysis from 4.4.

### Problem 5.9 Quarterly Analysis

The following performance information is available for the last five quarters for Ford and GM (in millions).

**Ford**

| | March 2002 | Dec. 2001 | Sept. 2001 | June 2001 | March 2001 |
|---|---|---|---|---|---|
| Revenue | $39,857 | $41,150 | $36,502 | $42,314 | $42,361 |
| COGS | 32,740 | 26,074 | 35,648 | 33,648 | 30,730 |
| Gross Profit | 7,117 | 15,076 | 1,333 | 8,666 | 11,631 |
| SG&A | 4,856 | 26 | 4,697 | 4,250 | 4,629 |
| Net Income | **–800 RF** | **–5,068 RF** | **692 RF** | **–752 RF** | 1,059 |

**GM**

| | March 2002 | Dec. 2001 | Sept. 2001 | June 2001 | March 2001 |
|---|---|---|---|---|---|
| Revenue | $46,264 | $45,950 | $42,475 | $46,220 | $42,615 |
| COGS | 38,326 | 24,385 | 34,866 | 37,181 | 34,510 |
| Gross Profit | 7,938 | 21,565 | 7,609 | 9,039 | 8,105 |
| SG&A | 5,621 | 6,131 | 5,926 | 5,855 | 5,390 |
| Net Income | **228** | 255 | **– 368 RF** | 477 | 237 |

Complete the following common-size and percentage change table.

**Ford**

| | Common-size | Common-size | Common-size | % Δ from Previous Qtr. | % Δ Same Qtr., 1 Year Ago |
|---|---|---|---|---|---|
| Period | March 2002 | Dec. 2001 | March 2001 | Dec. 2001 | March 2001 |
| Revenue | | | | | |
| COGS | | | | | |
| Gross Profit | | | | | |
| SG&A | | | | | |
| Net Income | | | | | |

**GM**

| | Common-size | Common-size | Common-size | % Δ from Previous Qtr. | % Δ Same Qtr., 1 Year Ago |
|---|---|---|---|---|---|
| Period | March 2002 | Dec. 2001 | March 2001 | Dec. 2001 | March 2001 |
| Revenue | | | | | |
| COGS | | | | | |
| Gross Profit | | | | | |
| SG&A | | | | | |
| Net Income | | | | | |

Does the quarterly analysis indicate any red flags? Explain

## CASES

### Case 5.1 Quarterly Analysis for Dell Computer

Quarterly operating data for Dell is summarized for the last sixteen quarters (in millions).

| Quarter | Revenue | Gross Profit | Net Income |
|---|---|---|---|
| Feb 2002 | $8,061 | $1,470 | $456 |
| 10/01 | 7,468 | 1,373 | 429 |
| 7/01 | 7,611 | 1,390 | **–101 RF** |
| 5/01 | 8,028 | 1,448 | 462 |
| 1/01 | 8,674 | 1,559 | 375 |
| 10/00 | 8,264 | 1,758 | 674 |
| 7/00 | 7,670 | 1,634 | 603 |
| 4/00 | 7,280 | 1,492 | 525 |
| 1/00 | 6,801 | 1,304 | 436 |
| 10/99 | 6,784 | 1,370 | 483 |
| 7/99 | 6,142 | 4,788 | 507 |
| 4/99 | 5,537 | 1,190 | 434 |
| 1/99 | 5,173 | 1,161 | 425 |
| 10/98 | 4,818 | 1,086 | 384 |
| 7/98 | 4,331 | 985 | 346 |
| 4/98 | 3,920 | 873 | 305 |
| 1/98 | 3,737 | 822 | 285 |
| 10/97 | 3,188 | 717 | 248 |
| 7/97 | 4,331 | 985 | 346 |

**a.** Calculate gross profit and net income as a percent of revenue for each quarter

| Quarter | Gross Profit ÷ Revenue | Net Income ÷ Revenue |
|---|---|---|
| 2/02 | | |
| 10/01 | | |
| 7/01 | | |
| 5/01 | | |
| 1/01 | | |
| 10/00 | | |
| 7/00 | | |
| 4/00 | | |
| 1/00 | | |
| 10/99 | | |
| 7/99 | | |
| 4/99 | | |
| 1/99 | | |
| 10/98 | | |
| 7/98 | | |
| 4/98 | | |
| 1/98 | | |
| 10/97 | | |
| 7/97 | | |

**b.** Calculate the percentage change for each quarter

| Quarter | % Δ, Revenue | % Δ, Gross Profit | % Δ, Net Income |
|---|---|---|---|
| 10/01 to 2/02 | | | |
| 7/01 to 10/01 | | | |
| 5/01 to 7/01 | | | |
| 1/01 to 5/01 | | | |
| 10/00 to 1/01 | | | |
| 7/00 to 10/00 | | | |
| 4/00 to 7/00 | | | |
| 1/00 to 4/00 | | | |
| 10/99 to 1/00 | | | |
| 7/99 to 10/99 | | | |
| 4/99 to 7/99 | | | |
| 1/99 to 4/99 | | | |
| 10/98 to 1/99 | | | |
| 7/98 to 10/98 | | | |
| 4/98 to 7/98 | | | |
| 1/98 to 4/98 | | | |
| 10/97 to 1/98 | | | |
| 7/97 to 10/97 | | | |

c. Analyze the results, including any red flags.

## Case 5.2 Eleven-year Summary Data for PPG

The following summary data is given from PPG's 2001 annual report (in millions, except for EPS).

| Year | Sales | Income before Tax | Net Income | Basic EPS |
|---|---|---|---|---|
| 1991 | $5,889 | $348 | $276 | $1.30 |
| 1992 | 6,042 | 538 | 319 | 1.51 |
| 1993 | 5,980 | 531 | 22 | 0.10 |
| 1994 | 6,570 | 840 | 515 | 2.43 |
| 1995 | 7,311 | 1,248 | 768 | 3.80 |
| 1996 | 7,466 | 1,215 | 744 | 3.96 |
| 1997 | 7,631 | 1,149 | 714 | 3.97 |
| 1998 | 7,751 | 1,267 | 801 | 4.52 |
| 1999 | 7,995 | 945 | 568 | 3.27 |
| 2000 | 8,629 | 989 | 620 | 3.60 |
| 2001 | 8,168 | 634 | 387 | 2.30 |

| Year | Current Assets | Current Liabilities | Total Assets | Stockholders' Equity |
|---|---|---|---|---|
| 1991 | $2,173 | $1,341 | $6,056 | $2,655 |
| 1992 | 1,951 | 1,253 | 5,662 | 2,699 |
| 1993 | 2,026 | 1,281 | 5,652 | 2,473 |
| 1994 | 2,168 | 1,425 | 5,894 | 2,557 |
| 1995 | 2,275 | 1,629 | 6,194 | 2,569 |
| 1996 | 2,296 | 1,769 | 6,441 | 2,483 |
| 1997 | 2,584 | 1,662 | 6,868 | 2,509 |
| 1998 | 2,660 | 1,912 | 7,387 | 2,880 |
| 1999 | 3,062 | 2,384 | 8,914 | 3,106 |
| 2000 | 3,093 | 2,543 | 9,125 | 3,097 |
| 2001 | 2,703 | 1,955 | 8,452 | 3,080 |

**a.** Calculate common-size information for PPG:

| Year | Sales | Income before Tax | Net Income |
|---|---|---|---|
| 1991 | | | |
| 1992 | | | |
| 1993 | | | |
| 1994 | | | |
| 1995 | | | |
| 1996 | | | |
| 1997 | | | |
| 1998 | | | |
| 1999 | | | |
| 2000 | | | |
| 2001 | | | |

| Year | Current Assets | Current Liabilities | Total Assets | Stockholders' Equity |
|---|---|---|---|---|
| 1991 | | | | |
| 1992 | | | | |
| 1993 | | | | |
| 1994 | | | | |
| 1995 | | | | |
| 1996 | | | | |
| 1997 | | | | |
| 1998 | | | | |
| 1999 | | | | |
| 2000 | | | | |
| 2001 | | | | |

**b.** Calculate the following ratios for each year:

| Year | Current Ratio | Debt to Equity | Return on Sales | Return on Assets | Return on Equity |
|---|---|---|---|---|---|
| 1991 | | | | | |
| 1992 | | | | | |
| 1993 | | | | | |
| 1994 | | | | | |
| 1995 | | | | | |
| 1996 | | | | | |
| 1997 | | | | | |
| 1998 | | | | | |
| 1999 | | | | | |
| 2000 | | | | | |
| 2001 | | | | | |

c. Calculate the following growth percentages for PPG:

| Year | Sales | Income before Tax | Net Income | Basic EPS |
|---|---|---|---|---|
| 1991–1992 | | | | |
| 1992–1993 | | | | |
| 1993–1994 | | | | |
| 1994–1995 | | | | |
| 1995–1996 | | | | |
| 1996–1997 | | | | |
| 1997–1998 | | | | |
| 1998–1999 | | | | |
| 1999–2000 | | | | |
| 2000–2001 | | | | |

d. Evaluate the trends for PPG for the last 11 years. Are there any red flags?

## INTERNET PROJECTS

### Project 5.1

Use the same company selected in Project 4.1. Gather the financial information you need from the company's annual report and other sources. Do a complete growth and trend financial analysis for the last six years, using the same format as above.

**Suggestions:** Summary financial statements can be found at www.hoovers.com; complete financial statements can usually be found on company Web sites and the SEC's EDGAR system. Considerable financial information can be found at various financial Web sites, such as Quicken (www.quicken.com) and Yahoo Financial (quote.yahoo.com).

### Project 5.2

Using the same company selected in Project 4.1, gather quarterly financial information for the last five quarters you need from the company's 10-Q and other sources. Do a complete quarterly financial analysis for the last five quarters, using the same format as above.

**Suggestions:** Limited quarterly data can be found at www.hoovers.com.

# CHAPTER 6

# Quantitative Financial Analysis Techniques: Incorporating Market Information

**Objectives**

- Evaluate the use and importance of stock price information.
- Describe the use of earnings per share (EPS) and distinguish between basic and diluted EPS. Explain how EPS forecasts are made and why they are important.
- Define price earnings (PE) ratios and how they can be used effectively.
- Define dividend yield and under what circumstances it is an important investment characteristic.
- Define market value and market-to-book and how these can be interpreted.
- Describe market activity measures.
- Define price earnings to growth (PEG) ratios and how these can be used to evaluate investment opportunities.
- Explain how earnings-based growth models can be used to value a firm.
- Apply intrinsic value per share as a valuation tool.
- Demonstrate when stock screening can be useful as an investment tool.

## INTRODUCTION

Basic financial analysis techniques were reviewed in Chapter 4. Most financial data analyzed came from the financial statements of the firm. Additional information essential to most financial analysis decisions comes from market information. Equity securities of large public firms trade on stock exchanges. With continuous buying and selling during trading hours, stock prices rise and fall constantly. When evaluating investment decisions, the current stock price is crucial. Market measures include price earnings (PE) ratios and dividend yields. PE and yield based on yesterday's closing price may suggest buying additional shares of a particular stock. But what if the stock price rises five points today (say a 7 percent increase from yesterday's price)? Should the stock still be bought? This is a perpetual problem (or opportunity) when evaluating investment decisions.

This chapter looks at the importance of stock prices, considers analysts' forecasts of earnings per share and other performance numbers, compares various sources of market information—especially sites available on the Internet, evaluates market-related ratios and how certain financial ratios can be recalculated based on market rather than book values, and demonstrates alternative valuation models for predicting stock prices. Stock screening is described as a tool to reduce market searches based on a few key items.

## Stock Prices

Major corporations trade on the New York Stock Exchange (NYSE), American Stock Exchange (Amex), and National Association of Securities Dealers Automated Quotations (NASDAQ). Daily closing prices for these are readily available in the *Wall Street Journal* and most newspapers the next day. Several Internet sites provide continual quotes during the day, usually with a slight delay from actual trading. A major source of market information is a set of graphs of the closing stock price of the company, along with competitors' averages and market averages. Stock price trends for the PC industry, compared to the Dow Jones Industrial Average (DJIA), for one and five years are presented in Exhibit 6.1. Note that Compaq also is presented for comparison. Compaq was a direct PC competitor until acquired by Hewlett-Packard in May 2002.

Daily trends over long periods can best be seen on a graph. Over the preceding 12 months, the **Dow Jones Industrial Average,** a measure of stock price performance for large corporations, dropped about 10 percent as of the first of May. The individual PC companies' stock prices varied considerably and had substantial volatility—much more than the DJIA. This is fairly typical of market averages compared to individual stocks. After a large dip from summer 2001, Dell ended with a slight price gain over twelve months. Apple had a similar summer dip and ended with a price decline of about 10 percent, essentially comparable to the DJIA. Gateway's price fell much of the year, for a total decline of about 70 percent.

Over the past five years, Dell has been a superlative performer—up almost 400 percent despite the decline in 2000 and 2001. Apple had somewhat similar performance with a net gain of about 200 percent. Gateway's performance was a roller coaster for the five-year period, rising for three years but down substantially over the last two years.

Exhibit 6.2 compares closing prices on May 1, 2002, with highs and lows for the previous twelve months and prices one and five years earlier.

This information demonstrates several important points. Both Dell and Apple were relatively close to their 52-week highs, while Gateway was close to its 52-week low. The high/low range indicates the stock price range over the period, which is substantial for all three companies (which is normal). The stock prices for Dell and Apple were relatively flat for one year and up substantially for five years. Gateway was down, based on any measurement. When the table information is combined with the stock charts (note that the amount of available data is large), a clearer picture emerges of historical stock prices. The question for potential investors is: what trends, if any, will continue?

The current stock price used for analysis is quickly out-of-date. Even yesterday's closing stock price and calculations of PE, yield, and market value become less useful once the market opens today. When making an investment decision, it is important to know the stock price

**EXHIBIT 6.1 CLOSING STOCK PRICES FOR THE PC COMPANIES**

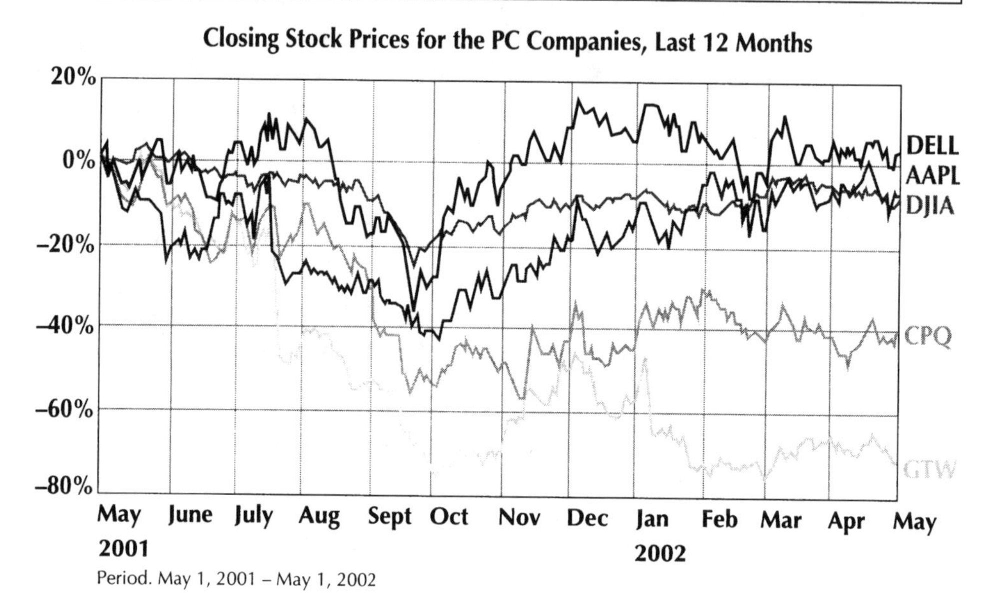


Period. May 1, 2001 – May 1, 2002

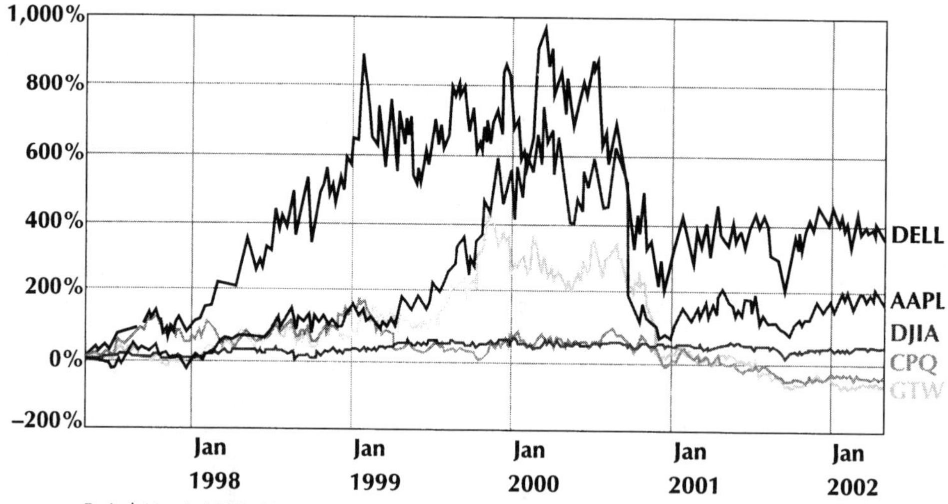


Period. May 1, 1997 – May 1, 2002

Source: www.quicken.com

expected at time of trade and at what price the transaction should no longer be consummated—alternatively, whether and when a hold recommendation becomes a buy (or sell).

Consider Gateway's stock price over the previous fifty-two weeks. As of May 1, 2002, it was down almost 70 percent from a year ago, but the price has been relatively flat for most of 2002. Does this mean that Gateway is on the way to recovery or is now a great time to drop the stock and avoid further losses?

**EXHIBIT 6.2 STOCK PRICE COMPARISONS FOR THE PC COMPANIES**

| | Dell | Gateway | Apple |
|---|---|---|---|
| May 1, 2002 | 26.48 | 5.33 | 23.98 |
| 52-week high | 30.52 | 19.35 | 26.17 |
| 52-week low | 16.01 | 4.24 | 14.68 |
| May 1, 2001* | 26.73 | 18.80 | 25.93 |
| May 1, 1997* | 5.42 | 14.47 | 8.50 |

*Adjusted for dividends and stock splits

Historical stock price trends are readily available and an important component for financial analysis. They can be used as a significant part of market analysis and the calculation and evaluation of several important ratios.

## EARNINGS PER SHARE AND ANALYSTS FORECASTS

For market analysis, net income can be converted to **earnings per share** (EPS), which is compared to stock price (stated on a per share basis) and other calculations. Historical EPS can be stated as basic or diluted, both of which are available from the income statement. **Basic EPS** is net income divided by weighted average of common shares outstanding. Basic EPS is the simplest to comprehend and will be used for most analysis in this chapter. **Diluted EPS** is an accounting artifact, used to consider the complex capital structure of major corporations when evaluating earnings. Basic and diluted EPS for Dell and competitors for the last three years (from the income statement) are shown in Exhibit 6.3.

The individual EPS number should not be overinterpreted. EPS depends on both net income and number of shares outstanding (and dilution potential) and fluctuates based on both. EPS becomes important when considering growth rates, when making comparisons to stock price and other measures, and when forecasting future EPS. Dell showed a consistent positive EPS over the three years, although down for 2002. Gateway had a downward trend and a substantial EPS loss of over $3 in 2001. Apple had a small 2001 loss, after two successful years. None of the companies had much dilution for the current year, although more substantial in earlier years. For example, dilution was $0.24 (2.42 – 2.18) or 9.9 percent for Apple in 2000.

Quarterly EPS is a number that stock market professionals evaluate almost immediately. Although quarterly and annual reports are not issued until about three months after the end of the fiscal period, earnings are announced a few days after the end of the period. Particularly important is the actual quarterly EPS compared to analysts' expectations or forecasts. If actual EPS is up from the previous quarter, but less than analysts' forecast, the price of the stock probably will fall. EPS numbers (diluted) for the last five quarters for Dell and competitors are shown in Exhibit 6.4.

Dell's quarterly earnings were slightly erratic, with a quarterly loss for the July 2001 quarter. To what extent this represents seasonal economic fluctuations versus current performance problems is an important question that calls for further analysis. Apple's EPS

**EXHIBIT 6.3 EPS COMPARISONS FOR THE PC COMPANIES**

| | Current Year | | Previous Year | | Two Years Ago | |
|---|---|---|---|---|---|---|
| | Basic | Diluted | Basic | Diluted | Basic | Diluted |
| Dell | $0.48 | $0.46 | $0.84 | $0.79 | $0.66 | $0.61 |
| Gateway | **–3.20** | **–3.20** | 0.75 | 0.73 | 1.36 | 1.32 |
| Apple | **–0.07** | **–0.07** | 2.42 | 2.18 | 2.10 | 1.81 |

*Fiscal year ended Feb. 1, 2002, for Dell; Dec. 31, 2001, for Gateway; and July 31, 2001, for Apple

**EXHIBIT 6.4 QUARTERLY EPS COMPARISONS FOR THE PC COMPANIES**

| Quarter | Current | –1 | –2 | –3 | –4 |
|---|---|---|---|---|---|
| **Dell: Current Quarter Is February 1, 2002** | $0.17 | $0.16 | **$–0.04** | $0.17 | $0.13 |
| **Gateway: Current Quarter Is March 31, 2002** | **–0.39** | 0.03 | **–1.61** | **–0.06** | **–1.56** |
| **Apple: Current Quarter Is May 31, 2002** | 0.11 | 0.11 | 0.19 | 0.17 | 0.12 |

Source: www.hoovers.com

numbers were relatively constant, but the last two quarters were somewhat lower than earlier quarters. Gateway's results were erratic and negative with only a single quarterly gain in the December 2001 quarter.

Perhaps the most useful earnings predictions are consensus **analysts' forecasts,** available from Zacks (www.zacks.com) and other sources. Using Analysts Ratings on Quicken (which uses Zacks, available from www.quicken.com), consensus quarterly forecasts for Dell and competitors for the next two quarters are shown in Exhibit 6.5.

Annual forecasts for the three firms are shown in Exhibit 6.6. Dell's forecasts suggest slight improvements from the current year, both quarterly and annually. Gateway's forecasts are consistently negative, although the red ink is expected to decrease. Like Dell's, Apple's forecasts suggest improvements. If these numbers are accurate, it suggests that current performance problems are solved for Dell and Apple, but Gateway's problems continue. Of course, the accuracy of forecasts is always somewhat questionable.

One problem is the existence of nonrecurring items and other transitory items that affect earnings. EPS numbers are calculated both before and after nonrecurring items. (Nonrecurring items, such as extraordinary items and discontinued operations, are covered in more detail in Chapter 7.) The question: which is more relevant? Generally, EPS numbers before transitory earning items are more useful. However, because of the earnings management potential of nonrecurring and similar items, these should be considered potential red flags and additional analysis conducted.

**EXHIBIT 6.5 QUARTERLY EPS ANALYSTS' FORECASTS FOR THE PC COMPANIES**

| | This Quarter* | Next Quarter† |
|---|---|---|
| **Dell** | $0.18 | $0.19 |
| **Gateway** | **–0.17** | **–0.10** |
| **Apple** | 0.12 | 0.17 |

*Quarter ended August 2002 for Dell, July 2002 for Gateway and Apple

†Quarter ended November 2002 for Dell and October 2002 for Gateway and Apple

## Calculating Market-Related Ratios

Market and financial numbers can be combined in additional ratios that are useful in evaluating investor perceptions of company operations, predictions, and other relevant factors. Four ratios are reviewed:

- Price earnings ratio (PE)
- Dividend yield (yield)
- Market value of firm
- Market to book ratio

**EXHIBIT 6.6 ANNUAL EPS ANALYSTS' FORECASTS FOR THE PC COMPANIES**

| | This Fiscal Year (2003/2002)* | Next Fiscal Year (2004/2003) |
|---|---|---|
| **Dell** | $0.77 | $0.90 |
| **Gateway** | −0.47 | −0.10 |
| **Apple** | 0.52 | 0.78 |

*Fiscal year ended February 2003 for Dell, December 2002 for Gateway, and July 2002 for Apple

## PRICE EARNINGS RATIO

The **price earnings ratio** (PE) is one of the most discussed ratios analyzed and easily misused. This ratio is the simple calculation of current stock price divided by EPS and best interpreted as the stock price "premium" for current (and future) EPS. A high PE usually is associated with a high growth company that is expected to generate substantial increases in EPS for the foreseeable future. A low PE usually is associated with companies where future earnings growth is expected to be low or erratic.

The PE numerator is stock price, which changes throughout the trading day and has a new closing price daily. The PE ratios fluctuate as stock prices change. When comparing PE ratios, the same date should be used for **closing stock price.** For example, closing stocks prices for May 1, 2002, are used throughout this book. The denominator is annual EPS. Which EPS should be used? Basic or diluted? The latest actual EPS, the last four quarters, EPS forecast one or two periods ahead? The preferred answer may be all of the above. The most common PE ratio used here will be basic actual EPS for the latest fiscal year, because this is based on actual information, not forecasts. Forecast EPS is more relevant to investors, but it is subject to prediction error. Consequently, PE ratios using other EPS numbers will be tabulated.

The PE ratio should not be overanalyzed. A high or low PE is not necessarily good or bad, just an indicator of investor confidence in future earnings growth. If EPS is expected to grow substantially soon, PE ratios using these future EPS numbers likely will be high. A drop in earnings or even earnings expectations (e.g., earnings are up, but not as much as expected) may result in a substantial drop in stock price. If a company has a year of poor earnings performance and the EPS drops substantially (but is expected to bounce back), the PE ratio may be high. This is not a measure of a huge price premium, but instead indicates that a higher EPS is expected in the immediate future. On occasion, stock price may be higher than expected based on current EPS, which could be associated with such things as substantial cash available or a high book value. In those cases the PE will signal a stock investor premium, which can be misleading and requires further analysis.

The basic EPS numbers for the PC companies are summarized (from above) in Exhibit 6.7. Only Dell had a positive actual EPS. Although the one- and two-year-ahead forecasts increased for all three companies, only Dell had consistently positive numbers. Apple has a small actual loss, but its forecast EPS were positive and increasing, suggesting a reasonable performance turnaround. Gateway had only red ink. The only good news is the red ink will decline, according to the forecasts.

Using the May 1, 2002, stock prices and the annual EPS numbers calculated above, the PE ratios for Dell and competitors are given in Exhibit 6.8. Dell's PE based on current (2002 actual) EPS is calculated as 26.48 ÷ 0.48 = 55.2. Apple's two-year-ahead forecast PE is 23.98 ÷ 0.78 = 30.7 (using 2004 forecast EPS). Gateway's PEs cannot be calculated, since EPS (the denominator) was negative. Market analysis is difficult when firms are losing money. Dell's PE numbers were "normal," in the sense that PE declines from current EPS to one- and two-year-ahead forecasts. This is caused by expected rising EPS in the near

**EXHIBIT 6.7 ANNUAL ACTUAL AND FORECAST EPS FOR THE PC COMPANIES**

| | Actual | One Year Ahead Forecast | Two Years Ahead Forecast |
|---|---|---|---|
| Dell | $0.48 | $0.77 | $0.90 |
| Gateway | **–3.20 RF** | **–0.47 RF** | **–0.10 RF** |
| Apple | **–0.07 RF** | 0.52 | 0.78 |

future. Apple's high one-year-ahead PE of 46.1 was really based on the anemic forecast EPS rather than a huge price premium. Using two-year-ahead forecasted EPS, the PE ratio was a more reasonable 30.7, which is still relatively high.

To better understand the range of PE ratios caused by stock price fluctuations, the 52-week high and low prices can be used to calculate PEs for Dell and Apple, as shown in Exhibit 6.9.

Stock prices can fluctuate substantially over one year, which indicates the potential spread available for analyzing PE ratios. At its high for the last fifty-two weeks, Dell had a PE over 63 based on current EPS (30.52 ÷ 0.48 = 63.6). The PE was only 17.8 at its stock price low using 2004 forecast EPS (16.01 ÷ 0.90 = 17.8). Similar results are apparent for Apple. Note that professional investors often wait for large stock market drops to buy securities and attempt to sell at relatively high prices. ("Buy low, sell high" is a market strategy that doesn't go out of fashion.) A purchase of Dell near its 52-week low would be considered a real bargain—a company with a projected 20%+ earnings growth rate at an average market premium.

A difficulty of PE ratios is determining what set of numbers to use. With fluctuating stock prices and actual and forecast EPS numbers, quite different results are possible. Note that Dell's PE ratio can be from 17.8 to 63.6, depending on what stock price and EPS numbers are used. Calculations are simple, but analysis can be tricky.

**EXHIBIT 6.8 PRICE EARNINGS RATIOS FOR THE PC COMPANIES**

| | Stock Price | PE Based on Current EPS | PE Forecast 1 Year Ahead | PE Forecast 2 Years Ahead |
|---|---|---|---|---|
| Dell | 26.48 | 55.2 | 34.4 | 29.4 |
| Gateway | 5.33 | NM* | NM* | NM* |
| Apple | 23.98 | NM* | 46.1 | 30.7 |

*NM: denominator is negative and ratio cannot be calculated

**EXHIBIT 6.9 PRICE EARNINGS RATIO COMPARISONS FOR DELL AND APPLE**

| | Stock Price | PE Based on Current EPS | PE Forecast 1 Year Ahead | PE Forecast 2 Years Ahead |
|---|---|---|---|---|
| Dell, High | 30.52 | 63.6 | 39.6 | 33.9 |
| Dell, Low | 16.01 | 23.4 | 20.8 | 17.8 |
| Apple, High | 26.17 | NM | 50.2 | 33.6 |
| Apple, Low | 14.68 | NM | 28.2 | 18.8 |

## DIVIDEND YIELD

Young, growing companies tend to pay little if any cash dividends. This is the case for the PC manufacturing companies described. Cash used to pay dividends is not available to reinvest in new plant and other investment opportunities. Mature companies that have limited growth prospects are more likely to pay a substantial portion of earnings in dividends. Certain industries, such as utilities, have historically paid large dividends. Investors that need current income (e.g., retirees) are likely to focus on stocks that pay high dividends, with earnings growth a lesser concern. From the investor perspective, the most useful calculation is **dividend yield,** defined as annual dividends per share divided by stock price.

Five companies in various industries are analyzed for dividend yield, as shown in Exhibit 6.10. Dell pays no dividend, typical of a high tech company. General Electric is a large "old economy" company that paid a nominal annual dividend of $0.72 a share and is usually considered a growth stock. Its yield of 2.3 percent (0.72 ÷ 31.70) is modestly attractive for income investors. Ford, an auto company and a cyclical (revenues and earnings rise and fall over the business cycle), cut its dividend to $0.40 per share, resulting in a yield of 2.4 percent ($0.40 ÷ 16.34). DuPont had a respectable 3.1 percent yield. The Southern Company, a utility, had a relatively large yield of 4.8 percent. DuPont and Southern have yields that make them potential acquisitions for investors needing income from investment portfolios. Corporations normally pay dividends quarterly, and yield is best calculated by using the accumulated dividends per share for the last four quarters.

## MARKET VALUE AND MARKET-TO-BOOK RATIO

The **market value** of a company (also called market capitalization or market cap) is calculated by multiplying the stock price by the number of shares outstanding. Dell had a market price (May 1, 2002) of $26.48 and 2,602 million shares outstanding, resulting in a market value of $68,874 million. The market value changes as stock price fluctuates and, less frequently, as number of shares outstanding change. A large market decline can reduce the market cap of big companies by billions of dollars.

The book value of the firm is total stockholder equity (also called net assets). Book value can be calculated on a per share basis by dividing net assets by number of shares outstanding. Dell had net assets of $4,694 million for fiscal year 2002. Dell's book value per share was $1.80 ($4,694 ÷ 2,602).

**EXHIBIT 6.10 DIVIDEND YIELD ANALYSIS FOR SELECTED COMPANIES, MOST RECENT FISCAL YEAR**

| Company | Annual Dividend | Stock Price on May 11, 2000 | Dividend Yield |
|---|---|---|---|
| Dell | $0.00 | $26.48 | 0% |
| General Electric | 0.72 | 31.70 | 2.3 |
| Ford | 0.40 | 16.40 | 2.4 |
| DuPont | 1.40 | 44.63 | 3.1 |
| Southern | 1.34 | 28.16 | 4.8 |

An important relationship is the **market to book** value ratio. This can be calculated on a per share basis as stock price ÷ book value per share. The alternative calculation is market value ÷ net assets, which gives the same answer. If net assets were a true representation of the economic value of the firm, then book value should be virtually the same as market value—a market to book ratio of 1. However, in most cases, the market values firms primarily on earnings potential, which results in a market premium over book value. Usually, the higher the market premium, the less useful is balance sheet information—additional information on such things as research and development success or manufacturing technology productivity will have to be analyzed from various sources.

The information for the market to book ratios for Dell and competitors is shown in Exhibit 6.11. Book value per share for Dell is 4,694 ÷ 2,602 = 1.80. All three firms have a market premium, but these range from 1.1× to 14.7×. Gateway's recent earnings problems are reflected in lower stock prices, and the firm now trades at little more than book value. Dell, on the other hand, is a relatively small firm based on assets, but it has a high market price at $69 billion based on earnings expectations. Consequently, the market-to-book is a substantial 14.7×. An important question is whether the earnings potential for Dell justifies this market premium relative to either Gateway or Apple.

## MARKET-RELATED RATIOS

Since market and book values can be quite different, several ratios can be restated using market information and compared with the similar book value counterparts. These include: debt to market equity, sales to net assets and sales to market value, and earnings growth rates to price earnings ratios.

### DEBT TO MARKET EQUITY

Debt to market equity (total liabilities at book value ÷ total equity at market value) is a leverage ratio reviewed in Chapter 4. Dell had high debt relative to equity based on book value, but when the market value of equity is used, leverage is small. The reason is the market premium on Dell's stock. Book value leverage ratios generally are more relevant than market value equivalents (especially for credit decisions, since cash generally is required to dispose of liabilities), but this does change the perspective and suggest the need for further analysis. The calculation of debt to market equity (total liabilities and shares outstanding are based on current fiscal year-end) is shown in Exhibit 6.12.

Debt to market equity for Dell is 8,841 ÷ 68,874 = .1284. The market premium has an impact on debt to market equity. Dell is highly levered (because of high current liabilities),

**EXHIBIT 6.11 COMPARISON OF MARKET TO BOOK VALUE FOR THE PC COMPANIES**

| | Stock Price, May 1, 2002 | Net Assets (millions) | Shares Outstanding (millions) | Book Value per Share | Market to Book Ratio |
|---|---|---|---|---|---|
| Dell | 26.48 | $4,694 | 2,602 | $1.80 | 14.7× |
| Gateway | 5.33 | 1,565 | 323 | 4.85 | 1.1 |
| Apple | 23.98 | 3,920 | 351 | 11.17 | 2.1 |

but debt to market equity is less than 13 percent. Gateway and Apple have higher ratios, consistent with lower market premiums.

## SALES TO NET ASSETS AND SALES TO MARKET VALUE

This is an activity comparison of equity at book and market. Sales to net assets is annual sales ÷ year-end total stockholders' equity, and sales to market value is annual sales ÷ (stock price × number of shares outstanding). The calculations for Dell and competitors are shown in Exhibit 6.13.

Dell's sales to net assets ratio is 31,168 ÷ 4,694 = 6.64, and its sales to market value is 31,888 ÷ 68,874 = .4630. The results are extremely different. Dell shows substantial efficiency in asset turnover at 6.6×, followed by Gateway at 3.9 and Apple lagging at 1.4. However, based on market value the results are almost reversed. Dell shows only a 46.3 percent "efficiency," with Gateway much higher at 3.5. This reinforces the concept of market premium. Dell's performance has been relatively good, and the stock market has responded (e.g., a PE of 55.2 for actual year 2001 EPS). But market value is more than double Dell's sales, a low efficiency measure on this scale. Can the analyst justify this high "market premium" if a buy decision is recommended? Gateway, on the other hand, has a market value not much higher than book value. Consequently, sales to net assets at 3.9 was almost the same as sales to market value (3.5).

## PRICE EARNINGS TO EARNINGS GROWTH RATES (PEG)

Generally, high PE ratios are associated with the expectations of high earnings growth rates. A possible rule of thumb for a buy recommendation is to look for an annual earnings growth rate greater than the PE ratio. The calculation is PE ÷ annual earnings growth rate. or PEG. The **PEG ratio** is an indicator of whether the stock is over- or undervalued. If the earnings growth rate is greater than the PE, PEG will be less than 1. Currently, a PEG less

**EXHIBIT 6.12 DEBT TO MARKET EQUITY ANALYSIS FOR THE PC COMPANIES**

| | Total Liabilities (millions) | Share Price (May 1, 2002) | Shares Outstanding (millions) | Market Value (millions) | Debt to Market Equity |
|---|---|---|---|---|---|
| Dell | $8,841 | 26.48 | 2,602 | $68,874 | 12.8% |
| Gateway | 1,422 | 5.33 | 323 | 1,722 | 82.6% |
| Apple | 2,101 | 23.98 | 351 | 8,417 | 25.0% |

**EXHIBIT 6.13 SALES TO NET ASSETS AND MARKET VALUE COMPARISON FOR THE PC COMPANIES**

| | Equity at Market Value* | Equity at Book Value† | Sales, Current Fiscal Year | Sales to Net Assets | Sales to Market Value |
|---|---|---|---|---|---|
| Dell | $68,874 | $4,694 | $31,168 | 6.6 | 46.3% |
| Gateway | 1,722 | 1,565 | 6,080 | 3.9 | 3.5 |
| Apple | 8,417 | 3,920 | 5,363 | 1.4 | 63.7 |

*In millions; see previous table.
†Current fiscal year end

than 1 is a relatively rare event, since PEs tend to be high. Various earnings growth rates are available from Quicken, Zacks, and other sources. Should historical earnings growth rates or projected earnings growth rates be used and for how long? Also, which PE ratio? Exhibit 6.14 shows historical earnings growth rates for the last five years and the five-year projected earnings (future) growth rates for Dell and its competitors.

These measures can quickly be found on Quicken. Historical rates are accurate, but they may not indicate future performance. Note that negative historic earnings for Gateway and Apple make PEG analysis meaningless. Forecasted rates are the important numbers, but how accurate are these projections? Earnings growth rates would be expected to be much lower with poor economic conditions. Dell's projected growth rate of 15.8 percent is slower than during the previous five years. It's unlikely that Dell could maintain its five-year historic rate of over 25 percent. Gateway's forecasted earnings growth is expected to be only 9.5 percent, much better than the negative historic rate of almost negative 200 percent. Gateway has had severe problems, so the concern is whether the firm will recover. Apple's historic rate cannot be calculated because of earlier net losses, but it is expected to have a respectable 10.2 percent annual earnings growth rate for the next five years.

What PE ratios should be used? A basic PE using last year's actual is an accurate number, but analysts forecasts for this and next year may be reasonably accurate. The PE ratios are summarized from earlier in this chapter in Exhibit 6.15.

Exhibit 6.16 shows PEGs for Dell and Apple calculated for (1) current PE and five-year historical earnings growth rates, (2) one-year-ahead PE and five-year projected growth rates, and (3) two-year-ahead PE and five-year projected growth rates.

The calculation for Dell using the five-year historical rate and current PE is 55.2 ÷ 27.2 = 2.03, substantially over 1. To meet the rule of thumb of a growth rate greater than PE, the ratio should be 1 or less. However, current PEs are relatively high, so a rule of thumb of 1.5 (or perhaps higher) may be appropriate. Using the two-year projected EPS, PE and five-year projected earnings growth (29.4 ÷ 15.8) gives a slightly lower 1.9, above the cutoff of 1.5. The calculations for Apple have very high PEGs. In summary, Dell and Apple appear overpriced using the PEG analysis. Gateway will have to have positive EPS numbers before PEGs can be calculated.

The matrix in Exhibit 6.17 can be used to compare price earnings to earnings growth rates (PEGs are estimated; for example, a stock with a 20 percent earnings growth rate with a PE of 40 would be in cell one, but PEG > 1.5).

**EXHIBIT 6.14 PRICE EARNINGS TO GROWTH (PEG) ANALYSIS FOR THE PC COMPANIES**

| | 5-Year Historical Growth Rates* | 5-Year Projected Growth Rates* |
|---|---|---|
| **Dell** | 27.2% | 15.8% |
| **Gateway** | **–197.0 RF** | 9.5 |
| **Apple** | NM | 10.2 |

*Available from www.quicken.com, Analysts Estimates

**EXHIBIT 6.15 PRICE EARNINGS RATIOS FOR THE PC COMPANIES**

| | PE, Current EPS | PE, 1 Year Ahead EPS Forecast | PE, 2 Years Ahead EPS Forecast |
|---|---|---|---|
| **Dell** | 55.2 | 34.4 | 29.4 |
| **Gateway** | NM | NM | NM |
| **Apple** | NM | 46.1 | 30.7 |

**EXHIBIT 6.16 PRICE EARNINGS TO GROWTH (PEG) RATIOS FOR DELL AND APPLE**

| | 5-Year Historical Earnings Growth, Current PE | 5-Year Projected Earnings Growth, 1-Year-Ahead PE | 5-Year Projected Earnings Growth, 2-Years-Ahead PE |
|---|---|---|---|
| **Dell** | 2.0 | 2.2 | 1.9 |
| **Apple** | NM | 4.5 | 3.0 |

Assume average PE is over 20 and average earnings growth rate is about 12 percent. Low PEGs are preferred. As a possible rule of thumb, PEG should be 1.5 or less: cells 2, 3, 5, 6, and 9. Growth funds would focus on cells 2 and 3 (and cell 1 as long as PEGs are not substantially higher than 1.5); that is, companies with high earnings growth rates. Stocks for value funds should be found in cells 5, 6, and 9 (stocks with earnings growth potential but with relatively low price premiums). Stocks for income funds require a high dividend yield. Beyond that, stocks in cells 5, 6, and 9 would be preferred (but PEG would be relatively less important). Dell and Apple are in cells 1 and 4, with high PEs and high earnings growth for Dell but average earnings growth for Apple.

## BETA (ß) ANALYSIS

As discussed in Chapter 2, ß is a calculation made from Sharpe's Market Model. Finance theory suggests that ß is a measure of nondiversifiable risk; that is, a well-diversified portfolio does not change the risks associated with ß—the overall market risks. If a particular stock (or portfolio) exactly matches the market's stock price changes over time, that stock's ß=1. A stock that moves "more slowly" than the market has a ß less than one and is considered less risky. Presumably, an investment portfolio can be established to be risky (with a ß greater than 1, consistent with a growth portfolio) or less risky (ß less than 1).

Although this is not an infallible technique, ßs are widely available and easily interpreted. One source is Quicken (www.quicken.com, Fundamentals). As of May 2002, ßs for the PC companies are: Dell = 2.14, Gateway = 2.15, and Apple = 1.54. As expected for high-tech companies, ßs are considerably greater than 1. It is recommended that ß analysis be used to corroborate other information. For example compare PEs and PEGs to ßs for the PC companies, as shown in Exhibit 6.18. Thus, the high s for Dell and Apple are consistent with PEs and PEGs.

An alternative measure of risk is Risk Grades (www.riskgrades.com), which calculates financial risk from 0 (no risk) to 1,000 (maximum risk) based on stock price variation and

**EXHIBIT 6.17 PEG ANALYSIS MATRIX**

| | High PE | Average PE | Low PE |
|---|---|---|---|
| **High Growth** | 1. PEG = 1.5 or greater | 2. PEG = 1.5 or less | 3. PEG < 1.5 |
| **Average Growth** | 4. PEG > 1.5 | 5. PEG = 1.5 | 6. PEG < 1.5 |
| **Low Growth** | 7. PEG > 1.5 | 8. PEG > 1.5 | 9. PEG = 1 or less |

volatility to a basket of global entities. The risk grades for the PC companies (May 2002) were Dell 286, Gateway 351, and Apple 229. Exhibit 6.19 compares these two risk measures for nine companies: three companies usually considered stodgy and low risk, the three PC firms, and three other high-tech companies with expected high risk.

The results suggest general comparability to expectation and risk grade to ß. The high-risk companies are most likely fits to growth portfolios. The key is corresponding earnings growth to go along with the high risk.

# VALUATION MODELS

Models are available to estimate market value of companies based on expected future performance. These are simplistic models, but they provide information that may be useful when determining what the market value should be. Generally, if the stock value calculation is greater than the current stock price, the stock is considered undervalued and this is a potential buy indicator. Two models will be considered: (1) an earnings-based growth model and (2) an intrinsic value calculation available from Quicken.

## EARNINGS-BASED GROWTH (DIVIDEND DISCOUNT) MODEL

Historically, companies were evaluated more on dividends than earnings. There were two primary reasons. First, companies were expected to pay out a large percentage of earnings as dividends, essentially to compete with bond interest payments. Second, dividend payments (presumably tied to cash flows) were considered more reliable than earnings numbers, especially before GAAP attempted to standardize income statement results. Therefore, the dividend discount model was considered a significant valuation technique. Today, earnings calculations are considered more reliable and dividend rates have declined dramatically. Despite this change in emphasis, the dividend discount model is still useful for companies paying dividends and is particularly important for investors seeking income rather than growth.

Under this approach a definition of earnings (E) is used as the numerator and the denominator is some rate of return (r). Therefore, valuation = E ÷ r. Under the simple **earnings-based growth model,** the purpose is to calculate stock price = P. The model used is $P = kE \div (r - g)$, where k is the dividend payout rate and g = growth rate. The growth rate can be estimated as $g = ROE \times (1 - \text{dividend payout rate})$.

Assume that ABC Co. has a current stock price of $60. Is this stock under- or overvalued? Assume that EPS is $8, annual dividends per share are $2 (thus the dividend payout is 25 percent), the discount rate (r) is 10 percent, and expected EPS growth is 8 percent. The calculation is: $P = kE \div (r - g) = (.25 \times 8) \div (.10 - .08) = \$100$. Therefore, based on this calculation ABC is

**EXHIBIT 6.18 COMPARISONS OF ß TO PE AND PEG RATIOS FOR THE PC COMPANIES**

| | ß | PE (2-Years-Ahead EPS Forecast) | PEG (2-Years-Ahead EPS Forecast) |
|---|---|---|---|
| **Dell** | 2.14 | 29.4 | 1.9 |
| **Gateway** | 2.15 | NM | NM |
| **Apple** | 1.54 | 30.7 | 3.0 |

**EXHIBIT 6.19 COMPARISONS OF RISK GRADE TO ß FOR SELECTED COMPANIES**

| | Risk Grade | ß |
|---|---|---|
| Procter & Gamble | 83 | 0.22 |
| DuPont | 113 | 0.73 |
| General Motors | 126 | 1.08 |
| Dell | 286 | 2.14 |
| Gateway | 351 | 2.15 |
| Apple | 229 | 1.54 |
| Cisco | 379 | 2.03 |
| Amazon | 379 | 3.32 |
| Yahoo | 356 | 3.78 |

undervalued by $40 per share. A limitation of this method is that the company must pay dividends.

The May 1, 2002, stock price of Procter & Gamble is $91.80. The projected stock price (P) can be estimated for Procter & Gamble with the following information: 2001 EPS was $2.07, 2001 dividends were $1.52, and the five-year projected annual earnings growth rate is 10.3 percent. The dividend payout ratio (k) was 1.52 ÷ 2.07 or 73.4 percent. Rate of return (r) is assumed to be 12 percent, roughly equivalent to the earnings growth rate of the average large corporation. Therefore; $P = kE \div (r - g) = (.734 \times 2.07) \div (.12 - .103) = \$89.41$. Therefore, Procter & Gamble is slightly overpriced at $91.80 by $2.39 or 2.6 percent of projected price, based on the assumptions used for this calculation.

### INTRINSIC VALUE PER SHARE

An **intrinsic value** calculator, called Evaluator, is available on www.quicken.com. The calculation begins with initial earnings, multiplied by the earnings growth rate and then discounted by some appropriate rate of return (r). Changing these assumptions results in quite different valuations. The calculation for Dell is $1,246 million (2002 net income) times an earnings growth rate of 15.8 percent (the five-year projected earnings growth rate) and discount rate of 11 percent (the Standard & Poor's 500 long-term earnings growth rate). The Evaluator calculation results in an intrinsic value of $18.72, below the stock price. The stock price to intrinsic value calculations for the three companies using comparable approximations are shown in Exhibit 6.20.

Annual earnings can be based on the net income for the latest fiscal year. Alternatively, it can be the accumulated net income for the most recent four quarters. When Apple's most recent four quarters of income is used, the company has a positive income and intrinsic value can be calculated. Based on the intrinsic value calculation, both Dell and Gateway are overvalued. Assuming that the analyst believes the estimates used are reasonable, this is a negative indicator for a buy/sell decision. Intrinsic value is a useful measure, but it depends on the confidence in the projected growth rate.

Evaluator can be used to compare different estimations. For example, what if Dell's annual earnings growth rate was 10 percent or 20 percent, rather than 15.8 percent? The results are intrinsic values of $12.11 and $25.85, respectively. At an annual growth rate of 20 percent, the intrinsic value is near the current stock price. This suggests that Dell must perform much better than predicted (above 20 percent annual growth in earnings) to justify its current stock price, again assuming these estimates are reasonable.

## STOCK SCREENING

Thanks to the Internet, stock screening tools are readily available to find stocks with specific investment criteria. **Stock screening** is a particularly useful way to choose a reasonable set of companies for further analysis. For example, to find stocks that pay high dividends (typical income fund investments), screen a group on dividend yield and perhaps additional criteria.

**EXHIBIT 6.20 INTRINSIC VALUE CALCULATIONS FOR THE PC COMPANIES**

| | Stock Price (May 1, 2002) | Annual Earnings (in millions)* | 5-Year Projected Earnings Growth Rate | Discount Rate | Intrinsic Value per Share | Stock Price to Intrinsic Value |
|---|---|---|---|---|---|---|
| **Dell** | 26.48 | $1,246 | 15.8% | 11% | $18.72 | 1.4 |
| **Gateway** | 5.33 | **–1,034** | 9.5 | 11 | NA | NA |
| **Apple** | 23.98 | **–25** | 10.2 | 11 | NA | NA |
| **Apple** | 23.98 | 205* | 10.2 | 11 | 14.19 | 1.7 |

*Annual earnings using net income for the latest four quarters, ending March 2002

Source: www.quicken.com/evaluator

Hoovers is one of several sites that have a useful stock screener (www.hoovers.com/search/forms/stockscreener). Users have dozens of options to choose from. For high dividend yield companies on the NYSE, search on NYSE and, say, a "dividend yield of 4 percent to ___." In May 2002 this listed 338 stocks with a yield of 4 percent or more. As an industry that typically pays high dividends, utilities had thirty-five firms with dividend yields of at least 5 percent. For a shorter list, a yield of 6 percent was selected (seventeen utilities). To ensure that these were earning a reasonable return, a 10 percent ROE has added. That pulled in seven domestic firms, shown in Exhibit 6.21.

This short list of potential high-yield utilities can be generated for further analysis. At the other extreme, a search for high-growth companies—20 percent earnings growth for one and five years, revenue growth of 20 percent on the NASDAQ, and large cap—found thirty-six companies. Any number of alternatives is available.

## SUMMARY

This chapter incorporates market information in the financial analysis process. Current stock prices and stock price trends are readily available in virtually any form desired. Assuming efficient markets, they are an unbiased estimate of the true value of the company. Therefore, stock price trends along with earnings and EPS projections provide considerable new information, new ratios, and valuation methods. The PE ratio defines the "market premium" relative to per share earnings, a fundamental starting point for market analysis. It is expected that PE should be related to a firm's long-term earnings growth potential, which can be approximated with PEG. Dividend yield is a basic measure of cash return, particularly important for investors seeking current income.

The market value of a corporation can be compared to book value, another measure of market premium. Valuing a firm can be difficult. Attempts to estimate its economic valuation include the dividend discount model and intrinsic value calculations. Finally, when looking for specific firm characteristics, stock screening can be useful.

**EXHIBIT 6.21 STOCK SCREENER RESULTS BASED ON DIVIDEND YIELD AND RETURN ON EQUITY**

| Firm | Yield | ROE |
|---|---|---|
| Aquila | 8.1% | 10.9% |
| Great Plains Energy | 6.9 | 13.3 |
| Northwestern | 7.0 | 11.2 |
| Reliant Energy | 9.7 | 13.4 |
| TransAlta | 6.7 | 11.4 |
| United Utilities | 7.6 | 15.1 |
| Xcel Energy | 6.9 | 12.7 |

## KEY TERMS

analysts' forecasts
basic EPS
closing stock price
diluted EPS
dividend yield
Dow Jones Industrial Average
earnings-based growth models
earnings per share (EPS)
intrinsic value
market to book
market value
price earnings (PE) ratio
PEG ratio
stock screening

## A SUMMARY OF MARKET RATIOS

Book value per share: Total stockholders' equity ÷ number of shares outstanding
Equity or net assets, as measured on the balance sheet

Earnings-based growth models: $P = kE \div (r - g)$, where E = earnings, k = dividend payout rate, r = discount rate, and g = earnings growth rate
Valuation models that discount earnings and dividends by a discount rate adjusted for future earnings growth

Intrinsic value: Internet calculation, based on net income and earnings growth rate, discounted at S&P 500 long-term growth rate (or other rate)
Per share valuation model available at Quicken; the value is compared with current stock price

Market to book: (Stock price × number of shares outstanding) ÷ total stockholders' equity
Measure of accounting-based equity

Price earnings ratio (PE): Stock price ÷ EPS
Measure of market premium paid for earnings and future expectations

Price earnings growth ratio (PEG): PE ÷ earnings growth rate
PE is compared to earnings growth rates as a measure of PE "reasonableness"

Sales to market value: Sales ÷ (stock price × number of shares outstanding)
A sales activity ratio based on market price

Dividend yield: Dividends per share ÷ stock price
Direct cash return on stock investment

## QUESTIONS

1. When is stock price information important? Is the major concern with current price or the price trend over a long period of time? Explain.
2. What is earnings per share? Should net income always be used as the measure of profitability? Explain. How important and how reliable are EPS forecasts?
3. Why are PE ratios important? Are they very general market premium indicators or precise, reliable measures?
4. Why are investor goals important when evaluating dividends and dividend yields?
5. When is market-to-book extremely important to an analyst? Is "the higher the better" a good rule of thumb? Explain.
6. Is a company with a PEG of less than one always a good investment? Explain.
7. What does it mean if the dividend discount model and intrinsic value give mixed signals?
8. When would stock screening be a useful tool?

## PROBLEMS

### Problem 6.1 Stock Price Charts

(Problems 6.1–6 relate to the chemical industry.)

Stock prices for three chemical companies [DuPont (DD), Dow, and PPG] and the Dow Jones Industrial Average (DJIA) are presented for one and five years.

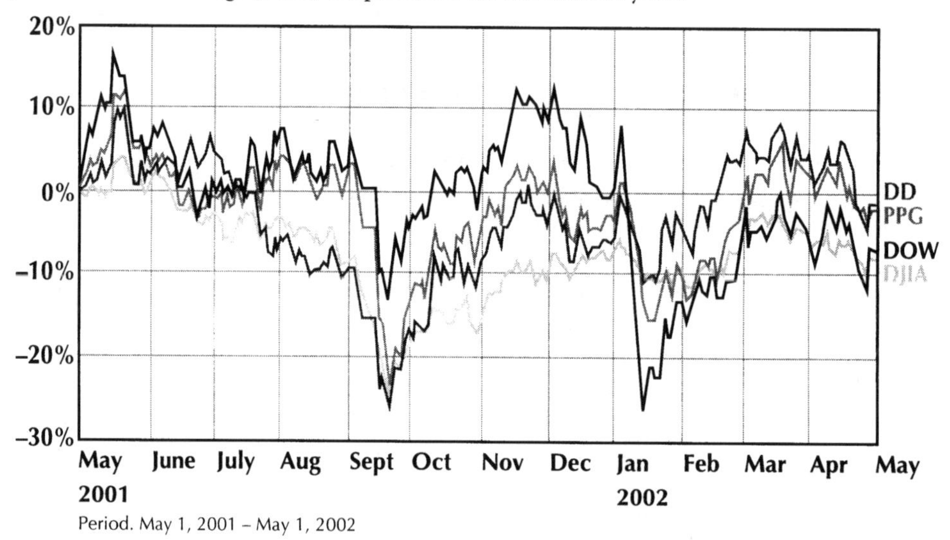


Period. May 1, 2001 – May 1, 2002

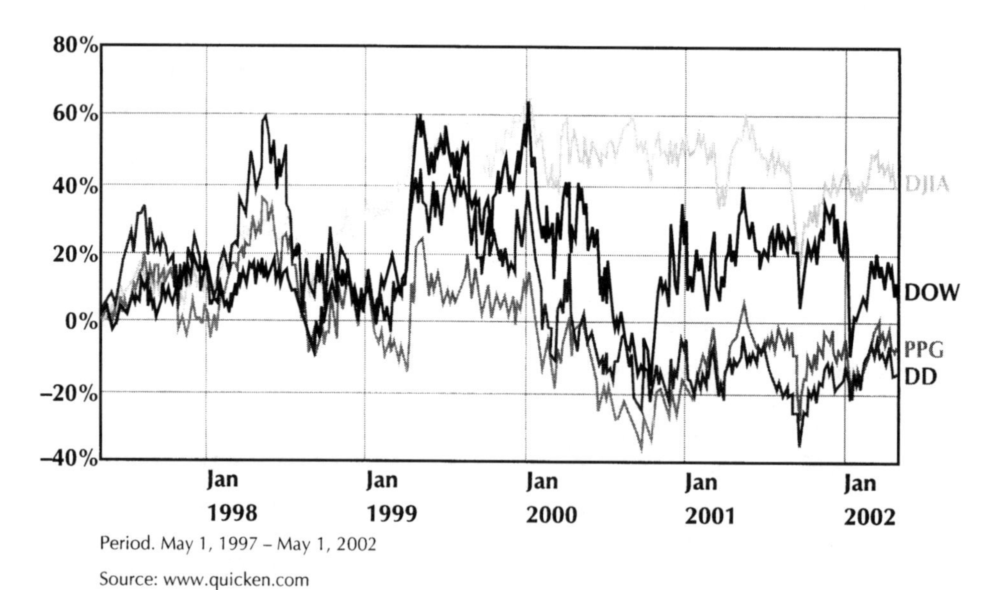


Period. May 1, 1997 – May 1, 2002

Source: www.quicken.com

Provide a brief analysis of stock prices for these companies relative to the DJIA.

### Problem 6.2 Price Earnings and Dividend Ratios

Given are stock prices (May 1, 2002, closing), EPS 2001 actual, 2002 forecast, 2003 forecast, and 2001 dividend yield:

| | Stock Price | EPS, Actual | EPS, 2002* | EPS 2003* | Dividend |
|---|---|---|---|---|---|
| DuPont | 44.63 | $4.15 | $1.75 | $2.38 | $1.40 |
| Dow | 31.49 | **–0.46 RF** | 1.01 | 2.37 | 1.34 |
| PPG | 52.22 | 2.29 | 2.73 | 3.50 | 1.68 |

*Zacks analysts' estimates from Quicken

Given the information above, calculate PE for the three definitions of EPS, dividend yield, and dividend payout:

| | Price/Actual EPS | Price/2002 EPS | Price/2003 EPS | Dividend Yield | Dividend Payout |
|---|---|---|---|---|---|
| DuPont | | | | | |
| Dow | | | | | |
| PPG | | | | | |

### Problem 6.3 PE to Annual Earnings Growth (PEG)

Given are annual earnings growth rates, both historical and projected.

| | 5-Year Historic Earnings Growth Rates* | 5-Year Projected Earnings Growth Rates* |
|---|---|---|
| DuPont | **–18.2%** | 11.0% |
| Dow | **–22.8** | 10.0 |
| PPG | **–7.1** | 8.0 |

*www.quicken.com, Analysts Estimates

Calculate PE to earnings growth rates (PEG), using the information above and calculations from Problem 6.2.

| | Current PE ÷ 5-Year Historic Growth | 1-Year-Ahead PE Forecast ÷ 5-Year Projected Growth | 2-Years-Ahead PE Forecast ÷ 5-Year Projected Growth |
|---|---|---|---|
| DuPont | | | |
| Dow | | | |
| PPG | | | |

Classify these companies by cell (1 to 9) based on the PEG matrix. Assume that the average PE is 20 and the average earnings growth is 12 percent.

## Problem 6.4 Market-to-Book and Sales Ratios

Given are stock price, net assets (total stockholders' equity), shares outstanding, and annual revenues for 2001 of the chemical companies.

**a.** Calculate book value per share and the market-to-book ratio for the chemical companies.

| | Stock Price | Net Assets (in millions) | Shares Outstanding (in millions) | Sales, 2001 (in millions) | Book Value per Share | Market-to-Book Ratio |
|---|---|---|---|---|---|---|
| DuPont | 44.63 | $14,452 | 1,002 | $24,726 | | |
| Dow | 31.49 | 9,993 | 905 | 27,805 | | |
| PPG | 52.22 | 3,080 | 169 | 8,169 | | |

**b.** Calculate the market value, the sales to net assets, and sales to market value ratios.

| | Market Value | Sales to Net Assets | Sales to Market Value |
|---|---|---|---|
| DuPont | | | |
| Dow | | | |
| PPG | | | |

## Problem 6.5 Earnings Growth (Dividend Discount) Model

Use the earnings growth model ($P = kE \div (r - g)$) to estimate projected stock price, assume the S&P 500 rate of return (r) is 12 percent.

| | Stock Price | EPS | Dividend Payout | 5-Year Earning Growth | Projected Price |
|---|---|---|---|---|---|
| DuPont | 44.63 | 4.15 | 33.7% | 11.0% | |
| Dow | 31.49 | **–0.46*** | 132.7 | 10.0 | |
| PPG | 52.22 | 2.29 | 73.4 | 8.0 | |

*Estimate using forecast EPS of 1.01

How do these compare to the May 1, 2002, stock price? Which are overvalued or undervalued?

## Problem 6.6 Intrinsic Value

Given the information below, calculate stock price to intrinsic value.

| | Stock Price, May 1, 2002 | Annual Earning (in millions)* | 5-Year Earnings Growth Rate | Discount Rate | Intrinsic Value per Share† | Stock Price to Intrinsic Value |
|---|---|---|---|---|---|---|
| DuPont | 44.63 | $4,322 | 11.0% | 11% | $81.59 | |
| Dow | 31.49 | 405 | 10.0 | 11 | 0 | |
| PPG | 52.22 | 383 | 8.0 | 11 | 44.39 | |

*Last four quarters, ending March 2002 †www.quicken.com, Evaluator

Given the information and calculations above, are these stocks overvalued or undervalued? Explain.

## Problem 6.7 Stock Price Charts

(Problems 6.7–12 relate to the hotel and resort industry.)

Stock prices for one and five years are shown for three hotel and resort companies—Hilton (HLT), Marriott (MAR), and Mandalay (MBG)—along with the Dow Jones Industrial Average.

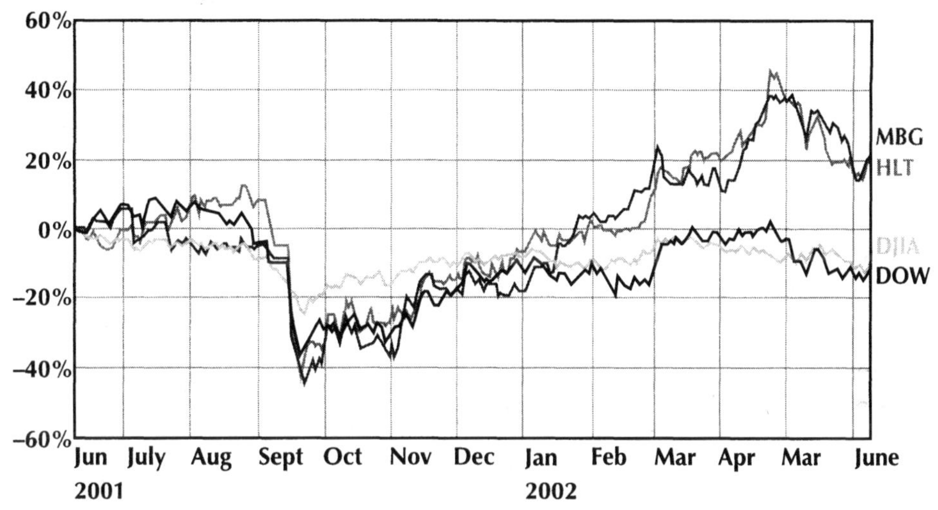


Period: June 11, 2001 – June 10, 2002

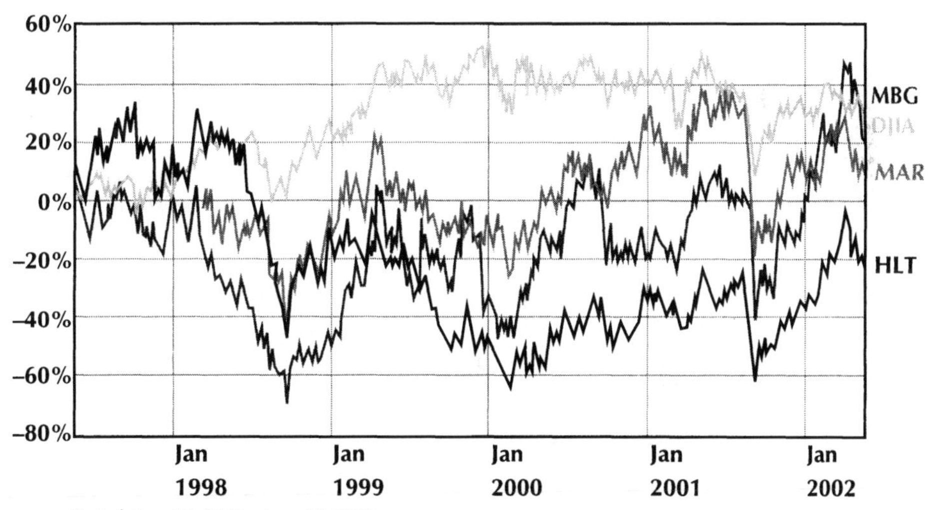


Period: June 10, 1997 – June 10, 2002

Source: www.quicken.com

Provide a brief analysis of stock prices for these companies relative to the DJIA.

## Problem 6.8 Price Earnings and Dividend Ratios

Given are stock prices (May 1, 2002, closing), EPS 2001 actual, 2002 forecast, 2003 forecast, and 2001 dividend yield:

| | Stock Price | EPS, Actual | EPS, 2002* | EPS, 2003* | Dividend |
|---|---|---|---|---|---|
| Hilton | 16.00 | $0.45 | $0.63 | $0.81 | 0.08 |
| Marriott | 44.03 | 0.92 | 1.68 | 2.07 | 0.28 |
| Mandalay | 7.13 | 0.71 | 1.87 | 2.20 | 0 |

*Zacks analysts' estimates from Quicken

Given the information above, calculate PE for the three definitions of EPS, dividend yield, and dividend payout:

| | Price ÷ Actual EPS | Price ÷ 2001 EPS | Price ÷ 2002 EPS | Dividend Yield | Dividend Payout |
|---|---|---|---|---|---|
| Hilton | | | | | |
| Marriott | | | | | |
| Mandalay | | | | | |

## Problem 6.9 PE to Annual Earnings Growth (PEG)

Given are annual earnings growth rates, both historical and projected.

| | 5-Year Historic Earnings Growth Rates * | 5-Year Projected Earnings Growth Rates * |
|---|---|---|
| Hilton | **–15.8%** | 13.9% |
| Marriott | 6.9 | 14.4 |
| Mandalay | **2.0** | 13.6 |

*www.quicken.com, Analysts Estimates

Calculate PE to earnings growth rates (PEG), using information above and calculations from Problem 6.8.

| | Current PE ÷ 5-Year Historic Growth | 1-Year-Ahead PE Forecast ÷ 5-Year Projected Growth | 2-Years-Ahead PE Forecast ÷ 5-Year Projected Growth |
|---|---|---|---|
| Hilton | | | |
| Marriott | | | |
| Mandalay | | | |

Classify these companies by cell (1 to 9) based on the PEG matrix. Assume that the average PE is 20 and the average earnings growth is 12 percent.

## Problem 6.10 Market-to-Book and Sales Ratios

Given are stock price, net assets (total stockholders' equity), shares outstanding, and annual revenues for 2001 of the hotel and resort companies.

**a.** Calculate book value per share and the market-to-book ratio for the chemical companies.

| | Stock Price | Net Assets (in millions) | Shares Outstanding (in millions) | Sales, 2001 (in millions) | Book Value per Share | Market-to-Book Ratio |
|---|---|---|---|---|---|---|
| Hilton | 16.00 | $1,783 | 369 | $2,632 | | |
| Marriott | 44.03 | 3,478 | 245 | 10,152 | | |
| Mandalay* | 7.13 | 941 | 68 | 2,462 | | |

*FYE January 2002

**b.** Calculate market value, the sales-to-net assets, and sales-to-market value ratios.

| | Market Value | Sales to Net Assets | Sales to Market Value |
|---|---|---|---|
| Hilton | | | |
| Marriott | | | |
| Mandalay | | | |

## Problem 6.11 Earnings Growth (Dividend Discount) Model

Use the earnings growth model ($P = kE \div (r - g)$) to estimate the projected stock price. Assume the S&P 500 rate of return (r) is 15 percent.

| | Stock Price | EPS | Dividend Payout | 5-Year Earning Growth | Projected Price |
|---|---|---|---|---|---|
| Hilton | 16.00 | $0.45 | 17.8% | 13.9% | |
| Marriott | 44.03 | 0.92 | 30.4 | 14.4 | |
| Mandalay | 7.13 | 0.71 | 0 | 13.6 | |

How do these compare to the May 1, 2002, stock price? Which are overvalued or undervalued?

## Problem 6.12 Intrinsic Value

Given the information below, calculate stock price to intrinsic value.

| | Stock Price, May 1, 2002 | Annual Earnings (millions)* | 5-Year Earnings Growth Rate | Discount Rate | Intrinsic Value per Share† | Stock Price to Intrinsic Value |
|---|---|---|---|---|---|---|
| Hilton | 16.00 | $145 | 13.9% | 11% | $0.13 | |
| Marriott | 44.03 | 197 | 14.4 | 11% | 8.40 | |
| Mandalay | 7.13 | 55 | 13.6 | 11% | 0 | |

*Last four quarters ending March 2002 (April 2002 for Mandalay) †www.quicken.com, Evaluator

Given the information and calculations above, are these stocks overvalued or undervalued? Explain.

## Problem 6.13 Stock Price Charts

(Problems 6.13–18 relate to the auto industry.)

Stock prices for Ford, GM, and the Dow Jones Industrial Average for one and five years follow.

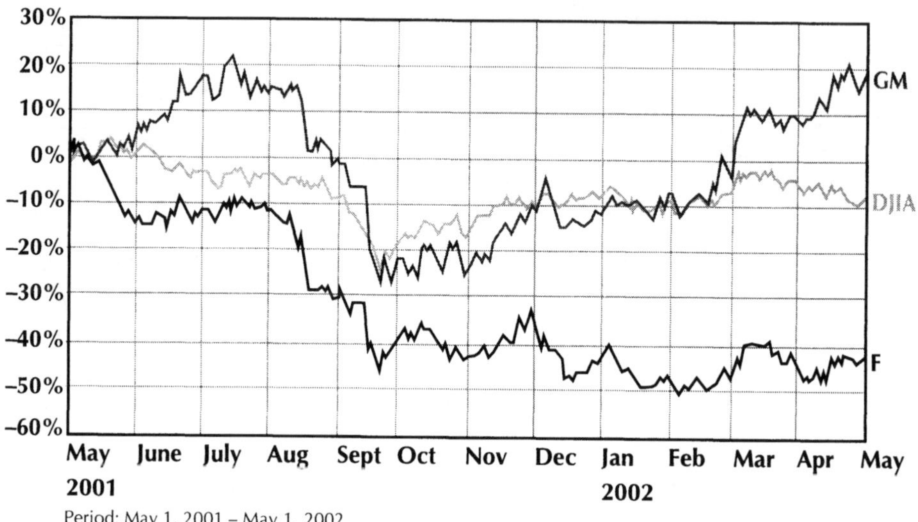


Period: May 1, 2001 – May 1, 2002

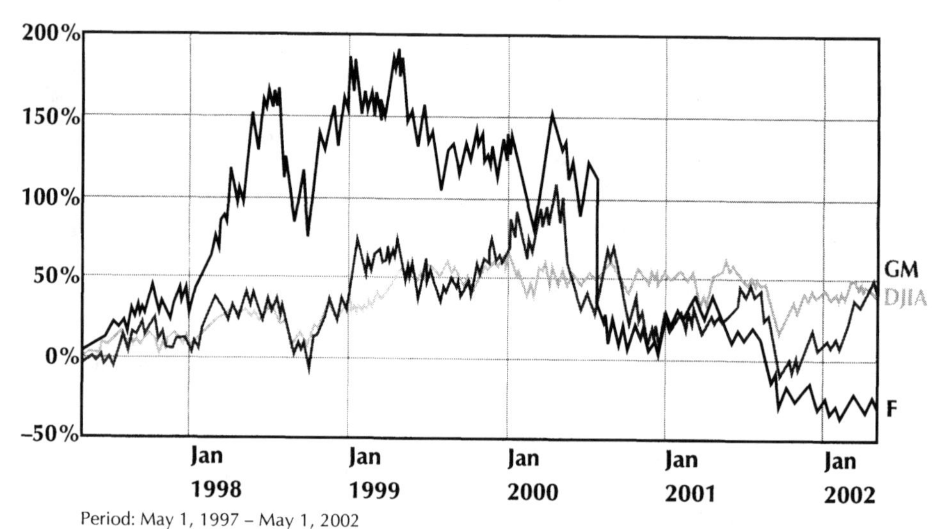


Period: May 1, 1997 – May 1, 2002

Source: www.quicken.com

Provide a brief analysis of stock prices for these companies relative to the DJIA.

## Problem 6.14 Price Earnings and Dividend Ratios

Given are stock prices (May 1, 2002, closing), EPS 2001 actual, 2002 forecast, 2003 forecast, and 2001 dividend yield:

| | Stock Price | EPS, Actual | EPS, 2002* | EPS, 2003* | Dividend |
|---|---|---|---|---|---|
| Ford | 16.34 | **−3.02 RF** | 0.16 | 0.89 | 0.40 |
| GM | 65.51 | **1.77** | 4.73 | 6.33 | 2.00 |

*Zacks analysts' estimates from Quicken

Given the information above, calculate PE for the three definitions of EPS, dividend yield, and dividend payout:

| | Price ÷ Actual EPS | Price ÷ 2001 EPS | Price ÷ 2002 EPS | Dividend Yield | Dividend Payout |
|---|---|---|---|---|---|
| Ford | | | | | |
| GM | | | | | |

## Problem 6.15 Market to Book and Sales Ratios

Given are stock price, net assets (total stockholders' equity), shares outstanding, and 2001 revenues of the auto companies.

**a.** Calculate book value per share and the market-to-book ratio for the chemical companies.

| | Stock Price | Net Assets (in millions) | Shares Outstanding (in millions) | Sales, 2001 (in millions) | Book Value per Share | Market to Book Ratio |
|---|---|---|---|---|---|---|
| Ford | 16.34 | 7,786 | 1,908 | 162,412 | | |
| GM | 65.51 | 19,707 | 1,437 | 177,260 | | |

**b.** Calculate market value, the sales-to-net assets, and sales-to market value ratios.

| | Market Value | Sales to Net Assets | Sales to Market Value |
|---|---|---|---|
| Ford | | | |
| GM | | | |

## Problem 6.16 PE to Annual Earnings Growth (PEG)

Given are annual earnings growth rates, both historical and projected.

| | 5-Year Historic Earnings Growth Rates * | 5-Year Projected Earnings Growth Rates * |
|---|---|---|
| Ford | **–170.4 RF** | 5.1 |
| GM | **–14.8** | 5.8 |

*www.quicken.com, Analysts Estimates

Calculate PE to earnings growth rates (PEG), using information above and calculations from Problem 5.8.

| | Current PE ÷ 5-Year Historic Growth | 1-Year-Ahead PE Forecast ÷ 5-Year Project Growth | 2-Years-Ahead PE Forecast ÷ 5-Year Projected Growth |
|---|---|---|---|
| Ford | | | |
| GM | | | |

Classify these companies by cell (1 to 9) based on the PEG matrix. Assume that average PE is 20 and average earnings growth is 12 percent.

### Problem 6.17 Earnings Growth (Dividend Discount) Model

Use the earnings growth model (P = kE ÷ (r – g) to estimate projected stock price. Assume the S&P 500 rate of return (r) is 12 percent.

| | Stock Price | EPS | Dividend Payout | 5-Year Earnings Growth | Projected Price |
|---|---|---|---|---|---|
| Ford | 16.34 | **–3.02*** | 250.0% | 5.1 | |
| GM | 65.51 | 1.77 | 113.0 | 5.8 | |

*Estimate using forecast EPS of $.16

How do these compare to the May 1, 2002, stock price? Are they overvalued or undervalued?

### Problem 6.18 Intrinsic Value

Given the information below, calculate stock price to intrinsic value.

| | Stock Price, May 1, 2002 | Annual Earnings (millions)* | 5 Year Earnings Growth Rate | Discount Rate | Intrinsic Value per Share† | Stock Price to Intrinsic Value |
|---|---|---|---|---|---|---|
| Ford | 16.34 | Neg | | | NA | |
| GM | 65.51 | 592 | 5.8 | 11.0 | 0 | |

*Last four quarters, ending March 2002

†www.quicken.com, Evaluator

Given the information and calculations above, are these stocks overvalued or undervalued? Explain.

## CASES

### Case 6.1 Market Analysis of the Chemical Industry

Conduct a comprehensive market analysis of the three chemical companies, based on the findings from Problems 6.1–6. Rate each category from 1 (poor) to 10 (excellent) and analyze the overall market. The primary consideration overall for growth stocks is whether the stock is overvalued or undervalued. The primary consideration for income stocks is yield, followed by dividend payout and over- or underevaluation.

| DuPont | Rating | Analysis |
|---|---|---|
| Stock Price Trends | | |
| PE Ratios | | |
| Dividends | | |
| Market-to-Book | | |
| PEG | | |
| Valuation: Dividend Discount Model | | |
| Valuation: Intrinsic Value | | |

| Dow | Rating | Analysis |
|---|---|---|
| Stock Price Trends | | |
| PE Ratios | | |
| Dividends | | |
| Market-to-Book | | |
| PEG | | |
| Valuation: Dividend Discount Model | | |
| Valuation: Intrinsic Value | | |

| PPG | Rating | Analysis |
|---|---|---|
| Stock Price Trends | | |
| PE Ratios | | |
| Dividends | | |
| Market-to-Book | | |
| PEG | | |
| Valuation: Dividend Discount Model | | |
| Valuation: Intrinsic Value | | |

## Case 6.2 Market Analysis of the Hotel and Resort Industry

Conduct a comprehensive market analysis of the three hotel and resort companies, based on the findings from Problems 6.7–12. Rate each category from 1 (poor) to 10 (excellent) and analyze the overall market. The primary consideration overall for growth stocks is whether the stock is overvalued or undervalued. The primary consideration for income stocks is yield, followed by dividend payout and over- and underevaluation.

| Hilton | Rating | Analysis |
|---|---|---|
| Stock Price Trends | | |
| PE Ratios | | |
| Dividends | | |
| Market-to-Book | | |
| PEG | | |
| Valuation: Dividend Discount Model | | |
| Valuation: Intrinsic Value | | |

| Marriott | Rating | Analysis |
|---|---|---|
| Stock Price Trends | | |
| PE Ratios | | |
| Dividends | | |
| Market-to-Book | | |
| PEG | | |
| Valuation: Dividend Discount Model | | |
| Valuation: Intrinsic Value | | |

| Mandalay | Rating | Analysis |
|---|---|---|
| Stock Price Trends | | |
| PE Ratios | | |
| Dividends | | |
| Market-to-Book | | |
| PEG | | |
| Valuation: Dividend Discount Model | | |
| Valuation: Intrinsic Value | | |

## Case 6.3 Market Analysis of the Auto Industry

Conduct a comprehensive market analysis of the auto companies, based on the findings from Problems 6.13–18. Rate each category from 1 (poor) to 10 (excellent) and analyze the overall market. The primary consideration overall for growth stocks is whether the stock is overvalued or undervalued. The primary consideration for income stocks is yield, followed by dividend payout and over- and underevaluation.

| Ford | Rating | Analysis |
|---|---|---|
| Stock Price Trends | | |
| PE Ratios | | |
| Dividends | | |
| Market-to-Book | | |
| PEG | | |
| Valuation: Dividend Discount Model | | |
| Valuation: Intrinsic Value | | |

| General Motors | Rating | Analysis |
|---|---|---|
| Stock Price Trends | | |
| PE Ratios | | |
| Dividends | | |
| Market-to-Book | | |
| PEG | | |
| Valuation: Dividend Discount Model | | |
| Valuation: Intrinsic Value | | |

## ETHICS CONSIDERATIONS

### Corrupt Corporate Governance and Wall Street

The following excerpts from *Fortune* ("Global Crossing, Emperor of Greed" by J. Creswell, www.fortune.com) illustrates corrupt practices that led to corporate failure:

> Gary Winnick had never worked in the telecom industry before he founded Global Crossing in 1997. He had never run a public company before either. Yet in the late 1990s, Chairman Winnick was hailed as an industry giant, the creator of a telco that a year after going public in 1998 was valued at $38 billion—more than Ford. A little over two years later, Global Crossing is in bankruptcy and fighting to survive, part of an industry collapse that wiped out $2.5 trillion in market value. Investors and regulators are struggling to figure out what went so wrong so fast.
>
> The answer captures all of the insanity and money fever of the telecom and dot-com bubbles, which saw billions of dollars vanish in pursuit of business that never materialized. Like a lot of other overreaching companies, Winnick's Global Crossing rose swiftly and fell even faster. Its business plan changed with the phases of the moon. So did its CEOs (there were five in four years). It had a huge market value and a teeny cash flow. Global Crossing inflated its revenues by swapping capacity with other carriers, say analysts, and lured customers and investors by overstating the reach and capabilities of its network—a $12 billion "state-of-the-art" system that, several former employees told Fortune, simply doesn't work that well. It exploited its relationships with both Wall Street and its bankers on a scale unrivaled in the industry.
>
> What's inarguable, as our story will document, is that billions of dollars flowed out of this company and into the pockets of insiders. Gary Winnick and his cronies are arguably the biggest group of greedheads in an era of fabled excess. Not only did Winnick sell off stock at huge profits while investors who jumped in later watched their stakes burn to nothing, but he treated Global Crossing from the get-go as his personal cash cow, earning exorbitant fees from consulting and real estate deals between Global Crossing and his own private investment company. In all, Winnick cashed in $735 million of stock over four years—including $135 million Global Crossing issued to his private company—while receiving $10 million in salary and bonuses and other payments to the holding company. Enron's Kenneth Lay doesn't even come close. He sold only $108 million of stock. (The telecom boom's cash-out king may be Qwest Chairman Philip Anschutz, who dumped $1.9 billion in stock. But Qwest, at least for now, is afloat.)
>
> Wall Street partners fared well too. Canadian firm CIBC World Markets, which was an early investor in Global Crossing and at one time had five employees on its board, earned $56 million in banking fees even before Global Crossing's 1998 IPO. It turned a $41 million investment into a $1.7 billion windfall and exited the board just as the telecom bubble was bursting. Global Crossing paid more than $420 million in fees to Wall Street firms in three short years. As one investment banker recalls, "People wanted to do business with Winnick because he was the best game in town."
>
> Needless to say, most outside investors never saw that kind of payday. Global Crossing's market valuation, which peaked at $47 billion in February 2000, deflated

to about $70 million when it filed for bankruptcy earlier this year. Investors and creditors have almost zero chance of recouping any of the $20 billion that Global Crossing raised. The company is seeking a buyer, but a bid from two Asian partners fell through at the end of May. It is looking to restructure now. In all likelihood, though, Global Crossing will be broken up and stripped for parts.

a. It seems that corruption works, at least for a while for those at the top. Is the problem with the system or mainly a matter of better regulations and enforcement?
b. Global Crossing went bankrupt. Part of the problems was earnings manipulation, especially aggressive revenue recognition (including transactions that seemed to have no economic basis except to book revenue). Is accounting practice the major problem or is it corporate governance?
c. Wall Street firms benefited from Global Crossing. Are they part of the problem?

## INTERNET PROJECTS

### Project 6.1 Internet Overview

a. Go to the Fortune site (www.fortune.com). Find the *Fortune* 500 and browse. What is the largest company on the list? What makes it the largest? Go to the *Fortune* 500 industry list and pick Pharmaceuticals. Which company has the largest ROE and ROA?
b. Go to Hoovers (www.hoovers.com) and search for Pfizer. Read the Pfizer Capsule. What is the ticker symbol? The Web address? Go to the abbreviated financials. Write down 2000 revenues, gross profit, and net income and calculate common-size percentages.
c. Go to Quicken (www.quicken.com). Enter the Pfizer ticker symbol. Use the year-to-date chart and compare Pfizer to the DJIA and Johnson & Johnson. How well has Pfizer done? Pull up the five-year chart and answer the same questions. Go to Analysts Ratings and look up EPS estimates for the next two years and the earnings growth estimated for the next five years. Compare Pfizer again to Johnson & Johnson.
d. Pull up Pfizer's 2000 10-K. Use the company's Web page (www.pfizer.com), Lexis/Nexis (www.lexisnexis.com/universe), or some other source. What is the CFO and pension amount shown on the balance sheet?

### Project 6.2 Stock Screener

Go to Hoovers (www.hoovers.com)—money/stock screener. Do this series of searches:

a. Large-cap, growth stocks, NYSE, all industries. Identify five companies from this list.
b. Large-cap value stocks, all exchanges, all industries. Identify five companies with a PE ratio below 10.
c. Use your own search to pick stocks. Explain your technique and results.

### Project 6.3

Use the company picked in Project 4.1. Gather information you need from the company's stock price, forecasts, annual report, and other sources. Do a complete market analysis, using the same format as project 6.1 and 6.2.

CHAPTER

# 7 An Accounting Analysis Perspective

**Objectives**

- Describe revenue recognition criteria and differentiate between conservative and aggressive recognition.
- Evaluate the matching principle and understand how it relates to revenue recognition.
- Distinguish nonrecurring items from continuing operations and evaluate the possible earnings management potential.
- Understand the difference between income from continuing operations, net income, and comprehensive income.
- Evaluate cash flow information, including cash flows from operations and basic ratios such as operating cash flows and free cash flows.
- Understand the self-interest incentives of managers and evaluate the earnings management potential of companies.
- Interpret the five-step detailed accounting analysis process, especially the importance of earnings management potential and red flags.
- Ascertain how accounting information can be updated using quarterly financial statements, especially 10-Qs.

## INTRODUCTION

Earnings issues are particularly significant to financial analysis, especially for equity investment decisions. This chapter begins with accounting issues involving the income statement, focusing on issues that affect how earnings information is best interpreted. Revenue recognition is fundamental. A company has flexibility especially as to when sales and other revenues are recognized. Particularly important from an earnings management perspective is conservative vs. aggressive recognition. Expenses are recognized relative to revenues based on the matching principal. In many cases, companies have flexibility on how and when expenses are recorded. **Earnings quality** generally is associated with conservative practices and focuses on continuing operations. Nonrecurring items by definition are unexpected and generally make analysis more difficult. There are several types and each one must be understood, especially in the context of earnings management. Various definitions of the "bottom line" are available, including net income, various definitions of operating earnings, and comprehensive income. In addition, companies can restate earnings on virtually any basis and call them *pro forma* earnings.

The cash flow statement supplements the analysis, with the exclusive focus on cash. Additional perspective is provided, which can be enhanced using ratio analysis. Significant ratios include (1) free cash flows, (2) cash from operations to total liabilities, (3) cash from operations per share, and (4) the cash flow adequacy ratio.

A formal structure is suggested for detailed accounting analysis as a five-step process. First, a general overview of financial accounting techniques can be used including a review of Note 1 on accounting policies. The company's reporting completeness should be evaluated. The annual report is fairly standardized, and companies are expected to use a common format and provide complete information. Analysts are always on the lookout for earnings management. Excessive earnings management can lead to distorted operating numbers and usually is referred to as earnings manipulation. All potential red flags should be reviewed for possible additional analysis. Finally, some accounting information may have to be reevaluated or restated.

For most of the year, annual report information is out of date and must be updated with the most recent reports and other information. A press release associated with earnings announcements usually is issued soon after the end of the accounting quarter. Within forty-five days of the end of the fiscal quarter, the company must file the 10-Q. Additional information can be found from the company press releases, the business press, and other reports, including include the proxy statement and 8-K filed with the Securities and Exchange Commission.

## Revenue Recognition

Performance evaluation begins with sales or other measures of revenue. Success depends on sales levels and growth. Major keys to understanding sales are the **revenue recognition** criteria used by the firm. According to the FASB's Conceptual Framework, revenue is recognized when (1) realized or realizable and (2) earned. "Realizable" means assets are received that are convertible into cash. Revenue is "earned" when exchange transactions (also called the earnings process) are substantially complete, usually by the time the product is delivered or service rendered.

In a complex business environment, managers must determine the appropriate time to recognize revenue. In addition, firm managers often have an earnings management incentive to recognize revenues as soon as possible to increase earnings in the current period. This is referred to as aggressive revenue recognition, and analysts typically view aggressive recognition with skepticism. Aggressive revenue recognition is usually accompanied by increasing receivables.

Revenue recognition is primarily a timing issue. Possible choices include recognition when a sale is made, when product is shipped, when product is received and accepted by the customer, or when cash payment is received. Will specific revenue be recognized this year or sometime in the future?

When should revenue be recognized? Dell's revenue recognition policy, described in Note 1 of the 2002 annual report, is:

> Net revenue includes sales of hardware, software and peripherals, and services (including extended warranty contracts and other services). Product revenue is recognized when both title and risk of loss transfer to the customer, provided that no significant obligations remain. The Company provides for an estimate of product returns and doubtful accounts, based on historical experience. ... (p. 37)

The SEC tightened recognition criteria with Staff Accounting Bulletin (SAB) 101 and Dell's recognition policy complied with this change. Previously, Dell recognized sales at date of shipment.

For a computer manufacturer like Dell, key sales events include the initial sale, shipment to the customer, customer billing, receipt and approval of the product by the customer, and cash payment. Dell's position on revenue recognition is defensible as realizable and earned, which are the Conceptual Framework's criteria, since the sale has been made, the product manufactured and delivered, and payment reasonably assured. Revenues from separate services and warranties are deferred until earned—the common practice when payment is received in advance. Although cash is received, revenue has not yet been earned. These are industry standards (Gateway and Apple have similar policies) and suggest no obvious earnings management from aggressive revenue recognition.

Different circumstances exist for revenue recognition. As with warranties and service contracts, prepaid items such as magazine subscriptions and insurance policies are deferred and revenue is recognized over the prepaid period. Engineering and construction companies build major capital and infrastructure project over several years. How should revenue be recognized in that case? Two alternatives are allowed: completed contracts (no revenue is recognized until the project is completed) or percentage of completion (revenue is recognized based on the estimated completion of the project). For example, Boeing uses both for aircraft construction. For commercial aircraft, revenues generally are recognized when deliveries are made (completed contracts). For government cost-reimbursement contracts, revenue is recognized based on scheduled milestones (percentage of completion). Both methods are used for government fixed-price contracts. The completed contracts method is more conservative, but both methods are considered reasonable.

## Conservative versus Aggressive Recognition

Dell's revenue recognition policy is conservative. It is defensible under the FASB criteria of realizable and earned, is consistent with industry practices, and comes relatively late in the sales event cycle. Analysts associate conservative revenue recognition with higher earnings quality and have more confidence in the earnings numbers.

Some companies treat revenue recognition aggressively. In this case, revenue is recognized early. This tends to increase current earnings, but it is shortsighted. Aggressive recognition reduces future recognition and is often a red flag (as an indicator of lower earnings quality) to analysts.

The giant telecommunications company Global Crossing sold fiber-optics capacity on its networks using long-term contracts. Global Crossing generally booked the entire contract amount as revenue, although the contracts often ran for twenty years. The company also bought capacity from other carriers, but it recorded these long-term costs as capital items rather than expenses. Despite these aggressive practices, Global lost billions and declared bankruptcy in 2001. Apparently, immediate recognition of revenues on long-term contracts was common in the industry.

Other examples are common. Xerox booked revenues from leased copiers (which should have been spread over the lease term) as if they were sold, leading to an SEC warning. Sunbeam in the late 1990s booked sales for products while still in the warehouses to show rising sales—that didn't exist. Microsoft, on the other hand, was accused of being too conservative, holding back revenues as cash reserves to smooth earnings from one quarter to the next.

## EXPENSES

Expenses are the costs associated with generating revenues. The key concept is the **matching principle.** Revenues recognized must be matched to related expenses during the same period. **Product costs** are a direct match, especially costs of goods sold related to sales. **Period costs** have no cause-and-effect relationship to sales, but they are consumed during the period. Marketing and advertising costs are period costs. As with revenues, timing is critical.

Perhaps the most important accounting topic in matching expenses to revenues is the accrual concept. Accrual accounting rather than the cash basis is used to determine appropriate expense recognition. These are the rules developed through GAAP on how expenses (as well as revenue and other items) are recorded. The costs of fixed assets are allocated to a specific time period using depreciation methods. Other allocation methods are used for long-term costs such as goodwill and other intangibles. Research and development costs, advertising, and human resource costs usually are expensed as incurred.

There are many difficult items for which the expense in a particular period may be hard to determine. Period expenses for defined benefit pension plans and other postretirement benefits are difficult to estimate, since the payout is based on many projections and assumptions into the distant future.

Consider an unusual item associated with airlines. The major airlines have frequent flier programs. Are these liabilities, and should expenses be recorded? That is not entirely obvious, since the cost of flying a plane is essentially the same whether it is full or partially empty. If the frequent flier tickets fill empty seats, it can be argued that there is no expense. On the other hand, the costs could be considered identical to the ticket price of paying passengers. Most airlines use a compromise approach. Continental Airlines is typical with its One Pass program. Continental records an estimated liability for the incremental costs of providing free transportation. AMR, the holding company for American Airlines, accrues the cost when specific award levels are reached.

Companies occasionally record "big bath" write-offs as part of continuing operations. A recent example was Cisco Systems, a maker of high tech routers and switches. Historically a high performance company (net income of $2.7 billion in fiscal year 2000), the company hit hard times in 2001. Losing money anyway, Cisco took two big bath write-offs for the April 2001 quarter. These included an excess inventory charge of $2.3 billion as part of cost of sales and restructuring costs and special charges of $1.2 billion for layoffs, closing buildings and reducing goodwill (recorded as a separate line item as part of operating income). Thus, there was a net loss of $2.7 billion on their 10-Q. Both write-offs were explained in Note 3.

## EBIT AND EBITDA

Two measures of current operating performance are (1) earnings before interest and taxes **(EBIT)** and (2) earnings before interest, taxes, depreciation, and amortization **(EBITDA).** EBIT (also called "operating earnings") excludes interest and taxes from earnings and can indicate a firm's ability to service its debt. EBITDA (also called "cash earnings") somewhat resembles cash flows from operations and can used for an alternative analysis of cash flows. Depreciation and amortization are noncash expenses and major expense categories at many large corporations.

Consider the PC companies for the current fiscal year (in millions), as shown in Exhibit 7.1. EBIT for Dell for 2002 was $1,760 million (1,246 + 485 + 29), $514 million (41.3 percent) above income from continuing operations (also net income since Dell had no nonrecurring items). EBITDA for Dell was $1,999 million (1,246 + 485 + 29 + 239), $753 million (60.4 percent) above income from continuing operations. Thus, earnings are much higher using these numbers. Both Gateway and Apple had losses from continuing operations and income was a "negative expense." Consequently, EBIT was roughly the same as income from continuing operations, since interest expense basically "offset" income tax. EBITDA for Gateway was $–828 million. However, EBITDA for Apple was $66 million, which seems much improved from the reported loss of $37 million.

A key question is whether these are useful numbers to evaluate earnings. They provide relevant information on operating cash flows and capital structure. These numbers will differ substantially from net income when (1) there are large nonrecurring items, (2) capital structure includes substantial interest-paying debt, and (3) the firm has a large fixed assets and intangible asset base, subject to depreciation and amortization.

Particularly when EBIT and EBITDA differ substantially from net income, profitability ratios can be recalculated using EBIT and EBITDA. Some alternative calculations for Dell for 2002 are shown in Exhibit 7.2.

The ratios for EBIT are 41 percent higher than net income and 60 percent higher for EBITDA. The EBIT and EBITDA numbers are sometimes presented as *pro forma* earnings (to be discussed shortly), since they are accepted as useful earnings numbers and can boost operating results considerably.

**EXHIBIT 7.1 INCOME STATEMENT ITEMS TO CALCULATE EBIT & EBITDA, PC COMPANIES**

| | Dell | Gateway | Apple |
|---|---|---|---|
| **Income from Continuing Operations** | $1,246 | $–1,014 | $–37 |
| **Provision for Income Tax** | 485 | –278 | –15 |
| **Interest Expense** | 29 | 294 | 16 |
| **Depreciation and Amortization** | 239 | 186 | 102 |

**EXHIBIT 7.2 EARNINGS RETURN RATIOS FOR DELL USING EBIT & EBITDA**

| | Using Net Income | Using EBIT | Using EBITDA |
|---|---|---|---|
| **Return on Sales** | 4.0% | 5.6% | 6.4% |
| **Return on Average Total Assets** | 9.2% | 13.1% | 14.8% |
| **Return on Average Equity** | 24.2% | 34.1% | 38.8% |

## NONRECURRING ITEMS

Revenues, cost of goods sold and most period costs are recurring items that are included in the calculation of income from continuing operations. **Nonrecurring items** are gains and losses that are unusual and expected to occur infrequently. Because of these characteristics, they don't provide much information to analysts about normal operations. They can be problematic and likely candidates for red flags.

Nonrecurring items include extraordinary items, discontinued operations, and accounting changes. According to Accounting Principles Board (APB) Opinion 30, extraordinary items are unusual in nature and infrequent in occurrence. They are recorded only if material in amount. These are reported separately after continuing operations, net of tax. Examples could be damage from floods or tornadoes where these are unusual or the expropriation of assets by foreign governments. The discontinuance or sale of a business component can be recorded as a discontinued operation under SFAS No. 144. This also is recorded as a separate line item net of tax. Cumulative prior period earnings changes on voluntary accounting changes usually are reported as separate line items net of tax (plus additional footnote disclosure). However, several exceptions to this are identified in APB Opinion 20, such as changes from last-in, first-out to other inventory methods (which require retroactive restatement).

In its 2000 annual report, DuPont recorded income from discontinued operations for 1997 and 1998, a gain on disposal of discontinued business in 1999 and 1998, and an extraordinary loss from early extinguishments of debt in 1998, all net of tax. These are described in more detail in Notes 9 and 10. The discontinued operation was the divestiture of Conoco. What makes this especially problematic is that nonrecurring items' amounts were larger than income from continuing operations (ICO). In 1999 ICO was $219 million, but net income was $7,690 million, thanks to the $7.5 billion gain on disposal. Net income showed healthy annual gains from 1997 ($2,407 million) through 1998 ($4,480 million) to 1999. But how useful is this big rise in earnings when analyzing DuPont? ICO dropped from 1997 ($1,432 million) to 1999 ($219 million). DuPont's return on sales for 1999 was a healthy 28.6 percent ($7,690 ÷ $26,918), but when ICO is substituted for net income the return on sales was only 0.8 percent. DuPont's ICO increased from $219 million in 1999 to $2,314 million in 2000. However, net income for 2000 also was $2,314 million, since no nonrecurring items were recorded. Consequently, ICO increased by $2,095 million (957 percent), but net income decreased by $5,376 million (70 percent).

In 2001 DuPont sold DuPont Pharmaceuticals to Bristol-Myers Squibb for $7.8 billion, booking a $6.1 billion pretax gain. DuPont treated this sale as part of continuing operations (the after-tax gain on the sale was $3.9 billion), rather than as a nonrecurring item. The result was 2001 net income of $4.3 billion, rather than a minuscule income of $0.4 billion (before the gain). This transaction seems similar to the earlier Conoco sale, but it was treated in a different manner. This appears to be obvious earnings management, and the financial analyst has to determine how to treat these sales and what further analysis is needed. At a minimum, performance measures should be made both before and after the sale.

Nonrecurring items require additional analysis, since they are unexpected and don't contribute to the understanding of normal operations. Some of these items may represent bad luck, such as damaging storms, while others may be problematic. Nonrecurring items may relate to troubled companies and poor management decisions in earlier periods. In most cases, the analyst should consider the possibility of earnings management. For example, management may have big bath incentives to write off large amounts of losses in poor performing periods when cash bonuses are not expected anyway. For example, TWA reported an operating loss for 1999 of $92.7 million. The airline then reported nonrecurring write-offs for discontinued European operations, leasehold improvements, special charges, and other items to arrive at a net loss of $353 million for the year. By taking large write-offs, earnings in future periods should be higher than without the write-offs. The managers benefit, but do the stockholders? In the case of TWA, the write-offs were ineffective, since the company filed for Chapter 11 bankruptcy in January 2001.

The largest nonrecurring item was AOL Time Warner's write-off of goodwill, based on the FASB's new pronouncement on intangibles, SFAS No. 142. AOL Time Warner wrote off $54.2 billion in the March 2002 quarter, turning a small loss of $1 million (income before the accounting change on the income statement) to a $54.2 billion net loss, roughly the gross domestic product of New Zealand. Consequently, equity fell from $152 billion to $98 billion. Was this a big bath write-off based on earnings management incentives or a required adjustment based on the application of a new pronouncement? There is more on this in Chapter 10.

## Net Income versus Comprehensive Income

Net income usually is considered the "bottom line," the most appropriate measure of profitability. Net income is a relatively complete measure, since it includes nonrecurring items in addition to normal operating income. However, not all gains and losses are included in net income, since a number of items are recorded directly to the balance sheet, resulting in the "dirty surplus" previously mentioned. SFAS No. 130 requires the presentation of comprehensive income to include net income plus all other gains and losses reported directly to stockholders' equity.

Dell reported fiscal year 2002 net income of $1,246 million plus a foreign currency translation gain of $2 million, a $39 million unrealized gain on derivatives, less a $65 million unrealized loss on investments, arriving at comprehensive income of $1,222 million. These figures are reported in the statement of stockholders' equity. These adjustments (marketable securities, derivatives, and foreign currency) probably are the most common categories of "dirty surplus." Another item that may be reported in comprehensive income is minimum pension liability adjustments. In addition to being presented within the statement of changes, comprehensive income may also be shown as part of the income statement or as a separate statement of comprehensive income.

Thus, analysts have several measures of profitability from measures of earnings before interest and taxes or other measures of continuing operations (before nonrecurring items), net income, or comprehensive income. All measures provide information and should be evaluated thoroughly. Net income is the most common measure. Comprehensive income considers all potential components. Income from continuing operations focuses on normal operations and ignores unusual items, which may best represent long-run earnings potential. All measures are subject to earnings management.

## *Pro Forma* Statements and S&P's Core Earnings

In addition to these accepted bottom-line measures (all part of GAAP), companies and analysts can "restate" earnings in various ways to emphasize certain features or components. ***Pro forma* earnings** are restated earnings, based on another perspective or based on future forecasts. When *pro forma* statements are prepared by management, the usual point is to put the company in a better light than under GAAP.

When PETCO announced first quarter 2002 financial results, the company reported that "*pro forma* earnings increased Three-fold to $0.15 per diluted share." Unfortunately, based on GAAP the company had a net loss of $29.7 million ($–0.57 a share). Earnings included an extraordinary loss, restructuring costs, legal and financing fees, and so forth. If these were excluded, then the *pro forma* earnings were $8.7 million or 15¢ a share. PETCO must present financial statements on a GAAP basis, but can explain a GAAP loss as positive earnings if certain information is ignored. It's up to the analysts and investors to determine if the restated, *pro forma* information is useful.

Unlike management-generated *pro forma* earnings, analysts generally restate earnings to make them reflect **economic reality.** Because of earnings management incentives and flexible GAAP, the claim is made that reported income numbers based on GAAP are exaggerated. In May 2002 Standard & Poor's (S&P) introduced its own measure to standardize income, called **"core earnings,"** "to return transparency and consistency to corporate reporting" (S&P press release, May 14, 2002). It includes certain expenses that are often not reported on the income statement and excludes certain income that it does not consider part of ongoing operations. Core earnings generally provides a lower earnings number than net income.

S&P's core earnings focuses on ongoing operations. The company's report on this concept (*Measures of Corporate Earnings,* Table 2) presents this table on what is included and excluded:

| Included in Core Earnings | Excluded from Core Earnings |
|---|---|
| Employee stock option grant expense | Goodwill impairment charges |
| Restructuring charges from ongoing operations | Gains and losses from asset sales |
| Write-downs of depreciable or amortizable operating assets | Pension gains |
| Pension costs | Unrealized gains/losses from hedging activities |
| Purchased research and development expenses | Merger/acquisition-related expenses |
| | Litigation or insurance settlements and proceeds |

In summary, major differences from net income are: employee stocks options are treated as an expense, pension asset investment gains are not part of income, and various gains and losses are excluded. A *Business Week* article recalculated earnings per share for General Electric, comparing reported 2001 EPS at $1.42 to core earnings, as shown in Exhibit 7.3 ("Earnings: A Closer Look," May 27, 2002, p. 37).

Thus, per share core earnings is $.31 or 21.8 percent lower than GAAP EPS. S&P's core earnings is a reasonable bottom line measure and is expected to be more conservative than net income in most cases. What's not clear is if this is a better bottom line measure. In any case, it is worth the effort to calculate a comparative measure.

## Analysis Using the Cash Flow Statement

Dell's 2002 Statement of Cash Flows (indirect method) shows (in millions):

| | |
|---|---|
| Cash Flows from Operating Activities | $3,797 |
| Cash Flows from Investing Activities | –2,260 |
| Cash Flows from Financing Activities | –2,702 |

This results in a net decrease in cash for the year of about $1.3 billion. Cash flow from operations (CFO) measures cash from operating activities beginning with net income ($1,246 billion) and adding back noncash revenues and expenses and other items. Thus, CFO for Dell is three times net income. Positive CFOs are expected in most cases. One exception may be rapidly growing companies, where negative CFOs are common. In most other cases this would be a red flag. Cash flows from investments (CFI) represents cash used to acquire assets and other investments. Consequently, a negative CFI is expected. Cash flows from financing (CFF) includes cash related to capital structure, both debt and equity. CFF is usually positive. It's negative for Dell primarily because the company repurchased outstanding shares with $3.0 billion.

Lucent Technologies showed a 2,000 percent net income of $1,219 million, reduced by a loss from discontinued operations of $462 million and down from 1999 net income of $4,789 million. But cash flow from operations suggested even more problems. Despite income from continuing operations of almost $1.7 billion, CFO was only $304 million. This was largely due to increases in accounts receivable of $1.8 billion and inventory of $2.3 billion. This is a potential red flag. Increases in accounts receivable suggest that the company was easing credit standards to customers to increase sales, with expected future increases in bad debts. Inventory increases may relate to slow-selling or obsolete items. By comparison, Lucent had a net loss of $16,198 million in 2001, but CFO was only a negative $3,421. The firm decreased both receivables and inventory.

**Free cash flows** (FCF) are a measure of cash available for discretionary uses after making required cash outlays. Although there are several potential calculations, the basic concept is cash from operations less capital expenditures required to maintain existing productive capacity. This can be estimated as cash from operations less cash from investments (CFO – CFI). Dell's FCF is 3,797 – 2,260 = $1,537 million, larger than net income. Thus, Dell is generating substantial operating cash to maintain and expand operating capacity. The results for Lucent Technologies were more serious for

**EXHIBIT 7.3 CORE EARNINGS FOR GENERAL ELECTRIC**

| | |
|---|---|
| **GE's 2001 EPS** | $1.42 |
| **Changes from Asset Sales** | –.06 |
| **Stock Options Expense** | –.04 |
| **Pension Gain** | –.19 |
| **Other Adjustments** | –.02 |
| **GE's Core Earnings** | **$1.11** |

2000. FCF was 340 – 2,480 = $–2,140 million, a negative amount almost double net income. This further highlights Lucent's operating problems.

Cash from operations ÷ total liabilities measures the company's ability to cover debt with current operating cash flows. The higher the ratio the better. The 2000 calculation for Lucent was 304 ÷ 22,620 = 1.3 percent, extremely low. By comparison, Dell's ratio for 2002 was 3,797 ÷ 8,841 = 42.9 percent. Dell seems to be generating substantial CFO to meet obligations.

Cash from operations per share can be compared to earnings per share and current stock price. Dell had 2,654 million shares outstanding at the end of fiscal year 2002, resulting in a CFO per share of 3,797 ÷ 2,654 = $1.43. This compares to a basic EPS of $0.48. Given Dell's May 1, 2002, stock price of $26.48, price to CFO per share was 26.48 ÷ 1.43 = 18.5 vs. a PE of 55.2. On a CFO basis the stock price seems considerably more attractive than on a PE basis.

The cash flow adequacy (CFA) ratio measures the ability to generate enough cash from operations for the most basic uses of cash: capital expenditures, inventory additions, and dividends. The can be calculated for the past three years (a longer period can be used) as: three-year sum of cash from operations ÷ (three-year sum of capital expenditures + inventory additions + cash dividends). Numbers usually come directly from the Statement of Cash Flows. Dell's CFA for 2000 to 2002 (Dell pays no dividends) was:

$$(3{,}797 + 4{,}195 + 3{,}926) \div [(303 + 482 + 401) + (278 + 400 = 301)] = 5.5\times.$$

A ratio of 1 or above indicates the company covered its basic cash needs internally. Consequently, Dell is in excellent shape.

The calculation for Lucent for 2000 was:

$$(304 - 962 + 1{,}452) \div [(2{,}701 + 2{,}042 + 1{,}615) + (2{,}340 + 1{,}699 + 199) + (255 + 222 + 201)] = 794 \div 11{,}274 = 0.070.$$

A ratio below 1 indicates insufficient internal cash to maintain internal growth and dividends. Consequently, Lucent's ratio of 7.0 percent is a major concern.

## Detailed Accounting Analysis

Beyond the calculations of financial ratios and other techniques, how can accounting information be used to better analyze firm performance, financial position, and future prospects? The annual reports provide additional information in notes and other sources such as management discussion and analysis. Further analysis provides information to evaluate the relative confidence to be placed on the financial statement information and the potential for earnings management. These factors can strongly influence how this information is used to arrive at projections of future performance.

The following five-step process is suggested for a detailed analysis of accounting disclosures:

1. Conduct a financial accounting overview
2. Evaluate reporting completeness
3. Evaluate the potential for earnings management
4. Consider potential red flags
5. Reevaluate or restate financial information

The basic process should be reasonably standard, but the time and effort on specific areas of analysis will vary by company and industry. Rapidly growing companies differ from troubled companies. High tech companies have different strategies and problem areas from automobile manufacturers.

## FINANCIAL ACCOUNTING OVERVIEW

The first step in the financial accounting overview is the analysis of Note 1, the accounting policies used by the company. What are the key accounting policies used by the company? Are they the same as used by competitors? Much of this note is "boiler plate," and descriptions will be similar from one company to the next. That's expected. Differences and unusual policies call for more analysis. Dell's Note 1 is similar to those of Gateway and Compaq. For example, Dell uses first-in first-out (FIFO) for inventory, capitalizes some software development costs, uses straight-line depreciation, amortizes goodwill over a period of three to eight years, recognizes revenue on sales at date of shipment to customers, and hedges foreign currency risks. Gateway and Compaq use FIFO and other similar accounting features. Revenues are recognized on sales at date of shipment. Compaq holds minority equity investments in technology areas. In summary, no major policy differences were detected.

## EVALUATE ACCOUNTING REPORTING COMPLETENESS

Since all firms are subject to GAAP and additional SEC rules, disclosures should be standardized. Right? This is generally the case, but incomplete or nonstandard reporting is possible. The key question is: does the company present the information expected, in a useful and timely form? As previously stated, quarterly earnings announcements should be reported in reasonable detail soon after the end of the quarter. Annual reports should be available within three months after the end of the fiscal year. Most of these reports are available on-line for major companies. Specific content must be perused carefully. Dell presents its 10-K as its available annual report; Gateway and Apple present annual reports separate from the 10-Ks.

Financial statement format will vary, primarily by industry. The three computer manufacturers use a standard format. Most companies, including these three, present relatively simple financial statements, with greater details in the footnotes. All have reasonable details presented in financial statements, notes, MD&A, and other components. Additional financial information is available on all companies in useful formats at their Web sites and standard financial sources.

## EVALUATE THE POTENTIAL FOR EARNINGS MANAGEMENT

Despite extensive GAAP requirements, earnings management techniques are practiced and expected. Management has incentives, especially (1) to increase current earnings to improve cash bonuses and (2) to give the appearance of continued steady earnings growth to boost stock prices. Analysts generally prefer relatively conservative accounting alternatives, including revenue recognition, preference for expensing rather than capitalizing costs, and recognizing all potential obligations. The analysis of Note 1 is an early clue to potential earnings management, if companies have policies that differ from industry counterparts. Nonrecurring items may indicate earnings management. How does management responds to bad news? Answers should be quick, accurate, and complete. Inventory policy, depreciation, revenue recognition, goodwill amortization, pension policies, and the existence of nonrecurring items are areas for analysis. Companies that are having performance problems are more likely to use earnings management.

## CONSIDER POTENTIAL RED FLAGS

**Red flags** can be found in any part of the financial analysis, but most are discovered when calculating financial ratios, common-size, and financial models. They usually come in bunches. If performance is poor, other problems usually are present. Gateway had quarterly losses in 2000, a red flag. This becomes a major focus for further analysis. Was this an unusual event, associated exclusively with the poor economy, or were problems more widespread? Gateway had a large net loss in 2001 and continues to have severe performance problems. Gateway's bonds were downgraded to junk bond status. The stock price reacted accordingly and dropped about 80 percent. Now the issue is potential bankruptcy, and Gateway becomes a potential investment buy only as a potential turnaround rather than a growth stock.

The existence of red flags doesn't automatically mean that the analysis is done and the answer is no: no loan, no investment, and sell if the stock is held as an investment. Opportunities may exist. The stock prices of the PC manufacturers dropped because of their recent problems, and a current purchase might represent a reasonable opportunity for any of the companies analyzed. However, the analyst should maintain skepticism and recommend a buy only if the evidence indicates that a company is undervalued.

What kind of red flags are likely, and what should an analyst look for? Poor performance, such as Gateway's, is a major candidate. Earnings management related to performance might include nonrecurring items, specific transactions to boost earnings such as assets sales, big increases in receivables that may suggest more aggressive revenue recognition or questionable credit sales, increasing differences between reported earnings and cash flows from operations, large fourth-quarter adjustments, or related-party transactions. DuPont's sale of major subsidiaries in 1999 and 2001 (a nonrecurring item for 1999 but part of continuing operations in 2001) greatly increased net income relative to income before these sales, a possible earnings management technique. Lucent's discontinued operations and low CFO in 2000 also indicated possible earnings management, likely related to Lucent's large net loss in 2001. Additional cash flow ratios indicated serious problems.

## REEVALUATE OR RESTATE FINANCIAL INFORMATION

Earnings management and other potential accounting distortions make financial statements less useful and reduce the confidence that analysts place in the specific financial numbers. In some cases it is possible to restate information and potentially reduce the distortion present. Earnings ratios can be restated before nonrecurring items or comprehensive income can be used rather than net income. For example, DuPont's profit ratios can be calculated both before and after the sales of major subsidiaries. Profit on a "before sale" basis suggests a poor performing firm. Using S&P's core earnings is another alternative. Restatements also can use statement of cash flow information and footnote details.

# Updating Annual Report Information

The most complete and complex accounting information for a company is presented in the annual report. The 10-K must be filed with the SEC within ninety days of the end of the fiscal year. (It is a potential red flag if companies don't meet this deadline.) Consequently, annual report information is outdated quickly. For example, Dell's fiscal year ended on February 1, 2002, and the 10-K was filed on May 1, 2001 (exactly ninety days later). The analyst has a number alternative sources for the most recent information. The tradeoff is timeliness for completeness. Companies usually announce earnings shortly after the end of the accounting period and provide at least limited financial data.

The most common reporting alternatives to the 10-K are earnings announcements; quarterly statements, including the 10-Q; the 8-K for unscheduled material events; proxy statements on items that require stockholder voting; prospectuses for new securities offerings to the public; and company announcements and updates, which can be issued at any time. This information typically can be found on the company Web site or in SEC filings or reported in the financial press.

Quarterly statements are issued after the end of the first, second, and third quarters. All reporting companies must file a 10-Q with the SEC for these quarters within 45 days of the end of the fiscal quarter. Dell's first quarter ended May 3, 2002, and its first quarter earnings announcement was issued on May 16. The announcement included a balance sheet and income statement, as well as limited analysis of results. Gateway's first quarter ended March 31, 2002, and the 10-Q was issued April 29. Comparative quarterly statements were the balance sheet, income statement, and statement of cash flows plus a limited set of footnotes.

There is usually a considerable amount of time between the end of the fiscal year and the SEC filing. However, companies typically issue an earnings announcement fairly quickly after the end of the period. Dell's earnings announcement for fiscal year 2002 was issued February 14, 2002, two weeks after the end of the fiscal year. This announcement is expected to include at least an abbreviated income statement and some details on operating results. The financial information would be unaudited and subject to change, but timely. Dell's earnings announcement included a fairly detailed income statement and balance sheet and relatively detailed information on operations and financial position. Dell's earnings announcement for the first quarter was May 16, 2002, less than two weeks after the end of the quarter.

## SUMMARY

Accounting analysis is the analysis of accounting policies and decisions beyond the financial statements. The ten elements of financial statements must be understood, and accounting analysis is usually based on these items. Firms have considerable flexibility with revenue recognition, expense recognition, and balance sheet items that need further evaluation. Revenue recognition can be conservative or aggressive, liabilities can be accurately and completely stated (or not), and nonrecurring items can be rare or common. Since managers have self-interest incentives, potential earnings management techniques must be evaluated.

The statement of cash flows restates information from a cash perspective. This adds to the analysis of both liquidity and performance and can provide information on earnings management. Part of this analysis is a set of financial ratios.

A five-step process is recommended for analysis:

1. Financial accounting overview
2. Evaluate reporting completeness
3. Evaluate the potential for earnings management
4. Consider potential red flags
5. Reevaluate or restate financial information

Accounting decisions by firms can a detriment to understanding financial statement numbers. The purpose of the detailed accounting analysis is to "undo" potential earnings management and better understand economic reality of the business firm. Accounting information also must be updated for the most recent information, using 10-Qs, quarterly earnings announcements, and other sources.

Annual reports can be updated from earnings announcements from the firms and quarterly with 10-Q filed with the SEC. Additional reports include proxy statements and 8-Ks. The business press and press announcements from the company are other possible sources of updated information.

## KEY TERMS

core earnings
earnings quality
EBIT
EBITDA
economic reality
free cash flows
matching principal
net assets
nonrecurring items
period costs
product costs
*pro forma* earnings
red flags
revenue recognition

## A SUMMARY OF FINANCIAL RATIOS

ICO Return: Income from continuing operations divided by sales, equity or total assets; alternative return ratios

CI Return: Comprehensive income divided by sales, equity or total assets; alternative return ratios

Free Cash Flows: CFO-CFI (can then be used for other liquidity-related ratios); can also be defined as CFO – capital expenditures

CFO to Liabilities: Cash Flows from Operations ÷ Total Liabilities

CFO per Share: Cash Flows from Operations ÷ Number of Shares Outstanding

Cash Flow Adequacy: CFO for past 3 years ÷ (Three Years of: Capital Expenditures + Inventory Additions + Cash Dividends)

## QUESTIONS

1. What is revenue recognition, and why is aggressive revenue recognition a potential problem when evaluating earnings quality?
2. How does the matching principle work, and what is its relationship to revenue recognition?
3. What are nonrecurring items, and why are they potential red flags?
4. Alternative definitions of the "bottom line" include EBIT, EBITDA, income from continuing operations, net income and comprehensive income. Is this complexity needed? Explain. Is S&P's core earnings a useful addition to bottom line analysis? Explain.

5. What are *pro forma* statements? When they are part of the annual report of a company, are they reliable? Why or why not?
6. Earnings management seems to be a major issue when evaluating accounting. Why?
7. How is the five-step detailed accounting analysis used to evaluate earnings management?
8. Assume that a financial analysis is made four months after the end of the fiscal year. How can the annual report information be updated to incorporate the most recent information available?

## PROBLEMS

### Problem 7.1 Financial Accounting Overview

(Problems 7.1–7.5 relate to the chemical industry.)

A review of Note 1 (Accounting Policies) of three chemical companies provides the following information:

| | DuPont | Dow | PPG |
|---|---|---|---|
| Revenue Recognition | Recognized when products are shipped and the title and risk of loss are transferred to customer | When risk and title are transferred to customer, generally at time of shipment | When goods are shipped and title to inventory passes to customers |
| Marketable Securities | Held-to-maturity | Trading, held-to-maturity, or available-for-sale | Valued at cost |
| Inventory | Last in, first out (LIFO) and first in, first out (FIFO) | LIFO, FIFO, and Average | LIFO and FIFO |
| Property, Plant, and Equipment | Recorded at cost, straight-line depreciation | Recorded at cost, straight-line depreciation | Recorded at cost, straight-line depreciation |
| Environmental Liabilities | Recorded as operating expenses when liability incurred and can be reasonably estimated | Recorded as operating expenses when probable | Probable that a liability has been incurred and amount of liability reasonably estimated |
| Hedging | Forward exchange contracts, interest rate swaps, commodities futures contracts | Interest rate swaps, foreign currency swaps, commodities futures, options, and swaps | Commodity swaps and options, foreign currency, and interest rates swaps |

Are there differences in accounting policies across these companies? Explain. Does this information suggest earnings management or the need for further analysis? Explain.

### Problem 7.2 EBIT and EBITDA

Given below are summary earnings numbers for the three chemical companies for 2001 (in millions):

| | DuPont | Dow | PPG |
|---|---|---|---|
| Net Income | $4,339 | **$–385** | $387 |
| Income from Continuing Operations | 4,328 | **–417** | 387 |
| Provision for Income Tax | 2,467 | –228 | 247 |
| Interest Expense | 590 | 733 | 169 |
| Depreciation and Amortization | 1,754 | 1,773 | 447 |

a. Based on this information, calculate EBIT and EBITDA and the percentage change over net income for EBIT [(Net Income – EBIT) ÷ Net Income] and EBITDA [(Net Income – EBITDA) ÷ Net Income].

| | DuPont | Dow | PPG |
|---|---|---|---|
| EBIT | | | |
| EBIT % Change from Net Income | | | |
| EBITDA | | | |
| EBITDA % Change from Net Income | | | |

Supplementary information for the current year (in millions):

| | DuPont | Dow | PPG |
|---|---|---|---|
| Sales | $24,726 | $27,805 | $8,169 |
| Average Total Assets | 39,872.5 | 35,753 | 8,788.5 |
| Average Equity | 13,875.5 | 10,916.5 | 3,088.5 |

b. Calculate alternative profitability ratios.

| | DuPont | Dow | PPG |
|---|---|---|---|
| Return on Sales | | | |
| Return on Total Assets | | | |
| Return on Equity | | | |

c. Based on the information above, evaluate the usefulness of EBIT and EBITDA as alternative earnings numbers.

### Problem 7.3 Alternative Bottom Line Ratios for DuPont

Given below is summary information from DuPont's income statement for the last three years (in millions).

| | 2001 | 2000 | 1999 |
|---|---|---|---|
| Sales | $24,726 | $26,268 | $26,918 |
| Income from Continuing Operations | 4,328 | 2,314 | 219 |
| Gain from Disposal of Discontinued Business (sale of Conoco) | | | 7,471 |
| Net Income | 4,339 | 2,314 | 7,690 |
| Translation Adjustment | –19 | –38 | 172 |
| Minimum Pension Liability Adjustment | –16 | 4 | 76 |
| Unrealized Gains on Marketable Securities | –24 | –21 | 51 |
| Comprehensive Income | 4,254 | 2,259 | $7,989 |

a. Calculate return on sales using (1) income from continuing operations (ICO ÷ sales); (2) net income (NI ÷ sales); and (3) comprehensive income (CI ÷ sales).

| | 2001 | 2000 | 1999 |
|---|---|---|---|
| ICO ÷ Sales | | | |
| NI ÷ Sales | | | |
| CI ÷ Sales | | | |

**b.** In 2001 DuPont sold DuPont Pharmaceuticals for a gain of $6,136 million ($3,866 million net of tax). This was recorded as a separate line item as part of continuing operations. How does this affect the analysis? (Note: consider recalculating profit excluding this transaction.) Is this an example of earnings management? Explain.

## Problem 7.4 Comprehensive Income

Given are summaries of comprehensive income tables for three chemical companies for 2001 (in millions):

| | DuPont | Dow | PPG |
|---|---|---|---|
| Net Income | $4,339 | $–385 | $387 |
| Unrealized Gains and Losses – Marketable Securities | –24 | 27 | 10 |
| Foreign Currency Translation Gains and Losses | –38 | –148 | –131 |
| Pension Liability Adjustment | –16 | –21 | –20 |
| Other | 6 | –45 | –51 |
| Comprehensive Income | $4,254 | –572 | 238 |
| Comprehensive Income ÷ Net Income | | | |

Calculate comprehensive income as a percentage of net income (comprehensive income ÷ net income) for these companies. Is this new information useful? Explain. Is it a better measure of the bottom line than net income? Explain.

## Problem 7.5 Contingencies

Given are highlights from contingency footnotes of three chemical companies.

DuPont (Note 25, 2001 annual report): Lawsuits outstanding alleging property damage from Benlate fungicide. Approximately 110 cases pending, DuPont denies claims. Environmental liability—company accrued $385 million in 2001, potential liability may be higher.

Dow (Note P, 2001 annual report): Breast implant litigation settlement from 1994 (for subsidiary Dow Corning—now bankrupt). Company still defendant in fourteen thousand breast implant product liability cases. Company considers further liability remote. Pesticide lawsuits (dibromochoropropane) primarily for ground water contamination/ Company considers further liability remote. Environmental liability—company accrued a total $444 million through 2001 (including Superfund). Asbestos claims through Union Carbide subsidiary, litigation accruals of $233 million.

PPG (Note 11, 2001 annual report): Lawsuits and claims on product liability, contract, patent, environmental, antitrust & other. Lawsuit for fixing prices on auto refinish & glass products; personal injury from exposure to asbestos (about 116,000 asbestos claims pending involving several companies). Company claims a successful defense and no responsibility. Trial court found PPG liable in 2002 in Texas, but PPG will appeal. Lost a lawsuit to Marvin Windows on breach of warranty. PPG will appeal. Environmental contingencies: PPG accrued $29 million in 2001 where liability probable as reserves (total reserves of $94 million). Possible environmental loss contingencies of $200–400 million considered reasonably possible (but unreserved).

Do these disclosures change your viewpoint on these companies as potential investments? Explain. How do these disclosures fit into (1) evaluation of earnings management, (2) red flag potential, and (3) reevaluation or restatement of financial statements?

## Problem 7.6 Cash Flow Analysis

The following information is given below for fiscal year 2001 (millions):

| | DuPont | Dow | PPG |
|---|---|---|---|
| Cash Flows from Operations | $2,419 | $1,789 | $1,060 |
| Cash Flows from Investments | 6,220* | –2,674 | –245 |
| Cash Flows from Financing | –4,043 | 831 | –816 |
| Total Liabilities | 23,443 | 25,522 | 5,250 |
| Number of Shares Outstanding | 1,089 | 981 | 168 |
| Net Income | 4,339 | –385 | 387 |
| Basic Earnings per Share | 4.18 | –0.46 | 2.30 |
| Stock Price, May 1, 2002 | 44.63 | 31.49 | 52.22 |

*Includes proceeds from sale of DuPont Pharmaceuticals for $7,798

**a.** Calculate the following:

| | DuPont | Dow | PPG |
|---|---|---|---|
| Free Cash Flows | | | |
| CFO ÷ Total Liabilities | | | |
| CFO per Share | | | |
| Price ÷ CFO per Share | | | |
| PE | | | |

The following additional information is given:

| | DuPont | Dow | PPG |
|---|---|---|---|
| CFO, 2000 | $5,070 | $1,214 | $870 |
| CFO, 1999 | 4,840 | 2,992 | 902 |
| Capital Expenditures, 2001 | 1,296 | 1,587 | 291 |
| Capital Expenditures, 2000 | 1,925 | 156 | 561 |
| Capital Expenditures, 1999 | 2,055 | 115 | 490 |
| Inventory Additions, 2001 | –362* | 34 | –187* |
| Inventory Additions, 2000 | 727 | –489* | 92 |
| Inventory Additions, 1999 | 384 | 79 | 7 |
| Cash Dividends, 2001 | 1,501 | 1,162 | 276 |
| Cash Dividends, 2000 | 1,465 | 783 | 276 |
| Cash Dividends, 1999 | 1,511 | 771 | 264 |

*Indicates decrease in inventory for the year

**b.** Calculate cash flow adequacy ratios:

| | DuPont | Dow | PPG |
|---|---|---|---|
| Cash Flow Adequacy | | | |

c. Analyze cash flows for DuPont relative to Dow and PPG.

## Problem 7.7 Financial Accounting Overview

(Problems 7.7–7.12 relate to the hotel and resort industry.)

A review of Note 1 (accounting policies) of three hotel and resort companies provides the following information:

| | Hilton | Marriott | Mandalay |
|---|---|---|---|
| Revenue Recognition | Recognized as services are performed; management fees and franchise fees based on contract | Management fees based on contract; distribution services when shipped and title passes to customer; timeshare when 10% of sales price received | Casino revenues, cash basis less incentives; hotel services as performed, less complementary allowances |
| Marketable Securities | Held-to-maturity | Trading, held-to-maturity, or available-for-sale | Held-to-maturity |
| Inventory | Time share properties | Not mentioned | FIFO and average |
| Property, Plant, and Equipment | Recorded at cost, straight-line depreciation | Recorded at cost, straight-line depreciation | Recorded at cost, straight-line depreciation |
| Insurance | Self-insured | Not mentioned | Not mentioned |
| Hedging | Forward exchange contracts, interest rate swaps | Not mentioned | Interest rate swaps |

Are there differences in accounting policies across these companies? Explain. Does this information suggest earnings management or the need for further analysis? Explain.

## Problem 7.8 EBIT and EBITDA

Given below are summary earnings numbers for the three hotel and resort companies for 2001:

| | Hilton | Marriott | Mandalay |
|---|---|---|---|
| Net Income | $174 | $236 | $53 |
| Income from Continuing Operations | 176 | 236 | 53 |
| Provision for Income Tax | 130 | 134 | 40 |
| Interest Expense | 237 | 109 | 230 |
| Depreciation and Amortization | 187 | 222 | 216 |

a. Based on this information, calculate EBIT and EBITDA and the percentage change over net income for EBIT [(Net Income – EBIT) ÷ Net Income] and EBITDA [(Net Income – EBITDA) ÷ Net Income].

| | Hilton | Marriott | Mandalay |
|---|---|---|---|
| EBIT | | | |
| EBIT % Change from Net Income | | | |
| EBITDA | | | |
| EBITDA % Change from Net Income | | | |

Supplementary information for the current year:

| | Hilton | Marriott | Mandalay |
|---|---|---|---|
| Sales | $2,150 | $10,152 | $2,639 |
| Average Total Assets | 8,962.5 | 8,672 | 4,142.5 |
| Average Equity | 1,712.5 | 3,372.5 | 1,005 |

**b.** Calculate alternative profitability ratios.

| | Hilton | Marriott | Mandalay |
|---|---|---|---|
| Return on Sales | | | |
| Return on Total Assets | | | |
| Return on Equity | | | |

**c.** Based on the information above, evaluate the usefulness of EBIT and EBITDA as alternative earnings numbers.

### Problem 7.9 Alternative Bottom Line Ratios for Hilton

Given below is summary information from Hilton's income statement for the last three years (in millions).

| | 2001 | 2000 | 1999 |
|---|---|---|---|
| Sales | $3,050 | $3,451 | $2,150 |
| Income from Continuing Operations | 166 | 272 | 176 |
| Accounting Change | | | –2 |
| Net Income | 166 | 272 | 174 |
| Translation Adjustment | –2 | –1 | –1 |
| Unrealized Gains on Marketable Securities | –9 | –17 | 25 |
| Comprehensive Income | 155 | 254 | 198 |

Calculate the return on sales using (1) income from continuing operations (ICO ÷ sales); (2) net income (NI ÷ sales); and (3) comprehensive income (CI ÷ sales).

| | 2001 | 2000 | 1999 |
|---|---|---|---|
| ICO ÷ Sales | | | |
| NI ÷ Sales | | | |
| CI ÷ Sales | | | |

### Problem 7.10 Comprehensive Income

Given are summaries of comprehensive income tables for three hotel and resort companies for 2001 (in millions):

| | Hilton | Marriott | Mandalay* |
|---|---|---|---|
| Net Income | $166 | $236 | $53 |
| Unrealized Gains and Losses – Marketable Securities | –9 | | |
| Foreign Currency Translation Gains and Losses | –2 | | |
| Pension Liability Adjustment | | –84 | 1 |
| Other | | | –16 |
| Comprehensive Income | 155 | 152 | 38 |
| Comprehensive Income ÷ Net Income | | | |

*Fiscal year ended January 2002

Calculate comprehensive income as a percentage of net income (comprehensive income ÷ net income) for these companies. Is this new information useful? Explain. Is it a better measure of the bottom line than net income? Explain

### Problem 7.11 Contingencies

Given are highlights from contingency footnotes of three hotel and resort companies.

> Hilton (Commitments & Contingencies Note, 2001 annual report): Various lawsuits are pending against us, not expected to be material.
>
> Marriott (Contingent Liabilities Note, 2001 10-K): Lawsuit from partners using RICO claims for kickbacks, concealing transactions, etc., seeking $140 million, outcome unknown.
>
> Mandalay (Note 16, 2001 10-K): Various lawsuits, including Detroit casino effort, outcome unknown.

Do these disclosures change your viewpoint on these companies as potential investments? Explain. How do these disclosures fit into (1) evaluation of earnings management, (2) red flag potential, and (3) reevaluation or restatement of financial statements?

### Problem 7.12 Cash Flow Analysis

The following information is given below for fiscal year 2001 (millions):

| | Hilton | Marriott | Mandalay |
|---|---|---|---|
| Cash Flows from Operations | $585 | $400 | $358 |
| Cash Flows from Investments | 154 | –481 | –160 |
| Cash Flows from Financing | –443 | 564 | –198 |
| Total Liabilities | 7,002 | 5,629 | 3,097 |
| Number of Shares Outstanding | 369 | 245 | 76 |
| Net Income | 166 | 166 | 53 |
| Basic Earnings per Share | 0.45 | 0.97 | 0.73 |
| Stock Price, May 1, 2002 | 16.00 | 44.03 | 7.13 |

a. Calculate the following:

| | Hilton | Marriott | Mandalay |
|---|---|---|---|
| Free Cash Flows | | | |
| CFO ÷ Total Liabilities | | | |
| CFO per Share | | | |
| Price ÷ CFO per Share | | | |
| PE | | | |

The following additional information is given:

| | Hilton | Marriott | Mandalay |
|---|---|---|---|
| CFO, 2000 | $589 | $850 | $436 |
| CFO, 1999 | 279 | 711 | 225 |
| Capital Expenditures, 2001 | 370 | 560 | 156 |
| Capital Expenditures, 2000 | 458 | 1,095 | 110 |
| Capital Expenditures, 1999 | 254 | 929 | 352 |
| Inventory Additions, 2001 | –19 | 1 | –20 |
| Inventory Additions, 2000 | –26 | –4 | 5 |
| Inventory Additions, 1999 | –30 | –17 | 0 |
| Cash Dividends, 2001 | 30 | 61 | 0 |
| Cash Dividends, 2000 | 29 | 55 | 0 |
| Cash Dividends, 1999 | 23 | 52 | 0 |

*Indicates decrease in inventory for the year

b. Calculate cash flow adequacy ratios:

| | Hilton | Marriott | Mandalay |
|---|---|---|---|
| Cash Flow Adequacy | | | |

c. Analyze cash flows for Hilton relative to Marriott and Mandalay.

## CASES

### Case 7.1 Contingencies at Microsoft

Microsoft's 1999 annual report reviewed contingencies in Note 17. Included is a discussion of the antitrust suit filed by the Justice Department and various state attorneys general in 1998. This lengthy discussion ends with: "Management currently believes that resolving these matters will not have a material impact on the Company's financial position or its results of operations" (p. 28).

On April 3, 2000, U.S. District Judge Thomas P. Jackson found that Microsoft had engaged in anticompetitive conduct in violation of antitrust laws. On June 7, he ordered the company split into two parts. On June 20, Jackson sent the Microsoft case directly to the Supreme Court, but he delayed imposing restrictions on Microsoft business practices.

Microsoft's stock chart for the year (from CNNFN) is:

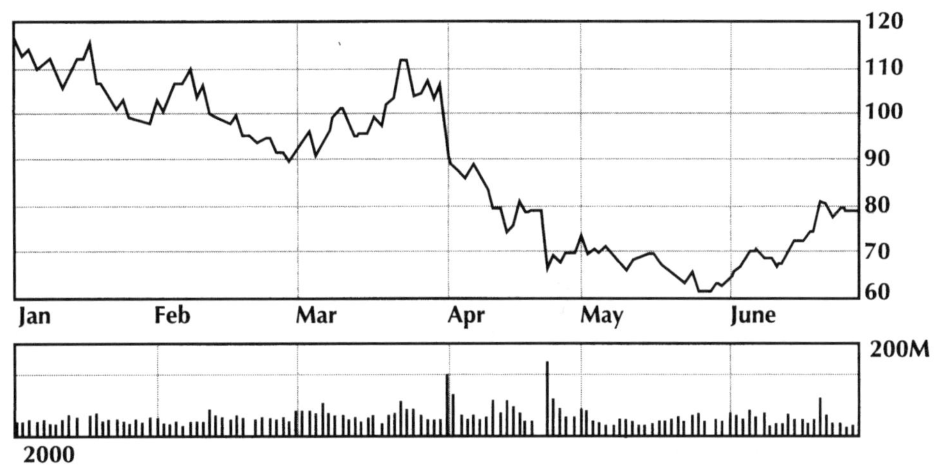


Period: January 3, 2000 – June 28, 2000

Source: www.quicken.com

Evaluate the adequacy of Microsoft's contingency disclosure, given the court actions. How did the market react to these events?

## Case 7.2 Revenue Recognition Associated with Frequent Flier Miles

Frequent flier miles were discussed earlier as a potential expense and liability. Airlines also sell mileage to hotels, car rental agencies, and credit card companies. This is a revenue item. How should these be recognized? Revenue recognition policies for five airlines follow:

| Airline | Revenue Recognition Policy |
|---|---|
| Continental Airlines | Revenue is deferred and recognized when transportation is provided. |
| AMR (American) | Revenue is deferred and recognized over the period approximating when mileage credits are used |
| UAL (United) | Revenue is recognized when the credits are sold (policy to change for future years) |
| Delta Airlines | Revenue is recognized as operating revenue at time of sale |
| US Airways Group | Revenue is recognized as other operating revenue when credits are sold |

Evaluate the revenue recognition policies or each airline given the revenue recognition criteria of the Financial Accounting Standards Board.

## Case 7.3 Restatement of Xerox Revenue

Xerox issued the following press release on June 28, 2002:

> Xerox Corporation (NYSE: XRX) announced that it expects to file today the company's 2001 10-K, which includes a restatement for the years 1997 through 2000 as well as adjustments to previously announced 2001 results. The restatement, required under the company's previously announced settlement agreement with the Securities and Exchange Commission, primarily reflects changes to the company's lease accounting under Statement of Financial Accounting Standards No. 13. As a result, adjustments have been made to the timing and allocation of equipment, service, rental and finance revenue streams. Approximately $1.9 billion of

revenue that was recognized over past years has been reversed and will be recognized in the company's future results, beginning in 2002. The monetary value of customers' contracts has not changed and there is no impact on the cash that has been received or is contractually due to be received.

For 1997 through 2001, the company reversed $6.4 billion of previously recorded equipment sale revenue offset by $5.1 billion of revenue that has been recognized and reported during the same period as service, rental, document outsourcing and financing revenues. Revenues for 1997–2001 have been reduced by 2 percent to $91 billion.

The 2001 Revised 10-K had the following reconciliation of revenue:

| | 2001 | 2000 | 1999 | 1998 | 1997 |
|---|---|---|---|---|---|
| Revenue, previously reported | $16,502 | $18,701 | $19,567 | $19,593 | $18,225 |
| Application of SFAS No. 13 | | | | | |
| Revenue allocations in bundled arrangements | 65 | (78) | (257) | (284) | (87) |
| Latin America—operating lease accounting | 187 | (58) | 57 | (358) | (461) |
| Other transactions not qualifying as sales-type leases | 73 | 57 | (60) | (119) | (152) |
| Sales of equipment subject to operating leases | 197 | 124 | (243) | 67 | (44) |
| Subtotal | 522 | 45 | (503) | (694) | (744) |
| Other revenue restatement adjustments: | | | | | |
| Sales of receivable transactions | 42 | 61 | (6) | — | — |
| South Africa deconsolidation | (66) | (72) | (71) | (60) | — |
| Other revenue items, net | 8 | 16 | 8 | (62) | (24) |
| Subtotal | (16) | 5 | (69) | (122) | (24) |
| Increase (decrease) in total revenue | 506 | 50 | (572) | (816) | (768) |
| Revenues, restated | $17,008 | $18,751 | $18,995 | $18,777 | $17,457 |

a. Calculate the percentage change in revenue for leases and total for each year ([revised – previous] ÷ previous).

| | 2001 | 2000 | 1999 | 1998 | 1997 |
|---|---|---|---|---|---|
| Leases | | | | | |
| Total | | | | | |

Pretax earnings were restated as follows.

| | 2001 | 2000 | 1999 | 1998 | 1997 |
|---|---|---|---|---|---|
| Pretax (loss) income, previously reported | $(137) | $(384) | $1,908 | $579 | $2,005 |
| Pretax income (loss), restated | $365 | $(367) | $1,288 | $(13) | $1,287 |

**b.** Calculate the dollar amount and percentage change in pretax earnings:

| | 2001 | 2000 | 1999 | 1998 | 1997 |
|---|---|---|---|---|---|
| Earning Change | | | | | |
| % Change | | | | | |

The impact on the 2001 income statement was reported as:

| | Previously Reported | As Adjusted |
|---|---|---|
| Year ended December 31, 2001 (millions) | | |
| Total Revenues | $16,502 | $17,008 |
| Sales | 8,028 | 7,443 |
| Service, outsourcing, financing and rentals | 8,474 | 9,565 |
| Total Costs and Expenses | 16,639 | 16,643 |
| Net Loss | (293) | (71) |
| Diluted Loss per Share | $ (0.43) | $ (0.12) |

**c.** Calculate the change and percentage change for these amounts:

| | $ Change | % Change |
|---|---|---|
| Total Revenue | | |
| Sales | | |
| Services, etc. | | |
| Total Costs and Expenses | | |
| Net Loss | | |

The stock chart year-to-date for Xerox compared to the Dow Jones average is:

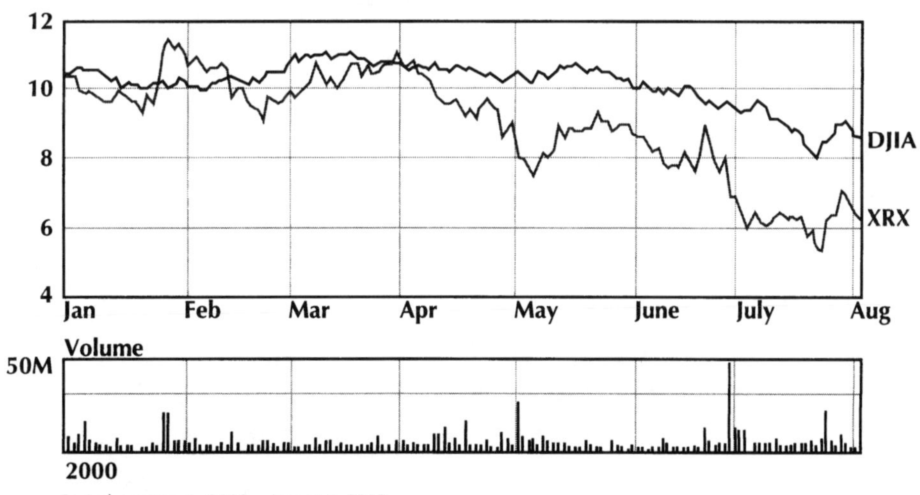


Period: January 1, 2002 – August 4, 2002

Source: www.quicken.com

**d.** Evaluate the impact of earnings management of revenue at Xerox in terms of performance and the evaluation of investors.

## ETHICS CONSIDERATIONS

### Operating Expenses Capitalized at WorldCom

On June 26, 2002, WorldCom announced that $3.8 billion in operating expenses had been misstated as capital items in the previous five quarters. Therefore, the $1.2 billion in earnings was wiped out and the company had a real loss of over $2 billion. It would have had to restate its earnings on the next 10-Q; however, the company filed for Chapter 11 bankruptcy instead on July 22. With assets listed at $107 billion, WorldCom became the largest firm ever to file for bankruptcy (beating out Enron, which had assets of $63.4 billion). At its peak in 1999, the company had a market capitalization of about $120 billion. This was earnings manipulation on a large scale, the only purpose of which was to camouflage real performance for as long as possible. Evaluate this use of manipulation from the perspective of the senior management, board of directors, investors, and the general public.

## INTERNET PROJECTS

### Project 7.1 Report Update Using the Internet

Using a company picked in earlier problems, search for the most recently available reports. Search the company's Web page for earnings or other announcements. Check the SEC filings for both 10-K and 10-Q reports. Describe the most recent information available, based on information completeness vs. timeliness.

CHAPTER 8

# Accounting Analysis: Specific Issues 1

**Objectives**

- Evaluate accounting for three categories of marketable securities and understand the different accounting requirements for each category.
- Distinguish among the alternative inventory methods and explain the use of lower-of-cost-or-market.
- Distinguish among the depreciation alternatives on fixed assets.
- Calculate and interpret the three fixed asset ratios.
- Analyze income tax allocation procedures and the use of deferred tax asset and liability accounts.
- Calculate and analyze effective tax ratios.
- Understand the use of operating and capital leases and the use of off-balance-sheet accounting. Recognize the earnings management potential of off-balance-sheet accounting.

## INTRODUCTION

Detailed information is required when evaluating the significance of many difficult accounting issues. Analysts want to determine economic reality relative to financial position and operations disclosed for a company. However, there are potential problems. Earnings management incentives could result in low-quality earnings; that is, performance seems to be driven by earnings manipulations and the analyst has a lack of confidence in the reliability of the financial statements.

This chapter considers six accounting issues for further analysis: marketable securities, inventory, fixed assets, income tax allocation, leases, and special purpose entities. These can be significant items for specific companies, and certain characteristics suggest the need for additional analysis. Quantitative analysis includes the relative significance of each category and specific ratios associated with fixed assets and effective tax rates.

## Marketable Securities

Firms with excess cash typically invest in interest-bearing **marketable securities** until the cash is needed for operations, expansion, or other purposes. Firms also can invest in equity securities in other companies for a variety of reasons. The section will focus on short-term debt instruments that are considered cash equivalents.

Accounting for marketable securities, which includes both debt and equity investments, is based on SFAS No. 115. This standard requires either cost or market, a hybrid approach, depending on the intentions of the investor. Three categories are described:

1. Debt securities **held to maturity.** If the investor has no intention of disposing of the securities before maturity, they are recorded at cost.
2. If the investor might sell the securities, they are classified as **available-for-sale** and reported at fair value. Unrealized gains and losses are reported as a separate component of stockholders' equity. This is a "dirty surplus" item and part of comprehensive income.
3. Investments that will be sold, such as held by a broker or dealer, are **trading securities** and reported at fair value. Unrealized gains and losses are reported on the income statement.

Dell recorded $3,641 million in cash and cash equivalents and $273 million in short-term investments for fiscal year-ended 2002 (total $3,914 million or 49.7 percent of current assets). Note 3 indicated $24,646 million in marketable securities (recorded at fair value), of which $4,311 million was debt securities and $355 in long-term investments. Cash and cash equivalents were recorded at cost, and investments were classified as available-for-sale securities (fair value). Net unrealized losses in investments for the year totaled $277 million and were reported in the consolidated statement of stockholders' equity as part of comprehensive income. Comparable information is shown for the three PC companies in Exhibit 8.1.

All three companies had considerable cash and short-term securities, but only Dell had considerable investments in long-term marketable securities (and losses for the year).

**EXHIBIT 8.1 MARKETABLE SECURITIES INFORMATION AND CALCULATIONS FOR THE PC COMPANIES**

| | Dell | Gateway | Apple |
|---|---|---|---|
| Cash and Cash Equivalents | $3,641 | $731 | $1,191 |
| Short-term Marketable Securities | 273 | 435 | 2,836 |
| Total Current Assets | 7,877 | 2,123 | 5,427 |
| Long-term Marketable Securities | 4,378 | 88 | 786 |
| Gains and Losses on Marketable Securities | –277 | 10 | 155 |
| (Cash and Marketable Securities) ÷ Current Assets | 49.7% | 54.9% | 74.2% |

Ford Motor Company recorded marketable securities in all three categories for the 2001 fiscal year:

| | |
|---|---|
| Trading securities, at fair value | $ 9,471 |
| Available-for-sale, recorded at fair value | 16,261 |
| Held-to-maturity, recorded at cost | 628 |
| Total (in millions) | $26,360 |

Marketable securities represented 9.5 percent of total assets. Cash and current marketable securities of $18,795 million were 51.8 percent of current assets. Given the complexity of classification used by Ford and the significant investment, there is some potential for earnings management. For example, how these securities are classified can depend in part on relative gains and losses in fair value, since there are three alternatives for recognizing these.

## INVENTORY

Basic accounting rules for inventory, and for depreciation, were established by the Committee on Accounting Procedure (CAP, the precursor to the APB) in the 1940s. Minor changes have been made since then. Multiple alternatives are allowed and rules are somewhat arbitrary. One reason for the status quo is IRS requirements, which limit the alternatives available to standard setters. For example, the Revenue Act of 1938 introduced the conformity rule, which allowed companies to use **last-in first-out** (LIFO) for tax purposes only if LIFO was also used for financial reporting.

When high costs and distinctive items are manufactured, separate inventory records are kept for each item. Most inventories are standardized such as barrels of oil and computer chips, and simplified calculations are used. The three basic methods are LIFO, **first-in first-out** (FIFO), and average methods. All are based on historical cost. Conceptually, FIFO suggests that the inventory item is perishable and that the first produced must be sold first (e.g., certain agricultural products). LIFO suggests that the most recently manufactured or acquired items are sold first. Or the inventory costs can be averaged over the period.

LIFO was allowed for tax purposes in 1938 as a compromise to businesses favoring current cost accounting. In a period of inflation the cost of goods sold (COGS) component comes close to matching current costs under LIFO, although inventory becomes understated on the balance sheet. LIFO is used when inventory prices are rising, since it usually reduces income tax expense. FIFO produces the opposite effect and tends to be used by companies when inventory costs are stable or declining, when inventory turnover is high, when there are restrictive debt covenants, and when the company needs to keep income as high as possible.

When prices are rising, LIFO results in higher COGS, lower net income, lower tax expense, higher cash flows (tax payments are lower), and lower working capital (lower inventory values more than offsets higher cash flows). The opposite is true when using FIFO.

GAAP requires the use of lower-of-cost-or-market (LCM) for inventories, one-direction current cost. Losses are recognized when inventory values decline and are booked (note that LCM cannot be used with LIFO for tax purposes). These write-downs are potential red flags to analysts.

Consider Dell's inventory compared to its competitors, as shown in Exhibit 8.2. Inventory policies are expected to be similar, since they're in the same industry. All use FIFO, primarily because of declining prices for components and finished goods. All have exceptionally low levels of inventory to current assets, a measure of production efficiency. Apple led the way with a minuscule fraction of 1 percent, including zero work in progress.

Inventory levels are expected to vary by industry. Retail chains are expected to have large inventories, as is heavy industry such as steel. Various service industries have no inventory, such as airlines. Exhibit 8.3 shows inventory comparisons for 2001 (in millions), and shows that inventory analysis is very much industry related.

## Fixed Assets (Property, Plant, and Equipment)

Historically, heavy industry has been invested in **fixed assets**—defined as property, plant, and equipment. These are recorded at acquisition cost and depreciated over the life of the assets. The purpose of depreciation is to allocate fixed asset cost over the life of the productive assets. The methods are arbitrary, but adequate for this purpose. Depreciation could represent a substantial percent of operating expense. Alternatives exist on depreciation methods, with straight line and double-declining balance being the most common. In most cases, straight line is used for financial accounting and double-declining balance (or other accelerated methods) used for tax purposes. This reduces tax expense in the early years of the assets' life, or continually for most growing companies that expand their infrastructure. Useful lives are set by IRS schedules.

**EXHIBIT 8.2 INVENTORY INFORMATION AND CALCULATIONS FOR THE PC COMPANIES**

| | Dell | Gateway | Apple |
|---|---|---|---|
| Primary Method | FIFO | FIFO | FIFO |
| Inventory (in millions) | $278 | $120 | $11 |
| Materials | 153 | 93† | 1 |
| Work in Progress | 125* | | 0 |
| Finished Goods | | 28 | 10 |
| Total Current Assets (in millions) | 7,877 | 2,123 | 5,143 |
| Inventory ÷ Total Current Assets | 3.5% | 5.7% | 0.2% |

*Dell combines work in progress and finished goods
†Gateway combines materials and work in progress

**EXHIBIT 8.3 INVENTORY TO CURRENT ASSETS FOR SELECTED COMPANIES**

| | Target (Retail) | Alcoa (Heavy Industry) | Delta Airlines (Service) |
|---|---|---|---|
| Inventory | $4,449 | $2,413 | $0 |
| Total Current Assets | 9,648 | 6,833 | 3,567 |
| Inventory ÷ Total Current Assets | 46.1% | 35.3% | 0% |

As a manufacturing company, Dell has a low level of fixed assets: property, plant, and equipment (net) for year 2002 were $826 million or 6.1 percent of total assets. The operating strategy is to assemble components manufactured by various suppliers around the world using the basic "wintel" system of the IBM de facto standard (including Microsoft software and Intel chips). Gateway's fixed assets were 20.4 percent and Apple's 9.4 percent of total assets. This suggests that Gateway has a somewhat different business strategy that involves greater direct manufacturing of components. All use straight-line depreciation for financial reporting.

Ford Motor is part of the old "rust belt" manufacturing economy with a substantial infrastructure. Net property for Ford's Automotive Services for 2001 was $33.1 billion or 37.5 percent of total Automotive assets. Note that Automotive Services represented only 31.9 percent of total assets—the bulk of the assets are in Financial Services.

Utilities have the majority of assets associated with fixed assets. For electric utilities this is the operating power base on which generating fees are based. Duke Energy, the largest utility in the *Fortune* 500, has the following fixed asset schedule (2001 fiscal year):

| | |
|---|---|
| Acquisition Cost (in millions) | $39,464 |
| Less Accumulated Depreciation | 11,049 |
| Net Fixed Assets | $28,415 |
| Total Assets | $48,375 |

Net fixed assets were 58.7 percent of total assets (acquisition cost was 81.6 percent of total assets).

Alcoa has net fixed assets of $11,982 million (accumulated depreciation of $10,933) or 42.3 percent of total assets. Note the large percentage of accumulated depreciation, indicating an older infrastructure. Older plants generally are not good news to investors, since older plants require more maintenance, are more likely to have work stoppages due to equipment failures, and are less productive than more modern plants and equipment.

Three ratios are useful in analyzing fixed asset age and useful life:

| Ratio | Definition |
|---|---|
| Average Age | Accumulated Depreciation ÷ Depreciation Expense |
| Average Age % | Accumulated Depreciation ÷ Ending Gross Investment |
| Average Depreciable Life | Ending Gross Investment ÷ Depreciation Expense |

Exhibit 8.4 shows the three items of information needed for the ratios. The PC companies' information, usually found in a fixed asset footnote, is in millions.

**EXHIBIT 8.4 DEPRECIATION INFORMATION FOR THE PC COMPANIES**

| | Dell | Gateway | Apple |
|---|---|---|---|
| **Accumulated Depreciation** | $ 612 | $ 440 | $ 360 |
| **Depreciation Expense*** | 239 | 200 | 102 |
| **Ending Gross Investment** | 1,438 | 1,048 | 564 |

* Includes amortization

The calculation of the ratios is shown in Exhibit 8.5. All three have very short estimated depreciable lives, suggesting both that the companies are relatively new and that they invest more heavily in equipment rather than plant and other buildings. Thus, although the average age percentage is rather high, the average age is 2–4 years old. Apple indicates a relatively "ancient" average age percentage of 63.8 percent (in other words, two-thirds depreciated), but the estimated average depreciable life is less than six years. Exhibit 8.6 shows the 2001 fixed asset information for the high-fixed-asset companies mentioned.

The calculations of the ratios are given in Exhibit 8.7. These fixed asset calculations demonstrate the differences across both companies and industries. The PC companies' numbers are all extremely low. The average age percentage of Duke is actually less than any of the PC companies, but the average useful life is much higher at almost thirty years. Alcoa's and Ford's fixed assets are half depreciated. The average depreciable life of assets varies from ten to thirty years. As expected for a utility, Duke Energy has the longest age life at 29.5 years. However, the average age is only 8.3 years and only 28.0 percent depreciated. Companies with the newest fixed assets are likely to be the productivity leaders.

## Income Tax Allocation

Objectives are different between financial reporting and tax regulations in the United States. Generally, managers want to minimize current taxes payable. Financial reporting

**EXHIBIT 8.5 DEPRECIATION RATIOS FOR THE PC COMPANIES**

| Ratio | Dell | Gateway | Apple |
|---|---|---|---|
| Average Age | 2.6 years | 2.2 years | 3.5 years |
| Average Age % | 42.6% | 42.0% | 63.8% |
| Average Depreciable Life | 6.0 years | 5.2 years | 5.5 years |

**EXHIBIT 8.6 DEPRECIATION INFORMATION FOR SELECTED COMPANIES**

| | Ford | Duke | Alcoa |
|---|---|---|---|
| **Accumulated Depreciation** | $27,510 | $11,049 | $10,933 |
| **Depreciation Expense** | 5,360 | 1,336* | 1,253* |
| **Ending Gross Investment** | 51,833 | 39,464 | 21,487 |

* Includes amortization

**EXHIBIT 8.7 DEPRECIATION RATIOS FOR SELECTED COMPANIES**

| | Ford | Duke | Alcoa |
|---|---|---|---|
| **Average Age** | 5.1 years | 8.3 years | 8.7 years |
| **Average Age %** | 53.1% | 28.0% | 50.1% |
| **Average Depreciable Life** | 9.7 years | 29.5 years | 17.1 years |

objectives are more complex, with user needs of economic reality tempered by earnings management incentives. GAAP (SFAS No. 109) requires **temporary tax differences,** or **interperiod tax allocation,** to be recorded as assets and liabilities. Also, nonrecurring and other items are reported net of tax, or **intraperiod tax allocation.**

## INTERPERIOD TAX ALLOCATION

Consider the following simple example, based on depreciation differences for tax and financial reporting. (Note that this example is oversimplified. Double-declining balance for tax purposes has a half-year requirement for the first year.) Assume that Bridget's Midget Widget has midget widget equipment with a four-year useful life. It costs $5,000 and has a $1,000 salvage value. Depreciation under straight-line and double-declining balance methods is shown in Exhibit 8.8.

Bridget's uses straight-line depreciation for financial reporting and double-declining balance for tax purposes, which minimizes current taxes payable. Bridget's tax calculations for year 1 under the two depreciation methods are shown in Exhibit 8.9.

Thus, there is a $525 tax difference under the two methods in year 1. For financial reporting, the tax expense of $5,950 is based on the financial reporting method (straight-line) and taxes payable of $5,425 (the amount actually owed to the IRS this year) uses double-declining balance. The journal entry for year 1 is:

| | | |
|---|---|---|
| Tax Expense | 5,950 | |
| Taxes Payable | | 5,425 |
| Deferred Tax Liability | | 525 |

**EXHIBIT 8.8 DEPRECIATION SCHEDULE COMPARING STRAIGHT-LINE AND DOUBLE-DECLINING BALANCE**

| | Straight-line | Double-declining Balance |
|---|---|---|
| **Year 1** | $1,000 | $2,500 |
| **Year 2** | 1,000 | 1,250 |
| **Year 3** | 1,000 | 250 |
| **Year 4** | 1,000 | 0 |

The difference between the two costs is a tax liability. Assuming that income before depreciation and tax is $18,000 each year, the tax for the four years is shown in Exhibit 8.10. Note that the timing differences reverses in year 3. The journal entry for that year is:

| | | |
|---|---|---|
| Tax Expense | 5,950 | |
| Deferred Tax Liability | 262.50 | |
| Taxes Payable | | 6,212.50 |

**EXHIBIT 8.9 INCOME STATEMENT INFORMATION COMPARING STRAIGHT-LINE TO DOUBLE-DECLINING BALANCE**

| | Straight-line | Double-declining Balance |
|---|---|---|
| **Income before Depreciation and Tax** | $18,000 | $18,000 |
| **Depreciation** | –1,000 | –2,500 |
| **Income before Tax** | 17,000 | 15,500 |
| **Tax (35%)** | 5,950 | 5,425 |
| **Net Income** | $11,050 | $10,075 |

**EXHIBIT 8.10 TAX LIABILITY COMPARISON USING STRAIGHT-LINE AND DOUBLE-DECLINING BALANCE**

| | Straight-line | Double-declining Balance |
|---|---|---|
| Year 1 | $5,950 | $5,425 |
| Year 2 | 5,950 | 5,862.50 |
| Year 3 | 5,950 | 6,212.50 |
| Year 4 | 5,950 | 6,300 |

In summary, the timing difference is temporary and "washes out" over the life of the depreciating asset. The deferred tax liability account for the four years is shown in Exhibit 8.11. Most firms keep growing and acquire more fixed assets. Their deferred tax liability grows over time.

Some timing differences result in a deferred tax asset. Generally, warranty costs are recorded as expenses at time of sale based on estimates from experience. However, actual warranty costs must be used for tax purposes. Since actual experience occurs with a lag, the difference between the two methods results in a deferred tax asset.

## INCOME TAX DISCLOSURES AND EFFECTIVE TAX RATES

U.S. corporations pay federal, state, and local taxes, and global companies pay taxes to foreign governments. The current federal corporate income tax rate is 35 percent, with companies attempting to reduce current taxes by such means as the accelerated depreciation illustrated above. Simultaneously, there are tax liabilities from the various other governments. Consequently, effective tax rates potentially can be quite high and analysts must consider the tax requirements as part of the financial analysis. On the other hand, corporations can be quite good at avoiding taxes and end up paying relatively little tax to the federal government in any given year. They also may pursue aggressive tax abatements to local governments. Critics refer to these and other deals with governments as corporate welfare. Perhaps such abatements are a debatable public policy issue, but they are a bonus for investors.

Considerable tax disclosure is presented in the financial statements. Deferred short- and long-term tax assets and liabilities are reported in the balance sheet. Tax expense is a separate line item in the income statement for continuing operations, while nonrecurring items are reported net of tax. An income tax note reconciles income tax amounts and provides additional information.

Dell's income statement reported an income tax expense of $485 million on income before tax of $1,731 million for fiscal year 2002. From this information the reported effective tax rate (income tax expense ÷ pretax income) can be calculated. Dell's reported effective tax

**EXHIBIT 8.11 DEFERRED TAX LIABILITY WHEN USING STRAIGHT-LINE FOR FINANCIAL ACCOUNTING AND DOUBLE-DECLINING BALANCE FOR TAX PURPOSES**

| | Journal Entry Amount | Deferred Tax Liability |
|---|---|---|
| After Year 1 | $525 Credit | $525 |
| After Year 2 | 87.50 Credit | 612.50 |
| After Year 3 | 262.50 Debit | 350 |
| After Year 4 | 350 Debit | 0 |

rate was 485 ÷ 1,731 or 28.0 percent, below the federal marginal tax rate of 35 percent. However, additional analysis is necessary on Dell's taxes, including more ratios.

Dell's income taxes are addressed in Note 4. Dell's provision for income tax is presented for the past three years. The 2002 fiscal year numbers (in millions) were:

| | |
|---|---|
| Current: | |
| Domestic | $ 574 |
| Foreign | 59 |
| Deferred | –148 |
| Provision for income tax | $ 485 |

Dell's deferred tax includes tax assets associated with inventory and warranty provisions, deferred service contract revenues, and provisions for product returns and doubtful accounts. The major tax liability is unrealized gains on investments. The effective tax rate was presented for three years. Dell's 2002 calculations were:

| | |
|---|---|
| U.S. federal statutory rate | 35.0% |
| Foreign income taxes at different rates | –6.6 |
| Other | –0.4 |
| Effective tax rate | 28.0% |

Alternative tax ratios include (1) taxes payable rate (taxes payable ÷ pretax income) and (2) taxes paid rate (income tax paid ÷ pretax income). Taxes payable are the current portion above ($574 + $59 = $633), and taxes paid was found in Note 9 on supplementary information. Tax ratios for Dell are shown in Exhibit 8.12. Dell has been successful in reducing current taxes. The actual cash outflow for tax was less than 7 percent.

In 2001, both of Dell's competitors had a net loss and essentially paid a "negative tax." Gateway had an income before tax of –$1,014 million and a tax rebate of $276 million, thus reducing the net loss for the year. Similarly, Apple had income before tax of $52 million and provision for tax of –$15 million. A tax footnote was still presented, but the ratios are not meaningful. To provide a better perspective on tax effectiveness, the tax rates for the previous year are shown in Exhibit 8.13.

The effective tax rates for Dell's competitors were higher for Gateway and lower for Apple. The taxes payable rates for Dell and Gateway were higher than their effective tax rates because deferred taxes were a net asset, and the situation was reversed for Apple. Dell's income tax paid for 2001 was –$32 million, and the taxes paid rate was –32 ÷ 2,451 = –1.0

**EXHIBIT 8.12 TAX RATE RATIOS FOR DELL**

| | Dell, 2002 |
|---|---|
| **Effective Tax Rate (Income Tax Expense ÷ Pretax Income)** | 485 ÷ 1,731 = 28.0% |
| **Taxes Payable Rate (Taxes Payable ÷ Pretax Income)** | 633 ÷ 1,731 = 36.6% |
| **Taxes Paid Rate (Income Tax Paid ÷ Pretax Income)** | 120 ÷ 1,731 = 6.9% |

**EXHIBIT 8.13 TAX RATE RATIOS FOR THE PC COMPANIES, PREVIOUS YEAR**

| | Dell, 2001 | Gateway, 2000 | Apple, 2000 |
|---|---|---|---|
| Effective Tax Rate (Income Tax Expense ÷ Pretax Income) | 958 ÷ 3,194 = 30.0% | 37.9% | 28.0% |
| Taxes Payable Rate (Taxes Payable ÷ Pretax Income) | 1,132 ÷ 3,194 = 35.4 | 51.3 | 4.2 |
| Taxes Paid Rate (Income Tax Paid ÷ Pretax Income) | –32 / 3,194 = –1.0 | 51.1 | NA |

percent. The reason for the negative number is not entirely explained in Dell's annual report, but tax loss carryforwards and unrepatriated foreign earnings are partial answers. Dell's tax rate ratios are difficult to evaluate and suggest the complexity associated with taxes. The various ratios differ from company to company. Perhaps the most useful number in this case is the effective tax rate for Dell of 28 percent in 2002 and 30 percent in 2001, which are below the statutory rate and similar to rates paid by competitors.

## LEASES

A **lease** is a contractual obligation to use an asset for a fee, with another entity owning the asset. A primary reason is **off-balance-sheet** financing, which avoids recording the asset and, especially, the obligation to pay for the asset. There are earnings management considerations here; avoiding high debt reduces the potential of technical default of debt covenants associated with leverage ratios. Footnote disclosure is the best source of information on the use of leases.

Conceptually, **operating leases** are short-term and allow the lessee use of fixed assets for a portion of its useful life. No assets or liability is recognized, and the cost is recorded as a rental expense as payments are made. This rental expense usually is constant over the lease term. The leased item is an asset of the lessor, who depreciates it over its useful life. **Capital leases** effectively transfer the risks and rewards of ownership to the lessee and are equivalent to sales with long-term financing. The assets and obligations are recorded by the lessee, who depreciates the assets and records interest expense associated with the periodic lease payments. Either straight-line or accelerated depreciation can be used. Finance charges are higher earlier in the lease, because the interest rate is based on the net present value (which declines over the useful life). Key questions are these: Under what circumstances should lease arrangements be capitalized? How are these contracts recorded on the financial statements?

Financial reporting is based on SFAS No. 13 and later statements. A lease meeting any of these four criteria is a capital lease:

1. Lease transfers ownership at the end of the lease term.
2. Bargain purchase option present.
3. Lease term equals 75 percent or more of estimated economic life.
4. Present value of minimum lease payments equals or exceeds 90 percent of the fair value of the leased property.

Since the criteria are specific, a capital lease can be avoided by not meeting these criteria. Thus, a long-term lease without transfer of ownership or bargain purchase whose term equals 74 percent of the economic life and present value of minimum lease payments are 89 percent of fair value is recorded as an operating lease. Thus, judgment of economic reality is not an issue. Critics call this "cookbook accounting" because quantitative rules rather than judgment apply.

Operating leases offer many advantages based on earnings management criteria, beginning with lower debt levels. Since capital leases have higher financing costs (and higher depreciation when accelerated methods are used) relative to the fixed payment schedules of most lease payments, operating leases result in lower interest expense and higher profitability in the early years (partially offset by potential tax advantages since these are tax-deductible items). In terms of ratios, the result of using operating leases is higher profitability and lower leverage. Since capital leases add both current and long-term liabilities, working capital and liquidity ratios are higher when using operating leases.

The three PC companies had operating leases related to production facilities and other plant and equipment. Most companies, including these three, report leases as a separate footnote. Exhibit 8.14 shows the future minimum lease payments for operating leases (not discounted) and the relative importance based on percentage of total assets.

The operating leases are off-balance-sheet and offer some earnings management potential. Assuming that 10 percent of total assets would be a minimum level for concern, this does not seem to be a major concern. Like earlier examples such as fixed assets, this is often an industrywide issue.

Airlines and retail department stores commonly lease their operating assets. Comparable lease information is presented in Exhibit 8.15 for three department stores: Target, Sears, and Federated. Based on the arbitrary 10 percent rule, Federated is a concern and further analysis is suggested, based on footnote information.

Federated reported lease information in Note 8 (2001 annual report) of: total minimum payments of capital leases of $100 million (present value $57 million) and operating

**EXHIBIT 8.14 MINIMUM LEASE PAYMENTS TO TOTAL ASSETS FOR THE PC COMPANIES**

| | Dell | Gateway | Apple |
|---|---|---|---|
| Minimum Lease Payments (millions) | $210 | $281 | $431 |
| Total Assets (millions) | 13,535 | 2,987 | 6,021 |
| Minimum Lease Payments ÷ Total Assets | 1.6% | 9.4% | 7.2% |

**EXHIBIT 8.15 MINIMUM LEASE PAYMENTS TO TOTAL ASSETS FOR SELECTED DEPARTMENT STORES**

| | Target | Sears | Federated |
|---|---|---|---|
| Minimum Lease Payments (millions) | $1,303 | $2,474 | $2,671 |
| Total Assets (millions) | 24,154 | 36,705 | 15,044 |
| Minimum Lease Payments ÷ Total Assets | 5.4% | 6.8% | 17.8% |

leases of $2,671 million. Thus, operating leases were 96.4 percent of total minimum lease payments (100 + 2,671 = 2,771 and 2,671 ÷ 2,771 = .9639). The capital leases were recorded as assets and liabilities of $57 million. The operating leases are not reported on the balance sheet and thus are subject to earnings management. The equivalent amount of operating leases can be added to assets and liabilities to recalculate leverage ratios. Assuming the same relationship of present value to total minimum payments (57 ÷ 100 = 57.0 percent), then the estimated present value of minimum lease payments of operating leases was .57 × $2,671 = $1,522 million. (This value may be overstated if operating leases are shorter than capital leases.) The adjusted calculations (in millions) are shown in Exhibit 8.16.

Higher liabilities are recognized, but equity remains unchanged, since leases involve only assets and liabilities. Thus, a high debt to equity ratio of 1.7 was made worse (to 2.0×) by this operating lease adjustment. Similarly, the debt ratio increased from 63.0 percent to 66.5 percent. A potential measure of earnings management has been found, through additional analysis of footnote details.

## Special Purpose Entities

The topic of special purpose entities (SPEs) became important with the financial collapse of Enron in 2001. In the October 2001 quarter 10-Q, Enron consolidated three SPEs in its financial statements, and income (by –$569 million) and equity (by –$1.2 billion) were restated. Then Enron filed for bankruptcy. Enron's financial collapse seemed to revolve around SPEs. Enron had hundreds, or perhaps thousands, of partnerships using SPEs, which were off-balance-sheet entities and unreported by the company before the third quarter 10-Q. What are SPEs? Can they be used to manipulate earnings on a massive scale? Are they common among America's largest corporations?

According to Financial Executives International, a **special purpose entity** is established by asset transfer to carry out some specific purpose. This entity could be a limited partnership, trust, or corporation. These can be used to access capital or manage risk. Examples include leasing, sales, and transfer of assets to an SPE, which issues debt obligations or equity for these assets, financing arrangements with third-party financial institutions, or various project development activities.

General Motors creates SPEs to redevelop closed factories with environmental problems. Airlines create SPEs to hold leases, keeping the liabilities off the balance sheet or even to **avoid disclosing them** in lease notes. Mortgage companies use them to consolidate and sell

**EXHIBIT 8.16 LEVERAGE RATIOS ADJUSTED FOR OPERATING LEASES FOR FEDERATED**

| | Balance Sheet | Operating Leases | Adjusted |
|---|---|---|---|
| **Total Liabilities** | $9,480 | $1,522 | $11,002 |
| **Total Assets** | 15,044 | 1,522 | 16,556 |
| **Total Stockholders' Equity** | 5,564 | – | 5,564 |
| **Debt to Equity** | 9,480 ÷ 5,564 = 1.7 | | 11,002 ÷ 5,564 = 2.0× |
| **Debt Ratio** | 9,480 ÷ 15,044 = 63.0% | | 11,002 ÷ 16,556 = 66.5% |

mortgages to investors. AOL Time Warner and Microsoft use SPEs to create synthetic leases to borrow funds from financial institutions to finance fixed assets or other asset acquisitions. Even Dell dabbled in SPEs, creating a joint venture with Tyco International for computer financing.

Accounting is difficult because the contracts and rules are complex and cover extremely diverse transactions. A key component is determining when SPEs have to be consolidated in the financial statements rather than off-balance-sheet (and unreported). Generally, a third party has to maintain a 3 percent equity interest at market value for the SPE to be off-balance-sheet. Apparently, this was violated at Enron, causing the restatement in the company's 10-Q. The FASB is considering tightening the rules by increasing the required equity interest to 10 percent.

## SUMMARY

This chapter reviewed six accounting issues: marketable securities, inventory, fixed assets, income tax allocation, leases, and special purpose entities. Each topic has unique issues and problems that may be specific to firms or industries. The importance of the each topic depends on the specific firm analyzed. An analysis of marketable securities is important for Dell, for example, but leases are not.

For most companies, marketable securities represent "near cash," a way to earn a return on excess cash until it is needed for capital investment or other purposes. This can be significant to analysts as an indicator of liquidity and potential for future dividends. An acquiring firm also can use this near cash. Firms typically use either LIFO or FIFO for inventory. This choice depends on changing prices, industry practice, and business strategy characteristics. Fixed assets are the productive assets of a firm, particularly important to most manufacturing firms. The amount of fixed assets and relative age can be important to analysts to evaluate manufacturing productivity. Income tax allocation is important to understand the effective tax rates that the firm pays. This is an area of earnings management particularly important to the investor, since tax payments should be minimized. A lease is an important earnings management tool. Where substantial operating leases are present, analysts may recalculate how these affect leverage ratios. A special purpose entity is another form of off-balance-sheet accounting that became well known only with the Enron debacle.

## KEY TERMS

available-for-sale securities
capital lease
deferred tax
first-in first-out
fixed assets
held-to-maturity securities
interperiod tax allocation
intraperiod tax allocation
last-in first-out
lease
marketable securities
off-balance-sheet financing
operating lease
special purpose entities
temporary tax difference
trading securities

## A SUMMARY OF FINANCIAL RATIOS

Average Age: Accumulated Depreciation ÷ Depreciation Expense
An estimate of how long the average fixed asset has been held

Average Age %: Accumulated Depreciation ÷ Ending Gross Investment
An estimate of the relative amount of fixed asset depreciation

Average Depreciable Life: Ending Gross Investment ÷ Depreciation Expense
An estimate of the average useful life of the average fixed asset

Effective Tax Rate: Income Tax Expense ÷ Pretax Income
A measure of the effective accounting tax rate (including local and foreign taxes)

Taxes Paid Rate: Income Tax Paid ÷ Pretax Income
A measure of the amount of tax paid in cash this year to the IRS and other taxing authorities

Taxes Payable Rate: Taxes Payable ÷ Pretax Income
Income tax payable to IRS and other taxing authorities

## QUESTIONS

1. Why are there three categories of marketable securities? How is each accounted for?
2. What are the alternative ways that inventory is accounted for? Why are alternatives allowed? What is lower-of-cost-or-market?
3. Straight-line depreciation is usually used for accounting purposes and accelerated depreciation for tax purposes. Why?
4. Why is the relative age of fixed assets important? How can age be estimated?
5. What is the statutory corporate tax rate? Why would the effective rate differ from the statutory rate? How can this be evaluated?
6. What is off-balance-sheet financing? Why is this related to earnings management?

## PROBLEMS

### Problem 8.1 Marketable Securities in the Chemical Industry

(Problems 8.1–8.5 relate to the chemical industry.)

Given below are the marketable securities totals and other asset information for two chemical companies for 2001 (in millions) [Note: PPG reports financial instruments but does not break out marketable securities]:

| | DuPont | Dow |
|---|---|---|
| Marketable Securities | $85 | $44 |
| Policy | Available-for-sale and held-to-maturity | Available-for-sale and held-to-maturity |
| Total Current Assets | 14,801 | 10,308 |
| Total Assets | 40,319 | 35,515 |

a. Calculate marketable securities as a percentage of current assets and total assets.

| | DuPont | Dow |
|---|---|---|
| Marketable Securities ÷ Total Current Assets | | |
| Marketable Securities ÷ Total Assets | | |

b. Evaluate the use of marketable securities accounted for both companies.

### Problem 8.2 Inventory in the Chemical Industry

Given below are the 2001 inventory and related information for three chemical companies (in millions).

| | DuPont | Dow | PPG |
|---|---|---|---|
| Inventory | $4,681 | $4,440 | $904 |
| Finished Goods, Work in Progress | 3,837 | 3,569 | 622 |
| Materials | 844 | 871 | 166 |
| Policy | LIFO, FIFO | LIFO, FIFO, Average | LIFO |
| Total Current Assets | 14,801 | 10,308 | 2,703 |

**a.** Calculate inventory as a percent of total current assets and finished goods and materials to total inventory percentages.

| | DuPont | Dow | PPG |
|---|---|---|---|
| Inventory ÷ Total Current Assets | | | |
| Finished Goods ÷ Inventory | | | |
| Materials ÷ Inventory | | | |

**b.** Analyze differences of ratios and policy based on business strategy and other financial analysis factors.

## Problem 8.3 Depreciation in the Chemical Industry

Given below are 2001 depreciation-related numbers for three chemical companies (in millions).

| | DuPont | Dow | PPG |
|---|---|---|---|
| Accumulated Depreciation | $20,491 | $22,311 | $4,101 |
| Depreciation Expense | 1,320 | 1,595 | 375 |
| Ending Gross Investment | 33,778 | 35,890 | 7,153 |

**a.** Calculate the following fixed asset age and useful life ratios:

| | DuPont | Dow | PPG |
|---|---|---|---|
| Average Age | | | |
| Average Age % | | | |
| Average Depreciable Life | | | |

**b.** Analyze these ratios with particular focus on what they mean across the three companies in this industry.

## Problem 8.4 Income Tax Allocation in the Chemical Industry

Given below is 2001 income tax-related information for three companies in the chemical industry:

| | DuPont | Dow | PPG |
|---|---|---|---|
| Pretax Income | $6,844 | $–613 | $666 |
| Income Tax Expense | 2,467 | –228 | 247 |
| Taxes Payable | 1,880 | – | 241 |

**a.** Calculate the reported effective tax rate and taxes payable rate for these companies.

| | DuPont | Dow | PPG |
|---|---|---|---|
| Reported Effective Tax Rate | | | |
| Taxes Payable Rate | | | |

**b.** Analyze these ratios for each company.

## Problem 8.5 Operating Leases in the Chemical Industry

Given below is 2001 lease information. Calculate minimum lease payments ÷ total assets.

| | DuPont | Dow | PPG |
|---|---|---|---|
| Minimum Lease Payments (millions) | $905 | $1,833 | $275 |
| Total Assets (millions) | 40,319 | 35,515 | 8,452 |
| Minimum Lease Payments ÷ Total Assets | | | |

**a.** Do any of these ratios raise a concern (10 percent or above)?

## Problem 8.6 Depreciation in the Hotel and Resort Industry

(Problems 8.6–8.8 relate to the hotel and resort industry.)

Given below are 2001 depreciation-related numbers for three hotel and resort companies (in millions).

| | Hilton | Marriott | Mandalay |
|---|---|---|---|
| Accumulated Depreciation | $1,154 | $559 | $1,162 |
| Depreciation Expense | 391 | 222 | 216 |
| Ending Gross Investment | 5,065 | 3,489 | 4,212 |

**a.** Calculate the following fixed asset age and useful life ratios:

| | Hilton | Marriott | Mandalay |
|---|---|---|---|
| Average Age | | | |
| Average Age % | | | |
| Average Depreciable Life | | | |

**b.** Analyze these ratios with particular focus on what they mean across the three companies in this industry.

## Problem 8.7 Income Tax Allocation in the Hotel and Resort Industry

Given below is 2001 income tax-related information for three companies in the hotel and resort industry:

| | Hilton | Marriott | Mandalay |
|---|---|---|---|
| Pretax Income | $250 | $370 | $93 |
| Income Tax Expense | 77 | 134 | 40 |
| Taxes Payable | 29 | 54 | 12 |

**a.** Calculate the reported effective tax rate and taxes payable rate for these companies.

| | Hilton | Marriott | Mandalay |
|---|---|---|---|
| Reported Effective Tax Rate | | | |
| Taxes Payable Rate | | | |

**b.** Analyze these ratios for each company.

## Problem 8.8 Operating Leases in the Hotel and Resort Industry

Given below is 2001 lease information. Calculate minimum lease payments ÷ total assets.

| | Hilton | Marriott | Mandalay |
|---|---|---|---|
| Minimum Lease Payments (millions) | $233 | $2,190 | $124 |
| Total Assets (millions) | 8,785 | 9,107 | 4,037 |
| Minimum Lease Payments ÷ Total Assets | | | |

**a.** Do any of these ratios raise a concern (10 percent or above)?

**b.** Calculate debt ratios and recalculate them adding operating leases for Marriott.

| | Balance Sheet | Operating Leases | Adjusted |
|---|---|---|---|
| Total Liabilities | $5,629 | $2,190 | |
| Total Assets | 9,107 | 2,190 | |
| Total Stockholders' Equity | 3,478 | | |
| Debt to Equity | | | |
| Debt Ratio | | | |

## CASES

### Case 8.1 Investment Income and Loss at Microsoft

Microsoft reported the following investment income information (in millions) in its 2001 10-K:

| | Year Ended June 30 | | |
|---|---|---|---|
| | 1999 | 2000 | 2001 |
| Dividends | $ 118 | $ 363 | $ 377 |
| Interest | 1,030 | 1,231 | 1,808 |
| Net recognized gains/(losses) on investments | 803 | 1,732 | (2,221) |
| Investment income/(loss) | $1,951 | $3,326 | $ (36) |

Microsoft went from a large gain of $3.3 billion to a $36 million loss. This had a dramatic effect on the income statement (selectively presented):

| | Year Ended June 30 | | |
|---|---|---|---|
| | 1999 | 2000 | 2001 |
| Revenue | $19,747 | $22,956 | $25,296 |
| Operating Income | $10,010 | $11,006 | $11,720 |
| Losses on Equity Investees and Other | (70) | (57) | (159) |
| Investment Income/(Loss) | 1,951 | 3,326 | (36) |
| Income before Income Taxes | 11,891 | 14,275 | 11,525 |
| Provision for Income Taxes | 4,106 | 4,854 | 3,804 |
| Income before Accounting Change | 7,785 | 9,421 | 7,721 |
| Cumulative Effect of Accounting Change (net of income taxes if $185) | — | — | (375) |
| Net Income | $ 7,785 | $ 9,421 | $ 7,346 |

a. The result of the investment loss in 2001 is that net income declined despite increasing operating income. Calculate common-size information below:

| | 1999 | 2000 | 2001 |
|---|---|---|---|
| Revenue | | | |
| Operating Income | | | |
| Investment Income (loss) | | | |
| Net Income | | | |

b. Evaluate the impact of Microsoft's investment income (loss) on overall operating results. Note that Microsoft also reported a $1.2 billion unrealized holding loss (net of taxes of $351 million) as part of comprehensive income. How important is this in determining a buy or sell equity decision?

## Case 8.2 Leases in the Airline Industry

Given below are minimum operating lease payments and total assets for three airlines (in millions).

| | American (AMR) | United (UAL) | Northwest (NWAC) |
|---|---|---|---|
| Minimum Lease Payments (millions) | $17,661 | $24,538 | $8,610 |
| Total Assets (millions) | 32,841 | 25,197 | 12,955 |
| Minimum Lease Payments ÷ Total Assets | | | |

**a.** Calculate the minimum lease payments ÷ total assets. Are these a concern? Explain.

**b.** Calculate the present value to total minimum payments for capital leases and using this percentage estimate the present value of operating lease payments:

| | AMR | UAL | NWAC |
|---|---|---|---|
| Capital Lease | $2,557 | $3,161 | $1,104 |
| Present Value of Capital Leases | 1,740 | 2,180 | 586 |
| PV to Total Capital Lease % | | | |
| Minimum Operating Lease Payments | 17,661 | 24,538 | 8,610 |
| Estimated PV of Operating Lease Payments | | | |

**c.** Given the information below, calculate the debt to equity and adjusted debt to equity ratios, assuming the present value of minimum lease payment for operating lease is the same as capital leases for each company.

| | AMR | UAL | NWAC |
|---|---|---|---|
| Total Liabilities, Balance Sheet | $27,690 | $22,164 | $13,386 |
| Total Assets, Balance Sheet | 32,841 | 25,197 | 12,955 |
| Operating Lease (at estimated PV) | | | |
| Total Liabilities, Adjusted | | | |
| Total Assets, Adjusted | | | |
| Total Stockholders' Equity | 5,373 | 3,033 | –431 |
| Debt to Equity Ratio | | | |
| Debt to Equity, Adjusted | | | |

**d.** Analyze the impact of operating leases on the debt to equity ratio. Does this suggest earnings management? Explain.

## Case 8.3 What Happened at Enron?

Enron was the seventh largest of the *Fortune* 500 early in 2001 and considered a successful energy-related company using derivatives to buy and sell not only energy, but also virtually anything, including the weather. The stock chart indicates the market reaction to Enron in 2001:

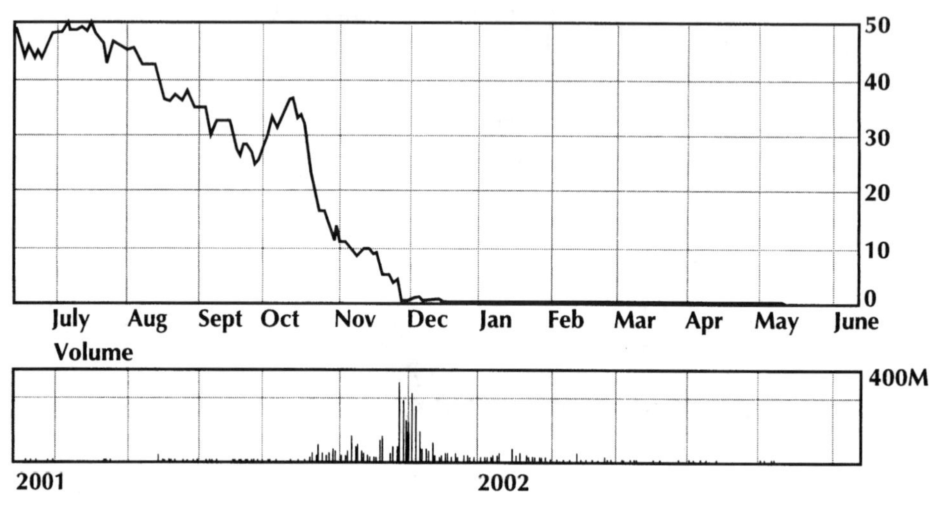


Period: June 13, 2001 – June 13, 2002
Source: www.hoovers.com

From a high over $90 in August 2000, the stock continued down over the entire second half of the year until Enron declared bankruptcy in early December 2001 when the price essentially went to zero. What happened? Until the third quarter 10-Q the financial statements weren't much help. They showed a profitable company, although leverage was high. What was not obvious was earnings manipulation on a vast scale. The third quarter results were announced October 16 and the 10-Q was released November 19. The SEC announced a formal investigation on October 31. Financial statements were restated from 1997, resulting in a decrease in stockholders' equity over $1 billion. The company filed for Chapter 11 bankruptcy on December 2. Note the large drop-off in price beginning around the October 16 announcement.

Here are highlights of Enron's third quarter 10-K. These tables show the restated net income and stockholders' equity since 1997 (in millions). Calculate the difference and percentage difference for each year.

| | 1997 | 1998 | 1999 | 2000 | 2001* |
|---|---|---|---|---|---|
| Net Income, Reported | $105 | $703 | $893 | $979 | $829 |
| Net Income, Restated | 26 | 564 | 635 | 842 | 869 |
| Difference | | | | | |
| % Difference | | | | | |

*First two quarters only

| | 1997 | 1998 | 1999 | 2000 | 2001* |
|---|---|---|---|---|---|
| Equity, Reported | $5,618 | $7,048 | $9,570 | $11,470 | $11,740 |
| Equity, Restated | 5,309 | 6,600 | 8,724 | 10,289 | 10,787 |
| Difference | | | | | |
| % Difference | | | | | |

*First two quarters only

Here is the third quarter earnings summary for 2001, compared to the same quarter in 2000 (in millions, restated). Calculate common-size percentages.

| | Third Qtr. 2001 | Third Qtr. 2001, Common-size | Third Qtr. 2000 | Third Qtr. 2000, Common-size |
|---|---|---|---|---|
| Revenues | $46,877 | | $29,834 | |
| Operating Income | –917 | | 533 | |
| Net Income | –644 | | 282 | |

Here is Enron's third quarter balance sheet summary for 2001, compared to December 31, 2000 (in millions, restated). Calculate common-size percentages.

| | Third Qtr. 2001 | Third Qtr. 2001, Common-size | Dec. 31, 2000 | Dec. 31, 2000, Common-size |
|---|---|---|---|---|
| Cash | $1,001 | | $1,240 | |
| Current Assets | 24,847 | | 30,027 | |
| Total Assets | 61,783 | | 64,926 | |
| Current Liabilities | 27,003 | | 28,741 | |
| Total Liabilities | 17,407 | | 18,452 | |
| Stockholders' Equity | 9,598 | | 10,289 | |

Calculate Enron's basic financial ratios, including cash, current, debt to equity, return on sales, and return on equity:

| | Third Qtr., 2001 | Earlier Period |
|---|---|---|
| Cash Ratio | | |
| Current Ratio | | |
| Debt to Equity | | |
| Return on Sales | | |
| Return on Equity | | |

Rate Enron from 1 to 10 based on this abbreviated quantitative analysis. How useful are the financial numbers in predicting the potential for bankruptcy for Enron? Based on the information presented, what is the most useful indicator of severe financial problems?

## ETHICS CONSIDERATIONS

### What Happened at Enron: Corporate Governance and Accounting

The chief executives at Enron all resigned and testified before Congress, although most of them took the fifth. The company's bankruptcy represented a financial failure. Who was at fault? Chairman and CEO Kenneth Lay claimed that all accounting issues were accepted by auditor Arthur Andersen. Many of the special purpose entities that now seem deceptive were developed by Andersen as part of its consulting operation. How much of the blame should be placed on Enron's corporate executives versus Arthur Andersen?

## INTERNET PROJECTS

### Project 8.1 Evaluating Enron

Access Enron's third quarter 10-Q and 2000 10-K and any other Enron information found on the Internet. Use the 10-Q to evaluate the three special purpose entities that were restated. Describe the use of earnings manipulation by Enron. Why was it effective? Can financial reporting be improved to better predict the presence of earnings manipulation? Explain.

CHAPTER 9

# Accounting Analysis: Specific Issues 2

**Objectives**

- Analyze the use of stock options, especially for management incentives and potential stock dilution.
- Evaluate business and geographic segments on the overall financial performance of companies.
- Understand the history and importance of foreign currency for multinationals and evaluate foreign currency accounting characteristics.
- Distinguish between defined benefit and defined contribution pension plans and analyze the impact of underfunded defined benefit plans.
- Evaluate other postemployment benefit obligations and the impact of these obligations.
- Defined various derivative instruments and analyze the potential impact based on their potential hedging or speculation functions. What potential risk is involved?

## INTRODUCTION

This chapter covers five complex but important accounting issues: stock options, segment information, foreign currency, pension and other postemployment benefits, and derivatives. The importance of these issues varies by company and industry. The most significant issue for Dell is stock options. Typical of high tech companies, Dell has issued a considerable number of options to managers and employees. On the other hand, Dell does not have a defined benefit pension plan; consequently, pensions are a minor issue for Dell. Dell does have foreign operations; so foreign currency and geographic segment information need analysis. Dell makes extensive use of derivatives.

Other companies would have a different set of significant accounting issues. For example, DuPont and other chemical companies have several divisions, so business segment information is important. They also have defined benefit plans and other postemployment benefit liabilities. On the other hand, stock options exist but are not extensive.

## STOCK OPTIONS

Corporations often grant managers and employees stock options. **Stock options** permit the holder to purchase stock at a set price (called the exercise price) over some fixed time period. The most common price is the closing market price of the stock at the option's issue date. At that price, the company records no compensation expense. SFAS No. 123 requires considerable disclosure of stock option information in the notes, but generally no compensation expense is recorded.

The use of stock options is a form of management compensation, widely used by high tech companies. Why would managers prefer stock options rather than higher salaries or cash bonuses? The advantage of the options is that is it a one-direction participation in the success of the company. As the stock price rises, the value of the options rises. If the stock price plummets, the manager does not exercise the option. Stock prices of high tech companies have a history of substantial stock increases (also many failures), so options have the potential to generate substantial wealth.

Why would a corporation want to use options? First, as long as the exercise price is the market price or higher at issue date, no compensation expense is recorded. In terms of the income statement, it is a zero-cost form of management compensation. Second, it should make the managers' incentives identical to the owners'. Since the benefit of options is future ownership and managers increase options value by increasing the value of the company, management incentives parallel owner incentives. Firms can recruit successful and high-priced executives and retain existing managers and employees by issuing stock options liberally. This can be a useful "low-compensation" strategy for high tech start-ups.

Is there is downside to stock options? Yes. There is a cost and it's recognized when evaluating stockholders' equity. Stock options that are issued and exercised increase number of shares outstanding, or stock dilution. The earnings of the company have to be spread over more shares, decreasing EPS. The impact of future dilution is estimated by using diluted EPS. If this has a potentially large effect on future EPS, it can represent a potential red flag. Since no compensation expense is recorded in most cases, the use of stock options can be considered a form of earnings management.

Dell summarizes its stock option plans, and related incentives, including stock appreciation rights, in Note 6 for fiscal year 2002. According to the note, stock options are generally issued at fair market value and must be exercised within ten years of the grant date. At the beginning of the fiscal year, 344 million shares were optioned. During the year sixty-three million shares were exercised, fifty-seven million canceled and an additional 126 million shares granted, resulting in 350 million options outstanding at year-end (with an average exercise price of $26.36). Exhibit 9.1 considers stock options outstanding at the end of the fiscal year relative to shares outstanding (in millions) for the PC competitors. Dell

**EXHIBIT 9.1 STOCK OPTION ANALYSIS FOR THE PC COMPANIES**

| | Dell | Gateway | Apple |
|---|---|---|---|
| **Stock Options Outstanding** | 350 | 64 | 97 |
| **Shares Outstanding** | 2,654 | 324 | 551 |
| **Options to Shares Outstanding** | **13.2%** | **19.8%** | **27.6%** |

stock option usage was lower but comparable to competitors. All the options indicate substantial potential dilution and should concern analysts.

Because of the potential dilution, pro forma calculations of the impact of stock options if treated as expenses are important. The necessary information is available from the stock options footnote, which presents Net Income—Reported compared to Net Income—*Pro Forma*, which includes the estimated stock options expense as if included in income. Dell's net income would have been reduced by $964 million, a reduction of $0.27 per share, as shown in Exhibit 9.2.

S&P's core earnings calculation includes stock options as an expense. This would be a major concern for these companies, all of which are affected. Dell's income fell by 77.4 percent, making it a much less attractive investment. Apple's options expense would move the earnings from a small loss to a substantial loss. Little impact was noticed on Gateway's earnings, since the substantial stock price decline left little potential benefit for exercising options.

## SEGMENT REPORTING

Large corporations have complex operations, often operate in separate **industry segments,** and have foreign components known as **geographic segments.** These are combined in the financial statements, but SFAS Nos. 14 and 133 require additional disclosure. According to SFAS No. 14, reportable segments are components that have 10 percent of any of three characteristics: total revenues, combined operating profits, or combined identifiable assets. Foreign operations also require disclosure, based on 10 percent criteria for sales or identifiable assets.

Dell reports limited industry segments (Note 10), but it does disclose geographic segments for: (1) the Americas, (2) Europe, and (3) Asia, the Pacific, and Japan. Summary geographic disclosures for fiscal year 2002 (in millions) are given in Exhibit 9.3.

**EXHIBIT 9.2 PRO FORMA NET INCOME ANALYSIS BASED ON STOCK OPTIONS FOR THE PC COMPANIES**

| | Dell | Gateway | Apple |
|---|---|---|---|
| **Net Income—Reported** | $1,246 | $–1,034 | $–25 |
| **Net Income—*Pro Forma*** | 282 | –1,106 | –396 |
| **Difference** | –964 | –72 | –371 |
| **% Difference** | –77.4% | NM | NM |

**EXHIBIT 9.3 OPERATIONS BY GEOGRAPHIC REGION FOR DELL**

| | Americas | Europe | Asia, Pacific, and Japan |
|---|---|---|---|
| **Total Sales** | $21,760 | $6,429 | $2,979 |
| **Operating Income** | 1,742 | 377 | 152 |
| **Identifiable Assets** | 2,319 | 1,220 | 499 |

To compare geographic segments, financial ratios include: (1) operating income ÷ total sales, a measure of profitability (also called operating profit margin); and (2) total sales ÷ identifiable assets, an efficiency measure (similar to total asset turnover). In both cases, the higher the better. The ratios for Dell are given in Exhibit 9.4.

Both ratios indicate better performance and efficiency for the Americas, compared to Europe and Asia. Since geographic expansion is part of Dell's business strategy, analysts should have some concern for the relative success of foreign operations.

Industry segments for Dell are Business and Consumer, but only for the American operations, which are summarized in Exhibit 9.5. The business segment was larger (79.4 percent) of sales and more profitable at 8.6 percent.

Gateway withdrew from most international operations in 2001, but it still reported three geographic regions: (1) United States; (2) Europe, the Middle East, and Africa (EMEA); and (3) Asia and the Pacific (A-P). The 2001 disclosures (in millions) are given in Exhibit 9.6.

Geographic segment ratios for Gateway are given in Exhibit 9.7. These ratios suggest that U.S. operations had lower returns and efficiency than Dell. Foreign segments had negative returns, red flags for both EMEA and A-P. It is clear why Gateway abandoned these foreign markets. Note that Gateway had over $1 billion in restructuring and other nonsegment expenses related to the withdrawal from foreign operations.

Like Dell, Gateway provided consumer and business segments, but only for the U.S. market. Those segments (in millions) are summarized in Exhibit 9.8. Gateway had a roughly even split between business (44.0 percent) and consumer (56.0 percent) sales, but the business segment was much more profitable.

Apple provides geographic segment information, but only sales by product as industry information. Geographic information in 2001 (in millions) is summarized in Exhibit 9.9.

Geographic segment ratios for Apple are given in Exhibit 9.10. Considerable variability existed by geographic segment. Unlike its competitors, the American market had the lowest operating return on sales, while Japan had the largest at 13.7 percent. Efficiency varied, with asset turnover from 3.5× for Other to 16.2× for Japan.

Segment reporting can be difficult to evaluate because presentation can vary substantially from one company to another and operations can vary by both operating and geographic segment. Since SFAS Nos. 14 and 133 allow considerable reporting flexibility, information may be difficult to compare across companies.

## FOREIGN CURRENCY

Until 1971 the United States and most of the world were on a gold exchange standard. The U.S. dollar was tied to gold—the **gold standard**—and currency fluctuations were minor. President Richard Nixon took America (and, effectively, the world) off the gold standard.

**EXHIBIT 9.4 OPERATING PERFORMANCE RATIOS BY GEOGRAPHIC SEGMENT FOR DELL**

| | Americas | Europe | Asia, Pacific, and Japan |
|---|---|---|---|
| **Operating Income ÷ Total Sales** | 8.0% | 5.9% | 5.1% |
| **Total Sales ÷ Identifiable Assets** | 9.4 | 5.3 | 6.0 |

The result is that all currencies are now **fluctuating currencies** and behave as commodities. Thus, fluctuating currencies have been an additional complexity for global business for thirty years. Since foreign currencies fluctuate to the U.S. dollar, the value of foreign assets and liabilities and operations for U.S. firms fluctuates in amount. The key question is how to value foreign operations and net assets and maintain economic reality. Because there are alternative valuation methods, compromises and additional disclosures are needed.

Because the FASB was formed in 1973, foreign currency became one of the first issues to deal with; in fact, SFAS No. 1 was on foreign currency. Two significant standards have been issued by the FASB (SFAS Nos. 8 and 52), and current accounting practices rest primarily on SFAS No. 52, Foreign Currency Translation.

SFAS No. 8 was considered conceptually sound, but finance officers of multinational corporations found it unworkable in practice.

## OPERATING IN FOREIGN COUNTRIES

Because this is a global economy, large U.S. corporations are multinational, often with more revenues from foreign operations than domestic operations. The advantages are new markets, growth opportunities and diversifying geographic risks. However, drawbacks exist. Foreign operations increase business and legal complexity. Companies face country-specific risks such as takeovers by hostile governments as well as foreign currency risks.

If a U.S. company has operations in Goravia (not a real country), what accounting issues exist? Goravian GAAP differs from U.S. GAAP, but year-end adjustments can compensate for these differences. The Goravian operations will have assets and liabilities denominated in Goravian gumboz (GG). How are GG translated into U.S. dollars for parent company financial reporting? Assets and liabilities can be short-term or long-term. They can also be **monetary items** (denominated in currency such as receivables or bonds)

**EXHIBIT 9.5 OPERATING ANALYSIS OF INDUSTRY SEGMENTS FOR DELL**

| | Business | Consumer |
|---|---|---|
| **Sales** | $17,275 | $4,485 |
| **Operating Income** | 1,482 | 260 |
| **Operating Income ÷ Sales (Operating Return on Sales)** | 8.6% | 5.8% |

**EXHIBIT 9.6 OPERATIONS BY GEOGRAPHIC SEGMENT FOR GATEWAY**

| | U.S. | EMEA | A–P |
|---|---|---|---|
| **Net Sales** | $5,528 | $229 | $322 |
| **Operating Income** | 235 | **–53 RF** | **–38 RF** |
| **Segment Assets** | 2,930 | 34 | 21 |

**EXHIBIT 9.7 OPERATING PERFORMANCE RATIOS BY GEOGRAPHIC SEGMENT FOR GATEWAY**

| | U.S. | EMEA | A–P |
|---|---|---|---|
| **Operating Income ÷ Net Sales** | 4.3% | **–23.1 RF** | **–11.9 RF** |
| **Net Sales ÷ Identifiable Assets** | 1.9 | 6.7 | 15.3 |

**EXHIBIT 9.8 OPERATING ANALYSIS OF INDUSTRY SEGMENTS FOR GATEWAY**

| | Business | Consumer |
|---|---|---|
| **Sales** | $2,431 | $3,097 |
| **Operating Income** | 220 | 15 |
| **Operating Income ÷ Sales (Operating Return on Sales)** | 9.0% | 0.5% |

and **nonmonetary items** (such as inventory or fixed assets). Operations as stated on the income statement are financial flows, representing events over the accounting period. These items can be stated at currency exchange rates from historical cost dates (if fixed assets were acquired in 1986, the 1986 exchange rate would be used), at the balance sheet date (for fiscal year ended December 31, 2001, the exchange rate at that date), or an average rate for the year.

Since currencies can fluctuate dramatically, different methods can substantially change results. Consider balance sheet results. If the foreign currency falls (the Goravian gumboz relative to the U.S. dollar, in this case), the foreign assets fall in value, but the liabilities are to be paid back in "cheaper dollars." Thus, matching foreign operation assets and liabilities (resulting in net assets of $0) is a natural hedge. This is unusual, and virtually all foreign operations have net asset positions subject to foreign currency fluctuations.

## ACCOUNTING FOR FOREIGN CURRENCY

**Foreign currency translation** represents the valuations of foreign financial positions and operations to U.S. dollars. The rules are somewhat complex and only the basics will be covered here. For most foreign operations the local currency is the functional currency. Thus, for the Goravian operations, the GG is the functional currency. The all-current method is used for translation. Under this method, all assets and liabilities are translated at the year-end balance sheet exchange rate. Common stock is translated using the translation rate at the date the common stock was issued. Retained earnings include the translated gains and losses from

**EXHIBIT 9.9 OPERATIONS BY GEOGRAPHIC SEGMENT FOR APPLE**

| | Americas | Europe | Japan | Other |
|---|---|---|---|---|
| **Net Sales** | $2,996 | $1,249 | $713 | $405 |
| **Operating Income** | 133 | 68 | 98 | 42 |
| **Segment Assets** | 334 | 137 | 44 | 115 |

**EXHIBIT 9.10 OPERATING PERFORMANCE RATIOS BY GEOGRAPHIC SEGMENT FOR APPLE**

| | Americas | Europe | Japan | Other |
|---|---|---|---|---|
| **Operating Income ÷ Net Sales** | 4.4% | 5.4% | 13.7% | 9.6% |
| **Net Sales ÷ Identifiable Assets** | 9.0× | 9.1× | 16.2× | 3.5× |

the income statement. All revenue and expenses use the weighted average exchange rate for the year. Unrealized foreign currency translation gains and losses are recorded as part of comprehensive income and a separate component of stockholders' equity.

Assume that the exchange rate at the beginning of the year is $1 = 1 GG; the average exchange rate for the year is $1 = 1.5 GG, and the year-end rate is $1 = 2 GG. The Goravian operation was started at the beginning of the year. Year-end financial statements, in GG and translated to U.S. dollars, are shown in Exhibit 9.11.

This example is oversimplified, but it indicates how foreign operations are translated and how unrealized foreign currency gains and losses are calculated.

The alternative approach is the temporal method, where the dollar is the functional currency and used when foreign operations are subject to hyperinflation. Under this method, nonmonetary assets and liabilities are translated using the historical rate. Monetary assets and liabilities are translated using the current rate. On the income statement, cost of goods sold and depreciation are based on the historical rate; all other items use the weighted average. Translation gains and losses are reported on the income statement.

## FINANCIAL REPORTING

Dell's segment reporting footnote indicates that over 30.2 percent of sales occur in Europe and Asia. Therefore, foreign operations are substantial. Note 1 indicates that foreign operations are translated using either the temporal or the all-current method. Dell's statement of stockholders' equity indicates a foreign currency translation gain of $2 million for fiscal

**EXHIBIT 9.11 FOREIGN CURRENCY TRANSLATION FROM GORAVIAN GUMBOZ TO U.S. DOLLARS**

| | Goravian Gumboz | Translation Rate | U.S. Dollars |
|---|---|---|---|
| **Cash** | 20 GG | 1 GG: $2 | $40 |
| **Inventory** | 30 | 1 GG: $2 | 60 |
| **Fixed assets (net)** | 50 | 1 GG: $2 | 100 |
| **Total** | 100 GG | | $200 |
| **Accounts payable** | 30 GG | 1 GG $2 | $60 |
| **Common stock** | 60 | 1 GG: $1 | 60 |
| **Retained earnings** | 10 | | 15 |
| **Unrealized translation gain** | | | 35* |
| **Total** | 100 GG | | $200 |

*Ending net asset position of $70 less (beginning net assets of $30 + net income of $15 = $45) = $35. This is part of comprehensive income.

| | Goravian Gumboz | Translation Rate | U.S. Dollars |
|---|---|---|---|
| **Sales** | 200 GG | 1 GG: $1.50 | $300 |
| **COGS** | 120 | 1 GG: $1.50 | 180 |
| **Other Expenses** | 70 | 1 GG: $1.50 | 105 |
| **Net Income** | 10 GG | | $ 15 |

year 2002. The company uses foreign currency exchange contracts to hedge its foreign currency risks (Note 1). Over three years (2000–02) Dell had an accumulated foreign currency translation gain of $16 million. This was an immaterial item for Dell, as it amounted to only 1.3 percent of net income for 2002. Both Gateway and Apple also used a combination of temporal and all-current methods for translations, but both had small foreign currency losses as part of comprehensive income.

## Pension and Other Postemployment Benefits

Pensions provide accumulated retirement resources. Larger employers generally provide some form of pension benefit. The two major categories are: (1) defined contribution plans and (2) defined benefit plans. Firms with defined benefit plans and a large labor force have substantial obligations, which may or may not be fully funded. Many corporations also have committed themselves to obligations for benefits to employees who have retired early or have left the firm for other reasons. SFAS No. 106 requires these commitments to be recognized as liabilities.

### PENSION PLANS

A **pension** is a long-term contract to provide retirement benefits to employees. Under a defined contribution plan, the employer makes periodic cash payment, usually based on a percentage of salary and often allowing or requiring employee matching. The funds are invested and the accumulated total investments plus portfolio earnings represent the retirement "fund," which is usually under the direction of the employees. The employer does not promise a specific level of future benefits. Defined benefit plans specify the retirement benefits the employee will receive. These are determined based on some definition of "final salary" and length of service. Assume Grumpy Gary's Gilmos's defined benefit plan provides 2 percent of final salary retirement benefit for each year of service. Foreman Mitty Smitty retires after thirty years, making a final salary of $60,000; therefore his annual retirement benefit is .02 × 30 × $60,000 or $36,000. The employer manages (directly or indirectly) the retirement fund, making cash payments to provide pension assets that are invested in securities portfolios and handling all pension-related calculations and journal entries. Thus, the employer specifies the commitment and bears all the risk associated with meeting the pension obligations. Pension plans come under federal law, based primarily on the Employee Retirement Income Security Act of 1974 (ERISA).

The incentives for pension plans are substantial. Pension contributions from both employer and employee are income tax–exempt, and earnings on invested pension assets are deferred until the employee retires. Only the employee is taxed, based on the pension annuities received by the employee—usually at a lower tax rate than when the employee was working. The pension can be considered part of the employee compensation package and may make employees more loyal to the company. In a defined benefit plan, dual incentives can exist. The company may feel paternalistic for employees' retirement and thus guarantee retirement benefits. Also, pension accounting for defined benefit plans allows considerable judgment, and there is substantial room for earnings management techniques.

## DEFINED CONTRIBUTION PLANS

**Defined contribution plans** are based on employer cash contributions, usually a percentage of an employee's salary and often tied to an employee's contributions. The employee typically has investment portfolio options and generally has "ownership" of the portfolio after some vesting period. The company essentially has no additional obligations.

Dell has a defined contribution complying with Section 401(k) of the Internal Revenue Code; a 401(k) plan is common in high tech industries. Dell matches 100 percent of employee contributions, up to 3 percent of the employee's salary. The compensation cost to the company was $40 million is fiscal year 2002 (0.1 percent of revenue). Gateway also has a 401(k) plan, allowing employees to contribute up to 20 percent of their compensation and receive a 50 percent matching contribution up to 6 percent of compensation. The 2001 compensation cost was $7.8 million (0.1 percent of revenue). Apple's 401(k) plan was similar, costing $17 million in 2001 (0.3 percent of revenue).

## DEFINED BENEFIT PLANS

In a **defined benefit plan,** the employer has an obligation for benefits to be paid to employees and for plan assets that are invested to meet these future obligations. Since the commitments are long-term and obligations recognized have to be estimated based on many assumptions, pension accounting is quite complex. This section will review only highlights and focus on basic investor concerns. Accounting procedures are based on SFAS No. 87, with additional disclosure requirements from SFAS No. 132.

The plan assets of a defined benefit plan represent the investment portfolio used to fund current and future retirement benefits. The plan assets essentially include the plan assets at the start of the period, plus or minus the earnings on investments (including changes in fair value), plus cash contributions from the employer, minus retirement payments. Pension plan liabilities include liabilities at the start of the period, plus increases in liabilities due to employee services and the passage of time, plus or minus actuarial gains and losses (based on assumptions), minus retirement payments. The net balance is recorded as a single item, either net plan assets (an overfunded plan) or liabilities (an underfunded plan).

Each year the employer recognizes the pension expense, which includes annual service cost and interest cost (roughly the increase in the projected benefit obligation) plus or minus other adjustments. Essentially, the entry is a debit to pension expense and a credit to pension liability. Some or all of this liability can be funded as a payment to the plan's assets. The entry would be a debit to pension liability and a credit to cash. The cash payment in any given year is based entirely on the discretion of management and, thus, is subject to earnings management incentives.

The most basic actuarial calculations are **accumulated benefit obligation** (ABO) and **projected benefit obligation** (PBO). ABO is the present value of amounts the employer expects to pay retired employees based on employee service to date and current-year salary levels, as adjusted by various actuarial assumption including average retirement age, mortality rates after retirement, number of employers staying to retirement, and so on. PBO is the same as ABO, except projections are based on expected future salary at retirement, rather than on the current salary. PBO will be higher than APO, except at employee retirement, when they will converge. How close ABO is to PBO is an indication of the average age of the workforce.

### REPORTING DEFINED BENEFIT PENSION PLANS

General Electric (GE) reported its pension plan under Note 6 of its 2001 annual report. Disclosure is extensive, but the most important information to the analyst usually is the net asset or liability position; that is, by how much the pension plan is over- or underfunded. According to Note 6, GE has a PBO at year-end of $30.4 billion and plan assets at fair value of $45 billion. The difference ($45 – $30.4) is the funding status of $14.6 billion. With other adjustments, the net pension asset position recorded in the balance sheet was $12.4 billion (as part of All Other Assets, see Note 17). This represented 2.5 percent of total assets. The pension expense for 2001 was a negative $1.5 billion (recorded as a "net cost reduction"), since service and interest costs were more than offset by expected return on plan assets. In other words, the pension plan increased net income by $1.5 billion for the year. Therefore, the pension plan for GE is a net positive. It should be noted that many analysts consider increase in net income from defined benefit plans a form of earnings management. Thus, these "pension gains" are excluded in S&P's core earnings (see Chapter 7).

Thanks largely to the rapid stock price increases in the 1990s, most defined benefit plans are overfunded. The amount of overfunding can be "claimed" by the company, but this is taxable. More likely, the overfunding would be used to decrease or eliminate further cash contributions to be pension plan. However, a corporate raider could use the excess funding to partially fund an acquisition of the firm.

### OTHER POSTEMPLOYMENT BENEFITS

Historically, companies have provided certain benefits to early retired and other former employees, with the costs recognized on a cash or pay-as-you-go basis. The most common benefits were health and other forms of insurance (the retired employees would be covered by Medicare at age 65). Particularly as health care costs rose, these obligations have increased. SFAS No. 106 requires the **other postemployment benefits** (OPEB) to be recognized as liabilities, with accounting and reporting similar to pensions. OPEB can be funded with invested assets, just like pensions, but they tend to be unfunded because the accrued OPEB costs are not tax deductible.

None of the three PC companies recognized any OPEB obligations in the most recent annual report. GE recognized a $2.7 billion OPEB liability as part of All Other Liabilities on its balance sheet. Note 5 shows accumulated postretirement benefit obligations of $6.8 billion and $1.8 billion in plan assets (note other adjustments of over $2 billion). An OPEB expense of $615 million for 2001 was disclosed. The $2.7 billion liability represents 2.5 percent of total assets, and the 2001 expense equals 0.5 percent of revenues. Therefore, this is only a minor concern for GE.

## DERIVATIVES

A **derivative** is a financial contract derived from another contract. Common derivatives involve options, futures, interest rates, foreign currency, and mortgage-backed securities. The two basic derivative strategies are hedging (attempting to reduce or manage various market risks) and speculating (essentially gambling on specific outcome or market direction). Derivative contracting is a huge part of financial markets and gets complex quickly. Since more and more companies rely on various derivatives, they are subject to financial analysis.

Definitions of common derivatives are:

- *Options*—Agreement that gives a party the right to buy (call) or sell (put) a specific quantity at a specific price (exercise price) until a specified maturity date. Examples include commodities, currencies, or stocks.
- *Forward contract*—Agreement between buyer and seller to deliver an asset in exchange for cash (or financial instrument) at a fixed price on a specific future date. Examples include commodities, currencies, or stocks.
- *Futures contract*—Standardized forward contract traded on an organized exchange. Same examples as with a forward contract.
- *Swaps*—Contract to exchange one series of payments for another.
- *Interest Rate swaps*—Contract to exchange fixed for floating interest payments on bonds and other credit agreements.
- *Currency swaps*—Agreement to make payments in one currency in exchange for the obligations in another currency.

Accounting for derivatives is based on SFAS No. 133. All derivatives are recorded on the balance sheet at fair value. Speculative derivatives are recorded at fair value, and unrealized gains and losses are recorded to net income. Accounting for hedging derivatives is more complex. In some cases, hedging derivative unrealized gains and losses can be recorded as part of comprehensive income ("dirty surplus") rather than net income (e.g., cash flow hedges such as floating-for-fixed interest rate swaps and certain foreign currency hedges).

Dell uses foreign currency hedging; interest rate swaps; equity options and forwards, and put obligations on Dell stock. These were described in various notes in the 2002 10-K, which is available at www.wiley.com/college/giroux. Note 1 states: "The adoption of [SFAS No. 133] did not have a material effect on the Company's financial condition or results of operations."

Note 3, "Long-term Debt and Interest Rate Risk Management," states that Dell used

> purchased option contracts and forward contracts as cash flow hedges to protect against the foreign currency exchange risk. ... The Company also uses forward contracts to economically hedge monetary assets and liabilities, primarily receivables and payables denominated in foreign currency. At February 2, 2002 the Company held purchased option contracts with a notional amount of $2 billion, a net asset value of $83 million and an unrealized deferred gain of $11 million, net of tax. ... The Company held forward contracts with a notional value of $2 billion, a net asset vale of $95 million and a net unrealized gain of $28 million, net of taxes.

Note 3 also states:

> Concurrent with the issuance of the Senior Notes and Senior Debentures [fixed rate], the Company entered into interest rate swap agreements converting the Company's interest rate exposure from a fixed rate to a floating rate basis to better align the associated interest rate characteristics to its cash and investment portfolio.

*The Wall Street Journal* (June 19, 2001) reported that Dell received premiums of $750 million over the previous 12 months associated with the puts. Under these put obligations, a premium paid to Dell (the buyer) allowed the sellers to sell Dell shares back to the company at an average price of $47. Since Dell's stock price dropped ($26.48 at May 1, 2002), Dell was forced to buy at this "inflated price."

## SUMMARY

This chapter reviewed five accounting issues requiring further analysis: stock options, segment reporting, foreign currency translation, pensions and other postemployment benefits, and derivatives. The impact of any of these items tends to be specific to the firm or industry. For an analyst looking at Dell, the first three issues and derivatives required analysis, but pension and other postemployment benefits were nonissues.

Stock options allow managers and employees the right to buy firm stock at a set price. Normally, no compensation expense is recorded, but substantial stock dilution is possible. Complex multinationals tend to have several divisions and major operations in foreign countries. Segment footnotes provide limited information on these activities. Foreign currency translation recognizes most holding gains and losses directly to stockholders' equity. Pension and other postemployment benefits are obligations to past and present employees. Major net liabilities may be a concern for these items. Derivatives are contracts that can be used for hedging or speculation. These should be analyzed for potential financial risks.

## KEY TERMS

accumulated benefit obligation
defined benefit plan
defined contribution plan
derivative
fluctuating currencies
foreign currency translation
geographic segments
gold standard
industry segments
monetary items
nonmonetary items
other postemployment benefit obligations
pension
projected benefit obligation
segment reporting
stock options

## QUESTIONS

1. What are stock options, and why are they issued to managers and employees?
2. Why is segment reporting useful when evaluating large corporations? Are current requirements adequate? Explain.
3. How did the gold standard work when it was the standard for all currency valuations? Compare that to the current system of fluctuating currencies. Is the present system superior or not? Explain.
4. How do fluctuating currencies influence foreign operations for domestic firms? What are the current accounting procedures for these activities?
5. What are the relative merits of defined benefit and defined contribution pension plans? What are the major accounting requirements for defined benefit plans?
6. Are other postemployment benefits liabilities? Explain. Contrast OPEB accounting with pension accounting.
7. What is a derivative? How can derivatives be used for hedging? How can derivatives be used for speculation? Can financial analysts effectively evaluate the risks associated with derivatives?

# PROBLEMS

## Problem 9.1 Impact of stock options and equity dilution in the chemical industry

(Problems 9.1–9.5 relate to the chemical industry.)

a. These three chemical companies have the following stock options outstanding and total common shares outstanding. Calculate the options to shares outstanding percentage for fiscal year 2001 (in millions).

| | DuPont | Dow | PPG |
|---|---|---|---|
| Stock Options Outstanding | 73.2 | 67.5 | 14.5 |
| Shares Outstanding | 1,089 | 981 | 168 |
| Options to Shares Outstanding | | | |

b. The chemical companies have the following net income and *pro forma* income numbers. Calculate the difference and percentage difference as if stock options were treated as an expense.

| | DuPont | Dow | PPG |
|---|---|---|---|
| Net Income—Reported | $4,339 | $–385 | $387 |
| Net Income—*Pro forma* | 4,249 | –444 | 24 |
| Difference | | | |
| % Difference | | | |

c. How significant is the potential dilution of stockholders' equity for these three chemical companies? Explain

## Problem 9.2 Segment Reporting in the Chemical Industry

DuPont reports the following industry segment information for 2001 (in millions):

| | Agriculture and Nutrition | Nylon | Perform Coating and Polymers | Pharma-ceuticals | Pigments and Chemicals | Polyester | Specialty Fibers | Specialty Polymers |
|---|---|---|---|---|---|---|---|---|
| Sales | $4,316 | $2,696 | $5,754 | $ 902 | $3,554 | $1,895 | $4,418 | $3,875 |
| Operating Income* | 19 | –75 | 319 | 3,924† | 439 | –349 | 356 | 372 |
| Net Assets | 8,998 | 1,838 | 3,927 | 102 | 1,732 | 2,042 | 4,213 | 2,513 |

*After tax

†Sold in 2001 for a gain

a. Calculate (1) operating income ÷ sales and (2) sales ÷ net (identifiable) assets.

| | Agriculture and Nutrition | Nylon | Perform Coating and Polymers | Pharma-ceuticals | Pigments and Chemicals | Polyester | Specialty Fibers | Specialty Polymers |
|---|---|---|---|---|---|---|---|---|
| Operating Income ÷ Sales | | | | | | | | |
| Sales ÷ Net Assets | | | | | | | | |

**b.** DuPont has the following geographic segment information for 2001 (in millions). Calculate sales ÷ net assets.

| | North America | EMEA | Asia-Pacific | South America |
|---|---|---|---|---|
| Sales | $13,613 | $6,431 | $3,657 | $1,025 |
| Net Assets | 8,952 | 2,732 | 1,292 | 311 |
| Sales ÷ Net Assets | | | | |

**c.** Evaluate the segment reporting information for DuPont.

## Problem 9.3 Foreign Currency in the Chemical Industry

**a.** Here are 2001 U.S. and foreign sales (in millions). Calculate foreign sales ÷ total sales.

| | DuPont | Dow | PPG |
|---|---|---|---|
| U.S. Sales | $12,054 | $11,725 | $5,469 |
| Foreign Sales | 12,672 | 16,080 | 2,700 |
| Foreign ÷ Total Sales | | | |

**b.** Calculate foreign currency translation as a percentage of net income and comprehensive income (stated in millions) for 2001.

| | DuPont | Dow | PPG |
|---|---|---|---|
| Net Income | $4,339 | $–385 | $387 |
| Translation Adjustment | –19 | –148 | –131 |
| Comprehensive Income | 4,254 | –982 | 238 |
| Translation Adjustment ÷ Net Income | | | |
| Translation Adjustment ÷ Comprehensive Income | | | |

**c.** Calculate cumulative foreign currency translations adjustment for the past three years and as a percent of 2001 comprehensive income (stated in millions).

| | DuPont | Dow | PPG |
|---|---|---|---|
| Translation Adjustment, 2000 | $–38 | $–188 | $–120 |
| Translation Adjustment, 1999 | $172 | $–121 | $ –40 |
| Total Translation Adjustment, 1999–2001 | | | |
| Total Translation Adjustment ÷ 2001 Comprehensive Income | | | |

**d.** Compare foreign operations and translation adjustments on the operations of these chemical companies.

## Problem 9.4 Defined Benefit Pension Plans Analysis for Chemical Companies

Given below is pension information for 2001 from pension footnotes and other sources (in millions). Benefit obligation at year-end is total pension liability based on PBO; pension expense is net periodic benefit cost; prepaid pension cost/obligation is net pension asset or liability position on the balance sheet (reported as part of other assets or other liabilities, if negative).

| | DuPont | Dow | PPG |
|---|---|---|---|
| Benefit Obligation at Year-end | $18,769 | $11,341 | $2,414 |
| Fair Value of Plan Assets | 17,923 | 11,424 | 2,423 |
| Net Periodic Benefit Cost (pension expense) | –374 | –95 | –53 |
| Prepaid Pension Cost (liability) | 1,693 | 177 | 825 |
| Total Assets | 40,319 | 35,515 | 8,452 |
| Net Income | 4,339 | –385 | 387 |

**a.** Calculate funding status (over- or underfunded, based on prepaid pension cost—O or U), pension obligation ÷ total assets; prepaid pension cost (obligation) ÷ total assets; and pension expense ÷ net income. Note: Net pension benefit cost is a negative expense for these companies (increases net income), because of positive expected return on plan assets.

| | DuPont | Dow | PPG |
|---|---|---|---|
| Over- or Underfunded? | | | |
| Benefit Obligation ÷ Total Assets | | | |
| Prepaid Pension Cost ÷ Total Assets | | | |
| Pension Expense ÷ Net Income | | | |

**b.** Compare the pension plans of the three chemical companies. Are there any concerns? Explain.

## Problem 9.5 Other Postemployment Benefits in the Chemical Industry

OPEB numbers are similar to defined benefit plans and are usually included in the same footnote(s). The 2001 year-end OPEB balances are stated below (in millions):

| | DuPont | Dow | PPG |
|---|---|---|---|
| OPEB Benefit Obligation | $5,832 | $2,035 | $823 |
| Fair Value of Plan Assets | 0 | 266 | 0 |
| Net Amount Recognized | –5,633 | –1,736 | –586 |
| Net Benefit Cost (pension expense) | 347 | 214 | 64 |

**a.** Calculate fund status (over- or underfunded, based on net amount recognized), OPEB obligation to total assets, net amount recognized to total assets, and OPEB expense (net benefit cost) to net income.

| | DuPont | Dow | PPG |
|---|---|---|---|
| Funding Status | | | |
| OPEB Obligation ÷Total Assets | | | |
| Net Amount Recognized ÷ Total Assets | | | |
| OPEB Expense ÷ Net Income | | | |

**b.** Evaluate OPEB obligations for these chemical companies and the relationship to pension obligations. Are there any concerns? Explain.

## Problem 9.6 Impact of Stock Options and Equity Dilution in the Hotel and Resort Industry

(Problems 9.6–9.10 relate to the hotel and resort industry.)

a. Hotel and resort companies have the following stock options outstanding and total common shares outstanding. Calculate the options to shares outstanding percentage for fiscal year 2001 (in millions).

| | Hilton | Marriott | Mandalay |
|---|---|---|---|
| Stock Options Outstanding | 33 | 20 | 10 |
| Shares Outstanding | 369 | 245 | 68 |
| Options to Shares Outstanding | | | |

b. Hotel and resort companies have the following net income and *pro forma* income numbers. Calculate the difference and percentage difference as if stock options were treated as an expense.

| | Hilton | Marriott | Mandalay |
|---|---|---|---|
| Net Income—Reported | $166 | $236 | $54 |
| Net Income—*Pro forma* | 150 | 187 | 43 |
| Difference | | | |
| % Difference | | | |

c. How significant is the potential dilution of stockholders' equity for these three hotel companies? Explain

## Problem 9.7 Segment Reporting in the Hotel and Resort Industry

a. Hilton reports the following industry segments information for 2001 (in millions).

| | Revenues | Operating Income | Assets |
|---|---|---|---|
| Hotel Ownership | $1,886 | $474 | $4,925 |
| Managing and Franchising | 120 | 113 | 680 |
| Timeshare | 144 | 22 | 315 |

b. Calculate (1) operating income ÷ revenues and (2) revenues ÷ assets.

| | Operating Income ÷ Revenues | Revenues ÷ Assets |
|---|---|---|
| Hotel Ownership | | |
| Managing and Franchising | | |
| Timeshare | | |

c. Evaluate the industry segment information for Hilton.

## Problem 9.8 Segment Reporting in the Hotel and Resort Industry

Marriott reports the following industry segment information for 2001 (in millions):

| | Revenues | Operating Income | Assets |
|---|---|---|---|
| Full-service Lodging | $5,238 | $294 | $3,394 |
| Select-service Lodging | 864 | 145 | 931 |
| Extended-service Lodging | 635 | 55 | 366 |
| Time Share | 1,049 | 147 | 2,107 |
| Senior Living | 729 | –45 | 690 |
| Distribution Services | 1,637 | –6 | 216 |

**a.** Calculate (1) operating income ÷ revenues & (2) revenues ÷ assets.

| | Operating Income ÷ Revenues | Revenues ÷ Assets |
|---|---|---|
| Full-service Lodging | | |
| Select-service Lodging | | |
| Extended-service Lodging | | |
| Time Share | | |
| Senior Living | | |
| Distribution Services | | |

**b.** Evaluate the industry segment information for Marriott.

## Problem 9.9 Foreign Currency in the Hotel and Resort Industry

**a.** Calculate foreign currency translation as a percentage of net income and comprehensive income (stated in millions) for 2001.

| | Hilton | Marriott | Mandalay |
|---|---|---|---|
| Net Income | $166 | $236 | $53 |
| Translation Adjustment | 0 | –14 | 0 |
| Comprehensive Income | 155 | 230 | 38 |
| Translation Adjustment ÷ Net Income | | | — |
| Translation Adjustment ÷ Comprehensive Income | | | — |

**b.** Calculate cumulative foreign currency translations adjustment for the past three years and as a percentage of 2001 comprehensive income (stated in millions).

| | Hilton | Marriott | Mandalay |
|---|---|---|---|
| Translation Adjustment, 2000 | $–1 | $–10 | $0 |
| Translation Adjustment, 1999 | –1 | –18 | 0 |
| Total Translation Adjustment, 1999–2001 | | | |
| Total Translation Adjustment ÷ 2001 Comprehensive Income | | | |

**c.** Compare foreign operations and translation adjustments on the operations of these companies.

### Problem 9.10 Defined Benefit Pension Plans Analysis for Hotel and Resort Companies

Here is pension information for 2001 from pension footnotes and other sources (in millions). Benefit obligation at year-end is total pension liability based on PBO; pension expense is net periodic benefit cost; prepaid pension cost/obligation is net pension asset or liability position on the balance sheet (reported as part of other assets or other liabilities if negative). (Marriott reported no information.)

| | Hilton | Mandalay |
|---|---|---|
| Benefit Obligation at Year-end | $ 248 | $ 55 |
| Fair Value of Plan Assets | 249 | 0 |
| Net Periodic Benefit Cost (pension expense) | 16 | 8 |
| Prepaid Pension Cost (liability) | 1 | –15 |
| Total Assets | 8,875 | 4,037 |
| Net Income | 166 | 53 |

**a.** Calculate funding status (over- or underfunded, based on prepaid pension cost—O or U), pension obligation ÷ total assets; prepaid pension cost (obligation) ÷ total assets; and pension expense ÷ net income. Net pension benefit cost is a negative expense for these companies (it increases net income) because of positive expected return on plan assets.

| | Hilton | Mandalay |
|---|---|---|
| Over- or Underfunded? | | |
| Benefit Obligation ÷ Total Assets | | |
| Prepaid Pension Cost ÷ Total Assets | | |
| Pension Expense ÷ Net Income | | |

**b.** Compare the pension plans of the two hotel and resort companies. Are there any concerns? Explain.

## CASES

### Case 9.1 Evaluating Stock Options and Pensions at General Electric

Chapter 6 discusses S&P's core earnings method and uses General Electric (GE) as an example for restating earning information. Two major items in core earnings are stock options (to be added to net income) and net cost of pensions (to be deducted from net income).

The following tables present GE's stock options information for 2001. Calculate (1) the dilution percentage (options outstanding ÷ total shares outstanding) and (2) pro forma difference percentage (net income difference ÷ net income reported):

| Options Outstanding | Common Stock Outstanding | Dilution % |
|---|---|---|
| 354 million | 9,926 million | |

| Net Income Reported | Net Income *Pro Forma* | Difference | Difference % |
|---|---|---|---|
| $13,684 | $13,388 | | |

GE had a net asset position for pension funding (i.e., the company is overfunded) of $12,415 million for 2001. The fair value of pension assets was $45,006 compared to PBO of $30,423. In addition, the income statement reported net cost reduction from pension funding of $1,480 million. Primarily, the expected return on plan assets was higher than pension expenses by this amount.

Restate earnings using these two components of S&P's core earnings:

| Net Income (reported) | |
|---|---|
| + Stock Option Expense | |
| – Pension Cost Reduction | |
| Core Earnings | |

Evaluate net income vs. core earnings (as identified) for GE.

For 2002, GE's net income is up from $12.7 billion to $13.7 billion, although revenues dropped from $130 billion to $126 billion. GE's stock price chart year-to-date shows the following:

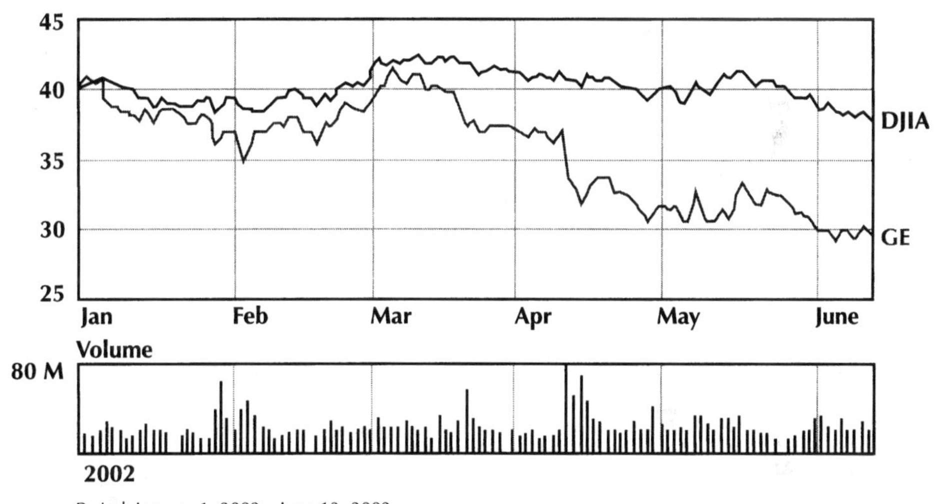


Period: January 1, 2002 – June 13, 2002
Source: www.quicken.com

Can the decline in stock price be best explained by revenues and sales for 2001 or by restatement such as S&P's core earnings? Explain.

## Case 9.2 Extensive Stock Option Reporting at Microsoft

Microsoft had the following disclosures in its 2001 10-K:

> The Company follows Accounting Principles Board Opinion 25, *Accounting for Stock Issued to Employees,* to account for stock option and employee stock purchase plans. An alternative method of accounting for stock options is SFAS 123, *Accounting for Stock-Based Compensation.* Under SFAS 123, employee stock options are valued at grant date using the Black-Scholes valuation model, and this compensation cost is recognized ratably over the vesting period. Had compensation cost for the Company's stock option and employee stock purchase plans been determined as prescribed by SFAS 123, *pro forma* income statements for 1999, 2000, and 2001 would have been as follows:

In Millions, Except Per Share Amounts

| | Year Ended June 30 | | | | | |
|---|---|---|---|---|---|---|
| | 1999 | | 2000 | | 2001 | |
| | Reported | Pro Forma | Reported | Pro Forma | Reported | Pro Forma |
| Revenue | $19,747 | $19,747 | $22,956 | $22,956 | $25,296 | $25,296 |
| Operating expenses: | | | | | | |
| Cost of revenue | 2,814 | 3,013 | 3,002 | 3,277 | 3,455 | 3,775 |
| Research and development | 2,970 | 3,479 | 3,772 | 4,814 | 4,379 | 6,106 |
| Sales and marketing | 3,238 | 3,445 | 4,126 | 4,468 | 4,885 | 5,888 |
| General and administrative | 715 | 841 | 1,050 | 1,284 | 857 | 1,184 |
| Total operating expenses | 9,737 | 10,778 | 11,950 | 13,843 | 13,576 | 16,953 |
| Operating income | 10,010 | 8,969 | 11,006 | 9,113 | 11,720 | 8,343 |
| Losses on equity investees and other | (70) | (70) | (57) | (57) | (159) | (159) |
| Investment income/(loss) | 1,951 | 1,951 | 3,326 | 3,326 | (36) | (36) |
| Income before income taxes | 11,891 | 10,850 | 14,275 | 12,382 | 11,525 | 8,148 |
| Provision for income taxes | 4,106 | 3,741 | 4,854 | 4,210 | 3,804 | 2,689 |
| Income before accounting change | 7,785 | 7,109 | 9,421 | 8,172 | 7,721 | 5,459 |
| Cumulative effect of accounting change | — | — | — | — | (375) | (375) |
| Net income | $ 7,785 | $ 7,109 | $ 9,421 | $ 8,172 | $ 7,346 | $ 5,084 |
| Basic earnings per share | $ 1.54 | $ 1.41 | $ 1.81 | $ 1.57 | $ 1.38 | $ 0.95 |
| Diluted earnings per share | $ 1.42 | $ 1.30 | $ 1.70 | $ 1.48 | $ 1.32 | $ 0.91 |

Included in this extensive disclosure is the increase in major expense categories if stock options had been recorded as expenses. Revenues remain unchanged, while net income declines from $7.4 billion to $5.1 billion.

**a.** Use this table to selectively calculate common-size information for the last two years:

| | 2000 Reported | 2000 *Pro Forma* | 2001 Reported | 2001 *Pro Forma* |
|---|---|---|---|---|
| Revenue | 100% | 100% | 100% | 100% |
| Operating expenses: | | | | |
| Cost of revenue | | | | |
| Research and development | | | | |
| Sales and marketing | | | | |
| General and administrative | | | | |
| Total operating expenses | | | | |
| Operating income | | | | |
| Income before income taxes | | | | |
| Net income | | | | |

b. Evaluate the use of stock options by Microsoft. How much does it affect performance?

c. If all companies prepared this level of detailed information in the stock option footnote, would it be necessary (as several commentators have proposed) to treat stock options as an expense in the income statement? Explain.

## Case 9.3 Compensation at Disney

Considerable discussion is made on the employment compensation of senior management, especially in difficult periods. A typical argument is that if shareholder value increases substantially (especially market value), managers should be richly compensated. Consider Michael Eisner, chairman and CEO of Disney. Under his initial employment contract in 1988, he was paid an annual salary of $750,000 plus a bonus based on performance, eight million stock option shares, and other compensation. Under the 1997 employment contract, base salary could be $1 million (the maximum allowed by IRS for tax deductibility), plus bonus, other compensation, and twenty-four million stock option shares. During much of Eisner's tenure, Disney has performed well. However, recent performance has suffered. Operating results for the last three years (in millions) are:

| | 2001 | 2000 | 1999 |
|---|---|---|---|
| Revenues | $25,269 | $25,402 | $23,402 |
| Gross Profit | 4,586 | 7,512 | 7,010 |
| Net Income | –158 | 920 | 1,300 |
| Total Assets | 43,699 | 45,027 | 43,679 |
| Stockholders' Equity | 22,672 | 24,100 | 20,975 |

a. Calculate return on sales, total assets and equity for the last two years:

| | 2001 | 2000 |
|---|---|---|
| Return on Sales | | |
| Return on Assets | | |
| Return on Equity | | |

Disney's market performance for the past five years, relative to the Dow Jones Industrial Average, is summarized in this stock chart:

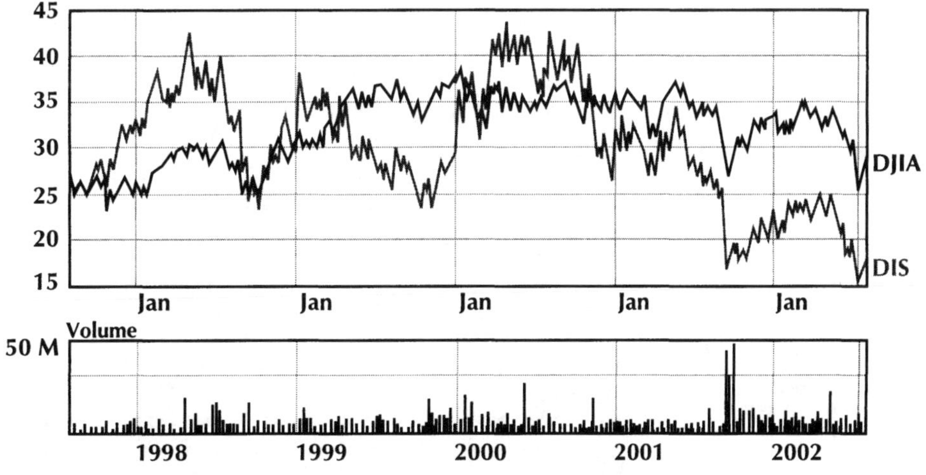


Period: August 1, 1997 – August 1, 2002

Source: www.quicken.com

**b.** Evaluate the relative performance of Disney over the past two years.

Eisner's compensation for the past three years is summarized (from the 2002 Proxy Statement) this way:

| Year | Base Salary | Bonus | Stock Options | Other | Total |
|---|---|---|---|---|---|
| 2001 | $1,000,000 | $ 0 | $ 0 | $ 4,020 | |
| 2000 | 813,462 | 8,500,000 | 387,060 | 3,004,020 | |
| 1999 | 750,000 | 0 | 0 | 3,820 | |

**c.** Calculate Eisner's total compensation over the last three years. Compare his compensation to the relative performance of Disney over the same period. Is he appropriately compensated, based on the information presented? Explain.

## Case 9.4 Financial Risks and the Use of Derivatives at Microsoft

The following comes from Microsoft's 2001 10-K:

> The Company is exposed to foreign currency, interest rate, and securities price risks. A portion of these risks is hedged, but fluctuations could impact the Company's results of operations and financial position. The Company hedges the exposure of accounts receivable and a portion of anticipated revenue to foreign currency fluctuations, primarily with option contracts. The Company monitors its foreign currency exposures daily to maximize the overall effectiveness of its foreign currency hedge positions. Principal currencies hedged include the Euro, Japanese yen, British pound, and Canadian dollar. Fixed income securities are subject to interest rate risk. The portfolio is diversified and consists primarily of investment grade securities to minimize credit risk. The Company routinely uses options to hedge its exposure to interest rate risk in the event of a catastrophic increase in interest rates. Many securities held in the Company's equity and other investments portfolio are subject to price risk. The Company uses options to hedge its price risk on certain highly volatile equity securities.
>
> **Foreign Currency Risk**
>
> Certain forecasted transactions and assets are exposed to foreign currency risk. The Company monitors its foreign currency exposures daily to maximize the overall effectiveness of its foreign currency hedge positions. Principal currencies hedged include the Euro, Japanese yen, British pound, and Canadian dollar. Options used to hedge a portion of forecasted international revenue for up to three years in the future are designated as cash flow hedging instruments. Options and forwards not designated as hedging instruments under SFAS 133 are also used to hedge the impact of the variability in exchange rates on accounts receivable and collections denominated in certain foreign currencies.
>
> **Securities Price Risk**
>
> Strategic equity investments are subject to market price risk. From time to time, the Company uses and designates options to hedge fair values and cash flows on certain equity securities. The security, or forecasted sale thereof, selected for hedging is determined by market conditions, up-front costs, and other relevant

factors. Once established, the hedges are not dynamically managed or traded, and are generally not removed until maturity.

**Interest Rate Risk**

Fixed-income securities are subject to interest rate risk. The fixed-income portfolio is diversified and consists primarily of investment grade securities to minimize credit risk. The Company routinely uses options, not designated as hedging instruments, to hedge its exposure to interest rate risk in the event of a catastrophic increase in interest rates.

**Other Derivatives**

In addition, the Company may invest in warrants to purchase securities of other companies as a strategic investment. Warrants that can be net share settled are deemed derivative financial instruments and are not designated as hedging instruments.

For the twelve months ended June 30, 2001, investment income included a net unrealized loss of $592 million, comprised of a $214 million gain for changes in the time value of options for fair value hedges, $211 million loss for changes in the time value of options for cash flow hedges, and $595 million loss for changes in the fair value of derivative instruments not designated as hedging instruments.

Derivative gains and losses included in [other comprehensive income] OCI are reclassified into earnings at the time forecasted revenue or the sale of an equity investment is recognized. During the twelve months ended June 30, 2001, $214 million of derivative gains were reclassified to revenue and $416 million of derivative losses were reclassified to investment income/(loss). The derivative losses reclassified to investment income/(loss) were offset by gains on the item being hedged. The Company estimates that $144 million of net derivative gains included in other comprehensive income will be reclassified into earnings within the next twelve months.

For instruments designated as hedges, hedge ineffectiveness, determined in accordance with SFAS 133, had no impact on earnings for the twelve months ended June 30, 2001. No fair value hedges or cash flow hedges were derecognized or discontinued for the twelve months ended June 30, 2001.

**a.** Evaluate the overall effectiveness of the financial risk strategy of using extensive derivative instruments.

**b.** Microsoft recorded 2001 losses from using derivatives. Evaluate the extent of these losses, given the net income for 2001 was $7.3 billion. Does this suggest that Microsoft was effectively hedging or engaged in speculative activity?

## ETHICS CONSIDERATIONS

### Stock Options and Ethics

A *Business Week* article (J. Byrne, "Restoring Trust in Corporate America," June 24, 2002, p. 34) indicates the problems with stock options:

Behind the sins of Enron and other corporations was the corrupting effect of stock options. They led to massive CEO pay inflation in the 1990s. But the toxic effects of that rise became clear only as the bull market began to ebb. Even while shareholders were losing millions of dollars, executive after executive seemed to be cashing in on an unsupervised lottery. At now-bankrupt telecom provider Global Crossing Ltd., Chairman Gary Winnick sold $735 million in company stock from 1999 to last November. At Enron, Chairman Lay sold more than $100 million in stock over the past three years—even while publicly insisting that he wasn't cashing out. The same was true at Tyco, where CEO Kozlowski and his chief financial officer unloaded more than $500 million in stock, quietly selling it back to the company, a trick that allowed them to delay any public disclosure of their sales (p. 34).

**a.** What is the major problem associated with stock options? Their existence? Their use by corrupt executives? Accounting issues, especially that compensation expenses are not recorded? Are there other issues?

**b.** What is the solution to stock options? Should they be disallowed? Regulated more stringently? Subjected to accounting reform, especially recording options as a compensation expense?

## INTERNET PROJECTS

### Project 9.1 Derivatives

**a.** Review the financial statements and notes of DuPont, Dow, and PPG to find out whether they use any of the following categories of derivatives:

| | DuPont | Dow | PPG |
|---|---|---|---|
| Options | | | |
| Forward or Futures Contracts | | | |
| Currency Swaps | | | |
| Interest Rate Swaps | | | |

**b.** Evaluate the use of derivatives for each company.

### Project 9.2 Derivatives

Using the company picked in earlier projects, review the 10-K of the company for use of derivatives and complete the following table. Evaluate the company's use of derivatives.

| | Check, If Applicable | Analysis |
|---|---|---|
| Options | | |
| Forward or Futures Contracts | | |
| Currency Swaps | | |
| Interest Rate Swaps | | |

CHAPTER

# 10 Business Combinations

**Objectives**

- Evaluate why mergers and acquisitions are common business events.
- Contrast pooling of interests and the purchase methods of accounting for business combinations.
- Explain the basic accounting procedures when using the purchase method.
- Evaluate two FASB pronouncements, SFAS Nos. 141 and 142.
- Determine when an acquisition is particularly desirable to the potential acquirer and to the potentially acquired firm
- Interpret the market (stock price) response to a merger announcement.
- Review the detailed accounting analysis process.

## Introduction

The history of big business for the last century and a half includes considerable merger activity. The economy was booming during and after the Civil War. John D. Rockefeller gobbled up competing oil refiners, and eventually Standard Oil had a 90 percent market share. His stated purpose was to maintain reasonable prices by eliminating cutthroat competition and ensure consistent quality of kerosene and other oil products. Other saw him as a ruthless robber baron. By 1902 J. P. Morgan, the most powerful banker in America, acquired Carnegie Steel and most of the rest of the industry to create U.S. Steel, the first billion-dollar corporation in the United States. U.S. Steel was formed by horizontal mergers on a vast scale. The financial reporting and auditing of U.S. Steel were excellent by the standards of the time, but they involved "watering the stock" by overvaluing assets (that is, not based on historical cost and not necessarily based on reasonable current value calculations) and other practices now illegal. The potential for misleading reporting has been a continual problem for business combinations.

**Mergers and acquisitions** can be used to increase economies of scale and reduce competition (**horizontal mergers** such as Standard Oil's), expand activities into related areas (**vertical mergers**), or diversify (**conglomerate mergers**). Henry Ford introduced the moving assembly line and the cheap, standardized Model T a century ago. Ford used a vertical merger strategy to acquire related firms: parts suppliers, ships and railroads for distribution, and mines and basic metal manufacturers. Ford owned most business components of auto manufacturing from mines to transportation to dealerships.

The advantages for diversification are well known. In theory, a manager can run a company in any industry effectively. The practice of owning a "portfolio" of unrelated businesses became particularly popular in the 1960s. James Ling took Ling Electronic public in 1955 and bought Temco and Chance Vought to form Ling-Temco-Vought, or LTV. Ling formed a holding company and proceeded to build an empire across multiple industries with borrowed money. Huge losses led to massive sell-offs and bankruptcy in 1986. LTV emerged from bankruptcy primarily as a steel company. There is less enthusiasm for the concept of conglomerate management, but conglomerates exist and many are successful. General Electric is one of the largest and most successful companies in the United States and it is essentially a conglomerate.

Mergers are every bit as common today as fifty or one hundred years ago. Merger strategy still includes all three types. DaimlerChrysler and ExxonMobil are recent horizontal mergers, AOL acquired Time Warner as a vertical merger, and U.S. Steel acquired Marathon Oil as a conglomerate merger (and became USX). Why are these important to analysts? When a company is announced as being acquired, the stock price can rise substantially. The stock price of the acquiring company can rise or fall. How does the merger fit the business strategy of the acquiring company? How does this merger affect the existing portfolio of the investor? How do mergers affect analysts' buy and sell decisions? Analysts working for investment bankers or large companies can become experts in mergers—as part of investment strategies, recommending merger targets, or designing strategies to avoid being acquired.

Since most large companies have acquired companies in the recent (and distant) past, how are the acquisitions accounted for? How does this affect the financial analysis? This chapter looks at the accounting for business combinations, considers the accounting for some recent acquisitions, and develops financial analysis techniques to better understand merger issues. As with most accounting issues, earnings management incentives are present.

## Accounting Issues

Accounting for acquisitions has been a continuing problem for standard setters. The basic methods used before SFAS Nos. 141 and 142 were issued in 2001 were (1) pooling of interests and (2) the purchase method. Both methods relied on valuations of existing assets and liabilities, rather than valuing the earnings capacity of the acquired firm. Conceptually, **pooling of interests** assumes a combination of two "near-equal" firms by exchanging stock. In 1950 Accounting Research Bulletin (ARB) No. 40 introduced four criteria for pooling: (1) continuity of ownership, (2) continuity of management, (3) relative size, and (4) similar businesses. Accounting was essentially "adding up" the combined book value. Under the **purchase method,** one firm acquires another, often for cash. The acquiring firm records the assets and liabilities of the acquired company at fair values. The difference between the acquisition price and the revalued net assets is goodwill—this is the only circumstance where goodwill is recorded.

Historically, both methods were allowed with few limitations. Pooling concepts were initially developed in the 1930s but seldom used before 1950. The method came to be accepted for most acquisitions by common stock, and by 1970 over 80 percent of mergers used pooling. The APB issued Opinion No. 16 in 1970, primarily to limit the use of pooling. Twelve criteria had to be met before pooling of interests was allowed. For example, the companies must be independent of each other, only voting common shares could be issued, and the combined company must not intend to dispose of significant portions of the business. This is another example of "cookbook accounting," or specific rules rather than judgment of economic reality. If an acquiring firm wanted to use pooling of interests, the 12 criteria must be met; otherwise the purchase method was required.

APB Opinion No. 16 eliminated some abuses and the number of poolings was reduced. The FASB issued a Discussion Memorandum on business combinations in 1976. Only sixteen comment letters were received, and the FASB dropped the project since little dissatisfaction existed. The issue of business combinations was added to the FASB addenda in 1996, and an exposure draft was issued in 1999. The main feature in the ED was the elimination of pooling of interests as an option.

Assume that Octopus, Inc., acquired Guppy Co. Guppy has the summary balance sheet information shown in Exhibit 10.1. Assume that Guppy was acquired for common stock with a fair value of $30 million and that the twelve criteria for pooling of interests are met. (Note that this was recorded before SFAS No. 142 went into effect.) The simplified journal entry (in millions) is this:

| | | |
|---|---|---|
| Accounts Receivable, net | 1.1 | |
| Inventory | 2.9 | |
| Fixed Assets, net | 8.0 | |
| Liabilities | | 2.0 |
| Equity | | 10.0 |

Thus, the company is recorded at book value. The economic substance of the transaction (i.e., Guppy effectively cost Octopus $30 million in stock) is ignored.

Alternatively, assume that Guppy was acquired for cash of $30 million and, therefore, the purchase method was used. The simplified journal entry is (in millions):

| | | |
|---|---|---|
| Accounts Receivable, net | 1.0 | |
| Inventory | 3.5 | |
| Fixed Assets, net | 10.6 | |
| Patents | 5.0 | |
| Goodwill | 11.9 | |
| Liabilities | | 2 |
| Cash | | 30 |

In this case, all assets and liabilities were recorded at fair value, including new intangible assets of patents and goodwill. Guppy was recorded at its economic cost of $30 million. Goodwill was created as an intangible asset and

**EXHIBIT 10.1 ABBREVIATED BALANCE SHEET FOR GUPPY CO.**

| | Book Value | Fair Value |
|---|---|---|
| **Accounts Receivable, net** | $1.1 million | $1.0 million |
| **Inventory** | 2.9 | 3.5 |
| **Fixed Assets, net** | 8.0 | 10.6 |
| **Patents** | 0 | 5.0 |
| **Liabilities** | –2.0 | –2.0 |
| **Net Assets** | $10.0 million | $17.5 million |

was a plug figure to balance debits and credits. Essentially, **goodwill** is the difference between the acquisition cost and fair value of net assets. Before SFAS No. 142, goodwill was to be amortized over a period of forty years or less.

Income tax consequences of business combinations are complicated. To the stockholders of the acquired firm, most pooling of interests acquisitions are nontaxable. The stockholders would exchange shares of stock. To these same stockholders, the purchase method is usually taxable no matter whether cash, stock or debt is involved. The stockholders must recognize gains and losses on the sale (generally taxable at capital gains rates).

## SFAS Nos. 141 and 142

The FASB passed SFAS No. 141, *Business Combinations,* and SFAS No. 142, *Goodwill and Other Intangible Assets,* in June 2001. The major change was the requirement that the purchase method be used for all business combinations after July 1, 2001. A primary reason was the lack of comparability between purchase and pooling. As stated in Paragraph B29:

> The purchase method is consistent with how the historical-cost accounting model generally accounts for transactions in which assets are acquired and liabilities are assumed or incurred, and it therefore produces information that is comparable to other accounting information. ... [U]sers of financial statements are better able to assess the initial costs of the investments made and the subsequent performance of those investments and compare them with the performance of other entities.

Generally, accounting for business combinations follows previous GAAP. Paragraph 37 of SFAS No. 141 states the valuation bases for assets and liabilities. For example, marketable securities are to be valued at fair value, raw materials at current replacement costs, and plant and equipment at current replacement cost for similar capacity. Intangible assets that meet the separability criteria (e.g., patents) are recognized separately from goodwill. Examples are listed in Paragraph A14.

Under SFAS No. 142, goodwill (and some other intangibles) is no longer amortized. Instead, goodwill is tested for impairment at least annually. Examples of impairment events (Paragraph 28) include adverse legal factors, unanticipated competition, or a loss of key personnel. An impairment loss is recognized if the carrying value is not recoverable and its carrying value exceeds its fair value. The second step is to measure the amount of the impairment loss. The impairment testing begins for fiscal year 2002 in most cases. Thus, impairment write-offs can be expected.

AOL Time Warner recorded a $54 billion loss for first quarter 2002. The write-off of goodwill turned a loss of $1 million to a net loss of $54,240 million. Since the loss was noncash, cash from operations was $1.8 billion. However, stockholders' equity declined from $208.6 billion to $160.4 billion, a loss of $48.2 billion or 23.1 percent. As stated in Note 3 of AOLTime Warner's First Quarter 2002 10-Q:

> Upon adoption of FAS 142 in the first quarter of 2002, AOL Time Warner recorded a one-time, noncash charge of approximately $54 billion to reduce the carrying value of its goodwill. ... The amount of the impairment primarily

> reflects the decline in the Company's stock price since the Merger was announced and valued for accounting purposes in January 2000.

AOL charged the impairment against specific segments, including Cable for $23 billion and Networks for $13 billion.

The elimination of the pooling of interest method will make financial analysis of business combinations somewhat easier, since all mergers will use the same method. However, the impairment charges to goodwill under SFAS No. 142 are problematic. It's not at all clear how fair value of goodwill can be determined or under what circumstances or when goodwill should be written off. The AOL Time Warner write-off suggests a "big-bath" earnings management strategy in a quarter that was losing money (although only a small $1 million loss). Further write-offs are likely from any number of firms. From an analyst's perspective, these will be hard to predict and may be hard to evaluate even after the fact.

## Impact on Financial Statements and Ratios

When an acquisition is made, the acquiring company is expanded in size and operations. How this affects specific balance sheet and income statement items as well as cash flows depends on the specific characteristics of the agreement: the exchange of voting common stock versus cash, debt instruments, or a combination of these; and before SFAS No. 141, whether it was accounted for as a pooling or purchase.

Under pooling of interests, financial statements were combined at book value. Balance sheet ratios changed only to the extent that the acquisition firm had a different asset and liability mix than the acquiring firm. The income statement showed "excess" growth solely because of the added operations of the acquired firm, but ratios differed only to the extent that the acquisition had different operating characteristics and efficiency. Equity was increased by the book value of the acquisition's net assets, although the composition of stockholders' equity will change. Under the pooling method, no cash flows took place for the acquisition and differences are the added cash flow transactions of the acquired firm.

The circumstances under the purchase method are more complex and variable. When the acquisition is cash (some or all the cash involved may be borrowed), the net asset (equity) position does not go up. Acquired assets and liabilities are recorded at fair values, which are offset by the cash paid. Balance sheet totals rise only to the extent that external financing is used. But asset and liability composition can change substantially. Patents, goodwill, and other intangibles are recorded; internally generated intangibles usually are expensed. Cash ratios will drop for the acquired firm, unless the acquisition was funded by new debt or equity, with liquidity ratios partially offset by the working capital position (at fair value) of the acquisition. Fixed assets and intangibles can rise substantially because fair values are used and goodwill recognized. Liabilities rise because of the acquisition's obligations and any debt used to finance the acquisition. Equity is unchanged in a cash or debt transaction. Consequently, leverage ratios will rise, perhaps substantially.

The income statement of the combined firm includes the acquisition's operations only after the effective date of the merger. Revenues rise because of the acquired firm's operations. Several negative results occur. Operating expenses usually are relatively larger because of write-ups of inventory to fair value of the acquisition; higher depreciation and other allocations, since fixed and other assets generally are written up; and because of the potential write-down of goodwill and other intangibles. Also, if the cash paid is from borrowed funds, additional interest expense is recorded. Consequently, profitability and activity ratios can suffer. That is, net income for the combined entity should be higher because of the acquired firm's operations, but performance ratios may decline because of increased expenses.

Under the purchase method, substantial cash flow effects result. The acquisition price paid in cash (less pre-acquisition cash held by the acquired firm) is recorded as cash used for investing (with any borrowing, cash represents cash flows received from financing). Requirements of SFAS No. 95 on the cash flow statement are relatively complex on acquisition and beyond the scope of this book.

The impact on financial statements is considerably different if equity is exchanged under the purchase method. Asset and liabilities are restated to fair value, and equity used also is recorded at fair value (unlike pooling of interests). Liquidity usually would be higher since cash is not used and inventory is generally restated upward. Fixed assets, intangibles, and other items are recorded the same whether cash or equity is used under the purchase method. Leverage ratios are lower when equity is used. There should be little difference under the alternative purchase method circumstances for the income statement. Interest expense would be higher if borrowed cash is used rather than equity.

## Characteristics of Potential Target Firms

What characteristics of companies make them likely targets for acquisitions? These characteristics are diverse and depend on complex economic, legal, and operating circumstances. Generally, larger companies acquire smaller companies (there are exceptions). Most would be classified as horizontal or vertical mergers, with the acquiring firm interested in expanding market share, combining complementary resources, and exploiting economies of scale. High-liquidity and low-leverage firms can be attractive acquisition targets. The acquiring firm can capture the cash and other liquid assets and benefit from the low debt. To some extent acquirers also can capture the benefits of substantially overfunded defined benefit pension plans of acquisitions.

Ironically, firms with financial difficulties may be attractive merger candidates. These may have income tax loss carryforwards that can be used by the acquirer. The acquirer may have management and other skills to turn around the troubled firm and provide additional financial resources. Price premiums of troubled firms typically are lower than successful firms, thereby representing a potential bargain. Somewhat related, low PE firms can be attractive targets, especially if the acquirers have higher PEs and can increase their own market price through the acquisition, in part by having the acquired net assets valued at the PE of the acquirer.

## Market Reaction to Acquisition Announcements

Acquiring firms typically pay a substantial premium over the current stock price to complete a merger. This is needed to persuade the target company's board of directors (presumably based on stockholder interests) to accept the offer and to fend off other potential acquiring firms. This market premium can top 50 percent of the current price, resulting in an immediate market reaction for both acquiring and target firms. Almost always, the stock price of the target approaches the announced acquisition price (discounted by the probability the combination will ultimately be completed). The price of the acquiring firm can go up or down, depending on how investors view the benefits of the acquisition relative to the premium paid.

Consider the announcement of the AOL acquisition of Time Warner on January 10, 2000. Exhibit 10.2 presents a stock chart is presented for both firms (Time Warner's ticker symbol is TWX). Time Warner received an immediate 30 percent rise in price, as expected. The early view of AOL was mixed, but skeptical (note the stock price was dropping before January 10). AOL's price went down slowly and by the middle of February had dropped 40 percent. AOL is a high tech communications company. Time Warner is a large, multifaceted communications company considered "old economy." An interesting point is that Time Warner is a much bigger company on virtually any measure except market value (market capitalization).

Analysts debated whether this was an appropriate move for AOL: (1) a brilliant vertical acquisition to combine old and new economy advantages or (2) an albatross that would drag AOL down to the low performance associated with old economy firms and added complexity of a diverse empire beyond the scope of AOL expertise. The stock price results suggest the latter view prevailed for the first three months after announcement.

The AOL Web site (www.aoltimewarner.com) called AOL the "first fully integrated media and communications company in the internet age." The effective date of the merger was January 11, 2001, almost exactly one year after the announcement of the merger. A year-to-date stock chart for the first six months indicated the initial market perspective to the merger, as shown in Exhibit 10.3.

The combined company had a substantial price rise for most of January and was up about 50 percent for the year through the end of May 2001. Since high tech was down (e.g. NASDAQ was down about 15 percent year-to-date, while the DJIA was essentially even), AOL's claims seemed correct.

The stock chart for the last twelve months has a different perspective, as shown in Exhibit 10.4. Both the Dow and NASDAQ were down, but AOL dropped from over $50 to

**EXHIBIT 10.2 STOCK CHART FOR AOL AND TIME WARNER, JANUARY TO MAY, 2000**

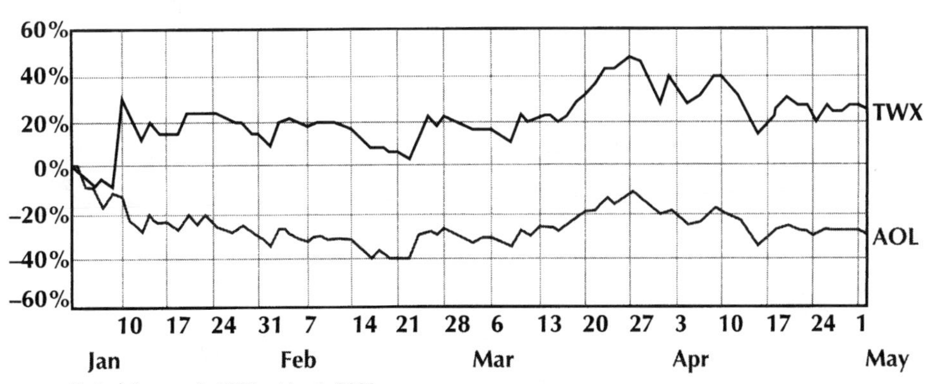


Period. January 2, 2000 – May 1, 2000

Source: www.hoovers.com

**EXHIBIT 10.3 STOCK CHART FOR AOL TIME WARNER, COMPARED TO DOW JONES AND NASDAQ, JANUARY TO JUNE, 2001**

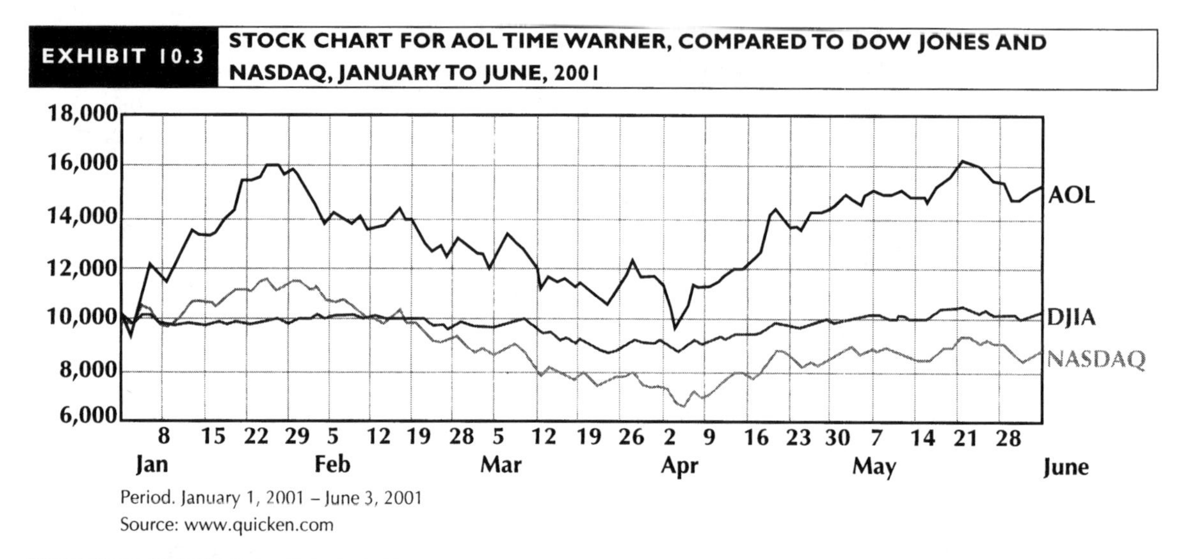


Period. January 1, 2001 – June 3, 2001
Source: www.quicken.com

**EXHIBIT 10.4 STOCK CHART OF AOL TIME WARNER, COMPARED TO DOW JONES AND NASDAQ, JUNE 2001 TO JUNE 2002**

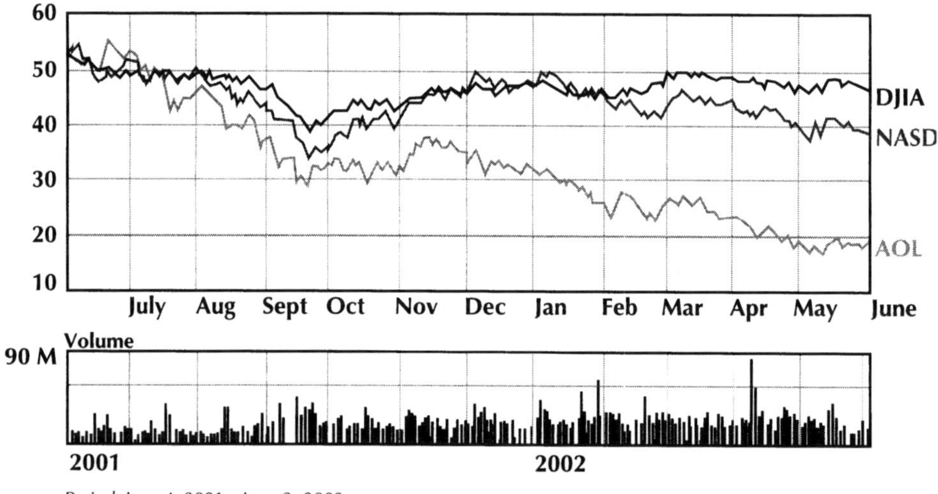


Period: June 4, 2001 – June 2, 2002
Source: www.quicken.com

less than $20, some 65 percent. This was reflected in the goodwill write-off of $54 billion. It becomes clear over the long term how perspective can change after the initial announcement and first results.

## Analysis and Forecasts of Merger Activity

Because of substantial market reaction, analysts must constantly consider potential merger activity. Investing in corporations that are likely to be acquired can often be lucrative, because of the substantial market premiums. Acquiring firms may not be as lucky, since stock prices often drop after the merger announcement. Therefore, forecasting future acquisitions is an important component of financial analysis. Analysts should review characteristics of firms that make them acquisition candidates. Which industries are likely to consolidate through merger activity? Which specific firms have a history of acquisitions? Which firms have characteristics that make them attractive targets, based on market share, technical expertise, attractive liquidity and leverage ratios, and relative market attractiveness (e.g., PE ratios and market-to-book values)?

## Public Policy Issues

Mergers by big business can greatly influence economic activity. One aspect is increasing market share and reduced competition, which involves potential antitrust violations. Declining competition also may reduce new innovation. Therefore, the Department of Justice, the Federal Trade Commission, and other federal regulators review mergers by major corporations. The regulators may disallow the merger or require certain structural changes, such as selling off certain market segments, to meet antitrust criteria.

The investor and analyst must evaluate antitrust and other legal characteristics of merger activity beyond the standard financial analysis. What is the probability that the merger will be denied? Will major restructuring or business segment sell-offs be required, making the merger less attractive? How should the investor react to these projections? How will mergers affect the competitiveness of the industry? These issues must be addressed case by case.

## Business Acquisitions by the PC Manufacturers

The PC industry has made few acquisitions since 1999. Dell Computer acquired ConvergeNet Technologies in October 1999 at a total cost of $332 million. Goodwill of $132 million was recorded, to be amortized over three to eight years. Gateway acquired a 20 percent interest in NECX Direct in 1999 for $78 million. The major development during this period was the acquisition of Compaq Computer by Hewlett-Packard.

Compaq Computer was the number one seller of PCs and a bigger company than Dell. Compaq also has been involved in a number of acquisitions (and divestitures). Particularly important for the analysis of Compaq was the acquisition of Digital Equipment Corporation (DEC) in June 1998. Compaq had continued problems with the DEC merger, partially because of restructuring charges that included consolidation of DEC facilities and workforce.

Hewlett-Packard (H-P) announced the acquisition of Compaq (CPQ) on September 4, 2001, for $19 billion in H-P stock (HWP). This was a vertical merger with the two companies in somewhat different market segments. Market reaction is given in the stock chart in Exhibit 10.5.

Unlike most mergers where the price of the acquired firm rises and the acquiring firm falls, the market reacted negatively to both stocks. There was a stock price reduction on September 4 for both firms, and the price dropped slightly over the next couple of months. There was considerable controversy at H-P over the acquisition, but the merger was approved and completed May 3, 2002. A stock chart for three months for H-P indicates that the market changed its mind and reacted favorably since the merger, pushing the stock price up from around $17 to $19, as shown in Exhibit 10.6.

**EXHIBIT 10.5** **CHART OF HEWLETT-PACKARD AND COMPAQ, COMPARED TO DOW JONES, AUGUST TO NOVEMBER 2001**

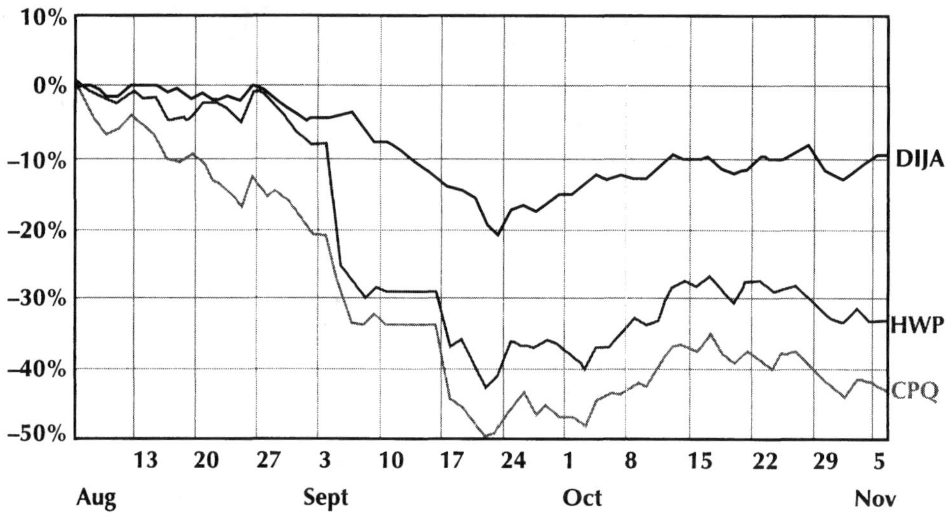


Period: August 6, 2001 – November 5, 2001
Source: www.quicken.com

**EXHIBIT 10.6** **STOCK CHART OF HEWLETT-PACKARD, COMPARED TO DOW JONES AND NASDAQ, MARCH TO JUNE, 2002**

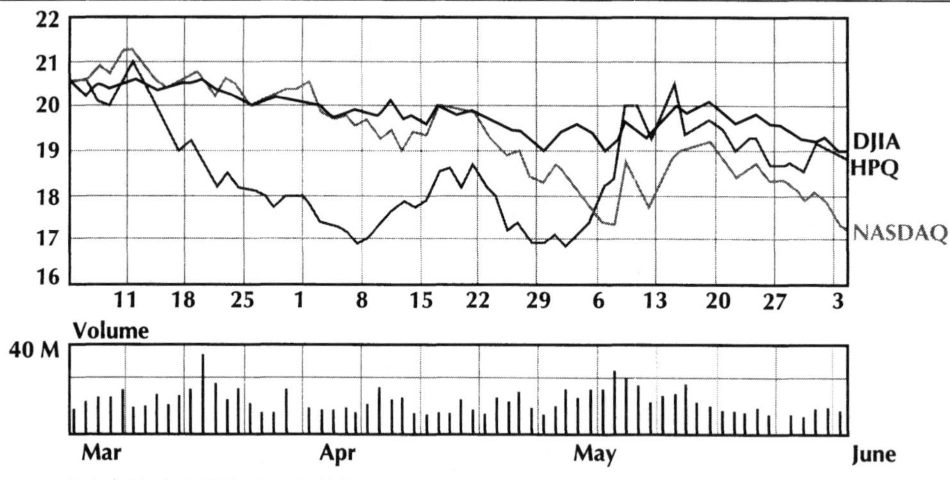


Period: March 4, 2002 – June 3, 2002
Source: www.quicken.com

Merger activity can be unexpected and difficult to evaluate. Both Compaq and H-P were PC competitors (although H-P had considerably more non-PC segments). It's not yet clear whether the combined company will be a stronger competitor to Dell, Gateway, and Apple.

## SUMMARY

Business combinations continue to be one of the major factors in big business and economic activity. Since acquisitions tend to increase market share and reduce competition, they have both investor and public policy aspects. The accounting for business combinations is complex and the analyst must understand the basic procedures and their impact on the financial position of the prospective merger. Current standards (SFAS No. 141 and 142) require companies to use the purchase method, which has substantively different affects on the financial statements and future operations (including tax aspects) than the previously allowable method of pooling of interests. The evaluation of past acquisitions (when both pooling and purchase were allowed) can be difficult and relies on previous financial statements, note disclosures, and analyst estimates. The ability to forecast prospective merger candidates may improve financial analysis recommendations. The stock market response represents investor judgment on the viability of the merger. In most cases, the stock price of the target rises.

## KEY TERMS

acquisition
conglomerate merger
goodwill
horizontal merger
merger
pooling of interests
purchase method
vertical merger

## QUESTIONS

1. Why were mergers common one hundred years ago? What type of mergers were most common?
2. Why are mergers common today? Are the types of mergers the same today as one hundred years ago? Explain.
3. Why is the purchase method the only accounting procedure now allowed for mergers (SFAS No. 141)?
4. What is goodwill? How is it accounted for according to SFAS No. 142?
5. Under what circumstances is an acquisition desirable to the potential acquirer? to the target firm?
6. What is the most typical market (stock price) response to the target firm in a merger announcement? Explain.
7. What should appear in the executive summary associated with the detailed accounting analysis process?

## PROBLEMS

### Problem 10.1 Goodwill in the Chemical Industry

(Problem 10.1 relates to the chemical industry.)

Here is information on goodwill, amortization, and relative size (in millions) for 2001:

| | DuPont | Dow | PPG |
|---|---|---|---|
| Goodwill | $ 3,746 | $1,129 | $ 3,130 |
| Amortization | 357 | 29 | 178 |
| Total Assets | 42,319 | 8,452 | 35,515 |
| Net Income | 4,339 | 387 | –385 |

a. Calculate amortization as a percentage of goodwill and of net income. Calculate goodwill as a percentage of total assets.

| | DuPont | Dow | PPG |
|---|---|---|---|
| Amortization ÷ Goodwill | | | |
| Amortization ÷ Net Income | | | |
| Goodwill ÷ Total Assets | | | |

**b.** Evaluate the impact of goodwill and amortization on the financial position of the industry.

### Problem 10.2 Goodwill in the Hotel and Resort Industry

(Problem 10.2 relates to the hotel and resort industry.)

Here is information on goodwill, amortization, and relative size (in millions) for 2001. No goodwill was reported by Marriott:

| | Hilton | Mandalay |
|---|---|---|
| Goodwill | $1,273 | $ 45 |
| Amortization | 77 | 12 |
| Total Assets | 8,785 | 4,037 |
| Net Income | 166 | 53 |

**a.** Calculate amortization as a percentage of goodwill and of net income. Calculate goodwill as a percentage of total assets.

| | Hilton | Mandalay |
|---|---|---|
| Amortization ÷ Goodwill | | |
| Amortization ÷ Net Income | | |
| Goodwill ÷ Total Assets | | |

**b.** Evaluate the impact of goodwill and amortization on the financial position of the industry.

## CASES

### Case 10.1 Merger Announcement by UAL and the Market Reaction

On May 24, 2000, UAL (the parent of United Airlines) announced a merger with USAir, at about a 50 percent premium over USAir's stock price of 40. According to *Fortune,* UAL is the second largest airline and USAir is No. 6 (ARM, the parent of American Airline, is the biggest). This horizontal merger would make UAL the largest airline and would increase UAL's market share in several key markets. How did the market react? A stock chart is presented below (USAir's ticker is U):

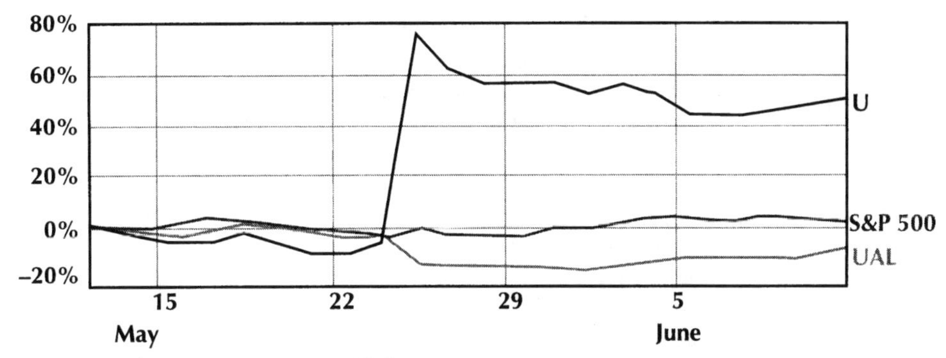


Period: May 11, 2000 – June 11, 2000

Source: www.quicken.com

a. Analyze the stock price reaction of USAir to the merger announcement.

b. Analyze the stock price reaction of UAL to the merger announcement.

## Case 10.2 Impact of Merger Announcements in the Airline Industry

The UAL-USAir merger announcement (from Problem 8.1) may affect the stock price of other airline companies. Both AMR and Delta (*Fortune*'s third largest airline) were rumored to be interested in acquiring No. 4 Northwest.

a. Without considering the actual stock price reaction, predict what stock prices should do for AMR, Delta, and Northwest.

Given below is the stock chart for these companies:

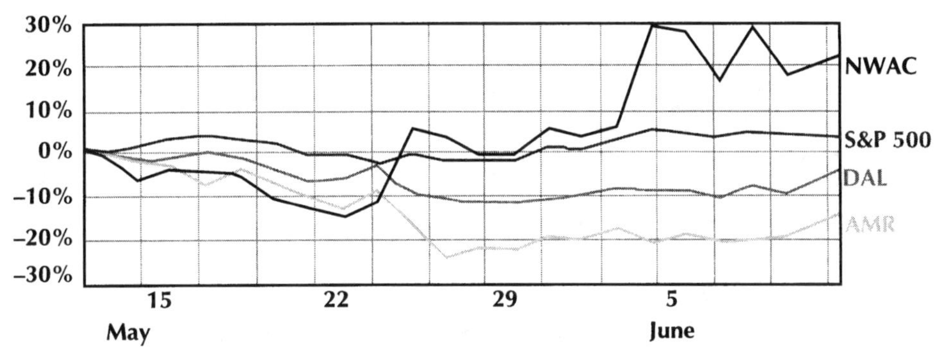


Period: May 11, 2000 – June 11, 2000

Source: www.quicken.com

b. Analyze the stock price reaction for these airlines.

c. Was the actual reaction the same as predicted? Explain.

## Case 10.3 DuPont's Acquisition and Divestment Strategy

The management discussion and analysis section of DuPont's 2000 annual report states: "As part of its strategy for growth, the company has made and may continue to make acquisitions and divestitures and form strategic alliances." Since 1999 the following activities have taken place:

**Acquisitions:** 1999 acquisition of 80 percent of Pioneer Hi-brands International not previously owned (price $7,684 million—$3,419 million cash plus $4,154 million in stock); Herberts Coating Business (cash of $1,588 million).

**Divestitures:** 1999 Conoco spin-off, trading Conoco shares for DuPont (a $7,471 million gain net-of-tax recognized as a discontinued operation); 2001 sale of DuPont Pharmaceutical to Bristol-Myers Squibb for $7,798 million (net assets sold of $1,411 million, resulting in a pre-tax operating gain of $6,136 million).

Consider basic financial statement numbers for 1999–2001:

| | 2001 | 2000 | 1999 |
|---|---|---|---|
| Sales | $25,370 | $29,202 | $27,892 |
| Income from Continuing Operations | 4,328 | 2,314 | 219 |
| Net Income | 4,339 | 2,314 | 7,690 |
| Total Assets | 40,319 | 39,426 | 40,777 |
| Stockholders' Equity | 14,452 | 13,299 | 12,875 |

Sales declined in 2001; income from continuing operations for 1999 was very low, but net income for 1999 was much higher than in later years; total assets declined in 2000, but they were up in 2001 to almost the 1999 level.

**a.** Analyze how much of these differences in performance and size is associated with these acquisitions and divestitures.

Analyzing companies that make frequent acquisitions and divestitures is particularly difficult. After the consolidation, it is difficult to determine the relative success of the parent, given these large business trades.

**b.** To what extent can large swings in performance and size be specifically identified as caused by acquisitions and divestitures? How can this be determined?

# ETHICS CONSIDERATIONS

## When Should Acquisition Be Made?

Strategic acquisitions can be an important component of a corporation's business strategy. However, there has been a merger frenzy with catastrophic results. Consider excerpts from a *Fortune* article (R. Charan and J. Useem, "Why Companies Fail: Acquisition Lust")

> WorldCom founder Bernard Ebbers liked to eat. He ate MCI. He ate MFS and its UUNet subsidiary. He tried to eat Sprint. Wall Street helped him wash it all down with cheap capital and a buoyant stock price. Pretty soon WorldCom was tipping the scales at $39 billion in revenues. But there was a problem: Ebbers didn't know how to digest the things he ate. A born dealmaker, he seemed to care more about snaring new acquisitions than about making the existing ones—all 75 of them—work together. At least Ebbers was up front about it: "Our goal is not to capture market share or be global," he told a reporter in 1997. "Our goal is to be the No. 1 stock on Wall Street."

a. Are there fundamental principles on when acquisitions make sense? Take a position and defend it.

b. WorldCom is still in business, but Bernard Ebbers resigned after a substantial drop in the stock price, then WorldCom declared bankruptcy. Why are some acquisitions successful and other a failure?

## INTERNET PROJECTS

### Project 10.1

Using the company picked in earlier chapters, complete an accounting analysis and prepare a summary table and executive summary.

# Appendix: Summary of Accounting Analysis for Dell and Its Competitors

Chapters 7–10 considered accounting issues that affect the financial analysis. Much of the discussion focused on Dell and its competitors. A table is used to summarize the information issued for fiscal year 2001 (2002 for Dell). An executive summary may be useful for highlighting key information. Items of particular importance are in bold (usually mentioned in the executive summary), and footnotes at the bottom of the table can be used for additional explanatory information.

## Accounting Analysis Summary
## Personal Computer Industry (Dell, Gateway, and Apple)
## Fiscal Year 2001 (fiscal year-end February 1, 2002, for Dell)

**Executive Summary**

Accounting related issues involve stock options, nonrecurring items, and underperforming segments. Stock options are extensive (14–20 percent of outstanding shares), substantial potential dilution of equity (but expected for this industry). All have restructuring charges, associated with declining sales (largely recession related). Overall, accounting is above average for Dell and average for Gateway and Apple. There are no other obvious accounting problems that would influence investment decisions.

| Issue | Dell | Gateway | Apple |
|---|---|---|---|
| Cash and Marketable Securities | High levels (49.7% of current assets), MS available for sale | High levels (54.9% of CA); MS available for sale and held to maturity | Very high levels (84.3% of CA) |
| Inventory, COGS, Accounts Receivable | Low levels of inventory (3.5% of CA), standard industry practices (FIFO); moderate level of AR (33.5% of CA) | Low levels of inventory (5.7% of CA), standard industry practices (FIFO); AR 10.4% of CA, moderate | Inventory stated at FIFO (0.2% of CA, very low); AR 9.1% of CA, low |
| Cash Flows | CFO of $4.2 billion | CFO of $0–270 million (RF); net increase in cash of $247 million; large net loss, but company has been accumulating cash | CFO of $185 million |
| Fixed Assets, Depreciation | Low amounts (6.1% of total assets), relatively new fixed assets (average age, 2.4 years), straight-line depreciation | Moderate level, 20.4% of TA; relatively new fixed assets (average age, 2.3 years), straight-line depreciation | Low levels (9.4% of TA); relatively new assets (average age, 3.5 years), straight-line depreciation |
| Revenue Recognition | Conservative, meets industry standards (revenue recognized on delivery with adoption of SAB 101) | Conservative, meets industry standards (on delivery, consistent with SAB 101) | Conservative, meets industry standards (on delivery, consistent with SAB 101) |
| Expensing vs. Capitalizing Costs | Consistent with industry | Consistent with industry; software capitalization; write-down of long-lived assets, $19 million | Capitalizes software development costs |

| Issue | Dell | Gateway | Apple |
|---|---|---|---|
| Income Tax | 28.0% effective tax rate | Income before tax negative and provision for tax also negative, operating loss carryforwards | Income before tax negative and provision for tax also negative, operating loss carryforwards |
| Stock Options | Substantial, about 14% of shares outstanding; dilution potential | Substantial, 19.7% of shares outstanding up from 15.0%; dilution potential | Operating leases $431 million, 7.2% of total assets |
| Operating Leases, Other Off-balance-sheet Items | Lease commitments exist, but minimal leases are outstanding | Operating lease obligations 9.4% of total assets (earnings management potential) | Operating leases $431 million, 7.2% of total sales |
| Commitments | Miscellaneous commitments reported, minimal amounts | Credit line—revolving line of credit of $300 million | None reported |
| Contingencies | Legal proceedings reported, but none considered material | Securities lawsuits, but not considered material | Litigation, not considered material |
| Retirement | 401(k) plan, no long-term obligations | 401(k) plan, no long-term obligations | 401(k) plan, no long-term obligations |
| OPEB | None reported | None reported | None reported |
| Segment Reporting | Industry segments not reported | None. Domestic reorganization combined business and consumer ops as a single entity | Sales by product includes Power Mac (31.0%) and iMac (20.8%) |
| Geographic Reporting | Operates in Americas, Europe, and Asia; operating margins for foreign operations are below U.S. margins (U.S., 7.9%; Europe, 6.2%; Asia, 5.3%) | U.S. operating income % = 4.3%; EMEA = –23.4% (RF); Asia=–11.6% (RF); company discontinued foreign operations in 2001 as part of restructuring | 44.1% of revenue from "Foreign Countries" |
| Nonrecurring Items | Nonrecurring charge of $105 million for job reduction and consolidation of facilities.* Accounting change for revenue recognition for SAB 101 had minor impact | Extraordinary gain on early extinguishments of debt, $4.3 million; cumulative effect of changing accounting principle, $–23.9 million | Accounting change for revenue recognition required by SAB 101 had minor impact |
| Comprehensive Income | Foreign currency marketable securities, not material | Foreign currency, marketable securities, not material | Foreign currency, marketable securities: net realized loss on derivatives |
| Business combinations | Minor acquisition activity | Minor acquisition activity | Minor acquisitions, including Power School and Spruce Technologies |
| Derivatives | Foreign currency hedging; interest rate sways; equity options, forward contracts, and put obligations on Dell stock | Foreign currency forward contracts under third quarter 2001 | Foreign currency forward contracts and options; interest rate swaps |
| Unusual Accounting Policies | Special charges of $482 million for job reductions etc. (part of income from continuing operations) | Restructuring charge of $876 million (part of continuing operations) | None |
| Auditor and Report | PriceWaterhouseCoopers; unqualified | PriceWaterhouseCoopers; unqualified | KPMG Peat Marwick; unqualified |
| Other | None | Strategic alliance with AOL for sales and distribution channels | None |

| Issue | Dell | Gateway | Apple |
|---|---|---|---|
| Analyst's Rating for Accounting Issues | 8; stock option dilution and recurring items are the only significant problems, based on information available | 5; stock option dilution potential; restructuring nonrecurring items, and operating leases are areas for potential earnings management | 8; substantial stock options |

## PROBLEMS

### Problem A.1 Industry Accounting Analysis

Using what you've learned about problems related to the chemical industry, especially in Chapters 7–10, complete an accounting analysis for the three companies discussed. Use the following matrix as a guide.

| Issue | DuPont | Dow | PPG |
|---|---|---|---|
| Cash and Marketable Securities | | | |
| Inventory, COGS, Accounts Receivable | | | |
| Cash Flows | | | |
| Fixed Assets, Depreciation | | | |
| Revenue Recognition | | | |
| Expensing vs. Capitalizing Costs | | | |
| Income Tax | | | |
| Stock Options | | | |
| Operating Leases, Other Off-balance-sheet Items | | | |
| Commitments | | | |
| Contingencies | | | |
| Retirement | | | |
| OPEB | | | |
| Segment Reporting | | | |
| Geographic Reporting | | | |
| Nonrecurring Items | | | |
| Comprehensive Income | | | |
| Business Combinations | | | |
| Derivatives | | | |
| Unusual Accounting Policies | | | |
| Audit Report | | | |
| Other | | | |
| Rating for Accounting Issues | | | |

**a.** Write an executive summary for your accounting analysis of the chemical industry.

### Problem A.2 Industry Accounting Analysis

Using what you've learned about problems related to the hotel and resort industry (especially in Chapters 7–10), complete an accounting analysis for the three companies discussed. Use the following matrix as a guide.

| Issue | Hilton | Marriott | Mandalay |
|---|---|---|---|
| Cash and Marketable Securities | | | |
| Inventory, COGS, Accounts Receivable | | | |
| Cash Flows | | | |
| Fixed Assets, Depreciation | | | |
| Revenue Recognition | | | |
| Expensing vs. Capitalizing Costs | | | |
| Income Tax | | | |
| Stock Options | | | |
| Operating Leases, Other Off-balance-sheet Items | | | |
| Commitments | | | |
| Contingencies | | | |
| Retirement | | | |
| OPEB | | | |
| Segment Reporting | | | |
| Geographic Reporting | | | |
| Nonrecurring Items | | | |
| Comprehensive Income | | | |
| Business Combinations | | | |
| Derivatives | | | |
| Unusual Accounting Policies | | | |
| Audit Report | | | |
| Other | | | |
| Rating for Accounting Issues | | | |

**a.** Write an executive summary for your accounting analysis of the hotel and resort industry.

# CHAPTER 11

# Capital Structure and Credit Risk

**Objectives**

- Define capital structure and explain the relationship of long-term debt to equity.
- Evaluate the importance of corporate debt, in the context of credit risk.
- Describe credit risk and distinguish between default risk and bankruptcy risk.
- Determine how financial analysis is used to evaluate credit risk.
- Describe Chapter 11 bankruptcy and predict failure potential.
- Define and describe Altman's Z-score as a measure of financial health.
- Explain bond ratings as defined by Standard & Poor's and Moody's.
- Distinguish between investment grade bonds and noninvestment grade bonds.

## INTRODUCTION

**Capital structure** refers to the relative mix and types of long-term debt and equity. Equity represents ownership. A key question is how much debt a corporation should acquire to support its asset base. Corporations assume debt for multiple reasons, from short-term payables of suppliers to long-term bonds for fixed assets acquisition and construction. The amounts and types of debt vary, based on the specific business strategy and the industry. Retailers have large investments in inventories and stores. Retailing also is a highly seasonal industry. Electric utilities have huge electric plant capacity, largely financed from long-term borrowing. Automobile manufacturing is a cyclical business with record levels of vehicles in boom years and substantial production drops during recessions. The structure of corporate debt will be reviewed for various industries.

Once firms assume liabilities, credit risk exists. Creditors expect timely cash payments and the fulfillment of other contract terms. This chapter considers two categories of **credit risk:** (1) **default risk,** the probability that a firm will miss cash payment of interest and principal when due; and (2) **bankruptcy risk,** the probability that the firm will declare bankruptcy. As credit risk increases, financial analysis becomes more crucial. This chapter evaluates two tools useful in assessing credit risk: (1) bankruptcy models developed by Edward Altman and (2) bond ratings, which indicate the relative financial strength of the rated companies.

## Corporate Debt

Large corporations have many global alternatives for borrowing funds, from overnight money to thirty-year and longer bonds. Suppliers of short-term credit include commercial banks and other financial institutions, as well as the commercial paper market. Commercial banks and other financial institutions provide multiple services for corporations and often specialize by industry and geographic area. By having a long-term direct relationship with companies, the bank can understand specific credit risks and opportunities for various services, including working capital and other borrowing needs. Types of loans include open lines of credit on demand up to some specific limit; revolving lines of credit, a longer credit relationship typically designed around the operating cycle of a business; term loans for a specific amount and time period; working capital loans, which are usually secured with inventory and/or accounts receivable; and leases, which may be for longer terms and are secured with the leased assets.

Dell Computer has relatively little plant infrastructure and relatively little long-term debt. Major liabilities by category for fiscal year 2002 are shown in Exhibit 11.1. Most liabilities for Dell were current, with long-term debt representing less than 4 percent of total liabilities. This was offset by current assets, although the current ratio of 1.0 was low. The long-term debt was senior notes and debentures, with maturities due in 2008 and 2028 (Note 3 in the annual report). The company also had a $250 million revolving line of credit (Note 3). In summary, there is little evidence of credit risk.

Liability ratios for the three PC companies for the current year are shown in Exhibit 11.2. The ratios of the companies are similar, with large accounts payable balances and most liabilities current.

**EXHIBIT 11.1 LIABILITY ANALYSIS FOR DELL**

| | In millions | As a % of Total Liabilities | As a % of Total Assets |
|---|---|---|---|
| **Accounts Payable** | $5,075 | 57.4% | 37.5% |
| **Total Current Liabilities** | 7,519 | 85.0 | 55.6 |
| **Long-term Debt** | 520 | 5.9 | 3.8 |

**EXHIBIT 11.2 LIABILITY RATIOS FOR THE PC COMPANIES**

| | Dell | Gateway | Apple |
|---|---|---|---|
| **Accounts Payable ÷ Current Liabilities** | 57.4% | 40.9% | 52.8% |
| **Current Liabilities ÷ Total Liabilities** | 85.0 | 93.3 | 72.3 |
| **Long-term Debt ÷ Total Liabilities** | 5.9 | 6.7 | 15.1 |

Ford Motor is a huge global company with both automotive manufacturing and financial service sectors. Debt includes both sectors, making credit analysis more complex. A financial summary of liabilities for fiscal year 2001 is shown in Exhibit 11.3.

Ford had a very high debt to equity ratio ($268,085 ÷ $7,786) of 34.4×; consequently, credit risk is problematic. Just over one third of the liabilities were automotive, while the remaining almost two thirds were financial services. Much of the debt ($107,266 or 40.1 percent of total liabilities) represented long-term debt associated with financial services. This included senior notes, bank debt, and subordinated indebtedness. The primary function of financial services is to finance vehicle purchases through Ford Credit and similar subsidiaries around the globe. This represents a partial explanation of Ford's high debt levels.

These numbers normally generate red flags in terms of credit risk, but they seem to be standard in the automobile business—because of financial services. (GM had total liabilities of $304 billion vs. equity of $20 billion.) This was a poor year for Ford, recording sales of $162 billion worldwide but a net loss of $5.5 billion (down from a net income of $3.5 billion in 2000). Performance plummeted in the recession year of 2001, another consideration for evaluating credit risk.

Although deregulation is in progress, utilities historically have been regulated monopolies with stable revenues and largely "guaranteed" earnings. They usually assume large amounts of debt, which increases return on equity, without substantial credit risk. Duke Energy (2001) had total liabilities of $35.5 billion compared to equity of $12.9 billion (debt to equity of 2.8×). American Electric Power had liabilities of $39.1 billion and equity of $8.2 billion (debt to equity of 4.8×). There are extremes. Microsoft had no long-term debt. TWA had more liabilities than assets, for a debt to assets ratio of 1.08×, and it declared bankruptcy. Thus, credit analysis depends on context.

## DEFAULT AND BANKRUPTCY RISK

Most liabilities require a specified cash payment at a stated due date. If a company fails to meet this deadline and usually after a reasonable grace period, the firm is in default. In most cases, the creditor will collect the amount owed. However, collection costs may be

**EXHIBIT 11.3 FINANCIAL SUMMARY OF LIABILITIES FOR FORD**

| | In millions | As a % of Total Liabilities | As a % of Total Assets |
|---|---|---|---|
| **Trade Payables, Automotive** | $ 15,677 | 5.8% | 5.7% |
| **Total Current Liabilities, Automotive** | 44,546 | 16.6 | 16.1 |
| **Long-term Debt, Automotive** | 13,492 | 5.0 | 4.9 |
| **Other Long-term Liabilities, Automotive** | 30,868 | 11.5 | 11.2 |
| **Total Liabilities, Automotive** | 92,980 | 34.7 | 33.6 |
| **Payable, Financial** | 3,095 | 1.2 | 1.1 |
| **Total Liabilities, Financial** | 175,105 | 65.3 | 63.3 |

high and, for troubled firms, the amount collected may be a small fraction of the original amount and received long after the original due date. Consequently, creditors evaluate credit risk carefully to minimize the potential for default.

Standard financial analysis techniques are used to evaluate default risk. Red flags associated with increasing risk include low liquidity, high leverage, poor or erratic earnings, declining sales, and negative cash flows from operations. When firms have operating or liquidity problems, earnings management techniques to camouflage existing problems are more likely. In most cases, multiple red flags will be present.

Various **failure events** can signal potential default problems. These include management restructuring, "big bath" write-offs, and unexpected nonrecurring items. Particularly serious events include troubled debt restructuring, bond rating downgrading, and going-concern audit qualifications.

Trans World Airlines (TWA) filed for Chapter 11 bankruptcy in 1995 and restructured. It was the eighth largest airline in the United States and traded on Amex. TWA recorded a net loss in 1999 of $353.4 million after losing $120.5 million in 1998. A negative stockholders' equity of $170.8 million existed, resulting in a debt ratio of 1.1 (that is, liabilities were greater than assets by 10 percent). Long-term liabilities totaled $1,347 million, of which $600.9 million were long-term notes paying interest rates of 7.5–15 percent. Cash flow from operations was a negative $3,212 million. Operating leases had minimum lease payments of $5,986 million (compared to capital leases with of $212 million). Net pension obligation total $12.6 million, while net postemployment benefit obligations were $502.1 million. Nonrecurring items included extraordinary items, discontinued operations, and special charges. Thus, TWA reported both failure events and other credit risk red flags. Not surprisingly, TWA declared bankruptcy and its assets were acquired by American Airlines.

More recently, Kmart filed for bankruptcy in January 2002. Trying to emulate Wal-Mart and expand its list of products, Kmart was unsuccessful. After losing $244 million in 2001 (January fiscal year-end) and $2.4 billion in 2002, Kmart filed for Chapter 11 protection in an attempt to reorganize under court protection from creditors.

## BANKRUPTCY

Probably the most desperate measure a corporation can take is to file for bankruptcy under Chapter 11 of the Federal Bankruptcy Code. The purpose of Chapter 11 is to seek court protection from creditors in an attempt to reorganize the firm. Perhaps 50 percent of firms filing under Chapter 11 survive and prosper after bankruptcy. However, equity investors in bankrupt firms seldom recover any of their investment. Creditors attempt to recover most of the principal amount, often by assuming an equity position in the firm. In most cases, creditors record losses from bankrupt companies.

Bankruptcy rates have been on the rise, especially large well-recognized corporations. As stated in a *Fortune* article (R. Charan and J. Useem, "Why Companies Fail," (**www.fortune.com**):

> How many more must fall? Each month seems to bring the sound of another giant crashing to earth. Enron. WorldCom. Global Crossing. Kmart. Polaroid. Arthur Andersen. Xerox. Qwest. They fall singly. They fall in groups. They fall with the heavy thud of employees laid off, families hurt, shareholders furious.

> How many? Too many; 257 public companies with $258 billion in assets declared bankruptcy last year, shattering the previous year's record of 176 companies and $95 billion. This year is on pace, with 67 companies going bust during the first quarter. And not just any companies. Big, important, FORTUNE 500 companies that aren't supposed to collapse.

Flagg and others (1991) identify a failure process beginning with two years of net losses. Failure events include troubled debt restructuring, dividend reduction and elimination, violation of debt covenants, going-concern auditor qualifications, bond rating downgrading below investment grade, and the ultimate failure event, filing for Chapter 11 bankruptcy. Financial ratios to predict bankruptcy were current ratio, earnings before interest and taxes (EBIT) ÷ total assets, retained earnings ÷ total assets, and total debt ÷ total assets. These ratios are similar to those used in the Altman model described below.

Most firms recover, but some continue to record failure events (Flagg et al., 1991). The purpose of evaluating bankruptcy risk is to ascertain the probability of future bankruptcy filings. Creditors expect to record losses when firms file for Chapter 11. As previously stated, traditional financial analysis techniques and additional red flags from a detailed accounting analysis signal potential bankruptcy. In addition, complex statistical models can be used to predict the probability of bankruptcy.

## Financial Leverage and Ratio Analysis

Financial leverage is the relative mix of long-term debt and equity. Long-term debt increases credit risk and has fixed (or variable) interest charges, which are additional expenses. The fixed charges associated with long-term debt reduce return on assets (ROA, calculated as Net Income ÷ Average Total Assets). However, they have two advantages. First, interest charges are tax deductible and the tax benefits increase cash flows from operations. Second, long-term debt (the use of leverage) increases return on equity (ROE). Consequently, it is the relative mix of debt to equity that is critical to analysis.

The **financial leverage index** (FLI) evaluates the relative returns: ROE ÷ ROA. An FLI greater than 1 can be interpreted as positive financial leverage. That is, the use of liabilities increases ROE relative to ROA. The solvency ratio from the DuPont Model is: Average Total Assets ÷ Average Common Equity. As a separate ratio, this is often called the **financial structure leverage ratio** (FSLR). The ratio can be used in conjunction with the FLI as part of the analysis of relative performance and credit risk. Other leverage ratios (reviewed in Chapter 4) also are useful credit risk evaluators.

Consider Dell's ratios (numbers are from Chapter 4):

| Ratio | Calculation | Result |
|---|---|---|
| Financial Leverage Index (FLI) | 39.8 ÷ 17.5 | 2.3 |
| Financial Structure Leverage Ratio (FSLR) | 13,485 ÷ 5,158 | 2.6 |
| Debt to Equity | 8,841 ÷ 4,694 | 1.9 |
| Interest Coverage | (1,246 + 29 + 485) ÷ 29 | 60.7 |
| Long-term Debt to Equity | 1,322 ÷ 4,694 | 28.2% |

As expected, Dell's ratios are above average. The FLI is 2.3, well above 1. The benefit of relatively high debt is the increase in ROE relative to ROA. The FSLR is a high 2.6, suggesting high leverage, as does the debt to equity ratio of 1.9. The interest coverage is very high, indicating considerable coverage ability. Long-term debt to equity is a low 28.2 percent, because most of Dell's liabilities are current. Thus, the interest coverage and long-term debt to equity ratio suggest relatively low credit risk.

## ALTMAN'S Z-SCORE

Several multivariate models have been developed to predict bankruptcy. Primarily, a sample of bankrupt firms is matched to a comparable sample of nonbankrupt firms and a set of ratios is used to classify firms as bankrupt or nonbankrupt. The best known of these models, **Altman's Z-score,** was developed 1968 to predict the failure of manufacturing firms. This original model was:

$$\begin{aligned} Z = {} & 1.2 \times (\text{working capital} \div \text{total assets}) \\ & + 1.4 \times (\text{retained earnings} \div \text{total assets}) \\ & + 3.3 \times (\text{EBIT} \div \text{total assets}) \\ & + 0.6 \times (\text{market value of equity} \div \text{book value of debt}) \\ & + 1.0 \times (\text{sales} \div \text{total assets}) \end{aligned}$$

The critical value of Z was 2.675. Firms having a Z-score below that were classified as failing. The "gray area" of Z-scores was 1.81–2.99, with firms in this range difficult to classify as failing or healthy. The model essentially represents a limited financial analysis model incorporating basic liquidity, leverage, and profitability ratios.

A more recent Altman Z-score model can be applied to a broader range of firms, including service firms (Altman, 1983):

$$\begin{aligned} Z = {} & 6.56 \times (\text{working capital} \div \text{total assets}) \\ & + 3.26 \times (\text{retained earnings} \div \text{total assets}) \\ & + 6.72 \times (\text{EBIT} \div \text{total assets}) \\ & + 1.05 \times (\text{book value of equity} \div \text{book value of debt}) \end{aligned}$$

Under this model the Z-score cutoffs are:

- Less than 1.1—Bankrupt
- 1.10 to 2.6—Gray area
- Greater than 2.6—Healthy

This Z-score model can be used as a general indicator of financial health. A Z-score below 1.1 doesn't mean the company will go bankrupt, but it is a red flag and suggests the need for further analysis of bankruptcy risk.

The 1983 Altman Z-score model will be used for further analysis. It is a more recent model and is more generalizable. The 1968 model was developed specifically for manufacturing firms. The 1983 model can be used for both industrial and service firms.

The following information is needed to calculate the Z-score for Dell's fiscal year 2002:

| | |
|---|---|
| Total current assets | $ 7,877 |
| Total current liabilities | 7,519 |
| Working capital | 358 |
| Total assets | 13,535 |
| Retained earnings | 1,364 |
| EBIT = income before tax of 1,731 + interest expense of 29 = | 1,760 |
| Total stockholders' equity | 4,694 |
| Total liabilities | 8,841 |

The calculation of Dell's Z-score is:

| Coefficient | Ratio | Calculation |
|---|---|---|
| 6.56 × | Working Capital ÷ Total Assets = 358 ÷ 13,535 | 0.174 |
| 3.26 × | Retained Earnings ÷ Total Assets = 1,364 ÷ 13,535 | 0.329 |
| 6.72 × | EBIT ÷ Total Assets = 1,760 ÷ 13,535 | 0.874 |
| 1.05 × | Book Value of Equity ÷ Book Value of Debt = 4,694 ÷ 8,841 | 0.506 |
| = | Z-score | 1.88 |

The calculation of working capital to total assets is 6.56 × (358 ÷ 13,535) = 0.174. Dell's Z-score of 1.88 (down from 4.02 in 2001) was less than the cutoff of 2.6, so Dell is classified in the gray area. The primary reasons were the drop in working capital and the fall in performance as measured by EBIT.

The Z-score calculations for the PC companies are tabulated as shown in Exhibit 11.4. Gateway had a large EBIT loss. Despite that, Gateway still was categorized in the gay area, although its score was below Dell's. The company compensated with substantial working capital and a relatively good leverage ratio. Apple had a large Z-score and was rated healthy. The only negative was a small EBIT loss. Thus, as credit risks both Dell and Gateway are minor concerns.

The evaluation of Trans World Airlines for default risk suggests a poor Z-score. The necessary information from TWA's 1999 financial statements is (in millions):

**EXHIBIT 11.4 Z-SCORE CALCULATIONS FOR THE PC COMPANIES**

| | Dell | Gateway | Apple |
|---|---|---|---|
| **Working Capital** | 0.174 | 2.146 | 3.950 |
| **Retained Earnings** | 0.329 | 0.672 | 1.224 |
| **EBIT** | 0.874 | –2.884 RF | –0.040 |
| **Equity ÷ Debt** | 0.506 | 1.337 | 1.959 |
| **Z-score** | 1.88 | 1.27 | 7.09 |
| **Category** | Gray area | Gray area | Healthy |

| | |
|---|---|
| Total current assets | $489.9 |
| Total current liabilities | 960.9 |
| Working capital | –471.0 |
| Total assets | 2,137.2 |
| Retained earnings | –899.7 |
| EBIT | –444.7 |
| Total equity | –170.9 |
| Total liabilities | 2,308.1 |

The Z-score calculation for TWA is:

| Coefficient | Ratio | Calculation |
|---|---|---|
| 6.56 × | Working capital ÷ total assets = –471.0 ÷ 2,137.2 = | **–1.45** |
| 3.26 × | Retained earnings ÷ total assets = –899.7 ÷ 2,137.2 = | **–1.37** |
| 6.72 × | EBIT ÷ total assets = –444.7 ÷ 2,137.2 | **–1.40** |
| 1.05 × | Book value of equity ÷ book value of debt = –170.9 ÷ 2,308.1 | **–.08** |
| = | Z-score | **–4.30 RF** |

TWA's Z-score of –4.30 indicates a failing firm. TWA filed for bankruptcy, not unexpected given its Z-score.

# Bond Ratings

**Bond ratings** are issued by bond rating agencies. The best known of these are Moody's and Standard & Poor's. These ratings indicated the agencies' evaluation of the credit worthiness of the firm. The ratings categories of the two firms are shown in Exhibit 11.5. Moody's adds "numerical modifiers" 1, 2, and 3 to each rating, with 1 at the high end and 3 at the low end of the rating. For example, DuPont's 2001 Moody's rating was AA3.

**EXHIBIT 11.5 BOND RATING CATEGORIES FOR STANDARD & POOR'S AND MOODY'S**

| | Standard & Poor's | Moody's | Category of Creditworthiness |
|---|---|---|---|
| **Highest Rating** | AAA | Aaa | Investment Grade |
| **Very High Quality** | AA | Aa | Investment Grade |
| **High Quality** | A | A | Investment Grade |
| **High Quality** | BBB | Baa | Investment Grade |
| **Speculative** | BB | Ba | Below Investment Grade |
| **Speculative** | B | B | Below Investment Grade |
| **Very Poor** | CCC | Caa | Below Investment Grade |
| **Very Poor** | D | C | Below Investment Grade |

Investors who are interested in bonds that have negligible credit risk would invest only in AAA and AA bonds, based on Standard & Poor's ratings. Most investors typically consider only **investment grade bonds,** those from BBB to AAA. Below that are speculative or **junk bonds** (most junk bonds are unrated). As the bond rating declines, the interest rate goes up to attract investors. Investors in speculative bonds receive a higher rate of interest but assume additional default risk.

Standard & Poor's reported bond rating information for 1999 (www.standardandpoors.com) as shown in Exhibit 11.6. Relatively few companies achieve high bond ratings, and more than half are below investment grade. Specific bond ratings seem to parallel relative size and standard financial ratios.

Bond ratings are an additional financial indicator for evaluation. Again, multiple techniques usually send the same signals. Successful companies according to financial ratios are expected to have healthy Z-scores and high bond ratings. A poor bond rating (generally below investment grade) is another potential red flag.

The current Moody's bond rating for the PC companies (May 2002) is:

| | Dell | Gateway | Apple |
|---|---|---|---|
| **Bond Rating** | A | Ba | Ba |
| **Status** | Investment Grade | Below Investment Grade | Below Investment Grade |

Somewhat inconsistent with the Altman results, only Dell has an investment grade rating. The three companies had different bond rating histories. In 1995 Dell had a B rating (junk), which was increased to Ba and Baa in 1997 and A in 1999. Gateway had an investment grade rating of Baa in 2000. Moody's changed its rating outlook to negative in July 2001 and downgraded Gateway senior debt to Ba, after poor earnings performance. Apple had investment grade bond status until 1996, when senior debt was downgraded to B. In 1997, it was lowered to Caa after performance difficulties. Bonds were upgraded to B in 1998 and Ba in 2000.

## SUMMARY

This chapter considered the liability structure of corporations and indicators of credit risk. As debt increases, credit risk also rises. The major categories are default risk (the probability of missing principal and interest payments on liabilities) and bankruptcy (the probability

**EXHIBIT 11.6 BOND RATING INFORMATION FOR STANDARD & POOR'S RELATED COMPANIES, 1999**

| | AAA | AA | A | BBB | BB | B | CCC |
|---|---|---|---|---|---|---|---|
| **% with Rating** | 1% | 4% | 13% | 20% | 24% | 32% | 4% |
| **Sales ($ millions)** | 14,028 | 8,367 | 4,242 | 2,082 | 731 | 276 | 42 |
| **Equity ($ millions)** | 7,519 | 3,010 | 1,697 | 794 | 228 | 64 | 21 |
| **Total Assets ($ millions)** | 16,015 | 8,043 | 3,560 | 2,230 | 824 | 374 | 254 |
| **Return on Capital** | 30.6% | 25.1% | 19.6% | 15.4% | 12.6% | 9.2% | –8.8% |
| **Operating Income ÷ Sales** | 30.9% | 25.2% | 17.9% | 15.8% | 14.4% | 11.2% | 5.0% |
| **Total Debt ÷ Capital** | 31.8 | 37.0 | 39.2 | 46.4 | 58.5 | 71.4 | 79.4 |
| **Total Debt ÷ Market Value** | 5.0 | 10.6 | 18.0 | 35.8 | 72.8 | 10.5 | 61.4 |

the firm will declare bankruptcy). Bankruptcy is devastating for both debtors and creditors and can lead to substantial creditor losses. Therefore, the prediction of bankruptcy potential is important.

In additional to traditional financial and accounting analysis, Altman's Z-score and bond ratings are useful tools for evaluating default risk. The Z-score was developed to predict bankruptcy, but it can be used also as a measure of overall financial health. Bond ratings are independent appraisals of relative credit worthiness and useful indicators of financial well-being.

## KEY TERMS

Altman's Z-score
bankruptcy risk
bond ratings
capital structure
credit risk
default risk
failure events
financial leverage index
financial structure leverage ratio
investment grade bond rating
junk bonds

## QUESTIONS

1. What are the major categories of debt and how do these relate to credit risk?
2. What is the relationship of default risk to bankruptcy risk when evaluating overall credit risk?
3. How is the financial analysis process used for evaluating credit risk? What measures are particularly important for this analysis?
4. What is Chapter 11 bankruptcy and how does it fit in the financial failure process?
5. What is Altman's Z-score and how can it be used in the credit analysis process?
6. What is a bond rating? Is this important in the credit analysis process? Explain.
7. What's the difference between an investment grade rating and a non-investment grade rating?

## PROBLEMS

### Problem 11.1 Financial Leverage and Solvency Ratios in the Chemical Industry

(Problems 11.1–2 relate to the chemical industry.)

Below are financial numbers for the three chemical companies.

| | DuPont | Dow | PPG |
|---|---|---|---|
| Net Income, 2001 | $ 4,339 | $ –385 | $ 387 |
| Total Equity, 2001 | 14,452 | 9,993 | 3,080 |
| Total Equity, 2000 | 13,299 | 9,686 | 3,080 |
| Total Assets, 2001 | 40,319 | 10,308 | 8,452 |
| Total Assets, 2000 | 39,426 | 27,645 | 9,125 |
| Common Equity, 2001 | 14,215 | 9,993 | 3,080 |
| Common Equity, 2000 | 13,062 | 9,686 | 3,097 |
| Total Liabilities, 2001 | 25,867 | 25,522 | 5,372 |
| Long-term Debt, 2001 | 5,350 | 9,266 | 1,699 |

a. Calculate the following ratios for 2001:

| | Formula | DuPont | Dow | PPG |
|---|---|---|---|---|
| Financial Leverage Index | ROE ÷ ROA | | | |
| Financial Structure Leverage Ratio | Average Total Assets ÷ Average Common Equity | | | |
| Debt ÷ Equity | Total Liabilities ÷ Total Equity | | | |
| Long-term Debt ÷ Equity | Long-term Debt ÷ Total Equity | | | |

b. Evaluate the financial leverage and credit risk of these companies, including a rating from 1 to 10.

| | DuPont | Dow | PPG |
|---|---|---|---|
| Financial Leverage | | | |
| Credit Risk | | | |

## Problem 11.2 Calculating Z-scores in the Chemical Industry

Below are the financial numbers for three chemical companies needed to calculate Altman's Z-score (1983) for 2001 (in millions):

| | DuPont | Dow | PPG |
|---|---|---|---|
| Total Current Assets | $14,801 | $10,308 | $2,703 |
| Total Current Liabilities | 8,067 | 8,125 | 1,955 |
| Total Assets | 40,319 | 35,515 | 8,452 |
| Retained Earnings | 13,517 | 11,112 | 6,551 |
| Earnings before Tax | 6,844 | 35 | 666 |
| Interest Expense | 590 | 733 | 180 |
| Total Stockholders' Equity | 14,452 | 9,993 | 3,080 |
| Total Liabilities | 23,443 | 25,522 | 5,250 |

a. Calculate Altman's Z-score for each company and rate each company as failing, healthy, or indeterminate.

| | DuPont | Dow | PPG |
|---|---|---|---|
| 6.56 × Working Capital ÷ Total Assets | | | |
| 3.26 × Retained Earnings ÷ Total Assets | | | |
| 6.72 × EBIT ÷ Total Assets | | | |
| 1.05 × BV of Equity ÷BV of Debt | | | |
| = Z-score | | | |
| Category | | | |

2001 bond ratings for the chemical companies are:

| | DuPont | Dow | PPG |
|---|---|---|---|
| Moody's | AA3 | A1 | A1 |
| Standard & Poor's | AA | A | A |

**b.** Evaluate the credit worthiness of these companies. Use Altman's Z-score, bond ratings, and previous financial analysis and rate the companies on a 1–10 scale.

| | Rating | Explanation |
|---|---|---|
| DuPont | | |
| Dow | | |
| PPG | | |

**c.** Are the signals from Altman's Z-score and bond ratings consistent? Explain.

## Problem 11.3 Financial Leverage and Solvency Ratios in the Hotel and Resort Industry

(Problems 11.3–4 relate to the hotel and resort industry.)

Below are financial numbers for the three hotel and resort companies.

| | Hilton | Marriott | Mandalay |
|---|---|---|---|
| Net Income, 2001 | $ 166 | $ 236 | $ 53 |
| Total Equity, 2001 | 1,783 | 3,478 | 941 |
| Total Equity, 2000 | 1,642 | 3,267 | 1,069 |
| Total Assets, 2001 | 8,785 | 9,107 | 4,037 |
| Total Assets, 2000 | 9,140 | 8,237 | 4,248 |
| Common Equity, 2001 | 1,783 | 3,478 | 941 |
| Common Equity, 2000 | 1,642 | 3,267 | 1,069 |
| Total Liabilities, 2001 | 7,002 | 5,629 | 3,097 |
| Long-term Debt, 2001 | 4,950 | 2,815 | 2,482 |

**a.** Calculate the following ratios for 2001:

| | Formula | Hilton | Marriott | Mandalay |
|---|---|---|---|---|
| Financial Leverage Index | ROE ÷ ROA | | | |
| Financial Structure Leverage Ratio | Average Total Assets ÷ Average Common Equity | | | |
| Debt ÷ Equity | Total Liabilities ÷ Total Equity | | | |
| Long-term Debt ÷ Equity | Long-term Debt ÷ Total Equity | | | |

b. Evaluate the financial leverage and credit risk of these companies, including a rating from 1 to 10.

| | Hilton | Marriott | Mandalay |
|---|---|---|---|
| Financial Leverage | | | |
| Credit Risk | | | |

## Problem 11.4 Calculating Z-scores in the Hotel and Resort Industry

Below are the financial numbers for three companies needed to calculate Altman's Z-score (1983) for 2001 (in millions):

| | Hilton | Marriott | Mandalay |
|---|---|---|---|
| Total Current Assets | $ 996 | $2,130 | $ 267 |
| Total Current Liabilities | 902 | 1,802 | 309 |
| Total Assets | 8,785 | 9,107 | 4,037 |
| Retained Earnings | 168 | 941 | 1,374 |
| Earnings before Tax | 250 | 370 | 93 |
| Interest Expense | 385 | 109 | 221 |
| Total Stockholders' Equity | 1,783 | 3,478 | 941 |
| Total Liabilities | 7,002 | 5,629 | 3,097 |

a. Calculate Altman's Z-score for each company and rate each company as failing, healthy, or indeterminate.

| | Hilton | Marriott | Mandalay |
|---|---|---|---|
| 6.56 × Working Capital ÷ Total Assets | | | |
| 3.26 × Retained Earnings ÷ Total Assets | | | |
| 6.72 × EBIT ÷ Total Assets | | | |
| 1.05 × BV of Equity ÷BV of Debt | | | |
| =Z-score | | | |
| Category | | | |

Bond ratings for the companies are:

| | Hilton | Marriott | Mandalay |
|---|---|---|---|
| Moody's | | | |
| Standard & Poor's | | | |

b. Evaluate the credit worthiness of these companies, using Altman's Z-score, bond ratings, and previous financial analysis. Rate the companies on a 1–10 scale.

| | Rating | Explanation |
|---|---|---|
| Hilton | | |
| Marriott | | |
| Mandalay | | |

c. Are the signals from Altman's Z-score and bond ratings consistent? Explain.

## Problem 11.5 Calculate Z-scores for Ford and GM

Below are the financial data needed to calculate Altman's Z-score (1983) for 2001 (millions):

| | Ford | GM |
|---|---|---|
| Total Current Assets | $ 37,833 | $208,920 |
| Total Current Liabilities | 43,327 | 63,156 |
| Total Assets | 284,421 | 303,100 |
| Retained Earnings | 17,884 | 10,119 |
| Earnings before Tax | 8,234 | 7,164 |
| Interest Expense | 9,519 | 9,552 |
| Total Stockholders' Equity | 18,610 | 30,175 |
| Total Liabilities | 265,138 | 272,925 |

a. Calculate Z-scores and rate each company as failing, healthy, or indeterminate.

| | Ford | GM |
|---|---|---|
| 6.56× Working Capital ÷ Total Assets | | |
| 3.26 × Retained Earnings ÷ Total Assets | | |
| 6.72 × EBIT ÷ BV of Debt | | |
| 1.05 × BV of Equity ÷ BV of Debt | | |
| = Z-score | | |
| Category | | |

The bond ratings for Ford and GM are:

| | Ford | GM |
|---|---|---|
| Moody's | A1 | A2 |
| Standard & Poor's | A | A |

b. Evaluate the credit worthiness of these companies, using Altman's Z-score, bond ratings, and previous financial analysis. Rate the companies on a 1–10 scale.

| | Rating | Explanation |
|---|---|---|
| Ford | | |
| GM | | |

## CASES

### Case 11.1 Debt Levels at General Electric (GE)

GE reported the following balance sheet information for the past two fiscal years (in millions). Calculate common-size information.

| | 2001 | 2001 Common-size | 2000 | 2000 Common-size |
|---|---|---|---|---|
| Total Assets | $495,023 | 100% | $437,006 | 100% |
| Short-term Borrowing | 153,076 | | 119,180 | |
| Current Liabilities | 198,904 | | 156,112 | |
| Long-term Borrowing | 79,806 | | 82,132 | |
| Total Liabilities | 434,984 | | 381,578 | |
| Stockholders' Equity | 54,824 | | 50,492 | |

Does the level of debt seem excessive?

A major part of GE is General Electric Capital Services (GECS), which is one of the largest financial services companies in the United States. Consequently, this subsidiary is funded primarily by debt. GE's balance sheet separates GE (manufacturing) from GECS. The same information as above for 2001 is presented for the two components. Calculate common-size information.

| | GE | GE Common-size | GECS | GECS Common-size |
|---|---|---|---|---|
| Total Assets | $109,733 | | $425,484 | |
| Short-term Borrowing | 1,722 | | 160,844 | |
| Current Liabilities | 36,072 | | 174,549 | |
| Long-term Borrowing | 787 | | 79,091 | |
| Total Liabilities | 53,961 | | 392,627 | |
| Stockholders' Equity | 54,824* | | 28,590* | |

* GECS equity is recorded as "Investment in GECS" in GE's balance sheet

GESC short-term borrowing is primarily commercial paper ($117,459 million); long-term borrowing is primarily senior notes due 2003–55 ($78,347 million). GECS has committed lines of credit of $28.6 billion. Part of the debt is foreign, and the company uses interest rate and foreign currency swaps as well as currency forwards and currency swaps.

Now evaluate the liabilities of the two components of GE.

### Case 11.2 Classifying Debt for Ford Motor Co.

The 2001 annual report for Ford reports the following liabilities on the balance sheet (in millions):

| | 2001 | 2000 |
|---|---|---|
| **LIABILITIES** | | |
| Automotive: | | |
| Trade payables | $ 15,677 | $ 15,075 |
| Other payables | 4,577 | 4,011 |
| Accrued liabilities (Note 10) | 23,990 | 23,369 |
| Income taxes payable | – | 449 |
| Debt payable within one year (Note 11) | 302 | 277 |
| Total current liabilities | 44,546 | 43,181 |
| Long-term debt (Note 11) | 13,492 | 11,769 |
| Other liabilities (Note 10) | 30,868 | 29,610 |
| Deferred income taxes | 362 | 353 |
| Payable to Financial Services (Note 1) | 3,712 | 2,637 |
| Total Automotive liabilities | 92,980 | 87,550 |
| Financial Services: | | |
| Payables | 3,095 | 5,297 |
| Debt (Note 11) | 153,543 | 153,510 |
| Deferred income taxes | 9,703 | 8,677 |
| Other liabilities and deferred income | 7,826 | 7,486 |
| Payable to Automotive (Note 1) | 938 | 1,587 |
| Total Financial Services liabilities | 175,105 | 176,557 |
| Company-obligated mandatorily redeemable preferred securities of a subsidiary T trust holding solely junior subordinated debentures of the Company (Note 1) | 672 | 673 |

**a.** Total liabilities were $268,757 million in 2001 and $264,780 million in 2000. A key question is what number to use when evaluating credit risk. The financial services sector has considerably more debt than automotive, which is expected for this type of activity. Calculate the percentage of liabilities for each sector.

| | Automotive % | Financial Services % |
|---|---|---|
| 2001 Liabilities | | |
| 2000 Liabilities | | |

**b.** Given the following information calculate debt to equity ratios and debt ratios for the two sectors and overall.

| | 2001 | 2000 |
|---|---|---|
| Total Assets | $276,543 | $283,390 |
| Stockholders' Equity | 7,786 | 18,610 |
| Debt to Equity Ratio | | |
| Debt Ratio | | |

c. Also, some liabilities can be excluded such as deferred income taxes. Note 10 has the following information on other liabilities from the automotive sector. Which of these should be excluded from leverage analysis?

| | 2001 | 2000 |
|---|---|---|
| NOTE 10. Liabilities—Automotive Sector (in millions) | | |
| Accrued Liabilities (Current): | | |
| Dealer and customer allowances and claims | $13,412 | $11,660 |
| Deferred revenue | 2,460 | 2,209 |
| Employee benefit plans | 1,790 | 2,029 |
| Postretirement benefits other than pensions | 1,230 | 1,076 |
| Other | 5,098 | 6,395 |
| Total accrued liabilities | $23,990 | $23,369 |
| Other Liabilities (Non-current): | | |
| Postretirement benefits other than pensions | $5,451 | $14,093 |
| Dealer and customer allowances and claims | 6,805 | 6,202 |
| Employee benefit plans | 3,853 | 4,145 |
| Unfunded pension obligation | 1,143 | 1,188 |
| Other | 3,616 | 3,982 |
| Total other liabilities | $30,868 | $29,610 |

The Automotive sector has current liabilities separated from long-term liabilities, but Financial Services does not. Note 11 has the following (interest-paying) debt information (summarized):

| Current Liabilities | Automotive, 2001 | Automotive, 2000 | Financial, 2001 | Financial, 2000 |
|---|---|---|---|---|
| Commercial Paper | | | $ 16,683 | $44,596 |
| Other Current | $ 302 | $ 52 | 29,594 | 21,796 |
| Long-term Notes and Bank Debt | 13,492 | 11,769 | 106,173 | 85,626 |
| Subordinated Debt (long-term) | | | 1,093 | 1,492 |

a. Calculate current and long-term (interest-paying) debt, total (interest-paying) debt, and relative percentages to total debt.

| | Automotive, 2001 | Automotive, 2000 | Financial, 2001 | Financial, 2000 |
|---|---|---|---|---|
| Current Debt ($) | | | | |
| Current Debt ÷ Total Debt | | | | |
| Long-term Debt ($) | | | | |
| Long-term Debt ÷ Total Debt | | | | |

What numbers should be used to calculate leverage ratios? Should the other liabilities from Note 10 be excluded? Should current liabilities be excluded? Should only interest-paying debt be included? How do the alternative definitions of debt or liabilities affect the credit risk of Ford?

## ETHICS CONSIDERATIONS

### How Much Risk?

A *Fortune* article (R. Charan and J. Useem, "Why Companies Fail: Overdosing on Risk," www.fortune.com) shows how incredible risk is assumed by CEOs:

> Some companies simply live too close to the edge. Global Crossing, Qwest, 360networks—these telecom flameouts chose paths that were not just risky but wildly imprudent. Their key mistake: loading up on two kinds of risk at once.
>
> The first might be called "execution risk." In their race to band the earth in optical fiber, the telco upstarts ignored some key questions: Namely, would anyone need all of this fiber? Weren't there too many companies doing the same thing?
>
> On top of execution risk was another kind, which we'll call liquidity risk. Global Crossing—run by Gary Winnick, formerly of the junk-bond house Drexel Burnham Lambert—loaded up on $12 billion of high-yield debt. This essentially limited Winnick to a cannonball strategy: one shot, and if you miss, it's bankruptcy.
>
> Bankruptcy it was. Given the utter violence of the telecom shakeout, you might say it was inevitable. But other telcos did manage to escape the carnage. BellSouth, dismissed as hopelessly conservative during the Wild West years, emerged with a pristine balance sheet and a strong competitive position. Its gentlemanly CEO, Duane Ackerman, was guided by a radical idea: "being good stewards of our shareholders' money."

**a.** There seems to be a relationship between corporate governance and bankruptcy risk. Is this reasonable? Are CEOs of these high-risk companies unethical?

**b.** What is the relationship of corporate governance and stewardship?

## INTERNET PROJECTS

### Project 11.1

Using the same company as in previous chapters, look up its bond rating and calculate Altman's Z-score. Compare it with one or more companies in the same industry. Go to Moody's Web site (www.moodys.com) and evaluate the bond rating history for this company.

CHAPTER 12

# Credit Analysis

**Objectives**

- Describe the six-step credit analysis process.
- Evaluate corporate loan considerations at commercial banks.
- Analyze credit-worthiness characteristics of corporations and other businesses.
- Apply the quantitative financial analysis and accounting characteristics associated with credit analysis.
- Discuss the use of the prime rate as a gauge for bank loan interest rates.
- Determine under what circumstances collateral or debt covenants are necessary for a commercial loan.

## INTRODUCTION

A primary source of commercial short-term loans is commercial banks and other financial institutions. Banks use **credit analysis** to determine **creditworthiness** and to recommend loan structure and interest rates. A six-step credit analysis process is suggested:

1. *Loan purpose*—The prospective borrower wants to borrow a specific sum of money for some purpose for a specified time period or establish a line of credit for some period.
2. *Corporate overview*—Analyze the industry and the company's business strategy for success.
3. *Quantitative financial analysis*—Based on (preferably audited) financial statements, the analyst will complete a thorough financial analysis focusing on the credit risk. Include Altman's Z-score and bond rating (if available). Evaluate both default risk and bankruptcy risk.
4. *Accounting analysis and forecasts*—Consider the confidence to be placed in the financial analysis above, based on earnings management incentives and specific circumstances involved. Is the prospective loan appropriate for the business strategy, or will it camouflage a cash shortage caused by operating problems? At

this point, forecasts of cash flows, sales, and profitability should be made for roughly the period of the prospective loan.

5. *Comprehensive analysis*—Summarize all components and consider the loan options. Should the loan be approved as stated by the customer, modified, or denied? At what interest rate? What specific contract terms, including debt covenants and collateral?
6. *Loan decision*—State specific recommendations, preferably as a written executive summary based on the comprehensive analysis.

The process is based on the financial analysis stated in Chapter 1, as modified for a credit decision.

## Loan Purpose

Commercial banks make short-term loans and lines of credit to *Fortune* 500 companies as well as smaller businesses. Banks prefer long-term relationships with established companies. Specific loan officers and credit analysts may be assigned to these firms, and their financial records are updated periodically. Revolving lines of credit and new loans would be quickly approved, based on standard terms. Banks also accommodate new customers, from successful firms wanting new banking relationships to those that walk in the door with a vague idea for a new business.

Typical commercial loans include working capital loans to finance the acquisition of inventory and receivables, lines of credit that allow borrowers to receive cash up to some limit as needed based on specified terms, term loans for intermediate or longer-term periods for equipment acquisition and similar purposes, or lease financing. These would usually be secured. For example, most retailing is seasonal, with a large percentage of sales around Christmas. Working capital loans or lines of credit are useful to build inventories for the Christmas period and expected accounts receivable balances after. These inventories and receivables often serve as collateral. Equipment purchased typically would secure term loans for equipment acquisition. Banks also may insist on compensating balances in the company's checking account; i.e., the loan would be credited to the company's account and some minimum balance in the account would be required.

Banks may specialize by industry, in which case loan officers and credit analysts with expertise in that industry would be hired or trained. Industry expertise gives the bank additional perspective on the unique circumstances and needs of that business. They also would be aware of pitfalls and the evaluation of potential red flags associated with operating problems and earnings management issues.

Assume that Piles of Tiles (PT), a local retailer of ceramic tiles and related products owned by sole proprietor Peter Piles, wants a ninety-day $100,000 working capital loan for inventory acquisition. He approaches Third National Bank, a medium-sized regional bank with assets of $250 million. The business is seasonal, with much of the business in the summer when construction and home remodeling takes place. PT is a Third National customer with a checking account and a previous borrower of short-term loans.

The information from Piles of Tiles establishes the purpose of the loan and the context for further credit analysis. The specific loan type is a working capital loan for a specific period. The potential borrower is a customer with an in-house credit history and a credit file. The credit analyst must determine what additional information is required to complete a financial analysis and must consider possible loan terms given the creditworthiness that will be determined. Much of the industry perspective and business strategy can be obtained from the owner and credit records of related businesses. In addition to what is available in PT's credit file, recent audited financial statements and tax returns are requested.

## Corporate Overview

Companies can be categorized by industry, by legal type, and by relative size. Each industry has unique characteristics related to seasonal factors (such as the agricultural growing season, retailing's Christmas sales, tourism's summer rush), economic characteristics (sales of durable goods such as automobiles fluctuate with the business cycle), geographic factors (oil and gas producing areas such as Texas and Oklahoma), and so on. Companies can be private, including sole proprietorships and partnerships, or public corporations. Corporations can be closely held or traded on major stock exchanges. Companies can range from global, billion-dollar giants that dominate industry segments to local sole proprietorships.

The *Fortune* 500 and other corporate giants depend on the largest commercial banks and bank consortiums for their borrowing. The companies also issue bonds for long-term borrowing and commercial paper for short-term requirements. They rely on commercial banks for revolving lines of credit (often based on their operating cycles) and other needs. These firms expect quick and excellent service and to borrow at the **prime rate,** the best (lowest) rate available to corporate borrowers. They typically have long-term relationships with major banks, often many banks around the world. They are in a position to require banks to compete for their business.

Smaller firms tend to be regional and more likely to deal with local or regional banks. These banks may specialize in certain industries. Many Houston banks specialize in the petroleum industry, while banks in Silicon Valley specialize in computer-related industries. Successful small firms usually have long-term relationships with one or more local or regional banks.

The credit analyst for Piles of Tiles should have a knowledge of specialty retailing, both local and national. What are the national and local circumstances associated with this business? What is the local or regional market for ceramic tiles and related products? What is the business strategy for PT? Who are PT's direct competitors? Is PT's strategy expected to be competitive? Assume that PT is the only specialized seller in the region, but two local merchandizing chains sell similar products. PT has a larger inventory, competitive prices, and more expertise useful to commercial and do-it-yourself buyers. The local economy is growing and PT has a track record of increasing sales. Will PT succeed in an economic downturn? Is that issue important for a short-term loan that's secured? These are some of the potential issues associated with the corporate overview.

## Quantitative Financial Analysis

The financial analysis for a credit decision doesn't differ fundamentally from the perspective of Chapter 4 (and Chapter 5 to a limited extent), except the focus is on the credit decision. Is the company creditworthy? To find out, relatively more emphasis is placed on liquidity and leverage measures. The main credit risks concern the ability of the company to pay back principal and interest as they come due. How much credit risk is the bank or other creditor willing to assume? To what extent is credit risk offset by collateral?

Creditworthiness can vary considerably and still be acceptable for commercial lending. The bank controls the terms of the loan and can adjust the interest rate and contract terms to compensate for increased credit risk. Blue-chip borrowers can receive prime rates without collateral and with few debt covenants. As credit risk increases, interest rates rise. These can be stated as prime rate plus 1 percent, 2 percent, or more. Collateral and compensating balances would be demanded and stringent debt covenants enforced. These can include maintaining certain minimum financial ratios (such as a current ratio above 1.5; debt to equity ratio below 2.0), limiting dividends, restricting further borrowing, compensating balances in the firm's checking account, and so on.

Liquidity and leverage analysis would begin with standard ratios, such as current and operating cash flow ratios, debt to equity, and interest coverage. Profitability and activity ratios are still important. Credit risk generally declines with increased profitability and efficiency. Both annual and quarterly results are important, as are growth rates. As with any financial analysis, particular concern is placed on red flags. Typically, red flags, when present, show up in several areas. A company with declining profitability should be expected to have poor profitability ratios, declining activity ratios, and problems related to specific liquidity and other ratios. Even profitable and growing companies can have red flags. For example, rising inventories and accounts receivables may indicate changing revenue recognition policies that suggest performance problems in the near future.

Assume that a complete financial analysis was performed on PT's audited financial statements and the most recent quarterly reports. Piles of Tiles has summarized ratios and other measures of performance, as shown in Exhibit 12.1. The credit analyst indicated that the financial history of the company was excellent, with no red flags.

## Accounting Analysis and Forecasts

A major concern is the confidence to be placed in the ratios and other financial analysis based on the financial statements of the company. These financial statements should represent economic reality, but owners and managers have earnings management incentives that could lead to financial distortion. Troubled companies have incentives to make the financial statements more attractive than they really are. Some issues for a credit decisions include: Does the company have incentives to inflate revenues (such as aggressive revenue recognition)? Are credit terms for sales too permissive? Do substantial unrecorded obligations, such as operating leases or contingencies, exist? Are inventories overstated, such as outdated inventories that should be written down to market?

**EXHIBIT 12.1 SELECTED FINANCIAL RATIOS FOR PILES OF TILES**

| | 2001 | 2000 |
|---|---|---|
| **Current Ratio** | 1.7 | 1.6 |
| **Operating Cash Flow** | 30.7% | 32.2% |
| **Debt to Equity** | 0.8 | 0.9 |
| **Interest Coverage** | 10.9 | 10.3 |
| **Inventory Turnover** | 14.6% | 14.1% |
| **Gross Margin** | 22.7% | 22.0% |
| **Return on Sales** | 3.1% | 2.9% |
| **Annual Growth Rate for Sales** | 5.1% | 3.4% |

Forecasts should be calculated for sales and profitability and future cash flows for roughly the period of the prospective loan. The primary key to forecasting is the projection of future sales. Sales growth rates usually indicate rising or falling profitability and future cash flows. Forecasts can range from simple projections based on historical trend as modified by expected economic conditions to sophisticated statistical forecasts based on time series or econometric analysis. Sales and earnings forecast are readily available from financial analysts for large firms, but they would have to be calculated for smaller firms.

The accounting analysis for Piles of Tiles would be based on information available from the financial statements and discussions with the accountant and auditor. The financial statement information should be compared to tax returns for the same period. It is expected that the numbers would be similar. If not, the differences would have to be explained. Projections for sales, profit, and cash flows can be based on historical growth rates, expected current sales trends, and local economic projections from the local chamber of commerce or other sources. Assume that last year's sales growth rate for PT was 5.1 percent. This represents the starting point for these projections.

## Comprehensive Analysis

At this stage the fundamental analysis has been completed and needs to be written up and summarized so recommendations can be made. The first key decision is creditworthiness. Is the credit risk level of the client low enough to consider a loan? Since the bank has considerable flexibility with loan terms, a reasonable level of risk can be assumed profitably. Assuming an adequate risk level, the loan terms can be considered, usually based on prime rate. What percentage rate above prime is adequate, given the credit risk level and what collateral required? For most small borrowers, the range may be from 1 percent to 4 percent above prime (4 percent for relatively high risk). **Collateral** typically is based on the loan purpose. A term loan for the purchase of equipment would usually require the equipment to serve as collateral. Potentially, any available assets with a market value can serve as collateral. Additional **debt covenants** may be required, especially for higher risk customers. These may include minimum liquidity and leverage ratios to be maintained, limiting dividends and other owners' withdrawals from the business, and limitations on further borrowing.

Piles of Tiles has minimum credit risk and should receive a relatively low interest rate and limited debt restrictions. The credit analyst recommends prime rate plus 1 percent, the lowest rate considered acceptable by the bank for a small sole proprietorship. Inventory and accounts receivable would be pledged as collateral, since this is a working capital loan. A compensating balance of 5 percent of the unpaid loan balance is required. No additional debt covenants are considered necessary.

## Loan Decisions

The loan officer responsible for the specific customer would make the final loan decision. A lending committee may have to approve loans over some minimum amount. For Piles of Tiles's application, an executive summary would summarize the financial analysis and recommendations. The agreement follows the credit analyst's recommendations. Since the loan is over $50,000, the final agreement has to be approved by the bank's Commercial Loan Committee.

Most major corporations use bank loans for at least some short-term reasons, usually as part of a larger liquidity perspective. Dell, for example (Note 3, 2002 10-K) has a $250 million revolving line of credit. DuPont borrows from non-U.S. banks in addition to using commercial paper and notes payable for short-term borrowing. DuPont reported (Note 20, 2001 annual report) an unused bank line of credit of $3.8 billion.

# Is This Dot-com Creditworthy?

Amazon.com is one of the most successful Internet companies. It is the world's biggest bookstore and attempts to sell or auction virtually anything. Its strategy is to expand as rapidly as possible to be the first and best and dominate these retail e-markets. But it is doing so without regard to current profitability. Does this make Amazon a viable candidate for a commercial loan? (This is a fantasy scenario to consider traditional financial analysis tools, not Amazon's real credit needs.)

Assume that Amazon wants a revolving line of credit for $500 million. Should this loan be made? The six-step process will be summarized to highlight key points.

1. *Purpose of loan*—$500 million line of credit to be used to finance seasonal inventory needs and other business opportunities.
2. *Corporate overview*—Amazon is unique. Founder Jeff Bezos established a bookselling Internet site with extraordinary success. The company has been growing and expanding into related businesses ever since. Competitors could include bookseller Barnes & Noble, a much bigger bricks and mortar company with its own entry onto the Internet; plus other dot-coms such as eBay. As stated on Amazon's Web site: "Our vision is to use this platform to build Earth's most customer-centric company, a place where people can come to find and discover anything and everything they might want to buy online."
3. *Financial analysis* (see below for financial summaries)—Substantial revenue growth from $610 million to $3.1 billion (1998–2001), a growth of over 400 percent in four years. This indicates the success of the company's strategy. The current ratio is a reasonable 1.8. But red flags abound. The 2001 net loss was $–567 million (a negative return on sales of 18.1 percent), but down from $1.4 billion in 2000. EPS forecasts call for a small loss in 2002, but a positive $0.13 EPS in 2003. Total equity was a negative $1.4 billion and the firm has substantial long-term liabilities. Stock price for the last 12 months increased about 10 percent. These numbers are similar to some dot-coms, but eBay was profitable ($90 million in 2001, a return on sales of 12.0 percent). Barnes & Noble resembled a typical old-economy company, with a 2001 net income of $64 million.
4. *Accounting analysis*—Cash from operations was $–120 million in 2001 and negative the past three years. Revenue is based on selling prices, which may overstate actual revenue (assuming Amazon essentially acts as an "agent generating commissions"). Minimum lease payments for operating leases totaled $511 million. The company increased long-term debt by $29 million in 2001 (to $2.2 billion). Substantial stock options exist; the net outstanding options at the end of 2001 were 66 million shares.
5. *Comprehensive analysis*—Amazon is successful given its business strategy of rapid expansion without concern for profitability. However, the result of emphasizing sales rather than profit is the existence of substantial red flags and a number of concerns about potential long-term success. Credit risk is substantial. Standard credit analysis suggests that the loan be rejected.
6. *Loan decision*—Reject based on traditional analysis. Accept if Internet companies are a specialty and the loan committee has faith in the business strategy of Amazon. Interest rate would be above prime rate and collateral would be required (e.g., the company has cash and marketable securities of almost $1 billion). Debt covenants should focus on limiting future long-term debt and projections of profitability.

Summarized financial statement information for Amazon.com and competitors (in millions) appears in Exhibit 12.2.

Here is how the dot-coms stocks did (percentage change) over one year.

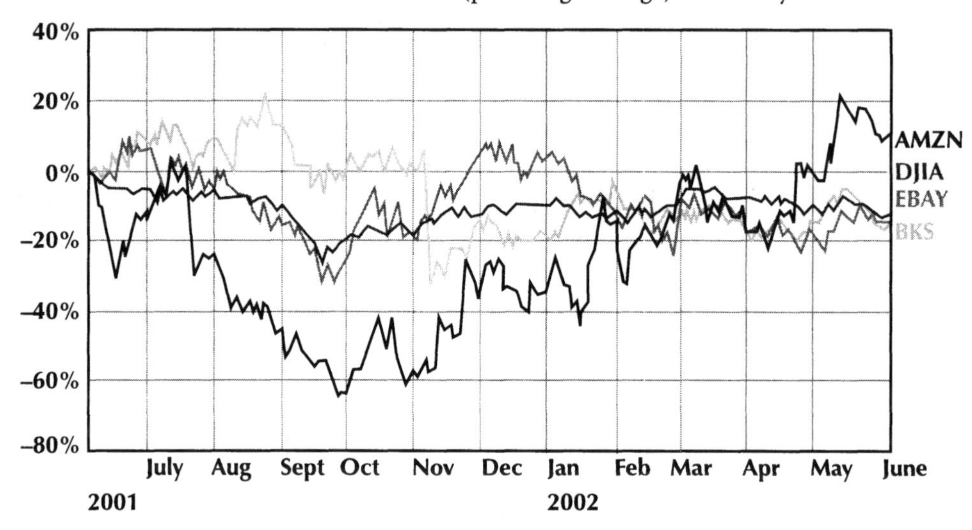


Period: June 5, 2001 – June 5, 2002

Source: www.quicken.com

Here is how the dot-coms did (percentage change) over five years.

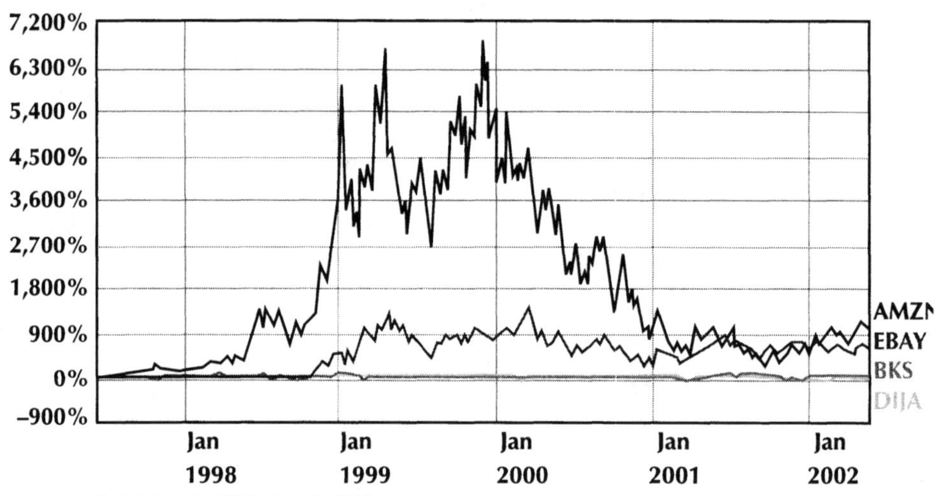


Period: June 5, 1997 – June 5, 2002

Source: www.quicken.com

The Amazon example illustrates the difficulty of evaluating young companies that are growing rapidly, typical of start-ups. The Internet represents an extraordinary growth area, but at substantial risk. Many companies ultimately will be successful, but which ones? The others likely will go bankrupt or be acquired at a relatively low price. Since bank lenders don't participate in equity growth but do sustain substantial losses for lending to failing companies, conservative decision making is expected.

**EXHIBIT 12.2 ABBREVIATED FINANCIAL INFORMATION FOR AMAZON.COM AND COMPETITORS**

| | Amazon 2001 | Amazon 2000 | Amazon 1999 | Amazon 1998 | Barnes & Noble 2001* | eBay 2001 |
|---|---|---|---|---|---|---|
| **Sales** | $3,122 | $2,762 | $1,639.8 | $610 | $4,870 | $749 |
| **Cost of Goods Sold** | 2,324 | 2,428 | 1,563.9 | 476 | 3,558 | 82 |
| **Gross Profit** | 799 | 334 | 75.9 | 134 | 1,312 | 667 |
| **SG&A** | 848 | 998 | 643.0 | 196 | 912 | 437 |
| **Net Income** | **–567 RF** | **–1,411 RF** | **–720 RF** | **–125 RF** | 64 | 90 |

| | Amazon 2001 | Amazon 2000 | Amazon 1999 | Amazon 1998 | Barnes & Noble 2001* | eBay 2001 |
|---|---|---|---|---|---|---|
| **Cash** | $ 997 | $ 822 | $ 117 | $ 26 | $ 108 | $ 524 |
| **Inventory** | 144 | 175 | 221 | 30 | 1,285 | 0 |
| **Total Current Assets** | 1,208 | 1,361 | 1,1012 | 424 | 1,591 | 884 |
| **Total Assets** | 1,638 | 2,135 | 2,472 | 649 | 2,623 | 1,679 |
| **Total Current Liabilities** | 921 | 975 | 739 | 162 | 1,140 | 180 |
| **Total Liabilities** | 3,078 | 3,102 | 2,205 | 510 | 1,735 | 249 |
| **Total Equity** | **–1440 RF** | **–967 RF** | 266 | 139 | 888 | 1,429 |

*Barnes & Noble's fiscal year ended January 2002

| | Amazon | Barnes & Noble | eBay |
|---|---|---|---|
| **Stock price, May 1, 2002, closing** | 16.49 | 31.00 | 54.06 |
| **Shares outstanding (millions)** | 373 | 67 | 277 |
| **EPS, 2001 actual** | **–1.56 RF** | 0.94 | 0.32 |
| **EPS 2002 forecast** | **–0.02** | 1.87 | 0.76 |
| **EPS, 2003 forecast** | 0.13 | 2.28 | 1.12 |

## SUMMARY

Commercial bank lending is an important segment of the capital markets and credit analysis a necessary step of lending decisions. A six-step process is suggested, based on the general process specified in Chapter 1 and using the techniques from all earlier chapters. The difference is focus and degree of analysis. The key is the evaluation of credit risk; specifically, the probability that principal and interest payments will be paid when they come due.

Quantitative financial analysis will be complete, but with special attention to evaluating liquidity and leverage. Accounting and forecasting analysis should pay particular attention to current and future cash flows. Since default is costly to creditors, lending contracts provide protection to the bank in the form of collateral, compensating balances, and debt covenants, as well as interest rates (usually based on the bank's prime rate) that factor in default risk.

## KEY TERMS

credit analysis
creditworthiness
collateral
debt covenants
prime rate

## QUESTIONS

1. Review the six-step process for a credit decision. Does it differ from other purposes (e.g., an equity investment decision)? Explain.
2. To evaluate credit risk, what are the main objectives of the credit analysis? How are these evaluated?
3. What credit-worthiness characteristics are associated with a commercial loan at the prime rate?
4. Give some examples of red flags that would cause a loan to be rejected.
5. Why are collateral and debt covenants often required for a bank loan?

## PROBLEMS

### Problem 12.1 DuPont Credit Analysis

Assume that DuPont's chief financial officer comes to your bank for a $2 billion revolving line of credit for two years at the prime rate. Complete the following credit analysis summary based on the calculations made from previous chapters.

| | |
|---|---|
| 1. Purpose of Loan | |
| 2. Corporate Overview | |
| 3. Financial Analysis | |
| 4. Accounting Analysis | |
| 5. Comprehensive Analysis | |
| 6. Loan Decision | |

### Problem 12.2 Hilton Credit Analysis

Assume that Hilton's chief financial officer comes to your bank for a $1 billion note for two years at the prime rate. This note will provide interim credit for the construction of new hotel facilities. Long-term financing will come later through long-term bonds or leases. Complete the following credit analysis summary based on the calculations made from previous chapters.

| | |
|---|---|
| 1. Purpose of Loan | |
| 2. Corporate Overview | |
| 3. Financial Analysis | |
| 4. Accounting Analysis | |
| 5. Comprehensive Analysis | |
| 6. Loan Decision | |

## Problem 12.3 Ford Credit Analysis

Assume that Ford's financial services sector director comes to your bank for a $5 billion unsecured ninety-day loan at the prime rate to cover a record temporary demand for Ford Credit loans. Complete the following credit analysis summary based on the calculations made in previous chapters.

| | |
|---|---|
| 1. Purpose of Loan | |
| 2. Corporate Overview | |
| 3. Financial Analysis | |
| 4. Accounting Analysis | |
| 5. Comprehensive Analysis | |
| 6. Loan Decision | |

# CASES

## Case 12.1 Credit Analysis for Amazon.com

Using the information from above, calculate the following for Amazon and its competitors:

**a.** Common-size statements.

| | Amazon, 2001, $ | Amazon, 2001, % | Amazon, 2000, % | Amazon, 1999 | Amazon, 1998 | Barnes & Noble, 2001 | eBay, 2001 |
|---|---|---|---|---|---|---|---|
| Sales | $3,122 | 100% | 100% | 100% | 100% | 100% | 100% |
| Cost of Goods Sold | | | | | | | |
| Gross Profit | | | | | | | |
| SG&A | | | | | | | |
| Net Income | | | | | | | |

| | Amazon, 2001, $ | Amazon, 2001, % | Amazon, 2000, % | Amazon, 1999 | Amazon, 1998 | Barnes & Noble, 2001 | eBay, 2001 |
|---|---|---|---|---|---|---|---|
| Cash | | | | | | | |
| Inventory | | | | | | | |
| Total Current Assets | | | | | | | |
| Total Assets | $1,638 | 100% | 100% | 100% | 100% | 100% | 100% |
| Total Current Liabilities | | | | | | | |
| Total Liabilities | | | | | | | |
| Total Equity | | | | | | | |

**b.** Calculate these ratios (additional information below table*):

| | Amazon 2001 | Amazon 2000 | Barnes & Noble 2001 | eBay 2001 |
|---|---|---|---|---|
| Current | | | | |
| Cash | | | | |
| Inventory Turnover | | | | |
| Total Asset Turnover | | | | |
| Debt to Equity | | | | |
| Debt | | | | |
| Debt to Market Equity | | | | |
| Gross Margin | | | | |
| Return on Sales | | | | |
| Return on Total Equity | | | | |
| Return on Assets | | | | |

* Additional information for Barnes & Noble for fiscal year 2000 (in millions): inventory $1,239, total assets $2,558, stockholders' equity $778; for eBay: inventory $0; total assets $1,182, stockholders' equity 1,104

c. Analyze the financial calculations for a commercial loan decision for Amazon.

## INTERNET PROJECTS

### Project 12.1

Go to the Standard & Poor's Web site (www.standardandpoors.com/Forum/RatingsAnalysis/CorporateFinance). See whether the company analyzed in previous chapters has been recently analyzed by S&P. If yes, give a brief analysis.

### Project 12.2

Using the company picked in earlier chapters and using the completed analyses done, do a credit analysis. Assume the company wants a $1 billion revolving line of credit, or develop another scenario that fits your company, and complete the credit analysis table below.

| | |
|---|---|
| 1. Purpose of Loan | |
| 2. Corporate Overview | |
| 3. Financial Analysis | |
| 4. Accounting Analysis | |
| 5. Comprehensive Analysis | |
| 6. Loan Decision | |

CHAPTER

# 13 Equity Investment Analysis

### Objectives

- Determine how an investment strategy and purpose are determined for an equity investment decision.
- Explain the reasons for investment portfolio diversification, especially related to the tradeoff of return and risk.
- Differentiate mutual fund categories and identify how they fit to specific investment objectives.
- Apply the six-step approach to analyze companies for equity investment decisions.
- Compare relative performance of Dow Jones Industrial Average companies.
- Evaluate the importance of an executive summary to provide an overview to the six-step process.
- Evaluate how a specific buy or sell investment decision is made.

## INTRODUCTION

Perhaps the most important financial analysis decisions involve equity investments. Virtually all of the necessary raw data are publicly available and almost all of the data are available on the Internet. This chapter uses all the techniques from previous chapters in the context of investment decisions for specific equity investment portfolios. Background materials are introduced including the purpose of investments and investment portfolios and the use of mutual funds. Then the six-step process is reviewed in the context of investment portfolio decisions. Dell Computer will be considered as a potential additional to a growth mutual fund.

## Purpose of Investments

The purpose of investing is to accumulate financial assets to be useful for some purpose. The investor earns a return by receiving interest and dividend payments and by selling the securities at a higher price than he or she paid for them, a capital gain (and hopefully avoids a capital loss). There are several investment-related risks. Corporate managers can reduce or stop dividend payments, the firm can default on its debt, interest rates can change, and stock prices can drop. The investor determines the investment goals to be met and the amount of risk to assume.

Most investors find several key features of strategy useful. Before individual investors seriously consider investment portfolios, it makes sense to pay off most liabilities and certainly all high-interest debt. There should be some minimum level of cash available in the form of bank or money market accounts and, as a rule of thumb, three to six months' salary should be kept in cash equivalents. Then an investment strategy should be considered. There may be short-term and long-term goals, income tax consequences, and consideration for employer-related retirement, stock option, or other investment plans.

Short-term goals might focus on the investor's education, buying a first house, the children's education, and so on. The most common long-range goal is retirement planning. Given the complexity of federal tax law, most retirement portfolios have significant tax consequences. Employer pension plans, stock options, and stock purchase plans should be the first consideration, followed by individual retirement accounts. Tax consequences are beyond the scope of this book, but they almost always are a consideration for investment planning. The primary focus here will be retirement planning, but without the detailed complexity of tax planning.

Retirement planning for young investors means a long investment horizon and, thanks to the magic of compound interest, the potential to accumulate a large pool of retirement savings. The primary goal in this case is long-term return. Historically, investments in common stock have the highest potential long-term return, and the investment strategy may include 100 percent investment in common stocks with a high potential for stock price growth. High growth common stocks are risky investments in the short run since stock prices can fall substantially at any time. The long-term trend is upward, and a diversified portfolio of growth stocks is much less risky. A more conservative strategy would include a diversified holding of bonds, cash equivalents (such as money market funds), and non–growth-oriented stocks.

For people in retirement or close to retirement, there should be more emphasis on investments that are less risky and that pay cash returns either in interest payments or dividends. There is still a place for high growth stocks, but the percentage holding would decline. A conservative strategy would also be suggested for shorter-term investment goals such as funding education costs within the next, say, ten years.

## An Investment Portfolio

Investment strategies seem almost unlimited, from holding only cash equivalents to high-flying dot-com companies. Investors can invest in individual securities or rely on mutual funds that are professionally managed. This chapter will consider alternative strategies but focus mainly on a growth fund (long-term approach) and an income fund (shorter-term or conservative approach) using the largest U.S. corporations, primarily the *Fortune* 500. This is only to simplify the analysis and is not necessarily the best investment strategy.

A possible long-term **investment portfolio**—a specific set of investments owned or managed for a person or entity—for retirement might include the fifty most attractive large firms that have earnings growth and stock price growth characteristics. The average investment for each firm would be 2 percent of the portfolio, with the firms having the best growth prospects representing 5 percent or more of the portfolio (5 percent is the maximum the SEC allows in a mutual fund). What characteristics would these stocks have? Obviously, firms expected to have the best stock price growth are favored. These would have the best earnings prospects, successful business strategies, efficient operations, and so on. Since other investors would also find these characteristics attractive, price earnings ratios (PEs) would likely be relatively high. The reason for high PEs is the large price premium on current earnings (that is, the stock price is discounted for expected earnings increases).

A possible short-term portfolio where cash will be needed soon might include 30 percent investment in cash equivalents, 30 percent investment in short- and medium-term bonds, and 40 percent investment in income-generating securities. Those income-generating securities would be perhaps thirty stocks that pay high dividends and seem to have relatively stable stock prices, or at least are unlikely to fall dramatically in a correction or bear market. The companies chosen for equity investments should have high dividend yields, relatively stable if unspectacular earnings growth, indications of strong balance sheets, and suitable business strategies. They probably will have relatively low PE ratios.

## Mutual Funds

A **mutual fund** is a portfolio of stocks, bonds and possibly other investments. They are regulated by the SEC and rated by various organizations such as Morningstar (www.morningstar.com). Investment professionals actively manage most funds. Annual fees are charged. "Load funds" charge commissions; "no load" funds don't charge commissions but do have annual fees.

Mutual funds have several advantages. First is **diversification.** The investor is buying a broad-based investment portfolio with each mutual fund, based on the specific investment strategy of the fund. Second is liquidity. Mutual funds can be converted to cash on request. Third, these are professionally managed. There are thousands of funds with different investment perspectives and, in theory, should represent a more preferred investment mix than one constructed by the individual investor. Fourth, it is possible to invest with small amounts of cash.

Drawbacks also exist. There are fees to pay, and this means that the average mutual fund returns about 2 percent less than the market averages, equivalent roughly to the fees charged by the funds (see Motley Fool's Web page, www.fool.com). Charges include annual management fees (also called investor advisory fees), administrative costs, 12b-1 fees (primarily for marketing), and commissions for load funds. Professional management also could be a drawback. The investor has no control of the funds. Most fund managers are actively buying and selling securities, which have capital gains and losses and other tax consequences. Perhaps an individual can develop a portfolio to better match his or her investment goals.

## MUTUAL FUND CATEGORIES

There are dozens of mutual fund companies running thousands of funds, so there are many fund categories. Here are the four major categories of investments:

- *Money market funds*—These invest in safe, short-term debt instruments that include Treasury bills, bank certificates of deposit, and corporate commercial paper. The investments are safe and earn a relatively low rate of interest. They are near cash, and investors usually can write checks against their balances.
- *Bond funds*—These invest in bonds and usually specialize in short-, intermediate- or long-term bonds. Bond categories include Treasury bonds, corporate bonds, municipal (tax exempt) bonds, and international bonds. These usually pay higher interest, but there is a risk associated with changing interest rates.
- *Stock funds*—These invest in equity issues of corporations and can specialize in almost any category: growth, income, value, industry sector, and so on. The long-term return for stocks has been higher than any other category, but stock prices can plummet at any time. Therefore, the short-term risk from stock investments is potentially high. Just like any stock, a specific mutual fund can generate a return much greater or lower than market averages.
- *Balanced funds*—These invest in a mix of stocks and bonds. The primary objective is income from interest and dividends, but with some stock appreciation potential. These are considered conservative investment portfolios, but they generally have higher risks than bond funds.

An investment strategy can incorporate investments in any combination of categories. For example, a beginning investor might start by investing in money market funds for liquidity, in bond or balanced funds for short-term goals, and in stock funds for retirement.

Stock funds can take many forms, so several attempts at fund categories will be considered. First, funds can focus on U.S. stock (domestic) or international (exclusively foreign or including U.S. stocks). Morningstar uses the following matrix to categorize mutual funds:

| | Value | Blend | Growth |
|---|---|---|---|
| Large | | | |
| Medium | | | |
| Small | | | |

Firms can be large, medium, or small capitalization (cap) firms. Morningstar considers the largest five thousand U.S. corporations based on market value (market price × number of shares outstanding). The top 5 percent (250 firms) are categorized as large, the next 15 percent as medium, and the bottom 80 percent as small cap. The matrix categories—value, blend, and growth—are based exclusively on price earnings (PE) and price to book (PB) ratios. The average PE ratio for the five thousand firms is given a value of 1, as is the average PB ratio. A weighted average is calculated for all PE and PB ratios, and these are added together for each firm. Thus, the average firm should score a 2. A value firm has a combined PE + PB less than 1.75 (i.e., the "relative price premium" is less than average), a blend firm 1.75 to 2.25, and a growth firm over 2.25. Therefore, the chart becomes:

| | Value < 1.75 | Blend 1.75–2.25 | Growth > 2.25 |
|---|---|---|---|
| Large Top 5% | | | |
| Medium Next 15% | | | |
| Small Bottom 80% | | | |

There are other categories and other ways to define mutual funds. Sector funds specialize in specific industries or other definitions of sectors. These include funds that specialize in banks, computers, pharmaceuticals, and utilities. Specialty funds are limited to such themes as social responsibility or convertible bonds.

Additional definitions of mutual funds include:

- *Asset allocation funds*—These funds spread the portfolio across a variety of investments, including domestic and foreign stocks and bonds, Treasury and other government securities, and cash equivalents. The purpose is to maximize investment diversity.
- *Index funds*—These are designed to mirror specific market indexes such as the Standard & Poor's 500. Fund fees are minimized because little stock trading occurs, and investors should come close to achieving the market return.
- *Income funds*—These are either stock funds or combination stock and bond funds. They maximize long-term cash payments in the form of dividends and interest payments. Generally, these are relatively conservative investments and have lower risks than more aggressive stock funds.
- *Aggressive growth funds*—These seek investments that have substantial growth opportunities, such as high tech start-ups. The potential for high earnings exists, but risk is equally high. High tech stocks, for example, rose substantially in the 1990s but crashed in 2000.
- *Sector funds*—These invest in specific sectors, usually based on industry such as pharmaceuticals, airlines, or utilities.
- *Regional funds*—These are based on geographic areas, usually specific countries or regions such as Latin America, Japan, or Eastern Europe.

This is not a complete list, but it indicates the alternatives available in mutual fund investing. Since there are so many funds, considerable research is needed to pick appropriate funds based on investment goals, performance history of the funds, and relative costs. Following SEC requirements, all mutual funds issue prospectuses, which should be reviewed before investments are made.

## THE GOTROCKS FUNDS

To illustrate the use of financial analysis for investment decisions, here are the Gotrocks Funds, a hypothetical mutual fund company. Its two mutual funds, the Gotrocks Growth Fund and the Gotrocks Income Fund, have the following characteristics:

- *Growth fund*—This fund invests in large capitalization "blue chip" domestic stock investments with the goal of maximizing long-term total market appreciation. Investments are mainly in *Fortune* 500 stocks. The fund has a market value of $45 million and invests in approximately fifty stocks. All have substantial earnings growth potential and are expected to earn a substantial market return. Each stock investment makes up at least 1 percent of the market value of the fund. The maximum holding is 5 percent.

- *Income fund*—This fund is invested 30 percent to 50 percent in intermediate- and long-term corporate and Treasury bonds and 50 percent to 70 percent in large capitalization "blue chip" stocks with the primary goal of maximizing cash return (interest and dividend payments) and, secondly, total return. The fund has a market value of $40 million, which is 65 percent invested in about thirty stocks.

It is assumed that 1 percent of the Growth Fund is invested in Dell Computer. A periodic review is made to recommend whether to (1) sell all Dell stock, (2) hold at the 1 percent level, or (3) buy more Dell stock, up to 5 percent of fund value. Since Gotrocks prefers 2 percent holdings of most stock, it is most likely that a buy or sell recommendation will be made.

## Equity Analysis

The six-step approach introduced in Chapter 1 is restated for the equity investment decision of reevaluating Dell Computer:

1. *Investment purpose.* What is the specific purpose of the investment decision? The focus usually is on an investment portfolio with a specific objective in mind. In this case the portfolio is the Growth Fund and the specific decision is whether to buy, hold or sell Dell.
2. *Corporate overview.* Dell manufactures and sells computers and has a specific business strategy. What are the prospects for this industry, and how successful will Dell's strategy be?
3. *Financial and market analysis.* A complete financial analysis has been done (especially in Chapters 3 and 4 and credit risk in Chapter 9). How is this analysis useful in the context of this specific investment decision?
4. *Detailed accounting analysis.* Dell's specific accounting policies and reporting decisions (based on the annual report and other sources) will be evaluated in terms of the fit to a growth fund investment. Are there any concerns about future operations and success based on this accounting review? Does any financial statement information have to be recalculated based on accounting specifics?
5. *Comprehensive analysis.* The analytical information must be evaluated in total to see how the information fits to the investment decision. Are there any obvious red flags or other concerns? How confident is the prediction of operating success and earnings? Is the stock over- or undervalued based on intrinsic value relative to the current stock price? Do economic conditions affect the analysis?
6. *Financial analysis decision.* A final recommendation must be made and defended: buy, sell, or hold based on current market price. Market timing can be an important consideration; that is, should the buy or sell decision be made immediately? Other recommendations or suggestions can be incorporated.

It should be emphasized that this is only a suggested format. It can be modified as needed for specific investment decisions.

# Investment Purpose

The list of alternative mutual fund categories indicates the vast number of potential investment goals that are available. Consider the difference between just two mutual fund types: growth and income funds. The growth fund is consistent with retirement investments, with a long-term focus and investments most likely to achieve a significant long-term rate of return with reasonable risk (or extreme risk associated with aggressive growth funds). The typical stocks in this fund should have high earnings growth rates. Consistent with earnings growth, sales growth is expected to be equally high, the industry and business strategy should suggest the potential for continued growth, PE ratios (note alternative calculations) are usually high to reflect a market premium for high growth, and the overall analysis should indicate a strong financial position and few if any accounting concerns. It should be noted that a PE below potential earnings growth is preferred (e.g., a PEG less than 1).

The income fund includes both bond and stock investments. The stocks should have a reasonably high dividend yield, at least above the average yield for large stocks and probably in the top quartile (25 percent). The goal is to maximize long-term cash dividends, so, in addition to yield, the company should have reasonable and stable earnings growth, a history of increasing dividends, an adequate financial position, and few accounting concerns. Earnings growth is expected to be in an average range, the company is likely is a mature industry, and this should be reflected in PE ratios at or below the market average.

## DOW JONES INDUSTRIAL COMPANIES

Initial selection of potential stocks for each portfolio can include an analysis of PEs, historical earnings growth rates, forecasted earnings growth rates, and dividend yield. Unless a company meets the basic criteria for fund investment, there is no reason to proceed. Consider ten stocks from the **Dow Jones Industrial Average** (DJIA), a stock price index of thirty industrial firms used as the indicator of stock market performance. Stock price, actual EPS (latest year), annual dividends (latest year), and five-year projected growth rates (available from www.quicken.com) are given in Exhibit 13.1.

From this information, PE ratios, PEG (PE ÷ 5-year growth rates), and dividend yield can be calculated, as shown in Exhibit 13.2. These are ten of the largest U.S. corporations, yet these basic market ratios differ from company to company. As a first pass to possible stock selection, which of these stocks seems to fit either the growth or income fund? The S&P 500 has an average five-year projected growth rate of 12.5 annually. Three of these firms have a growth rate above the S&P average. Intel has the highest projected growth rate at 18.2 percent, followed by GE at 15.4 percent and Microsoft at 14.7 percent. Average PE based on actual EPS is now about 25. As expected, all had relatively high PE ratios: GE at a reasonable 22.5, Microsoft at 38.2, and Intel at over 150 (because of low current EPS). These are the

**EXHIBIT 13.1 MARKET CHARACTERISTICS FOR SELECTED DOW JONES CORPORATIONS**

| Company | Stock Price, May 1, 2002 | EPS, actual 2001 | Annual Dividends, 2001 | Projected 5-Year Earnings Growth Rate |
|---|---|---|---|---|
| Alcoa (AA) | $34.00 | $1.05 | $0.60 | 12.0% |
| Coca-Cola (KO) | 57.62 | 1.60 | 0.80 | 11.6 |
| ExxonMobil (XOM) | 40.69 | 2.18 | 0.92 | 8.9 |
| General Electric (GE) | 31.70 | 1.41 | 0.72 | 15.4 |
| IBM (IBM) | 84.30 | 4.35 | 0.60 | 11.1 |
| Intel (INTC) | 28.63 | 0.19 | 0.08 | 18.2 |
| International Paper (IP) | 41.60 | **−2.37 RF** | 1.00 | NA |
| Merck (MRK) | 55.30 | 3.14 | 1.40 | 10.3 |
| Microsoft (MSFT) | 52.75 | 1.38 | 0 | 14.7 |
| Philip Morris (MO) | 55.38 | 3.88 | 2.32 | 12.5 |

most likely candidates for the growth fund. The lower the PEG, the more likely the stock is undervalued. Microsoft had a PEG of 2.6, Intel a PEG of 8.3, and GE a fairly reasonable 1.5. The S&P 500 has an average dividend yield of somewhat above 1 percent. If it assumed that stocks must have a dividend yield of 2 percent or more to be considered for the Income Fund, five stocks are a potential fit: ExxonMobil, GE, International Paper, Merck, and Philip Morris. Philip Morris would be the most likely candidate with a very high yield. As expected, Philip Morris has a relatively low PE at 14.3 and a low PEG of 1.1.

Analysis gets more difficult after this initial pass. Intel has current problems due to soft demand for chips. Microsoft still has antitrust problems. A thorough analysis is necessary to determine if this is a buying opportunity. Philip Morris seems a great income fund opportunity, with a high yield, a relatively high earnings growth rate, and a low PEG. But this is a tobacco company, subject to massive litigation. International Paper has a relatively attractive yield of 2.4 percent, but the company had a negative EPS, $−2.37. It's not clear if the company can continue to pay dividends. Consequently, a complete financial analysis is needed if International Paper is a potential investment.

**EXHIBIT 13.2 MARKET RATIOS FOR SELECTED DOW JONES INDUSTRIAL CORPORATIONS**

| Company | PE Ratio | PEG | Dividend Yield |
|---|---|---|---|
| Alcoa (AA) | 32.4 | 2.7 | 1.8% |
| Coca-Cola (KO) | 29.6 | 2.6 | 1.4 |
| ExxonMobil (XOM) | 18.7 | 2.1 | 2.3 |
| General Electric (GE) | 22.5 | 1.5 | 2.3 |
| IBM (IBM) | 19.4 | 1.7 | 0.7 |
| Intel (INTC) | 150.7 | 8.3 | 0.3 |
| International Paper (IP) | NM | NM | 2.4 |
| Merck (MRK) | 17.6 | 1.7 | 2.5 |
| Microsoft (MSFT) | 38.2 | 2.6 | 0 |
| Philip Morris (MO) | 14.3 | 1.1 | 4.2 |

## DELL'S FIT TO THE GROWTH FUND

How does Dell compare as a prospective growth fund candidate? Exhibit 13.3 shows the same basic information as earlier for Dell and its competitors (from Chapter 5). PE, PEG, and dividend yield are shown in Exhibit 13.4.

**EXHIBIT 13.3 MARKET INFORMATION FOR THE PC COMPANIES**

| Company | Stock Price, May 1, 2002 | EPS, Actual 2001 | EPS, Forecast 2002 | Annual Dividend | Projected 5-Year Growth Rate |
|---|---|---|---|---|---|
| Dell | $26.48 | $0.48 | $0.77 | $0 | 15.8 |
| Gateway | 5.33 | **–3.20 RF** | **–0.47** | 0 | 9.5 |
| Apple | 23.98 | **–0.07** | 0.52 | 0 | 10.2 |

**EXHIBIT 13.4 MARKET RATIOS FOR THE PC COMPANIES**

| Company | PE, Actual EPS | PE, 1-Year-ahead Forecast | PEG (Based on PE, 1-Year-ahead Forecast) | Dividend Yield |
|---|---|---|---|---|
| Dell | $55.2 | $34.4 | 2.2 | 0 |
| Gateway | NM | NM | NM | 0 |
| Apple | NM | 46.1 | 4.5 | 0 |

Only Dell seems a potential fit to the growth fund, with none a fit to the income fund. Dell has a projected five-year growth rate above the 12.5 percent S&P 500 average and an above average PE ratio. Dell has a high PEG of 2.2. If these were rated on a 1–10 scale, based on this limited data, all would rate 1 for the income fund, Dell probably 5 for the growth fund and Gateway and Apple a 3 or less. Two of the DJIA firms above, IBM and Intel, are computer-related manufacturing firms. Both also rank low for the income fund and higher for the growth fund. IBM has a five-year growth rate of 11.1 percent, a PE of 19.4, and a PEG of 1.7, making it an "average" S&P 500 firm. Thus, the initial ranking may be about a 5. Intel has a growth rate of 18.2 percent, a high PE of 150.7, and an unattractive PEG of 8.3, giving it perhaps a rank of about 3 for the growth fund.

## UTILITIES IN THE GOTROCKS INCOME FUND

Electric and other utilities are likely fits to the income fund. Historically, utilities have been highly regulated monopolies and have basically guaranteed a specific rate of return on operating assets. They have tended to have relatively high dividend payout ratios. Exhibit 13.5 shows basic data on the largest six *Fortune* 500 utilities.

PE, PEG, dividend yield, and payout ratios are shown in Exhibit 13.6. The five companies have attractive dividend yields, from 2.9 percent to 7.4 percent. Generally, these firms had other characteristics normally associated with income fund investments: high dividend payout rates, relatively low PE ratios, and moderate PEGs. TXU's and Southern's relatively high PEs, PEGs, and dividend payouts are problematic. Reliant had negative forecast earnings growth. The ratios of Duke Energy and Aquila seem attractive. None of these companies would rate above a 3 for the growth fund, but they may rate 5 or higher (perhaps much higher for Aquila) for the income fund. Again, a thorough analysis is needed before any investment recommendation can be made.

**EXHIBIT 13.5 MARKET INFORMATION FOR SELECTED COMPANIES**

| Company | Stock Price, May 1, 2002 | EPS, Actual 2001 | Annual Dividend, 2001 | Projected 5-Year Growth Rate |
|---|---|---|---|---|
| Duke Energy (DUK) | $37.86 | $2.56 | $1.10 | 10.2% |
| Aquila (ILA) | 16.32 | 2.42 | 1.20 | 7.5 |
| TXU | 54.17 | 3.12 | 2.40 | 8.7 |
| Reliant Energy | 25.71 | 3.14 | 1.50 | **–13.0** |
| Southern | 28.16 | 1.81 | 1.34 | 5.5 |

## Corporate Overview

The corporate overview should indicate an industry position and business strategy consistent with investment goals. High tech, high growth industries fit the Gotrocks Growth Fund. Companies in mature industries trying to maintain existing market shares are not a good fit to the growth fund, but they may be a fit to the Gotrocks Income Fund if they have a reasonably high dividend yield.

Dell's corporate overview was covered in Chapter 1. Quicken.com classifies Dell in the microcomputer industry, and the five-year projected earnings growth rate for that industry is 22.0 percent. Although the industry is experiencing rocky times, projected industry growth for the next five years is consistent with the growth fund. Within this industry classification, Dell has an evolving specific business strategy that has been very successful in the recent past and is projected to have continued success. The basic sources of information of Dell's business strategy can be found in Dell's annual report and Web site. The business press can be useful external sources that should be more objective. Here is a summary of key points: (1) Dell is the world's largest direct seller of personal computer equipment; (2) the business strategy is based on its direct business model; (3) increasing emphasis is on Internet sales; (4) Dell maintains a low-cost strategy emphasizing custom-built systems and customer satisfaction; and (5) Dell is increasing its range of products, with more emphasis on business products and enterprise systems such as workstations, servers, software, and peripherals.

Dell's two closest rivals in this competitive industry are successful and compete head-on with Dell. Gateway's business strategy is similar to Dell's, while Apple has a proprietary platform and software. Dell has demonstrated an ability to compete effectively, and the market information summarized above indicates market confidence for continued success.

## Financial and Market Analysis

Financial analysis techniques were reviewed in Chapters 3–5 and received additional analysis in other chapters. All of this should be incorporated in the equity analysis, but some categories of information are especially important and may require further effort. Particularly important are profitability, market analysis, analysis of quarterly data, and forecasts. Since there are so many equity securities available, it seems logical to avoid companies with red flags and other concerns when investing in growth and income funds. On the other hand,

**EXHIBIT 13.6 MARKET RATIOS FOR SELECTED COMPANIES**

| Company | PE | PEG | Dividend Yield | Dividend Payout |
|---|---|---|---|---|
| Duke Energy | 14.8 | 1.5 | 2.9% | 43.0% |
| Aquila | 6.7 | 0.9 | 7.4 | 49.6 |
| TXU | 17.4 | 2.0 | 4.4 | 76.9 |
| Reliant Energy | 8.2 | NA | 5.8 | 47.8 |
| Southern | 15.6 | 2.8 | 4.8 | 74.0 |

red flags and other concerns fit the investment strategy of certain types of portfolios. Value funds focus on stocks that are undervalued, many of which are so classified because investors have sold or stayed away from companies with major concerns. Indicators of a successful reorganization may make these potentially attractive investments.

### DELL'S FINANCIAL ANALYSIS

Basic financial ratios for Dell are consistently positive (see Chapter 3). The ratios can be converted into ratings from 1 (poor) to 10 (excellent). Ratings are judgment-based and determined relative to benchmarks, competitors, market averages, or other criteria. Ratings for Dell might be as shown in Exhibit 13.7.

Financial analysis focusing on financial statement information rates from average (only activity is excellent). There are few concerns except for relative performance. Dell's performance growth rates are slowing.

### DELL'S MARKET ANALYSIS

Market analysis for Dell (see Chapter 6) is more problematic than the financial analysis. The market paid a substantial premium for Dell's performance, but as growth slowed the stock price tumbled. Dell's stock price was down almost 40 percent over twelve months ended May 1, 2002. The stock still has a relatively high PE ratio, but it has been volatile on bad news. That is, the market expects consistent growth in revenue and income. Ratings should demonstrate this risk–reward tradeoff, as shown in Exhibit 13.8. Stock market price has shown long-term growth for Dell, but was flat for the previous twelve months. Dell seems overvalued at its current price, despite reasonable earnings growth projections.

## DETAILED ACCOUNTING ANALYSIS

The primary purpose of the detailed accounting analysis is to indicate how much confidence should be placed on the financial statement information presented. When faced with indicators of unreported commitments and contingencies, aggressive revenue recognition, capitalizing costs that normally are expensed, and other indicators of earnings management abuse, analysts place less faith in the information presented. As distrust in the statements increases, the analysis becomes more difficult. The concerns need to be explored in detail and, if possible, financial information restated based on more realistic information or estimates.

By *Fortune* 500 standards, Dell is a simple company and the annual report supports this. Dell's 2002 10-K indicates relatively conservative accounting policies, such as revenue recognition and other policies consistent with the industry, and few concerns. There are no indicators of earnings management abuse or Unreported commitments. The primary accounting concern is the number of stock options outstanding, a common issue with high tech companies.

**EXHIBIT 13.7 QUANTITATIVE FINANCIAL ANALYSIS RATINGS FOR DELL COMPUTER**

| Category | Rating | Discussion |
|---|---|---|
| Common-size, Income Statement | 6 | Adequate earnings, but down from the previous year |
| Common-size, Balance Statement | 5 | Large cash position, especially marketable sercurities; but substantial current liabilities and mediocre leverage |
| Liquidity Ratios | 5 | Adequate liquidity; high cash but low current ratio |
| Leverage | 6 | High liabilities, but primarily current; low debt to market equity |
| Activity | 9 | Consistently high turnover ratios, indicating efficient operations—only five days of inventory |
| Profitability | 6 | Average performance, with a return on sales of 4.0% |
| DuPont | 6 | Average with high solvency and ROE of 24.2%, lower than in 2001 |
| Growth, Historical | 6 | Excellent sales and earnings growth, last five yeras, but lackluster in last year or two |
| Growth, Projected | 6 | High growth projected, but lower than last five years |
| Quarterly Analysis | 5 | Adequate, but loss of $101 million in August 2001 quarter |

**EXHIBIT 13.8 QUANTITATIVE MARKET ANALYSIS RATINGS FOR DELL COMPUTER**

| Category | Rating | Discussion |
|---|---|---|
| Stock Price Growth, 5 Years | 9 | Tremendous price rise, almost 400%, despite market tumble since early 2000 |
| Stock Price Growth, 1 Year | 5 | Dell flat, but best of the three PC companies |
| EPS Growth, Last 2 Years | 2 | Down 45.2% from previous year |
| EPS Growth, 2-Year-Ahead Projection | 8 | Expected increase of almost 90% over the next two years |
| Quarterly Earnings | 4 | Dell has faltered in some recent quarters |
| PE, Actual | 2 | High PE of 55.2 |
| PE, 2-Year-Ahead Projection | 4 | High PE of 29.4 |
| Yield | 1 | No dividends paid |
| Market to Book | 3 | High ratio, indicating few "real assets" to support market price |
| Intrinsic Value (from CNNFN) | 3 | Intrinsic value on 70% of current stock price |
| PEG | 3 | PE double expected earnings growth |

A table of potential accounting issues and ratings from 1 (extremely problematic) to 10 (no concerns) can be used. An evaluation of Dell's accounting issues may be as shown in Exhibit 13.9. The only real concerns are special charges for reducing its workforce and the dilution of equity from stock options. Pro forma net income is down 77.4 percent for option expense.

## COMPREHENSIVE ANALYSIS

All components of the financial analysis have to be combined to form a complete picture. Virtually any firm has red flags and concerns of some kind, and these need to be put into perspective based on all available information. Concerns from any of the previous components may indicate the need for further analysis. For example, Dell is expanding into various business markets such as workstations and servers. An investor may want to investigate this business segment further to determine sales and earnings prospects.

Other considerations that can be addressed here are what-if questions on changing economic conditions, changing competitive circumstances, and potential "bad news" scenarios that could affect the company. For example, how would Dell be affected by a recession or by increased competition from IBM or other competitor?

A written report should be prepared. An **executive summary** is recommended to delineate the key points of the analysis, supported by the detailed information of the analysis. The executive summary should direct the reader to the details. An example of an executive summary for Dell appears in Appendix 1 of this chapter.

An economic analysis should be part of the comprehensive analysis or presented as a separate step. The economy is subject to the business cycle, and many economic factors such as interest rates, inflation rates, and personal consumption trends can greatly affect

**EXHIBIT 13.9 DETAILED ACCOUNTING ANALYSIS RATINGS FOR DELL COMPUTER**

| Category | Rating | Discussion |
|---|---|---|
| Revenue Recognition | 9 | Policies consistent with industry |
| Expensing vs. Capitalizing Costs | 9 | No obvious capitalizing of costs normally expensed |
| Unusual Accounting Policies | 9 | Policies consistent with industry |
| Stock Options | 3 | Substantial options outstanding, large equity dilution effect, but average for the industry |
| Nonrecurring Items | 8 | Accounting change associated with SAB 101 requirements (in 2001) |
| Business Combination Abuse | 9 | Minor acquisition activity, no obvious problems or abuse |
| Operating Leases, Off-balance-sheet Reporting | 9 | Lease commitments exist, but minimal leases outstanding |
| Commitments | 9 | Miscellaneous commitments reported, minimal amounts |
| Contingencies | 9 | Legal proceedings reported, but none considered material |
| Retirement | 10 | 401(k) plans only, no long-term obligations |
| Special Purpose Entitities, Partnerships | 7 | Partnership with Tyco International for financing computer sales |
| Other | 6 | Special charge to reduce workforce; share repurchase program including call options (company also has put options) |

specific companies and industries. Stock market timing may be difficult to gauge, but relative economic conditions can change market strategies. Cyclical stocks, such as automobile and steel manufacturers, may be great investments at the start of an economic boom but poor prospects at the end of the cycle. Better alternatives at the end of the cycle are such "defensive stocks" as food or pharmaceutical companies, which tend not to drop much in recessions.

By the middle of 2000 the U.S. economy had been in the longest peacetime boom ever recorded. Had the business cycle been eliminated? Unfortunately, no. The United States entered a recession in March 2001, according to the National Bureau of Economic Research, after a ten-year expansion. This was the eleventh recession since World War II ended in 1945. Third quarter gross domestic product (GDP) dropped, but fourth quarter GDP increased 1.7 percent and first quarter 2002 GDP rose 5.6 percent. The NBER forecasted a recovery beginning by mid-2002 (if not already in progress), assuming no major shocks.

The prediction of economic conditions can change investment strategy. Dell may be an excellent investment if a recovery is rapid. Dell's sales growth could rise, but Dell's success in a poor economy is suspect.

Economic indicators are mixed in mid-2002, and there's no guarantee that a recovery will benefit the stock market. Leading indicators were down in April 2002, after virtually no gain since January. The unemployment rate (a lagging indicator) was up to 6 percent in April from 5.6 percent in January. Industrial utilization was up to 75.5 percent, up less than 1 percent since January. In summary, the indicators suggest a struggling economy that is not yet in an obvious recovery. However, it should be pointed out that changing economic conditions are hard to predict.

## Investment Decision

The analyst makes a specific recommendation or decision. The basic investment decisions, based on the current market price, are buy, sell, or hold. Other considerations are possible. Investment timing can be important. Analysts or firms may believe they can predict economic conditions, imminent market downturns, or price directions of specific stocks, then put off specific decisions until the timing is right. For example, Gateway's stock price is relatively close to its 52-week low. If it is expected that Gateway's price will decline further in the next three months, analysts may recommend delaying an investment until then. If Gateway's short-term prospects look good to the analyst, then it may be a buying opportunity. It should be pointed out that many investors make no attempt to time the market, and these types of timing decisions would not be considered. To simplify the recommendation for Dell, no attempt will be made to consider timing decisions.

Most indications point to Dell as a successful company in the long-term, but it has been hit by setbacks in the industry and perhaps the stock is overvalued. Basic financial analysis indicators are moderately positive and no indications of deceptive earnings management exist, but the stock sells at a high PE. The basic investment question is this: given the current stock price and uncertainty for the industry and the economy as a whole, should investors hold or increase their position in Dell? The PE is high the forecast of annual earnings growth of 15.8 percent for the next five years. If that earnings growth is exceeded, Dell's stock price may rise (probably higher than market averages), and buying more shares now would be a correct and profitable decision. If Dell stumbles, even slightly, the stock price probably will fall. That's the risk–reward tradeoff.

Consistent with a growth stock, Dell's potential is reasonably good but real downside risk is assumed.

What is the decision? That depends on the confidence in the earnings forecast and alternative investment alternatives. Given the information presented, selling the current investment of 1 percent of the Gotrocks Growth Fund would be a reasonable recommendation. There are alternative investments available. Having said that, if the investor is expects high earnings potential, the recommendation should be to buy.

## SUMMARY

Equity investment analysis is one of the most basic decision-making tools available, for both the professional analyst and the individual investor. Decisions should be based on specific investment goals, from short-term to very long-term, and on the amount of risk that can be tolerated. Mutual funds are an important investment area, providing investment specialties, professional management, and diversified portfolios. The hypothetical Gotrocks Funds are used to consider growth fund and income fund analysis, using the basic six-step approach introduced in Chapter 1.

The primary focus is on Dell as an investment vehicle in the Gotrocks Growth Fund. Although Dell is the largest and lowest-cost producer of PCs and related products, analysis suggests that selling the fund's Dell shares may be a reasonable recommendation since it has a relatively large PE ratio and may be overvalued. On the other hand, it is the one company in this industry most likely to succeed over the long term. All decisions involve judgment, and it is the process of arriving at professional decisions that is significant.

## KEY TERMS

diversification
Dow Jones Industrial Average
executive summary
investment portfolio
mutual funds

## QUESTIONS

1. Why would an investor determine that maximizing long-term portfolio growth is the appropriate investment purpose?
2. Why would an investor rely on mutual funds rather picking individual securities? What are the problems associated with mutual funds?
3. Review the PE, PEG, and yield of the Dow Jones Industrial companies.
4. Which companies are likely to fit into a growth portfolio? An income portfolio? Explain.
5. Why is an executive summary important?
6. Ultimately, a buy or sell decision must be made. How is a comprehensive financial analysis useful for the actual decision?

## PROBLEMS

### Problem 13.1 Financial Analysis for DuPont

This problem is based on analysis from throughout the book.

a. Convert the financial analysis ratios to ratings from 1 (poor) to 10 (excellent) using the following table:

| Category | Rating | Discussion |
|---|---|---|
| Common-size, Income Statement | | |
| Common-size, Balance Statement | | |
| Liquidity Ratios | | |
| Leverage | | |
| Activity | | |
| Profitability | | |
| DuPont Model | | |
| Growth, Historical | | |
| Growth, Projected | | |
| Quarterly Analysis | | |

b. Convert the market analysis ratios to ratings from 1 to 10 using the following table:

| Category | Rating | Discussion |
|---|---|---|
| Stock Price Growth, 5 Years | | |
| Stock Price Growth, 1 Year | | |
| EPS Growth, Past 2 Years | | |
| EPS Growth, 2-Year-Ahead Projections | | |
| Quarterly Earnings | | |
| PE, Actual | | |
| PE, 2-Year-Ahead Projections | | |
| Yield | | |
| Market-to-Book | | |
| Intrinsic Value (www.quicken.com) | | |
| PEG | | |

c. Convert the accounting analysis to ratings from 1 to 10 using the following table:

| Issue | Rating | Discussion |
|---|---|---|
| Revenue Recognition | | |
| Expensing vs. Capitalizing Costs | | |
| Unusual Accounting Policies | | |
| Stock Options | | |
| Nonrecurring Items | | |
| Business Combination Abuse | | |
| Operating Leases, Off-balance-sheet Reporting | | |
| Commitments | | |
| Contingencies | | |
| Retirement | | |
| Segment Reporting | | |
| Other | | |

**d.** Prepare an executive summary for DuPont with the format used in Appendix 1 for Dell.

- ☐ *Investment purpose*—Which Gotrocks Fund is most likely the best fit? Why?
- ☐ *Corporate overview*—Summarize from Chapter 1.
- ☐ *Financial analysis*—Summarize the analysis from Chapters 3 and 4 and other sources.
- ☐ *Detailed accounting analysis*—Explain the major concerns associated with DuPont.
- ☐ *Comprehensive analysis*—Summarize all available information relative to the investment purpose.
- ☐ *Investment decision*—Buy, sell, or hold? Why? What are the other considerations?

## Problem 13.2 Financial Analysis for Hilton

This problem is based on analysis from throughout the book.

**a.** Convert the financial analysis ratios to ratings from 1 (poor) to 10 (excellent) using the following table:

| Category | Rating | Discussion |
|---|---|---|
| Common-size, Income Statement | | |
| Common-size, Balance Statement | | |
| Liquidity Ratios | | |
| Leverage | | |
| Activity | | |
| Profitability | | |
| DuPont Model | | |
| Growth, Historical | | |
| Growth, Projected | | |
| Quarterly Analysis | | |

**b.** Convert the market analysis ratios to ratings from 1 to 10 using the following table:

| Category | Rating | Discussion |
|---|---|---|
| Stock Price Growth, 5 Years | | |
| Stock Price Growth, 1 Year | | |
| EPS Growth, Last 2 Years | | |
| EPS Growth, 2-Year-Ahead Projections | | |
| Quarterly Earnings | | |
| PE, Actual | | |
| PE, 2-Year-Ahead Projections | | |
| Yield | | |
| Market-to-Book | | |
| Intrinsic Value (CNNFN) | | |
| PEG | | |

c. Convert the accounting analysis to ratings from 1 to 10 using the following table:

| Category | Rating | Discussion |
|---|---|---|
| Revenue Recognition | | |
| Expensing vs. Capitalizing Costs | | |
| Unusual Accounting Policies | | |
| Stock Options | | |
| Nonrecurring Items | | |
| Business Combination Abuse | | |
| Operating Leases, Off-balance-sheet Reporting | | |
| Commitments | | |
| Contingencies | | |
| Retirement | | |
| Segment Reporting | | |
| Other | | |

d. Prepare an executive summary for Hilton with the format used in Appendix 1 for Dell.

- ☐ *Investment purpose*—Which Gotrocks Fund is most likely the best fit? Why?
- ☐ *Corporate overview*—Summarize from Chapter 1.
- ☐ *Financial analysis*—Summarize the analysis from Chapters 3 and 4 and other sources.
- ☐ *Detailed accounting analysis*—Explain the major concerns associated with Hilton.
- ☐ *Comprehensive analysis*—Summarize all available information relative to the investment purpose
- ☐ *Investment decision*—Buy, sell, or hold? Why? What are the other considerations?

## CASES

### Case 13.1

Gotrocks has recently established a Value Fund to invest in securities of companies that are undervalued. These could be undervalued for a variety of reasons, but most are companies that have had recent financial and performance problems and a substantial decline in market price. There should be evidence of a successful restructuring in progress and, therefore, potential for stock price appreciation.

a. Review the list of the DJIA stocks in Exhibit 13.1. Do any stocks seem to meet the criteria of the Value Fund? Use various Internet sites to assist in the analysis. List these sites and explain the rationale for using them.

b. Pick one company from Case 13.1a and prepare an abbreviated executive summary:

1. Investment purpose
2. Corporate overview
3. Financial analysis

4. Detailed accounting analysis
5. Comprehensive analysis
6. Investment decision

## ETHICS CONSIDERATIONS

### Investing in Ethics

Even in the face of corporate corruption, the failure of auditors and other third-party reviews to limit excesses, and the lack of substantial new regulations, individual and institutions can fight back. Investors can avoid companies that have a record of poor corporate governance or problematic financial reports or dump them when new revelations indicate problems. Institutional investors are targeting the S&P 500 index on corporate governance and compensation issues. The New York Stock Exchange is tightening its listing requirements, emphasizing minimum standards of corporate governance and financial reporting. Following the lead of Merrill Lynch (which paid a $100 million settlement with the attorney general of New York), investment bankers are making reforms for a more unbiased focus on financial analysis, such as increasing the number of "sell" recommendations.

a. How can these actions by various users make a difference?
b. What other actions would you suggest?

## INTERNET PROJECTS

### Project 13.1

Use the company picked in earlier chapters and convert financial analysis to ratings similar to DuPont above. Prepare an executive summary for this company.

- Investment purpose
- Corporate overview
- Financial analysis
- Detailed accounting analysis
- Comprehensive analysis
- Investment decision

# Appendix 1: Executive Summary for Dell Investment Decisions

- *Investment purpose*—Dell currently is 1 percent of the Gotrocks Growth Fund. Stock is being evaluated for buy or sell recommendations. Growth fund stocks should have substantial earnings potential and other characteristics consistent with potential for stock price growth.
- *Corporate overview*—Dell is the leading direct marketer of personal computers and a S&P and *Fortune* 500 (NASDAQ) corporation. Dell leads the industry in Internet sales and is expanding into business hardware. Dell is a high tech, high growth, high PE firm that pays no dividends. This is a highly competitive industry, and there is the continued question of overall industry growth rates and Dell's market share. Currently, both are projected to be adequate.
- *Financial analysis*—**Market analysis:** Stock price is up substantially for the past five years but flat over the past twelve months. Given the expected five-year earnings growth of 15.8 percent, the stock has a high PE and PEG and is overvalued to intrinsic value calculations.

  **Financial statement analysis:** High cash position but low current ratios, relatively high leverage (almost all current), very high efficiency based on turnover ratios, and average profitability (4.0 percent return on sales, 24.2 percent ROE).
- *Detailed accounting analysis*—Dell's accounting policies are consistent with the industry and reasonably conservative overall. Significant issues are stock options, which are expected to result in equity dilution above 10 percent, and recent employee cutbacks.
- *Comprehensive analysis*—The corporate overview, financial analysis, and detailed accounting analysis indicate a strong company with reasonable earnings and future growth prospects. The major negative is the relatively high market premium, based on PE, PEG, and intrinsic value. In summary, Dell's success depends on meeting or exceeding earnings growth targets.
- *Investment decision*—**Sell.** Immediately sell the Dell holding of 1 percent of the Gotrocks Growth Fund. The current analysis indicates that the stock is overvalued based on earnings forecasts.

# Appendix 2: Alternative Investment Strategies

- *Index funds*—An investor can invest in index funds that exactly match a given index, such as the S&P 500. The investor will earn exactly that rate of return, less various mutual fund fees. Motley Fool (www.fool.com) is a proponent of this strategy.
- *Dollar-cost averaging*—Invest an equal sum regularly (say $100 on the first of each month) over a long period, perhaps in a growth mutual fund. Since investment timing is difficult (impossible?), this method helps smooth out market fluctuations in an investment portfolio.
- *Buy and hold*—According to the efficient markets hypothesis, all public information is available to the market and has been impounded in the stock price. Therefore, any diversified portfolio should perform about as well as any other (following the "random walk" theory). If this is true, buying and selling only increase brokerage costs and should be avoided.
- *Beta analysis*—Beta (ß) is a risk measure, where ß = 1 represents a stock moving with the market, ß > 1 represents a stock that moves faster than the market (in both directions), and ß < 1 means the stock moves less than the market. By building a portfolio where ß is significantly greater than 1, the investor should earn a larger return long-term but with increasing risk.
- *Dow Theory*—The Dow Theory is an example of technical analysis, or buying based exclusively on market movements. In a simplified form, the Dow Theory indicates a strategy of selling when the market goes higher than the last peak and buying when it drops below its previous valley.

# Appendix 3: Six Categories of Investments

In *One Up on Wall Street* (1989), Peter Lynch identifies six categories of investments that present a useful perspective on building portfolios.

- *Slow growers*—Usually companies in mature industries that pay substantial dividends, such as utilities. Investors have discounted this slow growth, so stock price changes should be sluggish.
- *Stalwarts*—Large, well-known companies that still have some growth potential and provide some protection during recessions. These are usually in mature industries. Names include Coca-Cola, General Electric, and Wal-Mart.
- *Fast growers*—Smaller, relatively new companies that are successful and growing rapidly. They may be in a growth industry or have a creative strategy in a mature industry. Dell was in this group (and may still be).
- *Cyclicals*—Companies whose sales and earnings rise and fall with the business cycle. Autos, airlines, and chemical companies are cyclicals.
- *Turnarounds*—Companies with severe financial problems and considerable credit risk. These are high-risk investments, but if the company can restructure successfully, substantial stock price gains are likely.
- *Asset plays*—Companies with valuable assets that could include cash, real estate, net pension assets, patents, or tax-loss carryforwards. Their stock price potential is based on these assets, rather than on operating performance.

Another key point is that a company may be in more than one category: a cyclical with financial problems may restructure to emerge as a turnabout.

# Appendices

## USEFUL WEB SITES

www.cnnfn.com: This is one of my favorite sites. By using the ticker symbol, users can get substantial financial information from CNNFN and other sites like Quicken.

www.hoovers.com: Especially useful for information companies' simplified financial statements (more information is available to members).

www.fortune.com/fortune: *Fortune* magazine. Site includes the *Fortune* 500 list.

www.fool.com: Motley Fools site. Includes Fool's School.

www.rutgers.edu/Accounting/raw: "Raw" stands for "Rutgers accounting web." Extensive list of accounting sites.

www.sec.gov: Securities and Exchange Commission site includes the EDGAR database.

www.fasb.org: Find recent actions of the Financial Accounting Standards Board.

wsj.com/: *Wall Street Journal*'s site.

www.businessweek.com: *Business Week*'s site.

www.thestreet.com: The Street, another big site.

www.sectorupdate.com: This site is a "retriever" for investment information.

cbs.marketwatch.com: CBS' contribution to investment information.

www.morningstar.com: Morningstar ratings and other useful information.

www.dnb.com: Dun & Bradstreet

www.moodys.com: Moody's Investor Service. Look for ratings on whether equities are investment grade.

www.standardandpoors.com: Standard & Poor's.

quote.yahoo.com: Yahoo's finance site.

moneycentral.msn.com: Financial news delivered by MSN (Microsoft).

www.quicken.com: Quicken's site. Considerable is information available.

www.10kwizard.com: Search engine for SEC filings

www.easystock.com: Stock charts and other financial data

www.stockselector.com: Stock and industry information, plus recommendations

www.bloomberg.com: Considerable information on stocks and other finance topics

zacks.com: Particularly useful for analysts' earnings forecasts

www.investorama.com: Links to hundreds of sites

www.census.gov: U.S. Census Bureau

www.bea.doc.gov: Bureau of Economic Analysis, useful for economic updates www.federalreserve.gov: Federal Reserve Board

acct.tamu.edu/giroux: My Web page includes the information on the financial analysis class, ACCT 447.

## Web Sites of Companies Analyzed

Dell: www.dell.com
Ford Motor Company: www.ford.com
DuPont: www.dupont.com
Hilton: www.hilton.com
Amazon: www.amazon.com
CDNow: www.cdnow.com
Aquila: www.aquila.com
Alcoa: www.alcoa.com
Boeing: www.boeing.com
Coca-Cola: www.cocacola.com
ExxonMobil: www.exxon.mobil.com
Home Depot: www.homedepot.com
Intel: www.intel.com
McDonald's: www.mcdonalds.com
3M Worldwide: www.mmm.com
Procter & Gamble: www.pg.com
Wal-Mart: www.walmart.com
Gateway: www.gateway.com
General Motors: www.gm.com
Dow: www.dow.com
Marriott: www.marriott.com
eBay: www.ebay.com
Duke Energy: www.duke-energy.com
TXU Energy: www.txu.com
American Express: www. americanexpress.com
Caterpillar: www.cat.com
Disney: www.disney.com
General Electric: www.ge.com
Honeywell: www.honeywell.com
International Paper: www.ipaper.com
Merck: www.merck.com
J.P. Morgan: www.jpmorgan.com
SBC Communications: www.sbc.com
Apple: www.apple.com
DaimlerChrysler: www.dcx.com
PPG Industries: www.ppf.com
Mandalay Resort Group: www.mandalayresortgroup.com
Barnes & Noble: www.barnesandnobleinc.com
PG&E Corporation: www.pgecorp.com
Southern Company: www.southernco.com
AT&T: www.att.com
Citigroup: www.citigroup.com
Kodak: www.kodak.com
Hewlett-Packard: www.hp.com
IBM: www.ibm.com
Johnson & Johnson: www.jnj.com
Microsoft: www.microsoft.com
Philip Morris: www.philipmorris.com
United Technologies: www.utc.com

# Fortune Top 10s by Size and Performance

Here are top 10 rankings in several categories. The rankings were available at www.fortunate.com/fortune.

## LARGEST FIRMS BY REVENUE

| Rank | Company | 2001 Revenue (in millions) |
|---|---|---|
| 1 | Wal-Mart | $219,812 |
| 2 | ExxonMobil | 191,581 |
| 3 | General Motors | 177,260 |
| 4 | Ford Motor | 162,412 |
| 5 | General Electric | 125,913 |
| 6 | Citigroup | 112,022 |
| 7 | Chevron Texaco | 99,699 |
| 8 | IBM | 85,866 |
| 9 | Philip Morris | 72,944 |
| 10 | Verizon | 67,190 |

## LARGEST FIRMS BY MARKET VALUE

| Rank | Company | 2002 Market Value (in millions) |
|---|---|---|
| 1 | General Electric | $401,499 |
| 2 | Microsoft | 331,520 |
| 3 | ExxonMobil | 295,762 |
| 4 | Wal-Mart | 277,543 |
| 5 | Pfizer | 251,155 |
| 6 | Citigroup | 251,112 |
| 7 | Intel | 207,592 |
| 8 | Johnson & Johnson | 196,235 |
| 9 | American International Group | 195,309 |
| 10 | IBM | 183,314 |

## LARGEST FIRMS BY BOOK VALUE

| Rank | Company | 2001 Assets (in millions) |
|---|---|---|
| 1 | AOL Time Warner | $152,071 |
| 2 | Citigroup | 81,200 |
| 3 | ExxonMobil | 73,161 |
| 4 | Viacom | 62,824 |
| 5 | Berkshire Hathaway | 57,950 |
| 6 | WorldCom | 57,930 |
| 7 | General Electric | 54,824 |
| 8 | American International Group | 52,150 |
| 9 | AT&T | 51,680 |
| 10 | Bank of America | 48,520 |

## MOST EARNINGS, 2001

| Rank | Company | 2001 Earnings (in millions) |
|---|---|---|
| 1 | ExxonMobil | $15,320 |
| 2 | Citigroup | 14,126 |
| 3 | General Electric | 13,684 |
| 4 | Philip Morris | 8,560 |
| 5 | Pfizer | 7,788 |
| 6 | IBM | 7,723 |
| 7 | AT&T | 7,715 |
| 8 | Microsoft | 7,346 |
| 9 | Merck | 7,282 |
| 10 | SBC Communications | 7,242 |

## PROFIT GROWTH PERFORMANCE—1997–2001 ANNUAL EPS GROWTH PERCENTAGE

| Rank | Company | Growth % |
|---|---|---|
| 1 | Northern Utilities | 182% |
| 2 | Calpine | 59 |
| 3 | Humana | 58 |
| 4 | Washington Mutual | 57 |
| 5 | Smithfield Foods | 47 |
| 6 | Best Buy | 47 |
| 7 | New York Times | 45 |
| 8 | Golden West Financial | 40 |
| 9 | Centex | 38 |
| 10 | CDW Computer | 37 |

## REVENUE GROWTH PERFORMANCE—1997–2001 ANNUAL REVENUE GROWTH PERCENTAGE

| Rank | Company | Growth % |
|---|---|---|
| 1 | USA Networks | 134% |
| 2 | AOL Time Warner | 104 |
| 3 | El Paso | 80 |
| 4 | Duke Energy | 66 |
| 5 | Express Scripts | 65 |
| 6 | Dean Foods | 64 |
| 7 | AES | 63 |
| 8 | Reliant Energy | 62 |
| 9 | American Electric Power | 60 |
| 10 | Aquila | 56 |

## RETURN ON EQUITY, 2001

| Rank | Company | Growth % |
|---|---|---|
| 1 | General Mills | 1,274% |
| 2 | Tricon Global | 473 |
| 3 | Maytag | 203 |
| 4 | Sara Lee | 202 |
| 5 | Colgate-Palmolive | 136 |
| 6 | Kindred Healthcare | 89 |
| 7 | Aramarly | 72 |
| 8 | Oxford Health Plan | 70 |
| 9 | Wyeth | 56 |
| 10 | Pitney Bowes | 55 |

## RETURN ON SALES, 2001

| Rank | Company | Growth % |
|---|---|---|
| 1 | Mellon Financial | 33% |
| 2 | Microsoft | 29 |
| 3 | Amgen | 28 |
| 4 | Bristol-Myers Squibb | 24 |
| 5 | Eli Lilly | 24 |
| 6 | Pfizer | 24 |
| 7 | Oracle | 24 |
| 8 | Cablevision Systems | 23 |
| 9 | Coca-Cola | 20 |
| 10 | Schering-Plough | 20 |

## TOTAL RETURN TO SHAREHOLDERS, 1997–2001 ANNUAL RATE PERCENTAGE

| Rank | Company | Growth % |
|---|---|---|
| 1 | Best Buy | 95% |
| 2 | AOL Time Warner | 73 |
| 3 | Echostar | 59 |
| 4 | Quest Diagnostics | 57 |
| 5 | Dell | 52 |
| 6 | Cablevision | 49 |
| 7 | Kohl's | 48 |
| 8 | Calpine | 46 |
| 9 | Advance PCS | 41 |
| 10 | Adelphic Communications | 40 |

# Glossary

**10-K** Annual report submitted to the Securities and Exchange Commission (SEC)

**10-Q** Quarterly report submitted to the SEC

## A

**accounting choice** Discretionary alternatives for reporting various financial items, such as depreciation or inventory method

**accumulated benefit obligation** Pension calculation under defined benefit plan: the present value of amounts employer expects to pay retired employees based on employee service to date and current salary levels

**acquisition** Acquiring the right to manage a company through a business combination or the acquisition of enough voting shares to have effective management

**activity ratio** Financial calculation to evaluate how effective corporate operations are

**agency costs** Contracting becomes more costly when there are agency costs, which include information asymmetries, adverse selection, and moral hazard

**agency theory** All contracts have a principal (e.g., owners) and an agent (e.g., managers); principals will attempt to write efficient contracts to maximize wealth and minimize agency and other transaction costs

**Altman's Z-score** Financial ratio model used to evaluate bankruptcy potential; can also be used to assess relative financial health

**analysts' forecasts** Specialist predictions of EPS (or other definitions of performance) for the forthcoming quarters and years

**assets** Probable future economic benefits based on past transactions or events

**available-for-sale securities** Marketable securities that, in the firm's judgment, may be sold before maturity; these are recorded at fair value and unrealized gains and losses recorded directly to stockholders' equity

## B

**bankruptcy risk** The probability that a firm will file for bankruptcy in the near future

**basic EPS** EPS measured as net income ÷ the weighted average number of common shares outstanding

**benchmarks** Comparison analysis of specific ratios and other techniques, based on rules of thumb, industry averages, and so forth

**beta analysis** Beta comes from the slope coefficient of the market model, which can be used to analyze relative systematic risk for stock selection. ß = 1 means the stock moves directly with the market

**bond ratings** Relative grades of "financial health" from highest (AAA for Standard & Poor's, Aaa for Moody's) to lowest (D for Standard & Poor's, C for Moody's)

**bounded rationality** Individuals are intendedly rational but limited in their knowledge and ability to process information

**business strategy** The key operating and financial strategies the corporation uses to compete in its industry

## C

**capital asset pricing model** Relationship of individual security return to the market return, based on the model $E(R_i) = R_f + ß[E(R_m) - R_f]$

**capital lease** Long-term lease, considered the equivalent of purchasing the asset and recorded by the lessee as an asset and a corresponding liability

**capital structure** The composition of long-term debt and equity, measuring relative leverage

**cash flows from operations** Cash flows directly associated with net income and other operating transactions, as reported on the Statement of Cash Flows

**closing stock price** The ending (last) stock price of the day for a security trading on a stock exchange

**collateral** Physical assets that the borrower pledges to the creditor in case of loan default

**common-size analysis** The conversion of balance sheet and income statement numbers to percentages of total assets and sales, respectively

**comprehensive income** Changc in equity during a period from all nonowner sources

**Conceptual Framework** The FASB's attempt to describe financial accounting theory into a coherent body as stated in the Statements of Financial Accounting Concepts (SFACs)

**conglomerate merger** Acquisition of a firm from an entirely different industry

**core earnings** S&P bottom line measure to better measure ongoing operations

**corporate overview** The qualitative analysis of specific corporations to identify key industry and business strategy characteristics

**credit analysis** The financial analysis process associated with evaluating the investment prospects of an investment in a debt instrument

**credit risk** The probability that a firm will either or both default on paying liabilities or declare bankruptcy

**creditworthiness** Analysis of credit risk and other factors to determine if the customer is acceptable for a loan (or other debt instrument) and under what terms

## D

**debt covenants** Contract terms mandated by the creditor to protect against possible loan default, such as minimum financial ratios or limitations on dividends

**default risk** The probability that a firm will not pay interest and principal when they come due

**deferred tax** The difference between the accounting calculation for tax expense and what is payable to the IRS; this is recorded as an asset or liability

**defined benefit plan** Pension plan committing an employer to pay specific benefits at an employee's retirement

**defined contribution plan** Pension plan committing employer to make specific cash payment to the employees' retirement accounts

**derivative** Financial contract derived from another financial instrument, including options, futures, and swaps

**detailed accounting analysis** The analysis of financial statements and other sources of information to further evaluate how corporations compete in complex environments; particularly important are the identification of earnings management potential and the "deconstruction" of financial information to make better comparisons across firms

**diluted EPS** Earnings per share with the number of shares adjusted for potential dilution (e.g., from stock options), which reduces EPS

**dirty surplus** Gains and losses, such as marketable securities and foreign currency translations adjustments, recorded directly to equity and not in the income statements

**diversification** Investment portfolio holding a broad base of securities, attempting to maximize the risk–return tradeoff

**dividend yield** Dividends per share divided by stock price, a measure of direct cash return on investment

**Dow Jones Industrial Average** A stock price average based on thirty of the largest industrial companies in America; the most well-known stock average

**due process** Procedures followed by the FASB and other bodies to allow public input during the various phases of the standard-setting process

**DuPont Model** Model to decompose return on equity relative to profit, activity, and solvency (leverage)

## E

**earnings-based growth models** Model for the valuation of the firm, based on dividend payout relative to earnings, discounted by some interest rate net of earnings growth rate; also called the dividend discount model

**earnings management** Operating and discretionary accounting methods to adjust earnings to a desired outcome; the incentives of corporate managers to manipulate earnings for their own best interests; accounting techniques include accruals to boost earnings (e.g., to increase bonuses) or smooth earnings over time

**earnings manipulation** Opportunistic use of earnings management to effectively "misstate" earnings to benefit managers

**earnings per share (EPS)** Net income (or some other measure of earnings) converted annually or quarterly to a per share basis, which can be calculated as basic EPS or diluted EPS

**earnings quality** The extent to which earnings represent economic reality, associated with conservative accounting and full disclosure

**earnings surprise** Actual reported earnings are greater or less than expected, usually measured by quarterly earnings announcements relative to analysts' forecasts

**EBIT** Earnings before interest and taxes (also called "operating earnings"), used to evaluate the firm's ability to service debt

**EBITDA** Earnings before interest, taxes, depreciation, and amortization (also called "cash earnings"), used to evaluate cash flows

**economic consequences** Sometimes-unintended consequences that occur after changes in regulations or other factors lead to actions by individuals and organizations

**economic reality** Financial information free of distortions that tend to hide the actual results of sales, expenses and other transactions

**efficient contracting** Writing contracts to maximize principal wealth and minimize transactions costs

**efficient markets** Markets in which prices adjust quickly to new information in an unbiased fashion

**equity** Residual interest in the assets after deducting liabilities; that is, ownership

**executive summary** Brief but formal overview of the six-step financial analysis process, stressing the key points for decision making

**expenses** Outflows from incurring liabilities or using up assets associated with sales and other central operations

**external financial analysis** The use of financial analysis techniques by analysts not affiliated with the company, such as for credit or investment decisions.

## F

**failure events** Signals of potential default such as troubled debt restructurings or going concern audit qualifications

**Financial Accounting Standards Board** Private sector standards-setting body responsible for promulgating financial accounting standards using due process

**financial analysis** The process of evaluating financial and other information for specific recommendations or decisions

**financial leverage index** A ratio of the impact of financial leverage on the performance of the firm, measures as return on equity ÷ return on assets

**financial structure leverage ratio** A leverage ratio measured as average total assets ÷ average common equity; the same ratios is used as the solvency ratio in the DuPont Model

**first-in first-out** Inventory method in which the first items recognized in inventory are released (sold) first

**fixed assets** Property, plant, and equipment, the basic infrastructure of the corporation

**fluctuating currencies** All currencies "float"; that is, their value is based on current market conditions compared to all other currencies

**foreign currency translation** Amount of gains and losses based on relative currency values of foreign operations of financial statement items and reported directly to stockholders' equity

**free cash flows** A measure of cash available for discretionary uses after certain cash outlays; a common calculation of FCF is cash from operations—cash from investments (CFO – CFI)

## G

**gains** Increase in net assets from peripheral transactions

**generally accepted accounting principles** The entire body of accounting standards that are in effect at any time

**geographic segments** Foreign operation footnote disclosure, including sales and identifiable assets

**gold standard** Historical system (no longer in use) in which currencies were pegged to gold by weight and currencies were redeemable in gold

**goodwill** Acquisition price of a target company less the fair value of the net assets of the target, used with the purchase method

**growth analysis** Multiple period (usually by year) comparisons of specific financial statement items (or ratios) to calculate periodic growth rates

## H

**held-to-maturity securities** Marketable securities that will be held to maturity and recorded at cost (or amortized cost)

**horizontal merger** Acquisition of a direct competitor, thus increasing market share and reducing direct competition

**hybrid securities** Securities that have characteristics of both debt and equity, such as convertible bonds

## I

**income from continuing operations** Operating income as measured before nonrecurring items

**income smoothing** Earnings management to smooth out erratic revenue and earnings behavior

**industry analysis** Identifying the industry a corporation competes in and evaluate the key characteristics and prospects of that industry

**industry segments** Industry or department segment disclosure for major divisions, including sales, operating income, and identifiable assets

**internal financial analysis** The use of financial analysis techniques by the entity for information or decision-making purposes

**interperiod tax allocation** Deferred tax items recorded as separate assets or liabilities on the balance sheet

**intraperiod tax allocation** The tax effect associated with specific nonrecurring items; these items are reported net of tax (i.e., the intraperiod tax allocation) on the income statement

**intrinsic value** A measure of per share value, calculated at www.quicken.com using Evaluator

**investment grade bond rating** The four highest bond rating categories (Standard & Poor's AAA to BBB), considered to have relatively low credit risk

**investment portfolio** A specific set of investments owned or managed by an individual or entity

## J

**junk bonds** Bonds with below investment grade ratings

## L

**last-in first-out** Inventory method in which the last items recognized in inventory are released (sold) first

**lease** Contract agreement for the use of assets on a rental or fee basis for a set period of time

**leverage ratio** Financial calculation to evaluate relative mix of equity to debt; also called solvency

**liabilities** Probable future economic sacrifices from present obligations

**liquidity ratio** Financial calculation to analyze cash and other current assets to determine if enough cash or current assets exist to pay off current liabilities

**losses** Decrease in net assets from peripheral transactions

**market model** Financial model to compare individual equity return with the market return for the same period, based on the model $R_{it} = \alpha_i + \beta_i R_{mt} + e_{it}$

## M

**market to book** A comparison of market value to book value (total stockholders' equity, also called net assets)

**market value** Also called market capitalization or market cap, stock price × number of shares outstanding, a measure of how the stock market values companies

**marketable securities** Debt and equity securities that are market traded and typically held for a short period of time as a cash equivalent

**matching principal** Recording expenses that are related to revenues recognized, both product and period costs

**merger** A combination of two companies into a single corporate entity

**monetary items** Assets and liabilities that are denominated in dollars (or other currencies) such as accounts receivable and corporate bonds

**mutual funds** Professionally managed investment portfolios, subject to SEC and other regulations and widely available as investment vehicles

## N

**net assets** Total assets minus total liabilities, equal to total stockholders' equity

**nonmonetary items** Assets and liabilities that are not denominated in currency such as inventory or fixed assets

**nonrecurring items** Gains and losses from peripheral transactions that are recorded as separate line items on the income statement and reported net-of-tax, such as extraordinary items and discontinued operations

## O

**off-balance-sheet financing** Contractual arrangements so that assets and liabilities are not recorded on the balance sheet; a likely source of earnings management

**operating lease** Short-term lease, with lease payments recorded as a periodic expense; obligation is off-balance-sheet

**opportunism** Individual behavior associated with self-interest with guile; that is, beyond the standard ethical norms

**other postemployment benefit obligations** Contractual obligations to retired or terminated employees, such as health insurance; must be recognized as liabilities

## P

**PEG ratio** PE divided by earnings growth rate, a measure of "reasonableness" of the PE ratio; a possible rule of thumb is a PEG equal to or less than 1 as a buy signal

**pension** Retirement plan that provides employees with income after retirement

**period costs** Expenses that relate to specific accounting periods, such as advertising

**pooling of interests** Accounting procedures for a business acquisition meeting specific criteria; no longer allowed by GAAP

**portfolio theory** The concept that financial risk is reduced in a large portfolio of securities relative to a single security

**price earnings (PE) ratio** Stock price divided by annual EPS, a measure of the "market premium" for earnings

**primary market** Capital market where new securities are initially issued

**prime rate** Bank lending rate to the "best" (or most creditworthy) corporate customers

**product costs** Expenses that related to specific revenues recognized, such as cost of goods sold

**profitability ratio** Financial calculation to evaluate profitability of the firm; also called performance ratio

***pro forma* earnings** Restated performance analysis to emphasize a perspective different from GAAP or to forecast future performance

**projected benefit obligation** Pension calculation under defined benefit plan: the present value of amounts an employer expect to pay retired employees based on employee service to date and expected salary at retirement

**purchase method** Accounting procedures now required for all business acquisitions; target is stated as actual market price

## Q

**quantitative financial analysis** A host of ratios, models, time series and forecasts to identify key financial characteristics, which can be compared to competitors or other standards

**quarterly analysis** Financial analysis on a quarterly rather than annual basis, almost always using a multiple-period approach

## R

**random walk** The concept that random selection of a securities portfolio is as effective as a professionally selected portfolio

**red flags** Signals of particularly poor performance or other matters of grave concern

**revenue recognition** Criteria for recorded revenues when revenue is (1) realized or realizable and (2) earned

**revenues** Inflows and other asset enhancements from sales and other central operations

## S

**secondary market** Capital market where previously issued securities can be bought or sold

**Securities and Exchange Commission** Federal agency that regulates the capital markets and the related financial accounting and reporting

**segment reporting** Footnote disclosures on industry and geographic segments

**special purpose entities** A unique legal entity to be used for a specific purpose, such as leasing arrangements or project development activities

**Standardized Industry Classification (SIC) codes** Comprehensive standards to identify specific industries, based on codes of one to four digits. In the process of being replaced by the North American Industry Classification System (NAICS)

**stock options** Employee benefits that allow employees to acquire a set number of shares or firm stock at a set price; options will be exercised only if the stock price is higher than the exercise price

**stock screening** Computer tool available at several Internet sites to find all stocks with specific investment criteria, such as all New York Stock Exchanges firms with an ROE greater than 15 percent

## T

**temporary tax difference** A tax difference between financial accounting and tax accounting that represents a timing difference and is recorded on the balance sheet (see deferred tax)

**trading securities** Marketable securities that are held (usually by a financial institution) for resale to another organization or individual; holding gains and losses are recognized on the income statement

**transaction cost** Cost of issuing and completing contracts, including agency costs

**treasury stock** Common stock acquired by the company in the open market and recorded as a negative equity item

**trend analysis** Multiple-period analysis by setting a base year equal to 100 and comparing financial statement items relative to the base year

## V

**vertical merger** Acquisition of an "indirect" competitor; that is, in the same basic industry but generally in a different market segment

## W

**working capital** Current assets less current liabilities, a widely used indicator of liquidity

# Bibliography


Altman, E., Corporate Financial Distress. New York: John Wiley, 1983.

Altman, E., "Financial Ratios, Discriminant Analysis, and the Prediction of Corporate Bankruptcy." Journal of Finance (September 1968), 589–609.

Flagg, J., G. Giroux, and C. Wiggins, "Predicting Corporate Bankruptcy Using Failing Firms." Review of Financial Economics (Fall 1991), 67–78.

Henry, D., "The Numbers Game." Business Week (May 14, 2001), 100–110.

Lynch, P., One Up on Wall Street. New York: Simon & Schuster, 1989.

Malkiel, B., A Random Walk Down Wall Street. New York: Norton, 1973.

Moody's Industrial Manual, 1999. New York: Moody's Investor Service 1999.

Palepu, K., P. Healy, and V. Bernard, Business Analysis & Valuation. Cincinnati: South-western College Publishing, 2000.

Paton, W., and A. Littleton, An Introduction to Corporate Accounting Standards. American Accounting Association, 1940 (reprinted 1970).

Penman, S., Financial Statement Analysis & Security Evaluation. Boston: McGraw-Hill, 2001.

Standard & Poor's, Standard Corporation Descriptions. New York: McGraw-Hill, various years, 1999–2000.

Stickley, C., and P. Brown, Financial Reporting and Statement Analysis. Orlando: The Dryden Press, 1999.

Watts, R., and J. Zimmerman, Positive Accounting Theory. Englewood Cliffs: Prentice-Hall, 1987

White, G., A. Sondhi, and D. Fried, The Analysis and Use of Financial Statements, 2nd ed. New York: John Wiley & Sons, 1994.

Williamson, O., The Economic Institutions of Capitalism. New York: The Free Press, 1985.

# Business Index

# Subject Index

B



C

## G